# Postinternationalism and the Rise of Heterarchy

Dana-Marie Ramjit
*St. Mary's University, Canada*

Published in the United States of America by
IGI Global
701 E. Chocolate Avenue
Hershey PA, USA 17033
Tel: 717-533-8845
Fax:  717-533-8661
E-mail: cust@igi-global.com
Web site: https://www.igi-global.com

Library of Congress Cataloging-in-Publication Data


CIP PENDING

ISBN13:  9798369335635
EISBN13: 9798369335642


Vice President of Editorial: Melissa Wagner
Managing Editor of Acquisitions: Mikaela Felty
Managing Editor of Book Development: Jocelynn Hessler
Production Manager: Mike Brehm
Cover Design: Phillip Shickler


British Cataloguing in Publication Data
A Cataloguing in Publication record for this book is available from the British Library.

All work contributed to this book is new, previously-unpublished material.
The views expressed in this book are those of the authors, but not necessarily of the publisher.

# Table of Contents

# Detailed Table of Contents

**Chapter 1**

The 21st century has ushered in a transformative era of global politics characterized by unprecedented interconnectedness, technological disruption, and the erosion of traditional state boundaries. As the world becomes increasingly interconnected, traditional notions of sovereignty and territoriality are being challenged. This new reality requires a rethinking of governance structures and international cooperation. This chapter explores the concept of a "postinternational world," a paradigm shift marked by the rise of transnational actors, the blurring of national borders, and a diffusion of power beyond traditional nation-states. The chapter delves into the key drivers of this postinternational shift, including technological advancements, globalization, and the emergence of non-state actors. It also examines the implications for international relations, security, and the future of global governance.

## Chapter 2

*Philip G. Cerny, University of Manchester, UK*

States have been the fundamental building blocks of modern world politics. They have formed a dualistic structure reminiscent of the role of the Roman god Janus. Statues of Janus were placed at the gates to the city. The god had two faces, one looking inwards to guard the social, economic and political life of the city, to give it unity and a sense of the common good and public interest. The second face looked outwards, to protect the city from external threats and predators, to pursue the city's interests in a hostile world and to interact with other cities. In today's collective choice literature, the first face or function of the state is said to be an 'arena of collective action' amongst its inhabitants and citizens. The second face or function was to permit the state to make—or break—'credible commitments' to other states, what Kenneth Waltz, in his magisterial Theory of International Politics, called 'like units' (Waltz 1979)—the capacity of a set of political institutions to play such 'two-level games' (Putnam 1988) effectively—is what is called 'statehood' (Brenner 2004).

## Chapter 3

*Richard R. Weiner, Rhode Island College, USA*

This chapter details how out of the Habermas-Luhmann epistemological and social debates of the 1970s through the 1990s, Günther Teubner moves us to mapping emergent properties amidst a complexity of contexts and temporalities in institutionalist analysis. Starting from respective theories of functional differentiation and complexity, Teubner's polycontexturality approach comprehends the emergence of self/ mutual referencing and self-enforcing reciprocity norms of non-state associations. We are guided by riddles: How does the relentless functional differentiation tend to multiple contextures in transnational policy making, rule-making and standard-setting.? How is it possible to coordinate resolution of overlapping or colliding autonomous systemic or subsystemic regime logics?

## Chapter 4

This chapter reviews approaches used to conceptualize postinternationalism and heterogeneity of actors in world politics: New Medievalism (NM), Spheres of Authority (SOAs), Hybrid Sovereignty (HS) and Heterarchy. All of them are the opposite of the Westphalian ideals of the international politics structured around domestically hierarchic nation-states interacting in the condition of anarchy. In this chapter, the point of departure is NM which is considered the most radical one. The chapter analyses the assumptions and the research praxis of new NM in International Relations (IR) theory, as coined by Hedley Bull (1977). However, the interactions among and between state and non-state actors (NSAs) can be approached and theorized in different ways.

## Chapter 5

This chapter explores the intersection of anarchism and heterarchical frameworks in the context of global governance, arguing that anarchistic principles provide valuable insights into the evolution of governance structures beyond the nation-state. By analyzing the theoretical underpinnings of anarchism and their applicability to heterarchical systems, this chapter illustrates how decentralized and non-hierarchical models can effectively address contemporary global challenges. It examines case studies of non-state actors and transnational movements that embody anarchistic principles, demonstrating their impact on global governance. The chapter further discusses the role of technology in facilitating anarchistic and heterarchical dynamics, shedding light on the reconfiguration of power dynamics and the challenges of legal governance in a postinternational world. Through a comprehensive analysis, this chapter contributes to the discourse on alternative governance frameworks, offering practical implications for future diplomacy and statecraft in a heterarchical global order.

This article is focusing on the development of heterarchical structures in the field of global health. It addresses the question to what extent heterarchical structures promote or inhibit crisis management of epidemic outbreaks. Essentially, heterarchy does both: in the health crises analyzed in this article, both fragmented and cooperative heterarchy are evident. While fragmented heterarchy is characterized by little cooperative interaction between relevant groups of actors and contestation, the second form of heterarchy - cooperative heterarchy - is characterized by collaborative problem-solving. This is based on the governance mode of orchestration, in which the WHO, as the leading actor (orchestrator), directs groups of actors (intermediaries), thereby achieving common goals in the form of crisis management in the interests of all. Orchestration is possible here on the basis of networks that can be activated and a fairly large problem-solving constraint (crisis management).

The Caribbean landscape is intertwined with threads of resilience, cultural richness, and a complex history marked by colonialism. The legacies of European domination continue to cast long shadows, shaping power structures and social relations across the region. Postcolonial scholarship has illuminated the enduring impact of colonialism on power dynamics, economies, and cultural identities (Parashar, & Schulz, 2021; Said, 1978; Anzaldúa, 1987). Colonial administrations established centralized control, privileging European elites, and marginalizing Indigenous and African populations. These hierarchies continue to influence land ownership patterns, political structures, and even social interactions in many Caribbean nations (Beckles, 2000; Ramjit, 2019). Heterarchy offers a compelling alternative to these entrenched power structures. Defined by anthropologists like Descola (2001) as a system that prioritizes collaboration and distributed power, heterarchy challenges the notion of a single, dominant authority.

# Chapter 8

This chapter argues that the European Union (EU) has gained empowerment through the fragmentation of the Common Commercial Policy (CCP), particularly focusing on investment governance. It highlights how the EU has utilized this altered policy landscape to enhance Brussels' capabilities in addressing investment issues. The argument posits that the CCP has become heterarchical due to politicization and geopoliticization, leading to a discussion on how the EU has navigated this new landscape to bolster its competencies in investment governance. Firstly, the chapter examines the adoption of an Investment Screening Mechanism (ISM), asserting its significance in shaping a Brussels-oriented perspective on investment-related risks. Secondly, it underscores the EU's revised approach to multilateral investment agreements, shifting from a state-centric demand for investment facilitation to a Brussels-centric framing of investment protection.

# Chapter 9

Globalization has been transforming the nature and characteristics of the present state-centric international system. Specifically, the process of fragmentation, decentralization, and internationalization associated with the promotion of neoliberal globalization altered the role of the state from being the only proactive player in the international arena to becoming more and more reactive. The proliferation of different specialized regimes into areas previously controlled and dominated by the state (e.g., trade law, environmental law, and human rights), international institutions sanctioned by intergovernmental organizations undermining the Westphalian constitutional concepts of state sovereignty, and the prevalence of internet governance and cybersecurity concerns reflect the emergence of post-internationalism and heterarchical governance as an alternative.

This chapter examines how African inter-state relations are shaped by the crisis
management initiatives of African International Organizations using the case of the
Economic Community of West African States. It leverages the insights of cybernetic
politics and heterarchy to decentre the dominant heuristic of hierarchy in the framing
of intra-African international politics given that it hardly accommodates transactions
beyond a one-dimensional understanding of power by. The chapter demonstrates
how ECOWAS member states use the logic of cybernetic politics and heterachy to
acquire flexibility and speed to pragmatically manage multiple episodes of authority
crisis in West Africa.

# Preface

In a world where the traditional boundaries of nation-states are increasingly blurred, the conventional understanding of global affairs is undergoing a profound transformation. The forces of globalization, rapid technological advancements, and the rise of new governance models are reshaping the landscape of international relations. It is within this context that *Postinternationalism and the Rise of Heterarchy* offers a timely and essential exploration of emerging paradigms that challenge and redefine the established order.

This volume brings together a diverse array of chapters that delve into the evolving dynamics of global governance, providing fresh perspectives on how power and influence are distributed in our increasingly interconnected world. By focusing on the concepts of postinternationalism and heterarchy, we seek to illuminate the complexities of contemporary global interactions, offering both theoretical insights and practical implications. Our contributors, hailing from various disciplines such as political science, international relations, sociology, economics, and law, present a multidisciplinary approach that underscores the relevance and urgency of these topics.

This book is not just an academic exercise; it is a call to rethink the structures and processes that define our global society. We aim to engage scholars, students, policymakers, and informed readers who are keen to understand and navigate the shifting realities of governance and politics. Whether you are an academic seeking to expand your research horizons, a policymaker grappling with the implications of these changes, or a curious reader eager to comprehend the forces shaping our world, this volume offers valuable insights and a compelling narrative.

In an era where the old certainties are fading, *Postinternationalism and the Rise of Heterarchy* invites you to explore the new paradigms that will shape the future of global governance.

# ORGANIZATION OF THE BOOK

## Chapter 1. Redefining Politics and Governance in a Postinternational World

The 21st century has ushered in a paradigm shift in global politics and governance, characterized by unprecedented levels of interconnectedness driven by rapid technological advancements. This chapter explores the concept of a postinternational world, where traditional state boundaries are increasingly blurred, and power is diffused beyond the conventional nation-state framework. By examining the rise of transnational actors and the changing dynamics of global governance, the chapter delves into how these transformations are fundamentally reshaping our understanding and practice of politics and governance in today's world.

## Chapter 2. The Reactive State in a Heterarchical World

States have long served as the foundational pillars of modern world politics, akin to the Roman god Janus with its dual faces: one turned inward to manage internal affairs, and the other outward to interact with external forces. This chapter examines the evolving role of states in a heterarchical world, where traditional state functions are increasingly influenced by the need to engage in complex, multi-level governance. Through the lens of collective action and credible commitments, the chapter explores how states navigate the challenges of maintaining authority and legitimacy in a global context marked by intricate interdependencies.

## Chapter 3. How Polycontexturality Goes Deeper than Polycentrism as the Approach to Exploring Heterarchic Space of Governance

Drawing from the intellectual debates of Habermas, Luhmann, and Teubner, this chapter delves into the concept of polycontexturality as a means of understanding the complexity of governance in a heterarchical world. By moving beyond polycentrism, the chapter maps out the emergent properties of non-state associations that operate within multiple, overlapping contexts and temporalities. Through a series of probing questions, the chapter investigates how functional differentiation and complexity shape transnational policy-making, rule-setting, and the resolution of conflicting systemic logics, offering a nuanced approach to understanding heterarchical governance.

## Chapter 4. Framing Postinternational Heterogeneous Order: New Medievalism and its Competitors

This chapter reviews various approaches to conceptualizing the postinternational and hcterogeneous nature of contemporary world politics. It begins with New Medievalism (NM), a radical departure from the Westphalian model of state-centric international relations, as conceptualized by Hedley Bull. The chapter critically analyzes the assumptions and methodologies of NM within International Relations theory, while also considering alternative frameworks such as Spheres of Authority (SOAs), Hybrid Sovereignty (HS), and Heterarchy. Through this comparative analysis, the chapter seeks to illuminate the diverse and often competing theories that attempt to make sense of the interactions between state and non-state actors in a postinternational world.

## Chapter 5. Anarchism and Heterarchy Rethinking Governance in a Postinternational Era: New Paradigms of Non-State Influence

This chapter explores the intersection of anarchism and heterarchical frameworks as they relate to global governance, positing that anarchistic principles offer valuable insights into the evolution of governance structures beyond the nation-state. By analyzing the theoretical foundations of anarchism and its applicability to heterarchical systems, the chapter illustrates how decentralized, non-hierarchical models can effectively address contemporary global challenges. Through case studies of non-state actors and transnational movements that embody anarchistic principles, the chapter highlights the role of technology in facilitating these dynamics and discusses the implications for diplomacy and statecraft in a postinternational world.

## Chapter 6. Crisis Management in Global Health: Heterarchy as Amplifier or Blocker of Effective Governance?

Focusing on the field of global health, this chapter investigates the role of heterarchical structures in crisis management during epidemic outbreaks. It contrasts two forms of heterarchy—fragmented and cooperative—highlighting their respective impacts on governance effectiveness. Fragmented heterarchy, characterized by minimal cooperation and contestation among actors, often impedes crisis management. In contrast, cooperative heterarchy, where collaborative problem-solving prevails, enhances the capacity to manage health crises. The chapter emphasizes the orchestration role of the World Health Organization (WHO) in directing actors within these networks to achieve common goals, providing insights into the conditions under which heterarchical governance can either amplify or block effective global health crisis management.

## Chapter 7. From Colonialism to Heterarchy: New Power Dynamics in the Caribbean

This chapter examines the lingering influence of colonialism on power dynamics in the Caribbean, where the legacies of European domination continue to shape social relations and governance structures. Through the lens of postcolonial scholarship, the chapter explores how heterarchy presents a compelling alternative to these entrenched hierarchies. By prioritizing collaboration and distributed power, heterarchical systems challenge the notion of a single, dominant authority, offering a pathway toward more equitable and inclusive governance in the region. The chapter provides a critical analysis of how heterarchy can help dismantle the colonial power structures that persist in Caribbean societies.

## Chapter 8. Navigating Regionalism in a Heterarchical Global Order: A Comprehensive Analysis of the EU's Empowerment in Global Investment Governance

This chapter argues that the European Union (EU) has gained significant empowerment through the fragmentation of its Common Commercial Policy (CCP), particularly in the realm of investment governance. By examining the EU's adoption of an Investment Screening Mechanism (ISM) and its revised approach to multilateral investment agreements, the chapter demonstrates how Brussels has leveraged heterarchical structures to enhance its competencies in addressing investment-related risks. The chapter provides a comprehensive analysis of how the EU has navigated the complexities of a heterarchical global order to assert its influence in global investment governance, highlighting the strategic shifts that have enabled its empowerment.

## Chapter 9. From a State-Centric System to a Cosmopolitan International System: Exploring Political Participation and the West Philippine Sea Issue in a Decentralized World

This chapter explores the transformation of the state-centric international system into a more decentralized, cosmopolitan order, driven by the forces of globalization and neoliberalism. Focusing on the West Philippine Sea issue, the chapter examines how the proliferation of specialized regimes and international institutions has undermined traditional notions of state sovereignty. By analyzing the role of non-state actors, international law, and cyber governance, the chapter sheds light on the emergence of postinternationalism and heterarchical governance as viable alternatives to the Westphalian model, offering insights into the evolving nature of political participation and state power in a decentralized world.

## Chapter 10. Crisis of Authority and the Cybernetic Politics of African International Organizations: The ECOWAS and its Institutional Circuits of Heterarchical Entanglement

This chapter investigates the role of African International Organizations, particularly the Economic Community of West African States (ECOWAS), in managing crises of authority within intra-African relations. By applying the concepts of cybernetic politics and heterarchy, the chapter challenges the traditional hierarchical understanding of international politics, demonstrating how ECOWAS member states utilize these frameworks to navigate authority crises. The chapter highlights the flexibility and speed with which ECOWAS operates within heterarchical entanglements, offering a novel perspective on the governance dynamics of African international relations and the role of regional organizations in addressing complex political challenges.

## IN CONCLUSION

As we reach the conclusion of this volume, it becomes evident that the traditional paradigms of global governance are undergoing profound transformations. The exploration of postinternationalism and heterarchy within these pages reflects a world in flux, where the once dominant structures of state-centric authority are being redefined by the complexities of a hyperconnected and multipolar global landscape.

Through the diverse contributions of our esteemed authors, this book has delved into the theoretical underpinnings, empirical case studies, and practical implications of these emerging frameworks. Each chapter has illuminated a different facet of how power, governance, and international relations are being reshaped in this new era, providing a comprehensive understanding of the evolving global order.

Our aim has been to challenge conventional wisdom and offer alternative perspectives on the future of global governance. As scholars, policymakers, and engaged readers, we are called upon to rethink the ways in which we navigate and influence the global stage. The concepts of postinternationalism and heterarchy are not merely academic constructs; they represent the lived realities of a world where authority is increasingly decentralized, and where collaboration across borders and sectors is both a necessity and an opportunity.

As you reflect on the insights presented in this volume, we hope you are inspired to contribute to the ongoing discourse and to play an active role in shaping a more just, equitable, and inclusive global order. The journey towards understanding and embracing these new paradigms is ongoing, and it is our collective responsibility to ensure that the future we build is one that reflects the diverse and interconnected world we inhabit.

**Dana-Marie Ramjit**
*St. Mary's University, Canada*

# Acknowledgment

I want to express my deepest gratitude to all who contributed to the completion of this project. A special thank you to the chapter authors, whose insightful contributions greatly enriched the content of this publication. I also sincerely appreciate the reviewers, whose expertise and thoughtful feedback were critical in refining each chapter, ensuring the highest quality, coherence, and clarity standards. Their collective efforts were invaluable in shaping this work into a meaningful and valuable resource. This publication would not have been possible without their dedication and commitment.

**Dana-Marie Ramjit**
*St. Mary's University, Canada*

# Introduction

The traditional notion of the nation-state as the dominant actor in global affairs is increasingly being questioned. Globalization, technological advancements, and new forms of governance have reshaped the international landscape, introducing complexities that challenge the established order. In this evolving environment, the concepts of *postinternationalism* and *heterarchy* emerge as promising frameworks for analyzing contemporary global dynamics.

*Postinternationalism* refers to a world where the dominance of nation-states is diminished, making room for a multiplicity of actors—both state and non-state—who operate across borders and influence global outcomes. *Heterarchy*, in contrast to hierarchy, refers to a system of governance where power is distributed, decentralized, and often organized through networks of cooperation rather than clear lines of authority. Together, these concepts offer critical insights into the diffusion of power and governance in today's world, providing tools to analyze the impact of non-state actors, transnational movements, and global economic trends.

This edited volume, *Postinternationalism and the Rise of Heterarchy*, brings together a collection of interdisciplinary contributions that examine how governance and power are being redefined in this new global order. Scholars from political science, international relations, sociology, law, and economics present theoretical perspectives, empirical case studies, and practical insights to unpack the implications of postinternationalism and heterarchy. The chapters in this book span a wide array of topics, including the evolution of the state, non-state actors, crisis management, and the role of technology in governance.

This volume is an essential resource for scholars, students, policymakers, and informed readers interested in governance, politics, and international relations. It appeals to political science and public policy academics, as well as general readers seeking a deeper understanding of the shifts in global governance.

**The opening chapter** sets the stage by exploring the fundamental shift in global politics, where borders blur, and power diffuses across multiple actors. The chapter delves into the theoretical underpinnings of a postinternational world and highlights how the proliferation of transnational actors and digital technologies is reshaping governance beyond the traditional nation-state framework. The second chapter discusses how states, once the core pillars of global politics, are transforming under the pressures of a heterarchical world. Drawing parallels with the Roman god Janus, the chapter highlights how states must navigate dual roles—managing internal governance while engaging in external diplomacy amidst complex interdependencies with non-state actors. Chapter 3 offers a deeper theoretical exploration of heterarchy by introducing the concept of polycontexturality, which explains how governance structures emerge within complex, overlapping contexts. Weiner presents a rich analysis of non-state associations and their roles in shaping transnational governance through functional differentiation and reciprocal norms. In the fourth chapter, the author reviews various approaches used to conceptualize the heterarchical nature of global governance. By focusing on concepts such as New Medievalism, Spheres of Authority, and Hybrid Sovereignty, the chapter analyzes the growing heterogeneity of actors in world politics, offering a critique of traditional Westphalian frameworks. Chapter 5 explores the intersection between anarchism and heterarchy, arguing that anarchistic principles can provide valuable insights into decentralized governance structures. The chapter examines non-hierarchical models of governance, using case studies of transnational movements to demonstrate the evolving role of non-state actors in global governance. The sixth chapter analyzes how heterarchical structures affect global health crisis management. Lange contrasts fragmented and cooperative forms of heterarchy and assesses how the World Health Organization and other global health actors navigate crises like pandemics. The chapter illustrates how orchestration networks facilitate or hinder crisis management. In Chapter 7, the editor examines the legacy of colonialism in shaping the power dynamics of the Caribbean and offers heterarchy as a compelling alternative to entrenched hierarchies. By focusing on collaboration and distributed power, the chapter provides insights into how heterarchical governance structures could address issues of inequality and resilience in postcolonial societies. Chapter 8 explores the European Union's adaptation to a heterarchical global order, focusing on the fragmentation of the Common Commercial Policy and the rise of Brussels' influence in investment governance. The chapter discusses how new legal mechanisms, such as the Investment Screening Mechanism, reflect the EU's shift toward a more flexible, heterarchical approach to global governance. In chapter 9, the author discusses the West Philippine Sea issue as a case study of how postinternational and heterarchical governance frameworks challenge state-centric models. Pactao highlights the role of international institutions, non-state actors, and cybersecurity in decentralizing governance and shaping political participation beyond state boundaries. **The last chapter** investigates the role of African international organizations, such as ECOWAS, in managing authority crises. Using the concept of cybernetic politics, the chapter reveals how heterarchical structures allow ECOWAS member states to flexibly address regional challenges, providing a pragmatic lens for understanding intra-African international relations.

This comprehensive overview of postinterntionalism and heterarchy provides a unique lens for understanding the transformation of global governance. By presenting both theoretical foundations and empirical analyses, this volume contributes to ongoing discussions on how power, authority, and governance are evolving in the 21st century.

As we move forward into a more interconnected and decentralized world, it is critical to rethink traditional frameworks and embrace new models of governance. *Postinternationalism and the Rise of Heterarchy* offers a vital contribution to this ongoing conversation, and we hope that readers will find the perspectives and analyses presented in this volume both insightful and thought-provoking.

# Chapter 1
# Redefining Politics and Governance in a Postinternational World

**Dana-Marie Ramjit**
https://orcid.org/0000-0003-1369-8121
*St. Mary's University, Canada*

## ABSTRACT

*The 21st century has ushered in a transformative era of global politics characterized by unprecedented interconnectedness, technological disruption, and the erosion of traditional state boundaries. As the world becomes increasingly interconnected, traditional notions of sovereignty and territoriality are being challenged. This new reality requires a rethinking of governance structures and international cooperation. This chapter explores the concept of a "postinternational world," a paradigm shift marked by the rise of transnational actors, the blurring of national borders, and a diffusion of power beyond traditional nation-states. The chapter delves into the key drivers of this postinternational shift, including technological advancements, globalization, and the emergence of non-state actors. It also examines the implications for international relations, security, and the future of global governance.*

## INTRODUCTION

The 21st century has witnessed a seismic shift in global politics, marked by unprecedented interconnectedness, technological disruption, and the erosion of traditional state boundaries. This new era, often called the postinternational world, is

DOI: 10.4018/979-8-3693-3563-5.ch001

characterized by blurring national borders, the proliferation of transnational actors, and a diffusion of power beyond traditional nation-states.

Departing from the Westphalian system of sovereign nation-states, the postinternational world is characterized by a more fluid and interconnected global order. Postinternationalism describes the growing number of interactions in world politics that occur without the direct involvement of states. These interactions create a state of turbulence in global affairs, a dynamic and complex environment filled with tension and constant change due to the involvement of diverse actors. Rosenau's (2003) concept of "distant proximities" highlights the inherent tension between the national and the transnational, characterized by contradictions, ambiguities, and uncertainties.

The rise of global challenges, such as climate change, pandemics, terrorism, and economic inequality, transcends national boundaries. These challenges demand collective action and cooperation among various actors, including states, non-governmental organizations (NGOs), multinational corporations, and international institutions. As a result, traditional notions of sovereignty, authority, and legitimacy are being challenged, paving the way for new decentralized, networked, and participatory forms of governance (Helberger, 2020).

This chapter explores these critical themes using theoretical frameworks and empirical evidence. It explores the rise of transnational governance networks, the increasingly important role of non-state actors in global politics, the impact of digital technology on political participation and accountability, and the challenges of reconciling global interdependence with national sovereignty. By navigating the winds of change in the postinternational world, the chapter provides insights into the evolving nature of power, authority, and governance in this new context. Ultimately, it aims to inform policy discussions to address the pressing challenges of the 21st century.

## Defining the Postinternational World

Focusing on the period following World War II to the present day, the concept of postinternationalism emerged in academic discourse in 1990 through the work of Rosenau (1990; 2003) and remains a pertinent framework for understanding contemporary political trends (Ansell & Trondal, 2017; Prichard & Cerny, 2017; Rosenau, 1990; 2003). Describing a context marked by evolving orientations and a redistribution of authority among various actors, postinternationalism captures the complexities of today's global landscape (Ferguson & Mansbach, 2007; Hobbs, 2000; Rosenau, 1990; 2003). This era of turbulence arises from the destabilization and restructuring of the structures that traditionally governed world politics (Rosenau,

1990; 2003). Consequently, postinternationalism offers a compelling framework for understanding contemporary politics.

The concept of the postinternational world represents a paradigm shift in global affairs, marked by the blurring of traditional boundaries and the emergence of a new geopolitical landscape characterized by heightened interconnectedness and interdependence among states, non-state actors, and supranational institutions. The postinternational world can be defined as a situation in which traditional concepts of sovereignty, territoriality, and authority are being challenged by transnational forces and processes that transcend national borders. Unlike the Westphalian system of sovereign nation-states that has dominated the international order for centuries, the postinternational world is characterized by fluidity, complexity, and interconnectedness, where issues and actors operate across multiple jurisdictions and levels of governance. This shift is driven by a myriad of factors, including globalization, technological advancements, and the rise of non-state actors, which have facilitated greater flows of people, goods, capital, and ideas across borders, thereby reshaping the dynamics of global politics and governance (Turnhout et al., 2020).

The implications of the postinternational world for politics and governance are profound and far-reaching. One of the central implications is the erosion of state sovereignty, as states increasingly find themselves constrained by transnational forces and unable to fully control events within their borders (Guazzone & Pioppi, 2022). This erosion of sovereignty is manifested in various ways, including the proliferation of international treaties and agreements that limit state autonomy, the rise of transnational governance networks that operate independently of state authority, and the increasing influence of non-state actors, such as multinational corporations, non-governmental organizations (NGOs), and international organizations, in shaping global policy agendas.

Moreover, the postinternational world is characterized by heightened global interconnectedness, facilitated by advancements in transportation, communication, and information technology (Topal, 2022). This interconnectedness has led to the emergence of transnational issues and challenges that defy national boundaries, such as climate change, pandemics, terrorism, and economic inequality (McEvoy, 2022). As a result, traditional notions of sovereignty and territoriality are being challenged, requiring new forms of governance that are more flexible, collaborative, and inclusive in nature. The postinternational world represents a fundamental reordering of global politics and governance.

## Turbulence

Turbulence emerges when decentralized multi-centric systems infiltrate state-centric systems, an intrusion that leads to a blurred delineation of power (Rosenau, 2003). The concurrent processes of globalization and localization give rise to distant proximities: globalization, with its expansive forces, pushes for greater global interconnectedness, while localization, with its localizing forces, advocates for stronger local identities (Rosenau, 2003). The tension between these opposing forces epitomizes contemporary society. Hence, localization symbolizes historical epochs, while globalization is the current environment that emerged post-World War II and endures today (Rosenau, 1990; 2003). This distinction is crucial for comprehending the postinternational world.

Alongside globalization and localization, the emergence of ideas like state-centrism, bipolarity, multi-centrism, and multipolarity are pivotal in explaining the shift from earlier epochs to the present era. Postinternationalism emerged as a response to the inadequacies of state-centric realism, which failed to explain the complexities of the dynamic, interdependent, and turbulent political landscape that emerged after World War II (Ferguson & Mansbach, 2007; Rosenau, 1990). For instance, the post-war era witnessed a surge in specialized labor, collective action, a shifting identity, and number of actors, evolving authority structures, diverse goals, and new arrangements, all within an accelerated and demanding global context (Ansell & Trondal, 2017; Rosenau, 1990; Weatherby et al., 2017). Moreover, the democratization process began in the 19th century with the extension of voting rights, coinciding with the rise of mass media, which meant that a multi-centric world had arisen (McNair, 2017). These developments blurred traditional boundaries, creating prolonged disequilibrium, and shaping political outcomes (Kibler, 2011; Rosenau, 2003).

These transformations constitute turbulence, manifesting at both micro (individuals and groups) and macro (new technologies) levels (Hobbs, 2000; Rosenau, 1990; Weatherby et al., 2017). This shift was further driven by the conflicting forces of stagnation and transformation, past and future, interdependence and dependence, and centralization and decentralization (Ansell & Trondal, 2017; Ferguson & Mansbach, 2007; Hobbs, 2000; Rogers, 2009; Rosenau, 1990).

A central aspect of turbulence was the restructuring of political structures. In turbulent or unbalanced environments, diverse actors or polities exist, each with its own goals, activities, and interactions (Hobbs, 2000; Ferguson & Mansbach, 2007; Kibler, 2011; Rosenau, 1990; 2003). This proliferation of non-state actors challenged national sovereignty and gave rise to a bifurcated or pluricentric world where states coexist with multiple actors (Ansell & Trondal, 2017; Bellamy, 2017; Moreno,

2000; Rogers, 2009; Rosenau, 1990; 2003; Weatherby et al., 2017). Multicentrism emerged as a defining characteristic of the postinternational world.

Simultaneously, the state's significance shifted. While the state remains a central actor in a postinternational world, its jurisdictional authority has diffused across an emerging, multi-level system of globalized governance (Hobbs, 2000; Trondal & Bauer, 2017; Lipshutz, 2000). In this framework, authority flows downward to regional and local levels and upward to the global. In many respects, the onset of postinternationalism coincided with the transformation of passive individuals into central actors, a shift facilitated by a revolution in communication and technology, empowering people with the information and skills necessary to make politically relevant judgments (Piacentine, 2022; Hobbs, 2000; Rosenau, 1990; Weatherby et al., 2017). Consequently, the postinternational citizen evolved into a self-governing utilitarian, challenging the state's traditional authority.

Turbulence reflects ongoing change, inconsistency, and diverse forces that constrain, weaken, and reconfigure existing systems (Rosenau, 2003). This complexity arises from the demands of relevant actors who must be accommodated and involved in decision-making (Ansell & Trondal, 2017; Bubolz & Sontag, 2009; Maull, 2011). Turbulence is evident in challenges such as climate change, global terrorism, financial crises, pandemics, nuclear proliferation, humanitarian crises, poverty, and migration. In the contemporary era, turbulence has become a norm due to the inability of existing structures to maintain control (Ansell & Trondal, 2017; Webster, 2017; Worth, 2017). Addressing turbulence requires cooperation not only among states but also with diverse actors.

## Distant Proximities & Fragmegration

Distant proximities are a phenomenon where individuals experience both a sense of closeness and distance simultaneously; what was once considered local is now part of the global sphere, leading to tensions in various dichotomies, such as core and peripheral countries, national and transnational identities, community, and cosmopolitan values, as well as cultural and subcultural norms, centralization and decentralization, spatial and temporal aspects, universal and particularistic values, and global and local perspectives (Andaya, 2017; Guy, 2009; Rosenau, 2003; Weatherby et al., 2017).

Fragmegration describes the dynamic interplay between fragmentation and integration (Rosenau, 2003). As social and geographic distances erode, individuals, organizations, and communities experience distance and proximity, resulting in fragmegration (Prichard & Cerny, 2017). Fragmegration has several underlying causes. First, the growth of technology and science led to the breakdown of traditional ideological belief systems (Rosenau, 2003). Consequently, individuals are increasingly insecure about the meaning of life, abandoning old identities and adopting new ones, which leaves them torn between the familiar and the distant global world (Rosenau, 2003; Weatherby et al., 2017). This uncertainty is emblematic of the broader conflict between individualism and collectivism in the postinternational world.

Second, the emergence of a new global environment characterized by subdivisions. The decline of traditional systems, norms, and rules has paved the way for forming ties, groups, and networks (Rosenau, 2003). Individuals have become more developed, flexible, and autonomous, embodying multiple and shifting identities; what were once distant developments have now become proximate (Galaz & Pierre, 2017; Rosenau, 2003). Those focused on the proximate occupy local worlds, such as landscapes, while those focused on the distant occupy global worlds, such as ethnoscapes, technoscapes, financescapes, mediascapes, ideoscapes, and landscapes (Rosenau, 2003). Consequently, the importance of the local has diminished as the global has taken precedence.

Third, several revolutions have contributed to fragmegration. An organizational revolution has shifted authority, influence, and power away from traditional structures (Prichard & Cerny, 2017; Rosenau, 2003; Weatherby et al., 2017). An economic revolution has transformed how goods, services, capital, and ownership are transported globally, making society superconnected, complex, and ultrafast (Prichard & Cerny, 2017; Galaz & Pierre, 2017). These changes have eroded borders and increased regional integration. Consequently, individuals are no longer tied to specific territories but have become more independent and skilled, weakening states and sharing authority among multiple polities (Ferguson & Mansbach, 2007; Rosenau, 2003; Weatherby et al., 2017). This newfound independence has expanded the boundaries of society.

Fragmegration has led to several global consequences. One of these is the weakening of states and territoriality (Prichard & Cerny, 2017; Rosenau, 2003). Although states remain legitimate, viable, and powerful entities, their struggle to adapt to rapid change has made fragmegration more pronounced (Ansell & Trondal, 2017; Rosenau, 2003). This loss of power has seen deterritorialization surpass territoriality (Prichard & Cerny, 2017; Rosenau, 2003). Increased mobility has resulted in a weakening of cultural ties and the transmission of values across cultures. However, there has also been a noticeable trend of reterritorialization due to increased migration and the formation of diasporic communities (Gordon, 2017; Rosenau, 2003). Indeed, the movement of people across borders is becoming increasingly prominent in our world.

Another consequence of fragmegration is the emergence of divided loyalties. The erosion of state sovereignty is evident in the waning loyalty of citizens and the rise of a vibrant array of non-governmental actors (Prichard & Cerny, 2017; Rosenau, 2003; Weatherby et al., 2017). Authority has shifted due to the decentralization of national governments, leaving many power vacuums that criminal organizations seek to fill, leading to bureaucratic disarray as individuals pursue their self-interests (Karns et al., 2015; Rosenau, 2003). A do-it-yourself approach becomes viable as people lose confidence in the state and seek alternative governance.

Fragmegration also led to the globalization of national economies, as it became increasingly impossible for economies to remain self-contained in an interdependent, postinternational world (Andaya, 2017; Ansell & Trondal, 2017; Rosenau, 2003; Prichard & Cerny, 2017). Economic globalization has been a critical feature of postinternationalism, leading to a multi-centric world characterized by global and transnational networks (Rosenau, 2003; Weatherby et al., 2017).

Moreover, fragmentation creates a conflict between individual and national interests, often prioritizing the former. This shift has presented global challenges, including environmental pollution, currency crises, the drug trade, terrorism, AIDS, and refugee movements, which require the cooperation and involvement of non-state actors, as states alone can often not provide adequate solutions (Ansell & Trondal, 2017; Prichard & Cerny, 2017; Rosenau, 2003).

Ultimately, postinternationalism illuminates two central realms of human existence: the global and the local. This distant proximity is characterized by interdependence and counteraction; the global sphere blurs boundaries, while the local sphere preserves them (Prichard & Cerny, 2017; Rosenau, 2003). The tension between globalization and localization gives rise to a crisis in the emergent era known as glocalization, or in Japanese terminology, dochakaku or global localization (Andaya, 2017; Guy, 2009; Rosenau, 2003).

## The Rhythm of Change

The landscape of global politics is no longer a static map, but rather a dynamic ocean in constant motion. The once-clear lines of authority separating national governments are blurring, replaced by a complex interplay of actors and forces operating across multiple levels. In ever-shifting landscape of postinternational politics, change is not just an occasional event, but the very essence of the system. A significant shift occurred with the transition from the industrial to the post-industrial world, moving from a tightly bipolar to a loosely bipolar to a multipolar political landscape (Ansell & Trondal, 2017; Rosenau, 1990; 2003). Change in postinternationalism is both endogenous and exogenous. It can be categorized under three global parameters: orientational or skill-based (such as individuals' analytical skills, compliance habits, legitimacy sentiments, and cathectic capacities), structural (including rules of governance, informal regimes, formal alliances, and legal conventions), and relational (encompassing class structures, balance of power, and dependency patterns)

(Ansell & Trondal, 2017; Rosenau, 2003). In essence, postinternationalism can be viewed as a theory of change.

Change is continuous, intense, transformative, and dramatic (Pierre & Galaz, 2017; Rosenau, 1990; Weatherby et al., 2017). Five key sources of change are central to this analysis. First, change was catalyzed by technology and the microelectronic revolution, which reduced distances and accelerated communication (Gordon, 2017; Rosenau, 1990; Weatherby et al., 2017). This technological advancement brought about global crises resulting from increased interdependence and transnational relations (Rosenau, 1990). Second, change manifested in the diminished ability of states to generate effective solutions to problems, leading to a loss of control over their citizenry, Third, change occurred through the weakening of the state and the empowerment of subsystems as decentralization superseded centralization. Finally, change was driven by increased analytical skills, engagement, and authority of citizens. These changes collectively contribute to the turbulence observed in world politics (Karns et al., 2016; Ansell & Trondal, 2017; Gordon, 2017; Rosenau, 2003).

In this elaborate environment, a conflict arose between change and continuity. As the world transformed, identities evolved, creating tensions between those embracing change and those seeking continuity (Ferguson & Mansbach, 2007; Rosenau, 2003). This confusion was further compounded by a bifurcation of global structures (Rogers, 2009). Bifurcation, in this context, refers to a division or split. In the realm of politics, this bifurcation of power occurred due to a multitude of factors, including the emergence of new actors, technological revolutions, economic globalization, loss of state sovereignty, increased interdependence, subgroups, a more educated and skilled population, and a widening gap between countries benefiting from globalization and those lagging (Bellamy, 2017).

As boundaries erode, sovereignty is challenged, building a new horizon where authority experiences fusion and fission (Ferguson & Mansbach, 2007; Rosenau, 1990; 2003). Fusion represents the growth of networks that connect and influence people globally, while fission involves fracturing political entities into localized and specialized units to address specific needs. However, amidst this constant flux, some underlying patterns remain. The quest for security, the pursuit of economic prosperity, and the yearning for a just world continue to shape the actions of both state and non-state actors. This dynamic nature policymakers to be agile in navigating turbulent political environments.

## Reimagining Governance Structures

Global transformations are inescapable, demanding a broader perspective from policymakers. This requires a departure from conventional and comfortable worldviews to make significant intellectual leaps in understanding the magnitude of global change (Rosenau, 1990). The proliferation of diverse actors has made it imperative to define this new environment and effectively address its challenges. Frameworks that integrate NGOs, domestic labor, conscientious individuals, corporations, and multilateral institutions into policymaking are crucial (Chong, 2002). While non-state entities face legitimacy challenges, they wield significant influence and skill, advocating for marginalized groups and serving as watchdogs in the political system (Aho, 2017).

Classifying the diverse actors involved is crucial to understanding the multi-centric world. Rosenau (1990) identified eight types of actors: three at the micro level (citizens, officials, private) and five at the macro level (states, subgroups, transnational organizations, leaderless publics, and movements). Chong (2002) elaborated on these actors, introducing two central concepts: resistance and complex multilateralism. Non state actors primarily campaign globally to establish an alternative dominion through opposition. This resistance highlights how globalization impacts power dynamics, compelling states to navigate behind the veil of globalization as they are overshadowed by contemporary demands (Teivainen & Trommer, 2016). Additionally, complex multilateralism is a global phenomenon that contributes to the decision-making processes of civil society (Sap, 2017). While this form of global rulemaking is popular and beneficial, it often leads to confused authority structures. Ultimately, a transformation of the policy process that considers the dimensions of globalization is necessary.

Postinternationalism has brought the roles of NGOs and the state to the forefront of analysis, suggesting that diverse actors are diminishing state effectiveness and autonomy. While the microelectronic revolution strengthened states' competence, it also enlarged the competence of individuals. The mobilization of individual efforts has, in turn, paralyzed states. Therefore, the most profitable survival strategy is a collaborative approach to politics.

## Multilevel Politics

The traditional, state-centric model of politics is struggling to address the complex challenges of our increasingly interconnected world. In this postinternational era, characterized by globalization, the erosion of state sovereignty, and the rise of non-state actors, a new understanding of political power and decision-making is necessary (Sellers et al., 2020). Multilevel politics recognizes the importance of governance structures operating at multiple levels – local, national, regional, and global – in addressing global challenges (Acharya, 2017; Pickett et al., 2024). This approach acknowledges that many issues transcend national boundaries and require coordinated action across different levels of government and governance institutions. Through cooperation and coordination among diverse actors at various levels, multilevel policymaking enables more effective and context-specific responses to complex problems.

The contemporary world faces superwicked, complex, and multidimensional challenges. Local authorities grapple with issues like climate change and pandemics, while regional blocs like the European Union exert significant economic and political influence. Meanwhile, powerful non-state actors, such as multinational corporations and non-governmental organizations (NGOs), increasingly shape global policy agendas and influence outcomes. This multilevel landscape presents both challenges and opportunities. Traditional mechanisms of international cooperation, often characterized by slow-moving bureaucracies and a focus on national interests, struggle to keep pace with the rapid flow of globalized issues (Saka-Olokungboye at al., 2023). Conversely, the emergence of new actors creates opportunities for more innovative and inclusive approaches to tackling shared challenges.

These challenges can be compared to a block of irregularly shaped Swiss cheese; the holes in Swiss cheese represent the gaps in governance waiting to be filled by private, governmental, non-governmental, transnational, and supranational actors (Hobbs, 2000). This opening of civic spaces for civil society to demonstrate their expertise and influence across boundaries is facilitated by social media and has been a primary avenue for these entities to create social impact (Ansell & Trondal, 2017; Milano, 2017; Weatherby et al., 2017). Technology has changed the landscape of politics, and this trend will continue. Governance requires collective efforts to identify, understand, and address our problems (Hobbs, 2000).

Governance in a multi-centric, bifurcated world is complex. It spans global, regional, sub-regional, national, provincial, local, and individual levels (Hobbs, 2000; Rosenau, 2003; Rogers, 2009). Governance must also consider the intersubjective, behavioral, and political levels (Rosenau, 2003). Several ideas become relevant to understanding this new configuration: hybrid sovereignty, where many actors negotiate sovereignty and territoriality alongside the state (Ramadan & Fregonese, 2017); participatory governance (Lovan et al., 2017); and scale shifting, which explores the diffusion of power among different networks (Tarrow, 2010).

Networked governance represents a departure from hierarchical, top-down approaches to governance, instead emphasizing decentralized decision-making and collaboration among diverse stakeholders (Zwitter & Hazenberg, 2020). In a networked governance framework, power and authority are distributed across interconnected networks of actors, including governments, non-governmental organizations (NGOs), businesses, and grassroots organizations (Sabatier, 2019; Jenkins-Smith & Sabatier, 1994). This model fosters flexibility, innovation, and adaptability, enabling stakeholders to respond effectively to complex, interconnected challenges.

Heterarchy, as an alternative governance structure, recognizes the non-linear distribution of power and authority among diverse actors, allowing for dynamic interactions and collaboration. Unlike traditional hierarchical models, heterarchy acknowledges the presence of multiple centers of influence and decision-making, facilitating adaptive responses to complex, interconnected challenges (Cerny, 2022; Ramjit, 2022). In a heterarchical framework, power is dispersed rather than concentrated, enabling more agile and context-sensitive governance arrangements.

While alternative governance models offer promising approaches to addressing global challenges and promoting responsive governance, their effectiveness depends on various factors, including context, implementation, and institutional capacity. Networked governance may foster innovation and collaboration but requires robust mechanisms for coordination and conflict resolution (Kapucu & Hu, 2020). Multilevel politics can enhance coordination and cooperation but may face challenges related to overlapping mandates and power struggles among different levels of government (Bianchi et al., 2021). Participatory democracy and heterarchy can enhance citizen engagement and adaptability but require investments in civic education, institutional mechanisms, and adaptive governance structures.

Despite these challenges, by embracing flexibility, inclusivity, and responsiveness, these models have the potential to address global challenges more effectively and promote greater citizen engagement and trust in governance institutions. However, realizing this potential requires careful consideration of context-specific factors and ongoing efforts to strengthen institutional capacity and democratic norms.

## CONCLUSION AND FUTURE IMPLICATIONS

Traditional concepts of power, governance, and policymaking face formidable challenges in modern society. Global interdependence blurs the lines of sovereignty, challenging the idea of absolute authority within national borders. As nations grapple with transboundary issues like climate change, pandemics, and economic disparities, the ability of individual states to unilaterally address these challenges is called into question. The notion of sovereignty must evolve to accommodate the modern world's shared responsibilities and interconnected realities. Moreover, the emergence of global interdependence requires a shift from hierarchical governance structures to more flexible and collaborative models. Traditional top-down approaches to governance prove inadequate in addressing complex, interconnected issues that transcend borders. Effective governance in a networked world requires inclusive decision-making processes that engage diverse stakeholders and leverage collective intelligence.

Pandemics and economic inequality are examples of global challenges that defy unilateral solutions. These issues transcend national borders and require collective action and cooperation among diverse actors, including governments, civil society organizations, businesses, and international institutions (Meuleman, 2021). Collaborative solutions that harness multiple stakeholders' collective expertise and resources are essential for addressing the interconnected challenges of the modern world. Confronted with multifaceted challenges, policymakers face the daunting task of formulating effective responses in a turbulent world. The interconnected nature of global issues demands holistic, cross-sectoral approaches that transcend traditional policy silos. Policymakers must navigate the complexities of interdependence, balancing national interests with global responsibilities and fostering cooperation among diverse actors.

# REFERENCES

Acharya, A. (2017). After Liberal hegemony: The advent of a multiplex world order. *Ethics & International Affairs*, 31(3), 271–285. DOI: 10.1017/S089267941700020X

Andaya, B. (2017). Glocalization and the Marketing of Christianity in Early Modern Southeast Asia. *Religions*, 8(1), 7. DOI: 10.3390/rel8010007

Ansell, C., Trondal, J., & Morten, O. (2017). *Governance in Turbulent Times*. Oxford University.

Bellamy, R. (2017). A European republic of sovereign states: Sovereignty, republicanism and the European Union. *European Journal of Political Theory*, 16(2), 188–209. DOI: 10.1177/1474885116654389

Bianchi, C., Nasi, G., & Rivenbark, W. C. (2021). Implementing collaborative governance: models, experiences, and challenges. *Public Management Review*, 23(11), 1581 1589. https://doi.org/DOI: 10.1080/14719037.2021.1878777

Byrne, D. (1998). *Complexity Theory and the Social Sciences: An Introduction*. Routledge.

Crumley, C. (2015). Heterarchy. In Kosslyn, S (Ed.), *Emerging Trends in the Social and Behavioral Sciences* (pp. 1–14). John Wiley and Sons. DOI: 10.1002/9781118900772. etrds0158

Curry, D. (2012). The Structure-Agency Paradox of New Forms of Non-Binding Governance: Actor Networks, Multi-Level Governance and Canadian and EU Lessons. Working Paper for 2012 84th Annual Conference of the Canadian Political Science Association, 13–15 June 2012, University of Alberta.

Curry, D. (2018). Multi-Level Governance in British Columbia. British Columbia, Canada. Retrieved from https://www.researchgate.net/publication/320085647 _Multilevel_Governance_of_Sustai ability_Transitions_in_Canada_Policy_Alignment_Innovation_and_Evaluation

Ferguson, Y., & Mansbach, R. (2007). Post internationalism and IR theory. *Millennium*, 35(3), 529–550. DOI: 10.1177/03058298070350031001

Gordon, S. (2017). *Online communities as agents of change and social movements*. IGI Global. DOI: 10.4018/978-1-5225-2495-3

Guazzone, L., & Pioppi, D. (2022). *The Arab State and neo-liberal globalization. the restructuring of state power in the Middle East*. (pp. 1–400). http://ci.nii.ac.jp/ncid/BB13295258

Guy, S. (2009). What is global and what is local? A theoretical discussion around globalization. *Parsons Journal for Information Mapping*. Retrieved from http://piim.newschool.edu/journal/issues/2009/02/pdfs/ParsonsJournalForInformationMpping_Guy-JeanSebastian.pdf

Harvey, D., & Reed, M. (1996). Social Science as the Study of Complex Systems. In Kiel, L. D., & Elliott, E. (Eds.), *Chaos Theory in the Social Sciences: Foundations and Applications*. University of Michigan Press.

Helberger, N. (2020). The Political Power of Platforms: How Current Attempts to Regulate Misinformation Amplify Opinion Power. *Digital Journalism (Abingdon, England)*, 8(6), 842–854. DOI: 10.1080/21670811.2020.1773888

Henning, C. (2009). Networks of Power in the CAP System of the EU-15 and EU-27. *Journal of Public Policy*, 29(2), 153–177. DOI: 10.1017/S0143814X09001056

Hobbs, H. H. (2000). *Pondering postinternationalism*. State University of New York.

Hofstadter, D. (1979). *Godel, Escher, Bach: An Eternal Golden Braid*. Basic Books.

Hutchins, E. (1994). *Cognition in the Wild*. MIT Press.

Jenkins-Smith, H., & Sabatier, P. (1994). Evaluating the Advocacy Coalition Framework. *Journal of Public Policy*, 14(2), 175–203. Retrieved May 5, 2021, from https://www.jstor.org/stable/4007571. DOI: 10.1017/S0143814X00007431

Kapucu, N., & Hu, Q. (2020). Network governance. In *Routledge eBooks*. DOI: 10.4324/9781351056540

Karns, M., Mingst, K., & Stiles, K. (2015). *International Organizations*. Lynne Rienner.

Kibbler, J. (2011). Cognitive disequilibrium. *Encyclopedia of Child Behaviour and Development*, 380-380. DOI: 10.1007/SpringerReference_179877

Kontopolous, K. (1993). *The Logics of Social Structure*. Cambridge University Press. DOI: 10.1017/CBO9780511570971

Maull, H. (2011). *World politics in turbulence*. Retrieved from library.fes.de: https://library.fes.de/pdf-files/ipg/ipg-2011-1/2011-1__03_a_maull.pdf

McCulloch, W. S. (1945). A heterarchy of values determined by the topology of nervous nets. *The Bulletin of Mathematical Biophysics*, 7, 89-93.

McEvoy, J. K. (2022). Power Shift: The global Political economy of energy Transitions. *International Journal, 77*(1), 153 155. https://doi.org/DOI: 10.1177/00207020221097998

McNair, B. (2017). *An introduction to political communication* (6th ed.). Routledge. DOI: 10.4324/9781315750293

Meuleman, L. (2021). Public Administration and Governance for the SDGs: Navigating between Change and Stability. *Sustainability (Basel)*, 13(11), 5914. DOI: 10.3390/su13115914

Minsky, M., & Papert, S. (1972). *Artificial Intelligence Progress Report* (AI Memo 252). Cambridge, MA: MIT Artificial Intelligence Laboratory.

Mouzelis, N. (1995). *Sociological Theory: What Went Wrong?* Routledge.

Papadopoulos, Y. (2010). Accountability and Multi-Level Governance: More Accountability, Less Democracy? *West European Politics*, 33(5), 1030–1049. DOI: 10.1080/01402382.2010.486126

Piacentine, C. (2022). Book Review: The Power of Platforms: Shaping Media and Society, by Rasmus Kleis Nielsen and Sarah Anne Ganter *Journalism & Mass Communication Quarterly*, 100(1), 216–218. DOI: 10.1177/10776990221129838

Pickett, S.T.A., Simone, A.T., Anderson, P. *et al.* The relational shift in urban ecology: From place and structures to multiple modes of coproduction for positive urban futures. *Ambio* **53**, 845 870 (2024). https://doi.org/DOI: 10.1007/s13280-024-02001-y

Pierre, J., & Galaz, V. (2017). Superconnected, compex and ultrafast: governance of hyperfunctionality in financial markets. *Complexity, Governance & Networks*, 12-28. doi:DOI: 10.20377/cgn-55

Prichard, A. (2010). *Rethinking anarchy and the state in IR theory: the contributions of classical anarchism*. Retrieved from University of Bristol: https://www.bristol.ac.uk/media library/sites/spais/migrated/documents/prichard0310.pdf

Rogers, D. (2009). *Postinternationalism and small arms control: theory, politics, security*. Ashgate.

Rosenau, J. N. (1990). *Turbulence in world politics: a theory of change and continuity*. Princeton University Press. DOI: 10.1515/9780691188522

Rosenau, J. N. (2003). Dynamics beyond globalization. New Jersey: Princeton University Press. 2016.1160599

Sabatier, P. (2019). Theories of the policy process. In *Routledge eBooks*. https://doi.org/DOI: 10.4324/9780367274689

Saka-Olokungboye, N., Ilugbami, J. O., & Olateru-Olagbegi, O. (2023). Traditional Institutions and Good Governance in Nigeria. *British Journal of Multidisciplinary and Advanced Studies*, 4(4), 27–39. DOI: 10.37745/bjmas.2022.0252

Stark, D. (2010). Ambiguous Assets for Uncertain Environments: Heterarchy in Postsocialist Firms. *Journal of Economic Sociology*, 1(2), 7–34. DOI: 10.17323/1726-3247-2000-2-7-34

Topal, R. (2022). The rise of digital repression: How technology is reshaping power, politics, and resistance. *The Information Society, 38*(1), 77 78. https://doi.org/DOI: 10.1080/01972243.2022.201422

Trondal, J., & Bauer, M. (2017). Conceptualizing the European multilevel administrative order. Capturing variation in the European administrative system. *European Political Science Review*, 9(1), 73–94. DOI: 10.1017/S1755773915000223

Turnhout, E., Metze, T., Wyborn, C., Klenk, N., & Louder, E. (2020). The politics of co production: Participation, power, and transformation. *Current Opinion in Environmental Sustainability*, 42, 15–21. DOI: 10.1016/j.cosust.2019.11.009

Wang, F. (2010). The Evolution of Hierarchy toward Heterarchy. *Frontiers of Business Research in China*, 515-540. doi:DOI DOI: 10.1007/s11782-010-0109-9

Weatherby, J., Arceneaux, C., Leithner, A., Reed, I., Timms, B., & Zhang, S. (2017). *The other world: issues and politics in the developing world* (10th ed.). Routledge. DOI: 10.4324/9781315543383

Worth, O. (2017). *Hegemony, international political economy and post-communist Russia*. Routledge. DOI: 10.4324/9781315253459

Zwitter, A. J., & Hazenberg, J. (2020). Decentralized Network Governance: Blockchain technology and the future of regulation. *Frontiers in Blockchain*, 3, 12. Advance online publication. DOI: 10.3389/fbloc.2020.00012

## KEY TERMS AND DEFINITIONS

**Distant Proximities:** Reflects the idea that world affairs are both distant and proximate; what was once remote is close-at-hand due to globalization.

**Fragmegration:** Reflects the interaction between fragmenting and integrating dynamics (how localization, decentralization and fragmentation are linked with globalization, centralization, and integration).

**Multi-Centric:** A theoretical perspective that views power and authority as distributed among multiple actors or centers of power from the from local to global.

**Multilevel Politics:** A framework that examines how power is distributed among various levels of government and other actors, including national, regional, local, and international entities. These actors often collaborate or compete to influence policy decisions.

**Postinternationalism:** Refers to the historical period which began after World War II and continues today, characterized by flux and transition, chaos, and coherence.

**State-Centric:** A theoretical perspective that views the state as the primary unit of analysis and the principal actor in politics. This perspective emphasizes the role of states in shaping policy outcomes.

**Turbulence:** Refers to tensions and changes which arise due to a rearrangement of world politics (state-centric systems invaded by a decentralized multi-centric system causing a confused conception of authority structures).

# Chapter 2
# The Reactive State in a Heterarchical World

**Philip G. Cerny**
*University of Manchester, UK*

## ABSTRACT

*States have been the fundamental building blocks of modern world politics. They have formed a dualistic structure reminiscent of the role of the Roman god Janus. Statues of Janus were placed at the gates to the city. The god had two faces, one looking inwards to guard the social, economic and political life of the city, to give it unity and a sense of the common good and public interest. The second face looked outwards, to protect the city from external threats and predators, to pursue the city's interests in a hostile world and to interact with other cities. In today's collective choice literature, the first face or function of the state is said to be an 'arena of collective action' amongst its inhabitants and citizens. The second face or function was to permit the state to make—or break—'credible commitments' to other states, what Kenneth Waltz, in his magisterial Theory of International Politics, called 'like units' (Waltz 1979)—the capacity of a set of political institutions to play such 'two-level games' (Putnam 1988) effectively—is what is called 'statehood' (Brenner 2004).*

## I. STATES AND STATEHOOD IN WORLD POLITICS

States have been the fundamental building blocks of modern world politics. They have formed a dualistic structure reminiscent of the role of the Roman god Janus. Statues of Janus were placed at the gates to the city. The god had two faces, one looking inwards to guard the social, economic and political life of the city, to give it unity and a sense of the common good and public interest. The second face looked outwards, to protect the city from external threats and predators, to pursue the city's

DOI: 10.4018/979-8-3693-3563-5.ch002

interests in a hostile world and to interact with other cities. In today's collective choice literature, the first face or function of the state is said to be an 'arena of collective action' amongst its inhabitants and citizens. The second face or function was to permit the state to make—or break— 'credible commitments' to other states, what Kenneth Waltz, in his magisterial *Theory of International Politics*, called 'like units' (Waltz 1979)—the capacity of a set of political institutions to play such 'two-level games' (Putnam 1988) effectively—is what is called 'statehood' (Brenner 2004).

'Statehood' therefore, is defined as the capacity to fulfill these two different and sometimes conflicting functions simultaneously. States frequently cannot do either of these tasks very well, much less do them both successfully at the same time. Today, a process of adaptation to what are sometimes loosely called 'global realities' has presented a challenge both to older post-feudal and quasi-states that have been absorbed into larger units, as in 18th-20th century Europe, and today to 'new' and 'postcolonial' states. We call this the 'dialectic of globalization and fragmentation' (Cerny 2023).

More powerful older nation-states like Britain, France, Germany and more recently the United States have normally been seen to have a comparative institutional advantage in terms of embodying 'statehood'. This advantage is said to be rooted in their long term historical development, their relative wealth and power in an industrializing world, their governments' increasing bureaucratization and state intervention and regulation to promote economic growth, prosperity and welfare—or what French social philosopher Michel Foucault has calindersandWoodlled 'biopolitics' (Foucault 2008; Gallarotti 2000)—and their inhabitants' sense of common sociological or ideological identity or belonging, whether instilled and indoctrinated from above or spontaneously emerging from below. In contrast, states that have *not* had strong centralizing institutions, political processes, economic development and/or cultural identity—'weak' states generally, especially what are today called 'failed' or 'collapsed' states—are seen as failing to fulfill the fundamental requirements of statehood (Badie and Birnbaum 1983; Migdal 1988).

Thus, the way most academic analysts as well as policymakers and mass publics conceive of 'modern' world politics has centered on the roles of states as the core political-organizational units or 'nodes' (see Cerny 2009b). Yet that very form of organization has been problematic from the start, and is becoming even more problematic in an age of globalization and fragmentation. In the 21st century, what is often called 'globalization' presents a particular challenge to this modern—'multifunctional' or 'proactive'—conception of the state and statehood through a range of top down and cross cutting structural transformations, from the integration of global markets and production chains to rapid technological innovation, the growth of complex 'multi-level governance' surrounding and cutting across the state, the convergence of economic policies around varieties of 'neoliberalism', the increasing influence of transnational interest groups and social movements, the emergence of a 'global village' linking societies and identities across borders and the like.

In the 21ˢᵗ century, then, the capacity of traditional nation states to act in effective 'state-like' fashion is increasingly being challenged by a range of factors. The transnational and global nature of the most pressing problems being faced by policymakers and publics, from globalized financial markets to endemic economic crises to the challenges of the environment, makes it difficult for state actors to make coherent and effective policy at the nation-state level. The transnationalities of technology, from the internet to transport to flexible production techniques, creates and strengthens all sorts of cross border economic, political and social linkages and processes. Changing political attitudes towards the human and economic costs of traditional interstate wars, from the rapid exhaustion of domestic public support to the rise of ethnic and religious conflict, including terrorism, means that the nature of warfare is undermining traditional state based military hierarchies and methods (Cerny 2012), a variable that seems to be confirmed by the Russian invasion of the Ukraine in 2022/3.

Furthermore, growing awareness of the complexity of political and social identities, from ever-increasing migration and multiculturalism to the capacity of groups to maintain and intensify of cross-border social and political linkages (for example, through the internet and the growing ease of international travel), challenges the fundamental sense of national identity and belonging that is essential to the social coherence and effectiveness of the 'nation' that the nation-state relies upon for stability, accountability and legitimacy. Transnational economic stresses and lifestyle issues from consumerism and the media 'global village' (McLuhan 1964) to today's 'green' consciousness make ordinary people, as well as elites, increasingly aware of the global and transnational significance and consequences of these challenges. But at the same time a fundamental two-dimensional shift is taking place, including mindless patriotism, jingoistic nationalism and Trump-style populism, on the one hand, to an awareness of the need for transnational and global responses to a whole range of other issues that were traditionally seen to be the job of nation states to tackle, on the other.

Indeed, various kinds of 'multi-level governance' crystallize and proliferate in a globalizing world. More formal international regimes, institutions and quasi-supranational bodies have been set up and are increasingly influential; however, they are still in somewhat fragmentary form, from the United Nations and the International Monetary Fund, the World Bank, the World Trade Organization, the Bank for International Settlements and the like to regional institutions like the European Union, as well as urban and other subnational or cross-national regions sometimes reaching across borders (Brenner 2004). A range of less formal transnational processes are also emerging, including the crystallization and intertwining of 'transgovernmental networks' among national regulators, legislators and legal specialists whose cross-border links increasingly take priority in terms of policy development over domestic hierarchies (Slaughter 2004), the development of 'global civil society', especially with regard to NGOs (non-governmental organizations), and the growing role of 'summits' and other *ad hoc* or semi-formal intergovernmental negotiating fora like the G7/8 and especially the G20 (Beeson and Bell 2009). 'Issue areas' are increasingly cut across in heterarchical fashion, including the convergence of public policies across borders through imitation, policy learning and 'policy transfer' (Evans 2005).

Thus there is a crisis of statehood in today's world. Some see the solution in resurrecting the nation state—whether through religious identity (Israel, Iran), 'nation-building' or 'state-building' (Fukuyama 2004), the reinvention of various forms of 'state capitalism' and the 'return of the state' (Plender 2008), or the renewal of American hegemony through 'soft power' or economic leadership (Nye 2008; Gallarotti 2009; Cerny 2006). Others look to a range of more specific organizational alternatives:

- strengthening existing international institutions;
- working through regional organizations like the European Union (de Larosière 2009);
- encouraging the development of a new multilateralism of 'civilian states' (Sheehan 2008) or a more pluralistic 'society of states' (Hurrell 2007);
- the creation of new forms of transnational 'regulatory capitalism' (Braithwaite 2008);
- the spread of such intermediate sub-state or cross-state organizational levels as urban, subnational and cross-border regional governance (Brenner 2004);
- 'global civil society' (Edwards 2004);
- the spread of democratization and cosmopolitanism (Held 1995; Archibugi 2008); and/or
- the 'bottom up' development of new forms translocal initiatives or 'glocalization', i.e., crosscutting local initiatives (Sassen 2007).

There are also more pessimistic interpretations that argue that we are entering a world of greater volatility, competing institutions, overlapping jurisdictions and greater instability reflecting a general 'disarticulation of political power' and statehood in a more open ended, destabilizing way sometimes referred to as 'neomedievalism' (Cerny 2000a).

I argue that future structural and organizational developments will depend on the kinds of political coalitions that can be built to confront and deal with those challenges, especially those involving cross-border networks, not only *multi-level* but also *multi-nodal* (Cerny 2010). States are enmeshed in increasingly dense webs of power and politicking, as well as economic and social connections, that diffuse 'statehood' unevenly This process sometimes leads to conflict and stalemate, but also sometimes to new, innovative forms of governance and a kind of multi-dimensional statehood within an ongoing process of construction and evolution.

## II. THE DISTORTED DEVELOPMENT OF THE NATION STATE AND THE STATES SYSTEM

Paradoxically, globalization itself in its earlier manifestations was primarily organized and structured by and through the division of the world into states. From the first European colonial empires in the 15th century to the spread of globalization in the late 20th century, the development and institutionalization of states as such and the states system has been inextricably intertwined a range of profound trans-formative changes at various levels:

- the spread of international trade and finance;
- the promotion of industrialization, economic growth and technological change;
- underdevelopment and development;
- the construction of social identity;
- the establishment of international institutions; and
- political modernization, including democratization.

Until the late 20th century, therefore, the very organization of world politics itself and the global political economy was rooted in the emergence, consolidation, and interaction of nation states. States also have deeply entrenched sources of institutional and organizational strength.

In long term historical perspective, of course, the nation state is only one of a wide range of alternative political-organizational forms, including village societies, tribal societies, city states, multilayered feudal and warlord dominated societies, federations and confederations of various kinds, and empires. However, with the emergence of new forms of complex interdependence in the late 20th and early 21st centuries—including global markets, networks of firms, transnational pressure groups (NGOs or non-governmental organizations), international regimes, the rise of world cities and urban regions, and the like—states have found themselves increasingly enmeshed in crosscutting or 'transnational' political, social and economic structures and processes. The nation state today is highly contingent and in flux (Brenner, Jessop, Jones and MacLeod 2003 rooted in what in France is called *raison d'État* or what others have called a 'shared mental model' (Roy, Denzau and Willett 2007) that takes the state for granted as the normal way to organize social life, effectively the only option (Foucault 2007 and 2008; Burchell, Gordon and Miller 1991).

State actors were able collectively to claim 'sovereignty' (Hinsley 1966). Sovereignty, originally rule or supreme power and authority from above, was a more legalistic, centralized, formal and normative version of what is here called statehood. The original European states derived key aspects of their power from the 1648 Peace of Westphalia, which ended decades of religious warfare in the wake of the collapse of feudalism and the Holy Roman Empire, indirectly enshrined the twin principles of (a) the territorial integrity of the state and (b) non-intervention in the internal affairs of other states. Together these principles have become the fundamental organizing doctrine of an international system rooted in the *de jure* sovereignty and *de facto* autonomy of states. Sovereignty in the ideal type sense has therefore been more a political objective than an fact on the ground, and the ideology of the sovereign nation state has been called a form of 'organized hypocrisy' (Krasner 1999). Nation states had to be consciously *constructed* precisely because they did *not* constitute self-evident 'natural containers'.

In this process, European states and later the United States and Japan turned themselves into 'Great Powers', whether through imperial expansion, political influence, economic clout or social imitation. Britain and France were the first effective nation states (Kohn 1955); much of their strength later came from their world-wide empires. Germany and Italy were only unified in the late 19th century but sought to become empires thereafter. Russia remained a loose, quasi-feudal empire until the Soviet era and retained many of its characteristics thereafter. The United States saw itself originally as a quasi-democratic continental empire that needed to avoid 'foreign entanglements' and had a complex federal structure, but it increasingly expanded outwards and centralized from the end of the 19th century. Japan moved rapidly from isolationist empire to expansionist empire in the 20th century. Therefore, imperial expansion was crucial in providing a resource base for 'core' states to spread the states system around the In turn, the most dramatic phases of the global extension of the state's system came with decolonization. Leaders of independence movements and postcolonial governments tried to emulate the European nation state model, what has been called 'nation-building' (Bendix 1964), although this process often did not include democratization.

In this context, attempts at post-independence democratization merely opened the way for zero sum social and economic struggles (Cerny 2009a). Only a few postcolonial states (especially India) stayed democratic for long, although since 1990 most former Communist states have become democratic and attempts to spread democracy in Asia, Latin America, Africa, and the Middle East have also multiplied in that time, sometimes successfully, sometimes unsuccessfully. International arrangements reinforced this trend, as the membership and institutional structures of United Nations and other formal international organizations are essentially composed of sovereign states. Ironically, it was at this time that the system of states started to decay.

## III. THE STATE AS A CONTESTED ORGANIZATION

The capacity of the state to embody and exercise effective statehood rests on two analytically distinct but inextricably intertwined foundations. In the first place, the state, as an *organization or institution*, is embodied in particular factors including: (a) a set of generally accepted 'rules of the game'; (b) the distribution of resources in a particular society; (c) a dominant ideology; and (d) the capacity of the state to use force, whether 'the monopoly of legitimate violence' (Max Weber) or a range of legal, economic and social sanctions, to impose particular decisions and ways of doing things upon both individuals and the society as a whole. In the second place, the state, like other organizations and institutions, is populated by a range of *actors* within and around the state apparatus. These 'state actors' make decisions and attempt to impose outcomes on non-state actors. The state is both a structured field of institutionalized power on the one hand and a structured '*playing field*' for the exercise of social or personal power on the other. They are—ostensibly at least—so-called '*differentiated*' organizations. In other words, ideal type states are organizationally distinct from families, churches, classes, races, and the like; from economic institutions like firms or markets; and indeed, from non-state political organizations such as interest and pressure groups or social movements. The state, in theory at least, stands on its own. Nevertheless, the state can be seen as contested on at least three levels.

Firstly, the state is an *economically* contested organization. It is organized around relationships of power as well as political ideas such as fairness and justice, whereas economic organizations like firms and markets are organized in principle at least around material criteria and relations of profit, exchange, and economic efficiency. Nevertheless, firms and markets also involve inherent *de facto* relationships of power. In particular, states and state actors have been increasingly involved historically in trying to promote economic growth and modernization. Secondly, the state is a *socially* contested organization. States are not natural, spontaneous organizations, but political superstructures historically constructed by real people and political forces around and over often deep divisions such as class, clans and extended families, ethnicity, religion, geography, gender, and ideology, usually in an attempt precisely to mitigate, counteract or even violently repress those divisions. 'Citizens' are made, not born. This often entrenches deep conflicts of identity and interest actually *within* the state itself. This is particularly true of postcolonial states— 'fake states', increasingly 'reactive' rather than 'proactive'. At the same time, older, more established nation states are coming under similar pressures. And finally, the state is a *politically* contested organization. States can be organizationally 'strong' in the sense that they can be rooted in widely accepted social identities and bonds, or that their institutions are effective and efficiently run, or that their 'writ' runs throughout the territory. They can also be powerful internationally. However, states can also be weak on both levels, often cutting across the so-called 'inside/outside distinction' (Walker 1992).

Nevertheless, as noted earlier, what is distinct about states in the modern world is that the state form of political organization has at least until recently prevailed historically over *other* forms, which have been relatively weak and vulnerable in comparison. The combination of hierarchical power inside the state and the spread of the state form of organized governance across the globe, leading to the wide-spread assertion and belief that states are, and should be, genuinely 'sovereign'. State organizations are said to represent a holistic concentration and centralization of generalized, overarching and legitimate political power that is unique among organizations—what the political philosopher Michael Oakeshott called a 'civil association', as distinct from an 'enterprise association' that has specific purposes and a limited remit (Oakeshott 1976). At the international level of analysis, there is supposedly no international 'state' or authority structure that has the kind of legal, political, social, economic or cultural reality, claim to primacy or legitimacy that the state possesses. The international *system of states* is seen as the norm. Each state is in principle, in international law, founded upon a unique base—a specific geographical territory, a specific people or recognized group of citizens, a specific organizational structure or set of institutions, a specific legal personality and a spe-cific sociological identity. Such distinctions, however, have historically often been constructed upon shaky foundations.

## IV. CONTEMPORARY CHALLENGES TO THE ORGANIZATIONAL CAPACITY OF THE STATE

Both dimensions of the inside/outside distinction are rooted in the *organizational capacity* of states. This is problematic in two main ways. On the one hand, various international, transnational and global structures and processes have competed with, cut across, and constrained—as well as empowered—states and state actors throughout modern history. As noted earlier, the most successful European states throughout the early modern and modern periods were ones whose power and pros-perity were rooted in international trade and imperial expansion as well as domestic consolidation. Indeed, globalization itself has often been seen as the externalization of a mix of hegemonic British and later American patterns of open capitalism, trade liberalization and monetary and financial hegemony, not to mention military success in defeating more authoritarian and state corporatist states like Germany and Japan and even the Soviet Union in the Cold War. However, state organizational power has paradoxically boxed itself in by promoting its own subsumption in the globalization process.

States and the states system thus do not exist in a vacuum, but are increasingly cut across by a range of 'complex interdependencies' (Keohane and Nye 1977). Globalization theorists suggest that these interdependencies constitute a rather different infrastructure of the international or global, based on *crosscutting linkages* that states have both ridden on the back of and struggled to control—whether multinational corporations, international production chains, the increasing international division of labor rooted in trade interdependence, globalizing financial markets, the spread of advanced information and communications technologies (Marshall McLuhan's 'global village'), rapidly growing patterns of migration and diasporas, and the emergence of diverse forms of 'global governance' and international regimes, not to mention the rapidly evolving field of international law. For example, the core of domestic state power— 'police power'—is becoming more problematic in this world, where borders are often helpless in controlling the movement of people, information, goods, and ideas (Mostov 2008). They are becoming increasingly institutionalized. They are often more structurally mobile and organizationally flexible than states.

On the other hand, states are rapidly evolving in their role as domestic or endogenous arenas of collective action in ways that also are inextricably intertwined with complex interdependence and globalization rather than holistic autonomy. Paradoxically, the world as a whole was only finally divided up into nation-states in the mid-to-late 20th century. However, many newer states, as well as older states that had in the past been part of quasi-imperial spheres of influence like that of the United States in Latin America or of Britain and France in Africa, have not 'developed' into bureaucratically effective, politically unified, socially homogeneous, or economically more prosperous and/or fairer societies. Some have thrown in their lot with regional organizations like the European Union, while others have stagnated and become more corrupt, for example suffering from the 'resource curse' or the 'aid curse' (Moyo 2009), and some have become 'failed' or 'collapsed' states, descending into quasi-anarchy, like Somalia.

States are also exogenously diverse and highly unequal. Even in relatively developed and powerful states like the United States, a combination of economic problems and the increasing difficulty of controlling external events has led to what the historian Paul Kennedy called 'imperial overstretch' (Kennedy 1987), not only the lack of capability to project military and economic power abroad, but also what in the Vietnam War was symbolized by the 'body bag syndrome'. Indeed, military historian James Sheehan has argued that Europe, that cauldron of international imperialism in the modern era, has simply lost its taste for war and evolved into a grouping of 'civilian states' (Sheehan 2008). However, at the same time, Putin's Russia is attempting to resurrect its neo-imperial role in the Ukraine.

In this context, states are also endogenously—domestically—diverse. They consist of a bewildering variety of institutions and practices—democratic, authoritarian, egalitarian, exploitative, etc.—that have very different consequences both for their inhabitants or citizens, on the one hand, or for other states and their inhabitants/citizens, on the other. Each state combines with and internalizes globalizing trends in somewhat different ways (Soederberg, Menz and Cerny 2005). Sometimes this enables them to exploit the opportunities presented by the opening up of particular international markets, for example the so-called 'BRICs' (Brazil, Russia, India, and China), but sometimes they find their international linkages exacerbating domestic problems by aggravating social or ethnic conflicts, hindering or even reversing economic development, or undermining political stability and leading to violent conflict, civil wars and terrorism. At the same time, these transnational linkages can lead to emergent groups, especially a new, increasingly globally aware and technologically skilled bourgeoisie, demanding a greater democratic say.

Of course, to paraphrase Churchill on democracy, states are still the central and predominant political organization of the modern era—compared with all the others. Markets and other economic organizational structures are concerned with material outcomes, not basic social or political organization. Ethnic groups pursue their own cultural goals, whether inside or outside existing political structures and processes. Only in theocracies do religious organizations claim political sovereignty, and even in the leading theocracy of the 21st century, Iran, religious claims to political authority are contested at various levels. International institutions and regimes are fragmented and lack sanctioning power, although a certain neoliberal hegemony increasingly pertains. Thus, the role of the state is increasingly contested both inside and outside.

## V. KEY ISSUES IN THE RELATIONSHIP BETWEEN GLOBALIZATION AND STATEHOOD

It is possible to identify a range of organizational issues crucial to any understanding of how states work both internally and externally (and in between) in this more complex environment. The first of these is what traditional 'Realist' International Relations theorists call 'capabilities'. This term originally covered mainly military resources but has been extended more and more to include social and economic organizations. States that could marshal concentrated military power to defend their national territory and, especially, to conquer or exercise effective influence over other states and/or power sources, have over the course of modern history been likely to exercise disproportionate influence over outcomes at the international as well as the domestic level. However, these states were also very vulnerable to complex shifts in the 'balance of power' and often found that others could 'balance' against them by forming alliances as well. Technological changes can also upset such existing balances or relations of capabilities. And diplomacy or international bargaining and politicking among states could constrain or effectively alter existing balances too (Little 2007).

Today it is often seen that other forms of capacity or effectiveness are far more important. People, especially in liberal democratic states, are more aware, particularly because of the development of the 'global village', not only of the downside of military involvement in other parts of the world but also of the possibilities of increased popular influence through pluralism, democratization and a 'new tribalism'. Paradoxically, this globalization and fragmentation of awareness has led to a growing unwillingness to get involved in military operations abroad unless they are relatively costless. However, these developments are currently being challenged by the Russian invasion of the Ukraine and the complex situation in Gaza.

At the same time, the costs of war, like the costs of empire in the 1950s, are increasingly seen by economists to be counterproductive of economic development, growth, and prosperity—in other words a drain on the state (and the country) rather than a benefit. Debates are still raging over whether the costs of the War in Iraq, often estimated at 2-3 trillion U.S. dollars, in turn prevented the United States from tackling a range of other problems, both domestic (health care, rebuilding infrastructure, social security, employment) and foreign (development aid, fighting disease, etc.) (Bilmes and Stiglitz 2008). The American failure in Afghanistan resurrected this issue, leading to the new isolationism of the Trump phenomenon. In this context, the maintenance or expansion of military and military related capabilities are increasingly seen as having negative consequences for state, society and economy, opening the state up to new international economic and institutional opportunities and constraints and in expanding the economic regulatory/domestic state. The 2008 financial crisis has accelerated awareness of these issues at all levels across the globe.

For these and other reasons, war as an instrument of statehood has generally declined dramatically since the Second World War. Some analysts stress the role of global awareness and the role of norms of peace and security in this previously understated development (Pinker 2011), while others stress—paradoxically, at first glance—the very success of the state's system itself. As state borders have become more fixed and mutually recognized, as states themselves have become more firmly rooted domestically and concerned with economic issues in a globalizing world, and as intergovernmental regimes have become more developed and accepted, foreign conquest, empire-building and other forms of war, have come to be seen as a pathological rather than normal state of affairs. Indeed, United Nations peacekeeping has played a significant role in this transformation, (Goldstein 2011). Whereas in the post-feudal European context, as Charles Tilly so famously wrote, 'war made the state, and the state made war' (Tilly 1975), today states—especially 'civilian states'—are expected to make peace and cooperate in order to grow and prosper (Kaplan 2012). 'The story is more one of war's containment than expansion' (Strachan and Scheipers 2011: 21).

The second major organizational issue facing the state in the 21$^{st}$ century involves the internal coherence and hierarchical effectiveness of states in both domestic and foreign policy-type decision making. States that are internally divided, bureaucratically weak, torn asunder by civil conflict, subject to the influence of special interests of various kinds, or fundamentally aggressive and neo-imperialist may either be ineffective and inefficient in pursuing so-called 'national interests' and may even be themselves the cause of destabilization processes that limit or even destroy state capacity and therefore undermine statehood itself, as may still happen in Russia. In an age of globalization and fragmentation, that conflict of interests is expanding rapidly.

The competition of interests has previously been analyzed primarily at domestic level but is becoming increasingly transnationals (Cerny 2010). Some critical analysts have identified the formation of a 'transnational capitalist class'—or at least a 'transnational elite' linked with multinational corporations, global financial markets, various transnational 'policy networks' and epistemic communities' and the like, and further associated with hegemonic opinion formers—especially in developed states (Sklair 2000; van der Pijl 1998; Gill 2003). These groups are said to have a common interest in the spread of a neoliberal model of globalizing capitalism. Not only do they have common goals across borders, but they also have resource power and a set of institutional bases and linkages that go from the local to the global (sometimes called 'glocalization'), not to mention the kinds of personal connections traditionally associated in domestic-level political sociology with class and elite analysis. Their common concern with developing transnational power bases gives them a kind of political muscle collectively that parochial domestic groups cannot match.

The most powerful interest groups are increasingly those that can mobilize resources transnationally and not just internally—multinational corporations, global financial market actors, social networks that cut across borders like ethnic and/or religious diasporas, and even consumers who don't care where particular goods are made provided the price and quality are right for the means at their disposal. The nation state represents sociological 'nations' less and less and increasingly resemble associations of consumers (Ostrom, Tiebout and Warren 1961) trying to get the best product at the best price in the international marketplace. They are characterized by what Rosenau calls 'fragmegration', or transnational integration alongside domestic fragmentation (Rosenau 2003).

The third major organizational issue of the 21$^{st}$ century concerns whether the state itself is increasingly becoming 'splintered' or 'disaggregated'. In studies of bureaucracy in the 20$^{th}$ century tradition of Max Weber, the key to effective rule was said to require a hierarchically organized state in which officials knew their roles and functions in the larger structure. Although a full command hierarchy in the authoritarian or Soviet planning modes was seen to be counterproductive, the state required a great deal of centrally organized institutional coherence and administrative efficiency in order to develop and prosper. Today, that logic has been turned on its head. The most effective bureaucratic structures and processes are those that link officials in particular issue areas with their counterparts in other countries, in order that they might design and implement converging international standards, whether for global financial market regulation, trade rules, accounting and auditing standards, and the like. Expanding 'transgovernmental networks' among regulators, legislators and legal officials are effectively transnationalizing such issue-areas, red-lining them from domestic protectionist interests, dominating policymaking processes, and globalizing the most important parts of the state in order to promote economic growth and other key policy goals (Slaughter 2004).

A fourth level of internal organizational change concerns the so-called 'competition state' (Cerny 2000b and 2009b). Modern nation-states, in the pursuit of the public interest or the general welfare', have traditionally sought to 'decommodify' key areas of public policy—to take them out of the market through some form of direct state intervention—in order to protect strategic industries or financial institutions, bail out consumers or investors, build infrastructure, counteract business cycles, and integrate workers into cooperating with the capitalist process through unionization, corporatism, the welfare state and the like. This process in the 20$^{th}$ century was linked with the growing social and economic functions of the state—the industrial state and the welfare state—and tended to come about through the expansion of what have been called 'one-size-fits-all' bureaucracies for the delivery of public and social services.

Today governments are more concerned not with decommodification of social and economic policy but with the 'commodification of the state' itself (Cerny 1990). This has two goals. The first is to promote the international competitiveness of domestically based (although often transnationally organized) industries. Only competitiveness in the international marketplace will do. The second is to reduce the costs of the state—what is called 'reinventing government'—or 'getting more for less' (Osborne and Gaebler 1992). These two processes are aimed both at streamlining and marketing state intervention in the economy and at reorganizing the state itself according to organizational practices and procedures drawn from private business. The welfare state is increasingly under cost pressure in the developed world, and developing states are often not able to provide meaningful welfare systems at all.

The 2008 financial crisis only exacerbated this trend, despite the partial return Keynesian stimulus policies, such as those followed by the Biden Administration in the United States, which are often seen as short-term remedies intended to 'save capitalism from the capitalists' (Cerny 2011). Thus this combination of complex interdependence, the transnationalization of interests, disaggregation of the state and the coming of the competition state has fundamentally transformed how the state itself works. There is a rapidly growing trend towards the erosion of national varieties of capitalism and the rise of a new neoliberal hegemony rooted in globalization (Soederberg, Menz and Cerny 2005; Cerny 2010).

## VI.  CONCLUSION: THE REACTIVE STATE IN A WORLD OF HETERARCHY HAS BECOME THE PREDOMINANT *PROBLÉMATIQUE* OF 21ST CENTURY WORLD POLITICS

Statehood is not a given, the exclusive property and distinguishing feature of modern nation states, but a *problématique* or analytical puzzle, the parameters of which are continually evolving. Organizationally strong states may to some extent be able both to internalize and to resist the pressures of economic, social and political globalization, although that capacity is increasingly hedged around by complex interdependence. Organizationally weak states are undermined by globalization and crisis becomes endemic. Most states are in between these two extremes, with state actors and various kinds of interest groups—crucial players in the international system of states as well as the expanding globalization process—seeking to alter, reform or completely restructure states in order to cope with the challenges of a globalizing/fragmenting world. Thus, effective statehood is becoming more and more difficult to achieve at the level of the nation state, while multi-level and multi-nodal politics are creating new and complex forms of latent, embryonic and indeed emergent forms of statehood that have increasingly come to dominate politics in the first decade of the 21st century. The statue of Janus increasingly resembles a kind of Gulliver, pinned down by the Liliputians of globalization, while people cast about for new ways of organizing their relationships and going about their business.

# REFERENCES

Archibugi, D. (2008). *The Global Commonwealth of Citizens: Toward Cosmopolitan Democracy*. Princeton University Press.

Badie, B., & Birnbaum, P. (1983). *The Sociology of the State* (Chicago, Ilinois: University of Chicago Press)

Barker, S. E. (Ed.). (1962). *Social Contract: Essays by Locke, Hume and Rousseau*. Oxford University Press.

Beeson, M., & Bell, S. (2009, Spring). The G-20 and International Economic Governance: Hegemony, Collectivism, or Both? *Global Governance*, 15(1), 67–86. DOI: 10.1163/19426720-01501005

Bendix, R. (1964). *Nation-Building and Citizenship*. Anchor Books.

Bilmes, L., & Stiglitz, J. (2008) *The Three Trillion Dollar War: The True Cost of the Iraq Conflict*. Norton.

Braithwaite, J. (2008). *Regulatory Capitalism: How it Works, Ideas for Making It Work Better*. Edward Elgar. DOI: 10.4337/9781848441262

Brenner, N. (2004). *New State Spaces: Urban Governance and the Rescaling of Statehood*. Oxford University Press. DOI: 10.1093/acprof:oso/9780199270057.001.0001

Brenner, N., Jessop, B., Jones, M., & MacLeod, G. (Eds.). (2003). *State/Space: A Reader*. Blackwell. DOI: 10.1002/9780470755686

Burchell, G., Gordon, C., & Miller, P. (Eds.). (1991). *The Foucault Effect: Studies in Governmentality*. University of Chicago Press. DOI: 10.7208/chicago/9780226028811.001.0001

Cerny, P. G. (1990). *The Changing Architecture of Politics: Structure, Agency and the Future of the State*. Sage.

Cerny, P. G. (1997, Spring). Paradoxes of the Competition State: The Dynamics of Political Globilization. *Government and Opposition*, 32(2), 251–274. DOI: 10.1111/j.1477-7053.1997.tb00161.x

Cerny, P. G. (2000a). Globalization and the Disarticulation of Political Power: Toward a New Middle Ages? In Goverde, H., Cerny, P. G., Haugaard, M., & Lentner, H. H. (Eds.), *Power in Contemporary Politics: Theories, Practices, Globalizations* (pp. 170–186). Sage. DOI: 10.4135/9781446219935.n9

Cerny, P. G. (2000b). 'Restructuring the Political Arena: Globalization and the Paradoxes of the Competition State,' in Randall D. Germain, ed., *Globalization and Its Critics: Perspectives from Political Economy* (London: Macmillan), pp. 117-138 DOI: 10.1007/978-1-137-07588-8_4

Cerny, P. G. (2006). 'Dilemmas of Operationalizing Hegemony', in Mark Haugaard and Howard H. Lentner, eds., H*gemony and Power: Consensus and Coercion in Contemporary Politics* (Lanham, MD: Lexington Books on behalf of the International Political Science Association, Research Committee No. 36 [Political Power]), pp. 67-87

Cerny, P. G. (2009a, May). Some Pitfalls of Democratisation: Thoughts on the 2008 *Millennium* Conference. *Millennium*, 37(3), 763–786. DOI: 10.1177/0305829809103243

Cerny, P. G. (2009b, April). Multi-nodal Politics: Globalisation is What States Make of It. *Review of International Studies*, 35(2), 421–449. DOI: 10.1017/S0260210509008584

Cerny, P. G. (2010). *Rethinking World Politics: A Theory of Transnational Neopluralism.* Oxford University Press. DOI: 10.1093/acprof:oso/9780199733699.001.0001

Cerny, P. G. (2011, May). "Saving Capitalism from the Capitalists?" Financial Regulation after the Crash. *St. Antony's International Review*, 7(1), 11–29.

Cerny, P. G. (2012). 'The New Security Dilemma Revisited', paper presented at the annual convention of the International Studies Association, San Diego, California, 1-4 April

Cerny, P. G. (2023). *Heterarchy in World Politics*. Routledge.

de Larosière, J. (2009). *The High-Level Group on Financial Supervision in the EU*, chaired by Jacques de Larosière (Brussels, 25 February 2009), https://ec.europa.eu/internal_market/finances/docs/de_larosiere_report_en.pdf

Edwards, M. (2004). *Civil Society*. Polity Press.

Evans, M. G. (2005). *Policy Transfer in Global Perspective*. Ashgate.

*Experiments with Global Ideas* (London and New York: Routledge)

Foucault, M. (2007). *Security, Territory, Population: Lectures at the Collège de France, 1977-1978* (French edition 2004). (Burchell, G., Trans.). Palgrave Macmillan.

Foucault, M. (2008). *The Birth of Biopolitics: Lectures at the Collège de France, 1978-1979* (French edition 2004). (Burchell, G., Trans.). Palgrave Macmillan.

Fukuyama, F. (2004). *State-Building: Governance and World Order in the 21ˢᵗ Century*. Cornell University Press.

Gallarotti, G. M. (2000, January). The Advent of the Prosperous Society: The Rise of the Guardian State and Structural Change in the World Economy. *Review of International Political Economy*, 7(1), 1–52. DOI: 10.1080/096922900347036

Gallarotti, G. M. (2009 forthcoming). *The Power Curse: Influence and Illusion in World Politics*. Lynne Rienner. DOI: 10.1515/9781685854355

Gill, S. (2003). *Power and Resistance in the New World Order*. Palgrave Macmillan.

Goldstein, J. S. (2011). *Winning the War on War: The Decline of Armed Conflict Worldwide*. Dutton.

Held, D. (1995). *Democracy and the Global Order: From the Modern State to Cosmopolitan Governance*. Polity Press.

Hinsley, F. H. (1966) *Sovereignty*. Watts.

Hurrell, A. (2007). *On Global Order: Power, Values and the Constitution of International Society*. Oxford University Press. DOI: 10.1093/acprof:oso/9780199233106.001.0001

James, A. (1986). *Sovereign Statehood: The Basis of International Society*. Allen & Unwin.

Kaplan, R. D. (2012). *Monsoon: The Indian Ocean and the Future of American Power*. Random House.

Kennedy, P. (1987). *The Rise and Fall of the Great Powers: Economic Change and Military Conflict from 1500 to 2000*. Random House.

Keohane, R. O., & Nye, J. S.Jr. (1977). *Power and Interdependence: World Politics in Transition*. Little, Brown.

Kohn, H. (1955). *Nationalism: Its Meaning and History*. Van Nostrand.

Krasner, S. D. (1999). *Sovereignty: Organized Hypocrisy*. Princeton University Press. DOI: 10.1515/9781400823260

Little, R. (2007). *The Balance of Power in International Relations: Metaphors, Myths and Models*. Cambridge University Press. DOI: 10.1017/CBO9780511816635

McLuhan, M. (1964). *Understanding Media: The Extensions of Man*. McGraw Hill.

Migdal, J. (1988). *Strong States and Weak States: State-Society Relations and State Capabilities in the Third World*. Princeton University Press.

Mostov, J. (2008). *Soft Borders: Rethinking Sovereignty and Democracy*. Palgrave Macmillan. DOI: 10.1057/9780230612440

Moyo, D. (2009). *Dead Aid: Why Aid Is Not Working and How There Is a Better Way for Africa*. Farrar, Straus and Giroux.

Nye, J. S.Jr. (2004). *Soft Power: The Means to Success in World Politics*. Public Affairs.

Oakeshott, M. (1976, August). On Misunderstanding Human Conduct: A Reply to My Critics. *Political Theory*, 4(2), 353–367. DOI: 10.1177/009059177600400308

Osborne, D., & Gaebler, T. (1992). *Reinventing Government: How the Entrepreneurial Spirit is Transforming the Public Sector, from Schoolhouse to Statehouse, City Hall to the Pentagon*. Addison-Wesley.

Ostrom, V., Tiebout, C. M., & Warren, R. (1961, September). The Organization of Government in Metropolitan Areas: A Theoretical Inquiry. *The American Political Science Review*, 55(3), 831–842. DOI: 10.2307/1952530

Pinker, S. (2011). *The Better Angels of Our Nature: The Decline of Violence in History and Its Causes*. Allen Lane The Penguin Press.

Plender, J. (2008). "The Return of the State: How Government Is Back at the Heart of Economic Life," *Financial Times* (August 22)

Putnam, R. D. (1988, Summer). Diplomacy and Domestic Policy: The Logic of Two-Level Games. *International Organization*, 42(3), 427–460. DOI: 10.1017/S0020818300027697

Rosenau, J. N. (2003). *Distant Proximities: Dynamics Beyond Globalization*. Princeton University Press. DOI: 10.1515/9780691231112

Roy, R., Denzau, A. T., & Willett, T. D. (Eds.). (2007). *Neoliberalism: National and Regional*

Sassen, S. (Ed.). (2007). *Deciphering the Global: Its Scales, Spaces and Subjects*. Routledge.

Sheehan, J. J. (2008). *Where Have All the Soldiers Gone? The Transformation of Modern Europe*. Houghton Mifflin.

Sklair, L. (2000). *The Transnational Capitalist Class*. Blackwell.

Slaughter, A.-M. (2004). *A New World Order*. Princeton University Press.

Soederberg, S., Menz, G., & Cerny, P. G. (Eds.). (2005). *Internalizing Globalization: The Rise of Neoliberalism and the Erosion of National Varieties of Capitalism.* Palgrave Macmillan. DOI: 10.1057/9780230524439

Spruyt, H. (1994). *The Sovereign State and Its Competitors: An Analysis of Systems Change.* Princeton University Press. DOI: 10.1515/9780691213057

Strachan, H., & Scheipers, S. (Eds.). (2011). *The Changing Character of War.* Oxford University Press. DOI: 10.1093/acprof:osobl/9780199596737.001.0001

Tilly, C. (Ed.). (1975). *The Formation of National States in Western Europe.* Princeton University Press.

United Nations Commission of Experts on Reforms of the International Monetary and Financial System. (2009). *Recommendations* (19 March 2009), https://www.un.org/ga/president/63/letters/recommendationExperts200309.pdf

van der Pijl, K. (1998). *Transnational Classes and International Relations.* Routledge.

Walker, R. B. J. (1992). *Inside/Outside: International Relations as Political Theory.* Cambridge University Press. DOI: 10.1017/CBO9780511559150

Waltz, K. (1979). *Theory of International Politics.* Addison-Wesley.

## KEY TERMS AND DEFINITIONS

**Dialectic of Globalization and Fragmentation:** This complex process has been underway since the post-Second World War period.

**Heterarchy:** The complex, multi-level and multi-nodal interaction of the concepts of Hierarchy and Anarchy. It refers to processes and institutions that operate above, below, and cutting across the state and the nation-state system. It replaces the field as defined in "neorealist" International Relations Theory and other "paradigms", where states are seen as hierarchical and relations between states are seen as anarchical. The approach has been developed in the fields of Sociology and Anthropology.

**Paradigm:** In science and philosophy, a paradigm is a distinct set of concepts or thought patterns, including theories, research methods, postulates, and standards for what constitute legitimate contributions to a field. The word paradigm is Greek in origin, meaning "pattern".

**Transnational:** Political, social, and economic processes that cut across the state and the states system in different social and economic sectors.

**Turbulence:** A term used by the postinternationalist theorist James Rosenau to describe and analyze the core problem of the Postinternationalist Era.

**World Politics or "Politique Mondiale":** A cross-cutting term to replace "International Relations".

# Chapter 3
# How Polycontexturality Goes Deeper Than Polycentrism as the Approach to Exploring Heterarchic Space of Governance

**Richard R. Weiner**
https://orcid.org/0000-0002-9995-1185
*Rhode Island College, USA*

## ABSTRACT

*This chapter details how out of the Habermas-Luhmann epistemological and social debates of the 1970s through the 1990s, Günther Teubner moves us to mapping emergent properties amidst a complexity of contexts and temporalities in institutionalist analysis. Starting from respective theories of functional differentiation and complexity, Teubner's polycontexturality approach comprehends the emergence of self/ mutual referencing and self-enforcing reciprocity norms of non-state associations. We are guided by riddles: How does the relentless functional differentiation tend to multiple contextures in transnational policy making, rule-making and standard-setting.? How is it possible to coordinate resolution of overlapping or colliding autonomous systemic or subsystemic regime logics?*

DOI: 10.4018/979-8-3693-3563-5.ch003

# 1. INTRODUCTION

This chapter focuses on heterarchy in the coordination of political economy outside the boundaries of the nation-state. Heterarchy is posed as an evolving decentered network re-regulation outside the de-regulating state in neoliberal political economy. Such de-centered re-regulation in private and social spheres emerges, amidst dispersed and different yet connected webs – webs of procedures and practices.

This is a study of the creation of traceable new spaces of unfolding institutionalizing practices. (Not the process tracing of multiple data points in political science input/ output analysis.) Precisely, emergence in the unfolding / evolving of non-state associations denoting movement and flow, circuits and circulation, the interconnexion of multiple network nodes, and the *emergence* of clustering relays of horizontally connecting multiple nodes.

*Polycentrism* is a conceptual framework – associated with The Indiana School of Elinor Ostrom (1990; 2010a; 2010b) -- providing analytical structure for studying many diffuse and different forms of self-organizing assemblages with different objectives, values and steering procedures. This amounts to sustaining and brokering mutual adjustment. Brokering rational choice amidst institutional fragmentation. Where the underlying *principe* (Montesquieu's term) is stabilization of some co-existing of multiple autonomous and closed centers of decision-making: both territorial and non-territorial; both muli-layered and multi-scalar.

The limitations of polycentricity approach have been denoted as:

(1) Issues of normative ambiguity regarding the legitimation/ justification of authority in reconciling and coordinating colliding and incommensurablee claims;
(2) Issues of how equilibrating groups can exploit each other while gaming some overarching order of rules and protocols; and
(3) Issues of how still other groups can remain latent and immobilized, or quietly emerging.

Can we go deeper in exploring heterarchic spaces of governance?

Complexity theory invites us to exchange equilibrating perspectives for a more expansive polycontextural perspective. One regarding how emergent intersecting parts combine with each other to assemble themselves and self-organize into new traceable and trackable space So as to develop an ordered whole. Grasping emerging patterns that tap into mutually constituting forces.is a conceptualized modality involving a meaning-making dimension.

For Günther Teubner, *polycontexturality* is a conceptualized modality --involving a meaning-making (i.e., phenomenological) dimension. Thus, would account for collaborative and sometimes reciprocal contact wherein web actors create their own frames as new spaces. New planes of self-reference and responsiveness are not reducible to its constituting parts. There is a tracing of conceptualized patterns of a self-referential/mutually referential and responsive circuits of interacting web domains. Polycontexturality thinking combines heterarchy with the emergence of coordinating multiple paths as complementary rather than just as interlocking.

Unlike *fragmegration* theorizing (Rosenau, 1990; 2010), we are moved by Günther Teubner beyond political scientists' often too simple equilibrating description of a polycentrism of transnational policy regime clusters. This is a distributive model of clustering in terms of patterned arrangements. Conceptually, the model of polycentrism is moved from the implicit rational-choice institutionalism of Elinor Ostrom's description of horizontal competition/cooperation among local governments and their civil society partners. Describing co-creating and providing both public goods and common goods.

Our key issue is the extent to which equilibrium thinking obscures the tracking movements and change in the contextualizing conditions of a complex system. Equilibrium is an idea that whatever the current unsettled condition – of a market, an economy, a society – there exists some configured fixed point with the property of persistence. It characterizes theorizing of balance wherein there is a presumed immanent order toward which a market, an economy, a society is supposed to tend, known as a steady state. (James K. Galbraith, 2024).

For Ping Chen (2010; 2023) economic equilibrium is an "illusion of self-stabilization" grounded in a mathematical principle -- an idea rather than empirical analysis of market movement and change. Chen talks of coordination games/ strategies *with multiple* equilibria / *multiple steady states*. And Galbraith (2025) grasps a sense of evolutionary economics, considering how the neoclassical economics at the foundation of NeoLiberalism/ OrdoLiberalism are rooted. Rooted in pre-evolutionary theories of equilibrating and optimizing "rational choice" starting with the Physiocrats and the Utilitarians. We should note here how Post-Keynesian models do not have built-in equilibrating mechanisms (Baccaro, Blyth, and Pontusson, 2022).

Teubner's approach starts from multiple equilibria where flows and circulation in multimodal networks return toward an institutionalizing trajectory of practical realizing and nonlinear complexity dynamics. Rather than a simple equilibrium of steady state among forces, a polycontexturality approach suggests we follow such institutionalizing trajectory as *interstitial*.

That is, *in between* **networks/ webs of governance** in coordinated procedures, practices, and meanings of expectations for mutual monitoring complementary webs of governance.

## 2. FROM FUNCTIONAL DIFFERENTIATION TO TRANSNATIONL WEBS OF GOVERNANCE

The cognate term "transnational" denotes mutually referential space by non-statist associations for standard-setting and rule-making protocols operating across nation-state borders. These serve as guidelines for iterative negotiations and bargaining -- to enable coordination and conflict regulation. Often dealing with colliding systemic and subsystemic rationales within an organization of recursive feedback relations.

Transnational space is a topography for webs of practices, procedures and meaning of seemingly incommensurable colliding discourses and operating logics. This is a space with a range of diverse landscapes, diverse contexts of norms and rules. The world has become so closely connected and yet so different.

Fragmentation is no longer understood solely in terms of territorial sphere -- as in the Westphalian Order. Rather, it is increasingly understood in terms of additional functional / sectoral spheres. This reflects a social evolution of normative and legal ordering towards reciprocity and reconciliation. Towards development that dilutes any attempt at integration from a given center or combination of hegemonic centers.

It is a space for interfaces of functioning, coding, and mutually referring relations among fragmented *webs*. Institutional relationality is key. Emergent associational properties cluttered around differentiated and dispersed issue areas. By webs, we metaphorically denote institutional development as networking configuration weaving together patterns of negotiations in a sort of *meshwor*k (DeLanda, 2016).

- Meshworks fostering norms of connectingness.
- Meshworks of participation in practices with normative commitment.

This involves heterarchical clustering and entangling rather than hierarchical embedding.

Functional differentiation is the driving force of modernity and is modernity itself. Niklas Luhmann (1982) understood "modernity as the primacy of functional differentiation" and was the first sociologist to shift the concept of functional differentiation to what he referred to as the "world society" of The Second Modernity. Luhmann considered nation-state limitation of functional differentiation as an arrangement of limited duration – which bears the seed of its dissolution in itself since unrelenting evolution leads toward another direction.

Relentless functional differentiation intensifies and accelerates social economic complexity of autonomous mutually regulating operative subsystems in cyberspace. A complexity within recursive heterarchies, comprehensible as metaphoric loops and loops within loops. Networks of interconnected autonomous and autopoietic subsystems of operative closure. These autonomous systems and subsystems involve what Eleanor Ostrom (1990) referred to as "self-enforcing reciprocal norms (SERNs)"

Space is being reinvented and realigned. What Ulrich Beck (1992) referred to as First Modernity's solidity/ solidarity is challenged, liquified and responded to. First Modernity appeared to be solid because of how the rapid centralization of institutional power became consolidated in a "project nation state" (Maier, 2023) stabilizing organized capitalism. The semblance of social solidarity – what socio- logical theorist Emile Durkheim referred to as functional organic society melts.

Solidity/Solidarity is challenged, liquified and responded to. In Second Modernity, what Zygmont Bauman (2000) has called Liquid Modernity, there is a movement away from perceived over-regulation of enterprises by territorially bounded project nation-states. There is a porous and diffuse condition of perpetual becoming. Space is being re-ordered into various hybrid combinations beyond verticality – re-ordered as horizontally, diagonally, centripetally, centrifugally, transversally, spherically, and fractally

As Philip Cerny (2013) argues, functional differentiation of the Second Moder- nity can be understood as leading to an explosion of transnational webs in post- international political economy Such web-like differentiation, Cerny (2013; 211) notes, "opens up a wide range of complex systems" with a bewildering diversity of contextual referents. These are organized metaphorically as Gilles Deleuze noted as grooves, creases, furrows, and folds

There is a wearing down of verticalism and hierarchy towards heterarchical and horizontal relationships. By heterarchy, we denote in transnational political economy self-critical space of increasingly decentered rule-making, standard-setting, and policy-making. Not in terms of superordination and subordination, but in terms of lateralized strategies occurring horizontally to reflect the increased differentiation of interstitial zones / zones of "in-between-edness" (what Teubner imaginatively refers to as the *Zwischenraum*).

These autonomous systems and subsystems involve what a Third Generation of Frankfurt School Critical Theory of Society (Forst, 2003, 2018) refers to as ***norma- tive order*** i.e., what Elinor Ostrom referred to as "self-enforcing reciprocal norms." As Helmut Willke (2007) discusses, transnational webs of governance and webs of capital – as noted in Appendix below - are constituted in a decentered *lateral* world system both criss-crossing and inter-connecting. Emerging non-state associational properties within emergent webs of networked self-reference.

Liquid Modernity challenges us to cope with seemingly incompatible and incom- mensurable modes of protocols and their contexts. We are challenged to seek a way to attain some approximation of institutional complementarity. Such complementarity

(1)  compensates for each other's deficiencies in instiyutionalizing some whole; and

(2) reciprocally reinforces each other to greater web resilience and the semblance of a solidarity of sustainability.


## 3. GÜNTHER TEUBNER'S POLYCONTEXTURALITY PROJECT

Out of the Habermas-Luhmann Debates of the 1970s through the 1990s [fn. 1], Günther Teubner significantly developed a framework of analysis for spatially framing and exploring emergent adaptive heterarchic governance. This is described as multi-nodal coupling. It is found within the de-centered/ multi-layered negotiating and coordinating of potentisl network complementarities. Webs of Capital Accumulation and Webs of Governance characterize the global capitalism emerging in the late 20th century. (See Appendix below.)

The Debates emerged during the 1960s. The two pulled their essays together and co-authored in 1971 the book *Theory of Society or Social Technology*. Habermas moves in the direction of cognitive and communicative capabilities *vis à vis* normative ordering, i.e., the legitimatory aspacts of social evolution. In contrast, Luhmann moves in the direction of the levels and scales of operations of sustainable self-organizing (autopoiesis) and self-referencing (reflexivity) of systems and subsystems.

Luhmann focuses on the closure of different systems and subsystems at the same time as there is a heightening interactive environment both of and between systems. Habermas in attempting to integrate insights of Luhmann's systems theory countered by arguing that within systems there is cognitive open-ness of normative differences rather than Luhmann's perceived closure between the systems.

Poul Kjaer (2006) significantly points out that Luhmann seems to have inadequately recognized the importance of context for the constitution of social phenomena. This is referred to as *the context dependency issue.* Luhmann incorporated: (1) Habermas's concept of an intersubjective lifeworld that counters the over-determination of technic/ technology -- – as the determining surroundings of system and subsystem; as well as (2) an appreciation of the existence of an inner framing and an external framing. But Luhmann is confronted with the issue of how context denotes meaning with which we frame our observations. This is the temporal problematic of historicity in Max Weber's *verstehen* sociology which Kjaer stringently take note of. Kjaer argues that beyond affirmation, Luhmann has trouble demonstrating how systems contain "a mechanism for determining what a system constitutes itself against." (Kjaer, p.80)

Günther Teubner seeks to break down the hardened fields as well as to develop the convergences within the Habermas-Luhmann debate. Seeking to mediate the philosophy of speech acts, phenomenology of meaning and normative ordering in

Habermas with Luhmann's sociological systems theory. Here emphasizing differentiation and a heterarchy of decentered forms of social discourses and knowledge within a web of networks – which cannot be tamed and overcome by nation-state politics. Teubner stresses how the complexity in systems and networks resist hierarchy of some single centralizing global integration. Like Luhmann, Teubner focuses on the levels and scales of operations and both the collective and the intersubjective processual practices of communication. This helps lead Teubner to analyze various forms of negotiations, relational contracts, negotiated network connecting contracts, mediation and arbitration – and the linkages between the nodes of different interconnected systems of communication

Teubner takes account of complex systems network theory that comes after Luhmann. Networks are comprehended as complex webs composed of nodes, interfaces and boundaries. Networks are interconnected systems capable of communicating and sharing information – as well as collaborating on tasks. Contextures of inter-legality, inter-normativity, inter-textuality with an eye on: (1) the necessary exchange of information through processual practices; (2) overlapping structures, and (3) the co-evolution of rule-making and standard-setting.

Necessary to facilitate efficient operation of global supply chains. Further, there are contextures of unpredicted disruption in finance, employment, climate, and public health, and technology spur novelty and innovation to enable adaptation.

Teubner points to the 21$^{st}$ century systems-oriented practice of "Learning by Monitoring" (Sabel, 1996; 2004). Reflexive heterarchic network governance (Voss and Kemp, 2006) involves inter-systemic contexts and inter-organizational contexts defined in multiple serial nodes, linkages, regularized interactions and regulation of collisions and conflicts. These webs of governance require organizational and institutional complementarity exerting a kind of hybrid heterarchical rather than hierarchical influences on other organizations, other institutions, other subsystems. Some examples:

* Mutual monitoring and learning among network participants and thus encouraging a sense of legitimacy and accountability;
* Adopting and monitoring performance standards, codes and protocols;
* Setting up and verifying information pooling for the network; and
* institutionalizing scheduled sanctions to guarantee both (1) transparency, and (2) that supply networks work

Concretely: transnational corporate codes of social responsibility; transnational environmental governance agreements; multilateral fisheries agreements; multilateral biodiversity agreements; multilateral carbon management standards; monitored transnational finance reporting; transnational standards of collectivized liability.

## 4. CONTEXTURES, COMPLEXITY AND COMPLEMENTARITY

The core puzzle posed by Teubner are the possibilities for self-constitutionalizing capacity of stable non-state associations as institutions of protocol-based regulation and resolution. (Thornhill, 2011). How can they be seen in a coordinating capacity in the form of the reflexive governance of both private law and non-state association socially constituted? It is puzzle Teubner considers as the "constitutionalizing of polycontexturality."

Self-constitutionalizing is not something particularly new because of globalization. The *Régulation School* of Robert Boyer and his colleagues in Paris (Boyer and Saillard, 2002) makes a distinction in self-constitutionalizing. Bargaining agreements ("solemn and binding") –- *réglementtions sollonels* which steer a field of enterprise. On the other hand, *régulation* refers to the decentered ensemble of rules, norms, procedures and sedimented practices that represent the underlying organizing principles (*principes*) that represent a political economy as a whole – be it territorially-based or non-territorially based. Teubner (2012) responds to discussions regarding the progress in the level of modelling coherence and tightening up in the studies of fragmented plural legal and socioeconomic spaces -- what he refers to as "*constitutional fragments*."

We can understand Teubner's over-arching methodological approach involves the supervenience of Polycontextual Logic (PCL)– a logic referring to the complementarity of seemingly incommensurable rationales of fragmented subsystems. This cybernetic perspective combines the need for coordinating heterarchy with a need for coordinating resolution of colliding autonomous subsystemic regime logics. Here the influence of Warren McCulloch (1945) and Niklas Luhmann. A PCL approach is multi-level, multi-scalar, tranversal and fractally multiplex—providing an imaginative projecting and rational reconstructing that enables us to conceptualize, frame and analyze/synthesize

A PCL approach uses sociological systems theorizing to study functional differentiation across multiple contextures in the making of policy, rules, standards, codes, protocols. This is a methodological approach to relentless differentiation resulting in self-regulating/ self-legitimating systemic proceduralism, practices and meanings. This is what is referred to as self-constitutionalizing within networks of trust and reciprocity—within Transnational Policy Regimes and the Transnational Law they co-create.

*The systems approach of Luhmann and the polycontexturality approach of Teubner recognize the impossibility of steering society from a single central control without regressive functional de-differentiation.* Resisting either a Carl Schmitt-like homogeneous or Talcott Parson-like / Hans Kelsen-like universalizing system of values/ forms of life. And overcoming seeing one's context from the blind spot in one's own non-state association. Not Durkheim's perspective of the collective representations of some *conscience collective,* but of social representations constantly negotiated and renegotiated (Moscovici, 2000).

*Here, Teubner (2011) takes us to a depth level beyond the pattern-arrangement equilibrating approach of polycentrism. This is the* level *of polycontextural policy and legal dynamics that relate to and reference the non-linearity of multiple equilibria. A complex causality of multiple contextures.*

By **contexture**, Teubner signifies:

*First*, the mediations of warranted assertions of purported legitimacy – rulemaking, standard setting; performance auditing; professional and scientific certifying and innovation. Contextures for decentered action. That is, law, standards, codes and protocols for conflict regulation, self-limiting constitutionalism, and political culture. Education, professions and the Internet come under Transnational Normative Orders beyond the constitutions of nation-states.

*Second*, as previously noted, conditions of unpredictable disruption or even chaos such as financial crises; unemployment, pandemics, and havoc caused by climate change.

Specifically, polycontexturality refers to the multiple and qualitatively different contextures embedded with each other, often referred to as "imbricated" (Bartmansky, 2021). We are moved from a rational-choice and compliance with functioning embeddedness. Moved to a more normative approach to institutions. Considering **the institutional facticity of norms, rules, and protocols, rather than the brute facticity of material forces.** (See here Neil MacCormick, 1998.) Here the institutional facts are the procedures, practices and meanings Transnational Policy Regimes (TPRs), Transnational Normative Order (TNOs), Transnational Law (TNLs), and Transnational Advocacy Networks (TANs). These are separate but aligned with both nation-states and international organizations like the United Nations.

We are challenged to represent a polycontextural sense of institutional complementarity – constituted by connecting institutions. Operating in the unfolding reflexive self-organization of a world civil society of networks. These are what Carl Schmitt referred to in German jurisprudence as *Konnexion Institüt* and what Poul Kjaer (2020) more recently refers to as *intermediary institutions* or bridge institutions. **Institutional complementarity** comes to be understood in terms of how we can facilitate and enforce both communications and obligations across boundaries – boundaries of nation-states, boundaries of function systems.

PCL complexity theorizing combines conceptualizing heterarchy with a need for:

- transcending functionally differentiated subsystems;
- responding to seeming incommensurability and the possibility of reconciling;

- offsetting the negative consequences (externalities) of function systems and subsystems in a world society of networks at large;
- regulating and coordinating the resolution of colliding discourses in autonomous self-constitutionalizing regimes (i.e., subsystemic economic constitutions); and
- interweaving, intermeshing, and in this way interconnecting colliding socio-economic and legal subsyetem rationalities.

Conceptually, the model of **polycentrism** is moved from the implicit rational-choice institutionalism characterizing Elinor Ostrom's description of horizontal mutually adjusting competition/cooperation among local governments and their civil society partners -- in the co-creating and providing of public goods and common goods (Ostrom 2010a, 2010b). Polycentrism can be understood as a concept and associated model in search of a deeper theory of complementarities and multiple equilibria.

We are moved by Teubner beyond polycentrism of policy regime clusters--- a distributive model of clustering in terms of patterned arrangements. We are moved toward emergent properties in terms of **homeorhesis**. *Not just in a sense of simply* equilibrating *distributions of power as homeostasis*. This involves complex mapping not just of the de-centered, but as well of the multi-centered: (1) where flows return to trajectory rather than to a steady state; and (2) a trajectory relating to and referencing many steady states, i.e., multiple equilibria

**This is not just a replacement umbrella term for polycentrism**. A polycontexturality (PCL) approach builds on the biological concept of heterarchy as logic of the non-aborescent.

Heterarchy is understood in terms of PCL denotes a homeorthetic model of multiple equilibria points/ multiple steady states -- where there is neither total disequilibrium or some integrative global equilibrium.

*PCL implies both the limits and range of equilibrating; it denotes innovation and* emergence. *Specifically, how expanding self-organizing flows exhibit* capability *for new elective affinities, i.e., assemblage.*

This is an understanding we can apply to a world system of law and political economy where there is a lurching from one unstable equilibrium to another. We need to resist thinking in terms of "rational choice" of describing change in one area, while everything else stays the same. Such polycentric thinking is inapplicable to studying historical processes and emergent socio-political and legal form where one change creates the *pressure on* and the *possibility for another*. Stabilization is understood in terms of coordinating some sense of institutional complementarity, rather than of a simple sense of balancing countervailing powers.

Thinking about normative and legal ordering can lead us to visualizing the crystallization of spatial institutional patterns. See Figure 1 just below for Crystallized Topology of Heterarchic Space extracted from Rakhyun E. Kim, 202

*Figure 1. Crystallized topography model of heterarchic space*

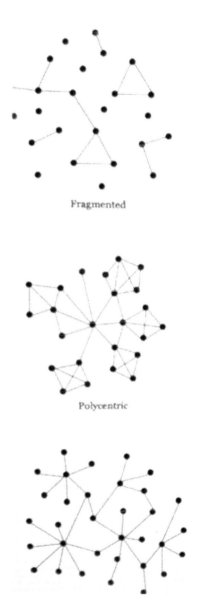

Fragmented

Polycentric

<< COMPLEXITY

Kim's model addresses the complexity of network governance. Interconnectedness is highlighted, rather than mutually adjusting equilibrium. Complexity is understood not merely as a metaphor, but as a quality characterizing a real world system that exhibits adapting and coordinating behavior even in the absence of a central hierarchical authority.

Teubner's polycontexturality approach approximates Kim's crystallized topography of a network of causality which channels complexity into novel paths of transition and transformative transition. Tipping points for abrupt change are reached. Emergent novelty spreads across interconnected systems and institutions within the adapting and coordinating network – cascading across different levels, different sectors and different scales, e.g., community, local, regional, totality.

## 5. THE EMERGENT COMPLEXITY OF HETERARCHIC SPACE

Andreas Duit and Victor Galaz (2008) further deepen our understanding of heterarchic space, introducing the concept of *Complex Adaptive System (CAS):* to better conceptualize and
   spatialize visually

(1)   the developing multiplication of linkages;
(2)   changes in contexts of legitimatio and innovation, and
(3)   changes that do not operate in a linear or predictable manner –as in a straight line between events -- as change accelerates and becomes faster and uncertain; and that have positive and negative feedback loops.

Complex Adaptive Network-Based Heterarchic Governance responds to non-linear unpredicted oscillating disruptions. Again: financial contextures of profit seeking expectations resulting in "irrational exuberance; ecological contextures; and epidemiological contextures of climate change warnings, floods; droughts as well as health hazard pandemics like avarian influenza and COVID; annihilation carnage and elimination, eradication/collapse like the destruction of the World Trade Center on 9/11 and their health hazard consequences; persistent poverty; precarity of gig era jobs; the fatalism of lowered expectations of youth; as well as the speed and distortion in information flows. Teubner comes to associate polycontexturality with "polycrises."

A sense of network architecture is moved --John Meyer (1997a) notes -- beyond both:

(1) the "complicatedness" of distributed power (Kim, 2020) in fragmented policy-making diffusion; and

(2) the patterned clustering of polycentrism with associated focus on equilibrating what is, rather than on what emerges (**emergence**).

Emergence rather than reductionism (Hasker, 1999). The dynamics of multiple disequilibrium responding to multiple contextures rather than mutual adjusting equilibrium. Emergent causal powers supervene. Novelty is added in terms of emergent causal interactions "which cannot be figured out just from the composition of the elements and environmental relations."

Specifically, complexity dynamics in system theorizing denote emergent self-organization and transformation. In Teubner's approach, an emergent metamorphosizing into reflexive and recursive network governance. Networks of negotiated relational contracts, comprehensible as intermeshed operating practices. Complexity theorizing explores how structural patterns emerge spontaneously. The result of interconnected and interactive networks of many parts operating without - overall guiding hands - giving rise to new forms and modes of collective behavior. We are led to visualize *node to node dynamics*

A more conceptually robust complexity approach to network architecture enables us to focus on (1) issues of interlinkages/ interconnections, self-organization and emergent properties; and (2) a sort of meta-law/ meta-normativity/ meta-governance (Jessop, 2020) of the co regulating of conflicting normative orders, conflicting rationalities, and the legal approach to "conflict of laws."

We turn to spatially comprehending – "mapping" -- the heterarchical space that takes us beyond the closure of function systems causing "mutual irritants" (Teubner, 1998). This heterarchical space characterizes the *self-enforcing reciprocal norms (SERNs)* apparent in the code-making and standard-setting of networks. This is what characterizes these re-regulating transnational webs of governance. (See Teubner, 2002; 2003/2004; 2007; 2012; 2015.) These are transnational policy regimes -- with each of their own transnational laws, procedures /codes and protocols; transnational norms for co-creating particular regime norms; codes and protocols.

Thus, we are moved toward a network architecture of ceaseless and cascading *emergent complexity -- a network of networks.* A ceaseless complexity of co-creating, ordering, processing and colliding. We are moved from a focus on co-creation toward issues of institutional coherence, compatibility, institutional complementarity, and multi-nodal network coordination. Self – regulating subsystemic governances –- that is, of governance regimes – with significant autonomy from nation-state governments. Heterarchical space emerges, ineractions in what Teubner refers to as the interstitial *realm of In-Between-edness (Zwischenraum).* What Pierre Bourdieu in *The Logic of Practice* (1990) referred to as *interstitial social space.*

Amidst multiple contextures subsystems interact –i.e., inter-textualities, inter-normativities and inter-legalities. For example, mediating/ arbitrating issues of "conflict of laws" regarding overlapping and colliding transnational orders (TNOs). And toward coordinating the multiple transnational law constitutions (TNLCs). Heterarchic space for Transnational Policy-Making and *Transnational Coordinating of Meshworks.* Grist for this hoped for coordination includes colliding regime discourses; overlapping or colliding legalities; and the clash of the respective rationalities of each autonomous normative system/ subsystem., that is, norms for the creation of norms (Teubner **1996;2003/2004**)

## 6. POLYCONTEXTURALITY CAPABILITY: SEEKING COMPLEMENTARITY AMIDST MULTIPLE EQUILIBRIA

An overarching theme of this chapter is how the equilibrium thinking involved in polycentrism models obscures contextualizing conditions. What Teubner has referred to as the context dependency issue. The deeper issue is normative -- the mutual referencing and responding involved in the mutual monitoring that goes on within polycentric patterns

What we call *polycontextural capability* is such a referencing and responding. A referencing of contextures. And a responsiveness to legitimation claims/ justifications that sustain and widen interlinked webs of governance.

Institutional complementarity refers to the way in which specified institutional patterns exert heterarchical rather than hierarchical influence. This is a complementarity ranging from "affect" to "mutual reinforcement" amidst the autonomous condition of non-state associations we describe as constituting mutual re-regulating regimes. The latter initially conceived as polycentric webs. Complementarity more than compatibility and interoperability lies at the heart of such a polycontextural capability -- gauging the multiple equilibria parts of interacting whole web patterns.

Introducing complexity theory offers new tools of non-linear dynamics and non-stationary time series. Such complexity theorizing involves how economy and society move through multiple equilibria – i.e., multiple complementary steady states --with stability tending to lead to instability and even chaos over time. Movement in complexity is not in a straight line relationship. Movement responding reflexively to contextures is non-linear and recursive-- returning over time to a trajectory rather than to a steady state.

Non-linear dynamics of unpredictable change diffusing through and across multiple equilibrium points are put forward in the evolutionary economics of Hyman Minsky [1986]. This precedes by more than 2 decades the issues of coordination games /with multiple equilibria advocated – at the start of this chapter – by Ping Chen [2010; 2023] and James K. Galbraith [2024; 2025].

Polycontextural capability dynamics respond not just for mutual adjustment. They reflexively respond to the plurality of fragmented contextures. Some of the latter are the codes and protocols that Teubner (2012) refers to as *"constitutional fragments"* Others are contextures of unpredicted disruption.

Polycontextural capability deals with coordinating **context steering procedures**, practices and meanings (Jessop, 2020: Chapter 1. pp. 35-64). It recognizes inter-connected nodes within a network of related autonomous regimes. Further, it recognizes legitimation claims both overlapping and colliding with each other a. polycentric re-regulating -as well as with the nation state. At a higher level, this is a capability which involves reinterpreting and even reconciling such overlapping and colliding inter-relations for mutual/ joint re-regulation. To hearken back to the sociologizing of Karl Mannheim, this is an emphasis on relationism rather than relativism.

So then, how do we re-interpret and reconcile the strategic selectivities of multiple context steering procedures? Best to inquire into how multiple isolated equilibria points in operationally closed autonomous systems can and at times converge. Inquiring how do heterarchies converge into lateral coordinating strategies? What is categorized in evolutionary economics as "coordination games" – with coordination costs [fn.2].

Complementarity rather than synchronicity. A complementarity where each heterarchy compensates for the deficiencies of other normative orders. Understanding how steering procedures/practices may complement each other in one particular set, but not in every other. Also understanding how institutional complementarities of OrdoLiberalism -- styled normative orders do not transfer to Japan.

Pulling this altogether, we can coordinate methodologically our analysis of polycontexturality in stages. Moving from a jurisprudential analysis of steering procedures and practices to what Robert K. Merton referred to as "middle range" theorizing as functional analysis, studying patterns, performances, outcomes, sequences, and consequences. And then to normative evaluation we can refer to as Critical Systems Theorizing [fn. 3] coping with and validating legitimation claims/ justifications.

# 7. CONCLUSION

Out of the Habermas-Luhmann epistemological and social science debates of the 1970s through the 1990s, Günther Teubner has significantly developed a critical sociology of law approach, which frames and explores emergent adaptive heterarchic governance. What has come to characterize decentered and multi-contextured negotiating and coordinating of potential complementarity of networks and the institutions that constitute them as "webs of governance."

The supervenience of polycontextural logic (PCL) characterizes Teubner's over-arching methodological approach to study functional differentiation of networks across multiple contextures of rules, standards, codes, and protocols. Networks in our emergent and fragmented global capitalism. Teubner focuses on: (1) how non-state associations reference each other and relate to each other; (2) how non-state associations operate their network code-making and standard-setting; as well as (3) how they fall into collisions of said codes and standards of each other. This is a focus on how non-state associations come to mutually regulate themselves in "webs of governance" outside the realm of what Charles S. Maier (2023) refers to as the project nation-state," managing themselves as recursive heterarchies facilitating *institutional complementarity*.

Polycontexturality is not just a replacement umbrella term for polycentrism. A PCL approach builds on the biological concept of heterarchy as a logic of non-aborescent multiple layers of neural networks – with multiple points of equilibria points (Mc-Colloch, 1945). Heterarchy understood in terms of PCL denotes a *homeorthetic model of multiple equilibrium points* – where there is neither total disequilibrium or some integrative global equilibrium. PCL implies both the limits and range of equilibrating; it denotes *innovation/ emergence*. Specifically, how expanding self-organizing flows exhibit capability for new affinities.

Polycontexturality 27

## Notes

1.  Habermas's focus has been on creating reciprocal learning opportunities, while Luhmann focused on the level of operations and the levels and scales of proces-sual communicative practices. Habermas initially mistook Luhmann's work as that of the first generation cyberneticians; manifesting a fear of how technology became integral in controlling interpersonal processes. (Referred to as the "in-tersubjective" in Habermas's conceptual language.) Habermas came to adapt parts of Luhmann's system theorizing in his 1975 book *Legitimation Crisis*. In his unfolding writings on epistemology, Habermas in *Truth and Justification* (2003) sees truth in communication having external veracity (i.e., through va-lidity claims). Conversely, Luhmann sees truth as contingent communicative symbols. Beyond Habermas's epistemological dissection and reconstruction, Luhmann in *The Differentiation of Society* (1982) had moved toward sociology and the need to build on recognizable developmental trends that can be realized in recurrent patterns of practices. He noted the plurality of logical domains, labeling them contextures following Gotthard Günther in his 1980 work *Life as*

*Polycontexturality* and Warren McColloch (1945) before him. A "coordination game" in evolutionary economics regarding complementarities and multiple equilibria describes the practice where players choose *context dependent* strategies to achieve a common outcome. Cf. Pure matching or Schelling coordination games; as well as Nash equilibrium games. The latter denoting simultaneous games where there is cooperation considering the decisions of other players, even when it is not the optimum outcome response to do so

2. A "coordination game" in evolutionary economics regarding complementarrities and multiple equilibria describes the practice where players choose *content dependent* strategies to achieve a common outcome. Cf. Pure matching or Schelling competition games, as well as Nash equilibrium games. The latter denoting simultaneous games where there is cooperation considering the decisions of other players, even when it is not the optimum outcome response to do so.

3. Rudolf Wiethölter (1972, 1985/99, 1986; 2013; cf. Habermas,1989; Teubner, 2024; Goldoni and Wilkinson, 2016, 2024). Wiethölter tried to lay the foundations of what he referrred to as a Critical Systems Theory. He uses the term "critical" in terms of tracing the transformational normative potential of institutionalizing trajectory developing within the conflict of social and economic rationalities within nation state-based society and what Luhmann and Teubner dub as "world society." Beyond the routinized fulfillment of the equilibrating functionalist autopoiesis regarding conflicts over social rationalities, our attention is directed (1) to grasping what both normatively and materially underlies collisions of rationalities and conflict of laws between functional systems and subsystem; as well as to grasping compatibility and complementarity of systems, subsystems and institutions.

# REFERENCES

Albert, M., Buzan, B., & Zürn, M. (Eds.). (2013). *Bringing Sociology to International Relations: World Politics as Differentiation Theory*. Cambridge University Press. DOI: 10.1017/CBO9781139856041

Aligica, P. D., & Tarko, V. (2014). Institutional Resilience and Economic Systems: Lessons from Elinor Ostrom's Work. *Comparative Economic Studies*, 56(1), 52–76. DOI: 10.1057/ces.2013.29

Amable, B. (2016). Institutional Complementarities in the Dynamic Comparative Analysis.'. *Journal of Institutional Economics*, 12(1), 79–103. DOI: 10.1017/S1744137415000211

Ansell, C. (2006). Network Institutionalism. In Rhodes, R. A. W. (Ed.), *The Oxford Handbook of Political Institutions*. Oxford University Press.

Avdagic, S. Rhodes, M. & Visser, J., (Eds.). (2011). *Social Pacts in Europe" Emergence, Evolution and Institutionalization*. Oxford University Press

Baccaro, L., Blyth, M., & Pontusson, J. (Eds.). (2022). *Diminishing Returns: The New Politics of Growth and Stagnation*. Oxford University Press. DOI: 10.1093/oso/9780197607855.001.0001

Bäckstrand, K. (2006). Multi-stakeholder Partnerships for Sustainable Development. *European Environment*, 16(5), 290–293. DOI: 10.1002/eet.425

Bartmanski, D. (2021). "Imbricated -A Conceptual Morphology of Contextuality," *Sozialraum.de*. Special Issue/ 2021 ISSN 1868-2596. https://www.sozialraum.de/imbricated-a-conceptual-morphology-of-contextuality

Bauman, Z. (2000/2010). *Liquid Modernity*. Polity Press.

Beck, U. (1992). *Risk Society: Towards a New Modernity. Theory, Culture and Society*, 1st Edition. Sage.

Berger, P., & Luckmann, T. (1966). *The Social Construction of Reality*. Doubleday.

Black, J. (2008). Constructing and Contesting Legitimation and Accountability in Polycentric Regulatory Regimes. *Regulation & Governance*, 2(2), 137–164. DOI: 10.1111/j.1748-5991.2008.00034.x

Boyer, R., & Saillard, Y. (Eds.). (2002). *Regulation Theory: The State of the Art* Shread, C., Trans.). Routledge.

Catá-Backer, L. (2012). *The Structure of Global Law: Fracture, Fluidity, Permeability, Polycentrism*. CPE Working Paper n. 2012-7/ Penn State Law Research Paper 15-20

Cerny, P. (2013). Functional Differentiation, Globalization, and Transnational Neo-pluralism. In Albert, M., Buzan, B., & Zürn, M. (Eds.), *Bringing Sociology into International Relations* (pp. 205–227).

Cerny, P. (2023). Heterarchy in an Age of Intangibles and Financialization. In Cerny, P. (Ed.), *Heterarchy in World Politics*. Routledge.

Chen, P. (2010). *Economic Complexity and Economic Illusion: Essays on Market Instability and Macro Vitality*. Routledge.

Chen, P. (2023). "Interview," *Commentaries.Newsletter of The World Economic Association.*, 3(2), 8–11.

Crocker, D. (2008). *Ethics of Economic Development: Agency, Capability and Deliberative Democracy*. Cambridge University Press.

Crouch, C. (2005). Dialogue on 'Institutional Complementarity and Political Economy,'. *Socio-economic Review*, 3(2), 359–382. DOI: 10.1093/SER/mwi015

DeLanda, M. (2016). *Assemblage Theory*. Edinburgh University Press. DOI: 10.1515/9781474413640

Duit, A., & Galaz, V. (2008). Governance and Complexity: Emerging Issues in Governance Theory. *Governance: An International Journal of Policy, Administration and Institutions*, 21(3), 311–335. DOI: 10.1111/j.1468-0491.2008.00402.x

Dukes, R. (2014). *The Labour Constitution: The Enduring Idea of Labour Law*. Oxford University Press. DOI: 10.1093/acprof:oso/9780199601691.001.0001

Dybvig, P. (2022) *Multiple Equilibria*. Nobel Lecture in Economic Sciences, 8 December 2022.

Falk, R. (1987). The Global Promise of Social Movements: Explorations at the Edge of Time. *Alternatives*, 12(2), 173–196. DOI: 10.1177/030437548701200202

Fischer-Lescano, A., & Teubner, G. (2012). Critical Systems Theory. *Philosophy and Social Criticism*, 38(1), 3–23. DOI: 10.1177/0191453711421600

Forst, R. (2002). *Contexts of Justice* (Farrell, J., Trans.). University of California Press.

Forst, R. (2018). *Normativity and Power* (Cronin, C., Trans.). Oxford University Press.

Galbraith, J. K. (2024), "Entropy, the Theory of Value, and the Future of Humanity," *Economic Democracy Initiative*. Rubric 7., https://www.postneoliberalism.org/articles/entropy-the-theory-of-value-and-the-future-of-humanity

Galbraith, J. K., & Chen, J. (2025). *Entropy Economics: The Living Basis of Value and Production*. University of Chicago Press.

Gleckman, H. (2018). *MultiStakeholder Governance: A Global Challenge*. Routledge. DOI: 10.4324/9781315144740

Goldoni, M., & Wilkinson, M. (2016). The Material Constitution. *The Modern Law Review*, 18(4), 1–31.

Gunningham, N. (2012). Regulatory Reform and Reflexive Regulation: Beyond Command and Control. In T. Dedeurwaerdere, T. & Siebenhüner, B. (Eds.) *Reflexive Governance for Global Public Goods*. MIT Press. DOI: 10.7551/mitpress/9780262017244.003.0103

Günther, G. (1980). Life as Polycontexturality. In *Beitrage zur Grandlegung einer operationsfuhien Dalekth* (Vol. 3). Felix Meiner Verlag.

Habermas, J. (1985). Law as Medium and Law as Institution. In Teubner, G. (Ed.), *Dilemmas of Law in the Welfare State* (pp. 203–220). DeGruyter.

Habermas, J. (1989). Der Philosoph als wahrer Rechtslehrer: Rudolf Wiethölter. *Kritische Justiz*, 22(2), 138–196. DOI: 10.5771/0023-4834-1989-2-138

Hall, P. A., & Soskice, D. (Eds.). (2013). *Varieties of Capitalism: The Institutional Foundtions of Comparative Advantage*. Oxford University Press.

Hartse, G. (2021). *The Habermas-Luhmann Debate*. Columbia University Press.

Hasker, W. (1999). *The Emergent Self*. Cornell University Press.

Heath, J. (2001). *Communicative Action and Rational Choice*. MIT Press. DOI: 10.7551/mitpress/1955.001.0001

Hobbs, H. (Ed.). (2000). *Pondering Postinternationalism; A Paradigm for the 21st Century*. SUNY Press.

Kelsen, H. (1945). *General Theory of Law and the State* (Wedberg, A., Trans.). Harvard University Press.

Kim, R. E. (2020). Is Global Governance Fragmented? Polycentricity or Complexity? The Art of the Network Approach. *International Studies Review*, 22(4), 903–931. DOI: 10.1093/isr/viz052

Kjaer, P. (2006). Systems in Context: On the Outcome of the Habermas/ Luhmann Debate, *Ancilla Juris*: 66-77.

Kjaer, P. (2013). Transnational Normative Orders: The Constitutionalization of Intra- and Trans-formative Law. *Indiana Journal of Global Legal Studies*, 20(2), 777–803. DOI: 10.2979/indjglolegstu.20.2.777

Kjaer, P. (2016). From the Crisis of Corporatism to the Crisis of Governance. In P. Kjaer and N. Olson (Ed) *Critical Theories of Crisis in Europe*. Rowman and Littlefield.

Kjaer, P. (Ed.). (2020). The Law of Political Economy: Transformation in the Function of Law. Cambridge University Press.

Jessop, B. (2020). The Governance of Complexity and the Complexity of Governance. In B. Jessop, *Putting Civil Society in Its Place: Governance, Metagovernance and Subjectivity* (chapter 2). Policy Press. DOI: 10.1017/9781108675635

Lenoble, J., & Maesschalck, M. (2003). *Toward a Theory of Governance: The Action of Norms*. Hague: Kluwer.

Levi-Faur, , D. (2005). The global diffusion of regulatory capitalism. *The Annals of the American Academy of Political and Social Science, 598*(1), 12-32.

Luhmann, N. (1982). The Differentiation of Society (Trans. S. Holes and C. Larmore). Columbia University Press. DOI: 10.7312/luhm90862

Francot-Timmermans, L., & Christodoulidis, E. (2011). The normative turn in Teubner's systems theory of law. *Rechtsfilosophie & Rechtstheorie, 40*, 187.

MacCormick, N. (1998). Norms, Institutions and Institutional Facts. *Law and Philosophy*, 17, 301–345.

MacCormick, N. (2007). *Institutions of Law: Law, State and Practical Reason*. Oxford University. DOI: 10.1093/acprof:oso/9780198267911.001.0001

MacCormick, N., & Weinberger, O. (1986). *An Institutional Theory of la*. Springer. DOI: 10.1007/978-94-015-7727-4

Maier, C. (2023). *The Project State and Its Rivals: A New History of the Twentieth and Twenty First Centuries*. Harvard University Press.

Mannheim, K. (1936). *Ideology and Utopia*. Trans. Edward Shils. Harcourt, Brace.

Mansbach, , RFerguson, , Y. (2007). Postinternationalism and International Relations Theory, *Millenium. Journal of International Students*, 35, 529–549.

Massey, D. (1995). *Spatial Divisions of Labour* (2nd ed.). Routledge. DOI: 10.1007/978-1-349-24059-3

McColloch, W. (1945). A Heterarchy of Values. *The Bulletin of Mathematical Biophysics*, 7, 89–93. PMID: 21006853

McDonald, K. (2002). From Solidarity to Fluidarity: Social Movements Beyond 'Collective Identity' —The Case of Globalization Conflicts. *Social Movement Studies*, 1(2), 109–128. DOI: 10.1080/14742830022000010637

Meyer, J., Boli, J., Thomas, G. M., & Ramirez, F. O. (1997a). World Society and the Nation-State. *American Journal of Sociology*, 103(1), 144–181. DOI: 10.1086/231174

Meyer, J., Frank, D. J., Hironaka, A., Schofer, E., & Tuma, N. B. (1997b). The Structure of a World Environmental Regime, 1870-1990. *International Organization*, 57(4), 623–681. DOI: 10.1162/002081897550474

Minsky, H. (1986). *Stabilizing an Unstable Economy*. Yale University Press.

Moscovici, S. (2000). *Social Representation: Explorations in Social Psychology* (Duveen, G., Trans.). Polity Press.

Nus, E. (2016). *Strategies, Critique and Autonomous Spaces/15M from an Autonomous Perspective*. <https.//www.degrowth/de/em/dim/degrowth-in-movemrnts/15M>

O'Connor, T. (1994). Emergent Properties, *American Philosophical Quarterly* 31:18ff

Orts, E. (1995). A Reflexive Model of Environmental Regulation. *Business Ethics Quarterly*, 5(4), 799–794. DOI: 10.2307/3857414

Ostrom, E. (1990). *Governing the Commons; The Evolution of Institutions of Collective Action*. Cambridge University Press. DOI: 10.1017/CBO9780511807763

Ostrom, E. (2010a). A Long Polycentric Journey. *Annual Review of Political Science*, 13(1), 1–23. DOI: 10.1146/annurev.polisci.090808.123259

Ostrom, E. (2010b). Polycentric Systems for Coping with Collective Action. *Global Environmental Change*, 20(4), 550–557. DOI: 10.1016/j.gloenvcha.2010.07.004

Perez, O., & Stegmann, O. (2018). Transnational Network Constitutionalism. *Journal of Law and Society*, 45(S1), 13–62. DOI: 10.1111/jols.12107

Postone, M. (1997). *Time, Labor and Social Domination: A Reinterpretation of Marx's Critical Theory*. Cambridge University Press.

Rosenau, J. (1990). *Turbulence in World Politics*. Princeton University Press. DOI: 10.1515/9780691188522

Rosenau, J. (2010). Fragmegration. In J. Rosenau. *Along the Domestic-Foreign Frontier*: *Exploring Governance in a Turbulent World* (Chapter 6, pp.89-117). Cambridge University Press.

Sabel, C. (1994). Learning by Monitoring: The Institutions of Economic Development. In Smelser, N., & Swedberg, R. (Eds.), (pp. 137–168). Princeton University Press.

Sabel, C. (1996). Constitutional Orders: Trust Building and Response to Change," In Hollingsworth, R. & Boyer, R. (Eds.) eds. *Contemporary Capitalism; The Embeddedness of Institutions* (pp.54-188). Cambridge University Press

Sabel, C. (2004. Beyond Principal-Agent Governance: Experimentalist Organizations, Learning and Accountability. In E. Engelen, E. & M. Sie Dhahien Ho, (Eds.). *Die Staat van de Demokratie. Demokratie voorbij die Staat.* (pp.173-195). WRR. Verkenning 3. University of Amsterdam Press.

Sabel, C., & Dorf, M. (1998). A Constitution of Democratic Experimentalism. *Columbia Law Review*, 98(2), 267–473. DOI: 10.2307/1123411

Sen, A. (1982). Development as Capability Expansion. *Journal of Development Planning*, 19(1), 41–58.

Smismans, S. 2004). Reflexive Law in Support of Directly Deliberative Polyarchy/ Reflexive Deliberative Polyarchy as a Normative Frame for OMC." In O. DeSchutter, O. and S. Deakin, (Eds.) *Social Rights and Market Forces:* The Future of Social Europe. Brussels; Bruylant

Stark, D., & Sabel, C. (2006). *Heterarchies: Distributed Intelligence and the Organization of Diversity*. Santa Fe Institute.www.santafe.edu/research/heterarchies.php

Ter Horst, P. (2009).Multiscalar Institutional Complementarity and the Scaling of Clusters," *Belgian Journal of Geography*https://doi.org/ pp. 43-64.DOI: 10.40/belgec7075

Teubner, G. (1992). Regulatory Law: Chronicle of a Death Foretold. *Social & Legal Studies*, 1(4), 451–475. DOI: 10.1177/096466399200100401

Teubner, G. (1996). De Collisione Discursuum: Communicative Rationalities: Law, Morality and Politics. *Cardozo Law Review*, 17, 901–918.

Teubner, G. (1998). Legal Irritants: Good Faith in British Law or How Unifying Law Ends Up in New Divergences. *The Modern Law Review*, 61(1), 11–236. DOI: 10.1111/1468-2230.00125

Teubner, G. (2002). Hybrid Laws: Constitutionalizing Private Governance Networks. In R. Kagen, R., Krygier, M., & Winston, K. (Eds.). *Legality and Community: On the Intellectual Legacy of Philip Selznick*. Berkeley: Berkeley Public Policy Press

Teubner, G. (2003/2004). *Coincedentia Oppositorium: Networks and the Laws Beyond Contract and Organization. Storrs Lectures*. Yale Law School.

Teubner, G. (2004). Societal Constitutionalism: Alternatives to State-Centered Constitutional Theory, Iin Transnational Governance and Constitutionalism, In C. Joerges, I-J. Sand, & Teubner (Eds.). Oxford: Hart.

Teubner, G., & Fischer -Lescano, , A. (2004). Regime Collisions: The Vain Search for Legal Unity in the Fragmentation of Global Law. *University of Michigan Journal of International Law*, 25(4), 999–1046.

Teubner, G. (2007). In the Blindspot: Hybridization of Contracting. *Theoretical Inquiries in Law*, 8, 51–72.1.

Teubner, G. (2011). "Constitutionalizing Polycontexturality." *Social and Legal Studies* 20 (2) 209-252. With Christodoulides, E. et al. (Eds.).

Teubner, G. (2012). *Constitutional Fragments: Social Constitutionalism and Globalization* (Norbury, G., Trans.). Oxford University Press. DOI: 10.1093/acprof:oso/9780199644674.001.0001

Teubner, G. (2015). Transnational Constitutionalism in the Variety of Capitalism. *Italian Law Journal*, 1(2), 219–248.

Teubner, G. (2024). Self-Justifying Law of Constitutionalism. In M. Goldoni & M. Wilkinson, *The Material Constitution in Rudolf Wiethölter's Critical Systems Theory* (Chapter 10, pp. 150-168), Cambridge University Press.

Teubner, G. (2024). *Environmental Law and Ecological Responsibility: The Concept and Practice of Ecological Self-Organization*. With L. Farmer and D. Murphy, (Eds.). Wiley

Teubner, G., & Collins, H. (2011). *Networks as Connected Contracts*. Ed./Intro. H. Collins. Trans. Michelle Everson. Oxford: Hart.

Theise, N. (2023). *Notes on Complexity: A Scientific Theory of Connection, Consciousness and Being*. Spiegel and Grau.

Thornhill, C. (2011). *A Sociology of Constitutions" Constitutions and State Legitimacy in Historical-Sociological Perspective*. Cambridge University Press. DOI: 10.1017/CBO9780511895067

Veldman, J. (2017). Self-Regulation in International Corporate Codes. In DuPlessis, J. & Low. (Eds.). *Corporate Governance Codes in the Twentieth Century* (pp.77-95). Springer.

Voss, J -P. & Kemp, R. (Eds.). (2006). *Reflexive Governance for Sustainable Development*. Cheltenham: Edward Elgar. DOI: 10.1007/978-3-319-51868-8_4

Weinberger, O. (1991). *Institution and Legal Politics. Fundamental Problems of Legal Philosophy and Social Philosophy*. Reidel.

Weinberger, O. (1994). Habermas on Democracy and Justice: Limits of a Sound Conception. *Ratio Juris*, 7(2), 239–253. DOI: 10.1111/j.1467-9337.1994.tb00178.x

Wiethölter, R. (2005). Justifications of a Law of Society. Paradoxes and Inconsistencies in the Law, 65, 71.

Wiethölter, R. (1972). *Rechtswissenschaft in Kritik und als Kritik,*.tudienerlin: https://doi.org/DOI: 10.1515/9783

Wiethôlter, R. (1988). Materialization and Proceduralism in Modern Law. In Teubner, G. (Ed.), *Dilemmas of the Welfare State*. DeGruyter., >DOI: 10.1515/9783

Wiethülter, R. (2013). Politische Rechtstheorie Revisited Rudolf wiethölter zum 100.Semester, In C. Joerges, C. & Zumbansen, P. (Eds.). Zentrum für Europäische Rechts (ZERP) Universitat Bremen

Willke, H. (2007). *Smart Governance: Governing the Global Knowledge Society*. Campus Verlag.

Zolo, D. (1992). *Democracy and Complexity: A Realistic Approach*. Penn State University Press.

Zumbansen, P. (2016). Where the Wild Things Are: Journey into Transnational Legal Orders, University of California, Irvine *(UC, Irvine) Journal of International, Transnational and Comparative Law, Vol. 1 Symposium: Transnational Legal Ordering and Private Law,"* Article 8. [1]

## KEY TERMS AND DEFINITIONS

**Contexture:** Contextulizing conditions. Both the encompassing mediations of warranted assertions of purported legitimacy / illegitimacy, as well as unpredictable disruptions.

**Emergence:** Innovative patterns and behaviors that arise from latency and manifest themselves in complex systems.

**Heterarchy:** A formal system or structure of connected nodes with links usually represented by a diagram of where the elements therein are organized non- hierarchically without any single permanent node.

**Homeoheresis:** Operating not in a sense of simply mutual equilibrating adjustment and return to a steady state, as in homeostasis.

**Polycontexturality:** Refers to the multiple and qualitatively different contextures embedded with each other. A logic referring to the complementarity of seemingly incommensurable rationales of fragmented subsystems.

**Webs of Capital:** Mediate the complexities of continuing capital accumulation, capital investment, commercial exchange (i.e., trade), and market competition *vis à vis* establishing mutually agreed standards and mutually agreed standards and protocols with enforceable sanctions to regulate collisions in commerce. Outside the purview of nation-state government these webs back up the enforcement of standards with threshold indicators, benchmarking, and performance audits. The intermediate and connecting institutions (Kjaer, 2020) within webs of capital transcend the *negotiated social pacts* of nation-state coordinated tripartite neocorporatism of the 1970s and 1980s Avdagic, Rhodes and Visser, eds, 2011) and reoriented toward new "coupling" modes of corporatism-steering and stabilizing to the challenges of regulating transnational complexities.

**Webs of Governance:** Can be understood as being beyond a web of state-initiated international organizations such as The United Nations, the World Health Organization, the International Monetary Fund, the World Bank (what we can label W/G1). This second type of web of governance (which we label W/G2) can be better referred to as Webs of Reflexive Governance (Voss & Kemp, 2006) --have a wider social project, one that mediates complexities with a commitment to the "institutional thickness" of social solidarity (Jessop, 2020). Such reflexive governance webs are rooted in network connected relational contracts (Teubner & Collins, 2011). New constellations of social partnership are evident in a focus on green transnational loops of inter-scalarity and multi-scalarity, as well as in environmental monitoring. Now further enhanced by focusing on epidemiological monitoring, monitoring greenhouse gases (GHGs), and climate control monitoring. The capability of monitoring such global common goods is provided in transnational advocacy networks (TANs), international non-governmental organizations (INGOs), and multi-stakeholder sustainable pacts (MSSPs). (See Bäckstrand, 2006; Orts, 1998; Gunningham, 2012.) They are bootstrapping standard-setting practices from the bottom up. They involve what Charles Sabel (1994, 1997) refers to as social learning and social constitutionalizing in mutual monitoring.

# Chapter 4
# Framing Postinterntational Heterogeneous Order:
## New Medievalism and Its Competitors

**Aleksandra Spalińska**
https://orcid.org/0000-0002-2494-858X
*University of Sussex, UK*

## ABSTRACT

*This chapter reviews approaches used to conceptualize postinternationalism and heterogeneity of actors in world politics: New Medievalism (NM), Spheres of Authority (SOAs), Hybrid Sovereignty (HS) and Heterarchy. All of them are the opposite of the Westphalian ideals of the international politics structured around domestically hierarchic nation-states interacting in the condition of anarchy. In this chapter, the point of departure is NM which is considered the most radical one. The chapter analyses the assumptions and the research praxis of new NM in International Relations (IR) theory, as coined by Hedley Bull (1977). However, the interactions among and between state and non-state actors (NSAs) can be approached and theorized in different ways.*

DOI: 10.4018/979-8-3693-3563-5.ch004

# INTRODUCTION: EMBRACING POSTINTERNATIONALISM AND HETEROGENEITY

This chapter reviews approaches used to conceptualize postinternationalism and heterogeneity of actors in world politics: New Medievalism (NM), Spheres of Authority (SOAs), Hybrid Sovereignty (HS) and Heterarchy. All of them are the opposite of the Westphalian ideals of the international politics structured around domestically hierarchic nation-states interacting in the condition of anarchy. In this chapter, the point of departure is NM which is considered the most radical one. The chapter analyses the assumptions and the research praxis of new NM in International Relations (IR) theory, as coined by Hedley Bull (1977). However, the interactions among and between state and non-state actors (NSAs) can be approached and theorized in different ways. There are four other frameworks that need to be discussed as they paint the same phenomena: Spheres of Authority (SOAs), Hybrid Sovereignty (HS), Polycentricity, and Heterarchy. Considering this as well as the gaps and pitfalls in the literature on NM, this chapter compares the assumptions and aims of NM with four other frameworks that paint the same phenomena, that is, the Spheres of Authority (SOAs), Hybrid Sovereignty (HS), Polycentricity and Heterarchy. This discussion is necessary to analyze NM's advantages and disadvantages in terms of how it frames the world politics in comparison to competing ideas. Interestingly, SOAs provide a more detailed picture of authority construction than NM, whereas HS, Polycentricity and Heterarchy picture the further implications of overlapping authorities and multiple loyalties in world politics.

## New Medievalism in International Relations Theory

New Medievalism (NM) is a conception and future scenario of the world order after globalisation. It describes the fragmentation of the state system, and the states themselves (Bull, 2002; Spalińska, 2023). The neo-medieval order is s a system of 'overlapping authority and multiple loyalty,' emerging as a consequence of globalization, fragmentation of polities and internationalization of power (Bull, 2002). Hedley Bull has identified several neomedieval 'trends' whose advances would lead to the emergence of NM. These trends include: the regional integration of states; the disintegration of states; the restoration of private international violence and coercion; the emergence and growing impact of transnational organizations, and the technological unification of the world (Bull, 2002, pp. 254-266). All these trends result from advancing globalization and simultaneous fragmentation.

NM is a metaphor based on a historical analogy in which the globalized world politics is considered functionally similar to the European Middle Ages (Spalińska, 2023). NM suggests that the globalized world order will be similar to the medieval one due to the lack of the sufficient territorial and political control, and consequently centralized and functionally similar political entities. The purpose of neo-medieval analogy is to envision "modern and secular counterpart" of the European Middle Ages "that embodies its central characteristic: *the system of overlapping authority and multiple loyalty*" (Bull, 2002, pp. 245). That means that NM aims at describing the order within which no government or ruler can be sovereign like it was in medieval Western Europe, where authority was shared "with vassals beneath, and with the Pope and (in Germany and Italy) the Holy Roman Emperor above" (Bull, 2002, pp. 245). Sovereignty refers here to "the sense of being supreme over a given territory" (Bull, 2002, pp. 245). According to Bull, a neo-medieval could only be a world order in which sovereignty would be uncertain both in theory in practice (Bull, 2002, pp. 256).

However, Hedley Bull was not the first one to call out the emerging NM in world politics. At the peak of the Cold War, Arnold Wolfers (1962, pp. 242) noted a trend of blurring of boundaries between the international and the domestic domains before Bull, and describe it as "new medievalism.".For him this trend was an outcome of the rivalry between internationalist ideologies (communism and capitalism) and the nation-state, resulting in wars for influence that were difficult to classify as external or internal and which exposed the vulnerability of the state. A definition similar to Bull's was proposed also by Philip Cerny who described NM as a system of "competing institutions with overlapping jurisdictions" (Cerny, 1998).

Furthermore, Jörg Friedrichs (2001, pp. 475-502) has contributed to the NM literature by elaborating on the rivalry of the universal and superior forces in world politics. As a result, he conceptualized NM as – "a system of overlapping authority and multiple loyalty, held together with the duality of competing universalistic claims" (Friedrichs, 2001, pp. 475-502; Spalińska, 2023). Friedrichs has built his take on NM on the critique of Bull's approach. Namely, according to Friedrichs (2004), Bull did not acknowledge the "profound unity of medieval order established by dual universalism of Empire and the Church" (pp. 16). In response to this gap, Friedrichs includes universal powers in his take on NM. In the Middle Ages, these powers were the papacy and the empire; today there are the global economy (universal and borderless), and the nation-state (a politically universal body) (Friedrichs, 2001, p. 486.

Beyond IR, NM is used in examining European integration and, specifically, in the model of the European Union (EU) as the neo-medieval empire (Zielonka, 2006). When applied to the EU, NM gives a more precise account for framing and researching politics and order within this supranational entity. In Zielonka's research, NM is a conceptual basis for crafting the category of the neomedieval empire for the research on the enlarged EU. The research is based on the 'ideal-types' approach (both concepts of empire were ideal types), and extensive empirical data (Zielonka

2006). Zielonka's take on NM inspired Andreas Faludi to propose the neomedieval project for spatial planning within the EU as an alternative to territorialism. Faludi develops there NM normatively as a viable alternative to national territorialism in spatial policy and spatial planning within the EU. This alternative would empower local authorities and municipalities, and facilitate their development. Specifically, Faludi proposes the project of neo-medieval governance through parallel over-lapping spatial plans. In Faludi's vision, cross-cutting, ever-more complex spatial configurations would be a response to the 'existing territorial mosaic of politico-administrative units' (Harrison, 2013, pp. 55-74). Fulling this vision would create the neo-medieval polycentricity.

The research praxis of NM, however, looks differently than the visions of world order that neo-medieval thinking inspires. NM is used to explore the logics of or-ganization, mechanisms of ordering, and characteristics of involved actors (Kobrin, 1998, pp. 365-366). NM has received increasing attention in the last thirty years, becoming a conceptual frame for the analysis of qualitative changes in world politics (Ferguson and Mansbach 2021: 580). That happens due to trends and transitions that are identified with NM, that is, the qualitative changes in world politics identified with the consequences of globalization, the end of Cold War, postmodernity, and the rise of non-state actors (NSAs) (Spalińska, 2023). As a result, NM has become a heuristic device and a framework to analyze NSAs (Télo, 2012; Brütsch, 2013), consequences of globalization and neoliberalism (Rapley, 2006), geopolitical condi-tions of the post-Westphalian world (Doboš, 2020), statehood and the statelessness where power is increasingly employed by paramilitaries or gangs (Norell, 2003; Kan, 2019).

Interestingly, NM is used in research dedicated to the outcomes of the neomedi-eval trends, not the causes. Instead of a close analysis of different kinds of author-ities, their interplay, loyalties, ways of unifying the world, or claims to supremacy/ universal rule in relation to globalization or other processes, NM appears in more specific investigations on a variety of issues identified with the consequences of globalization, deregulation of economies or the EU. In the existing definitions of NM the position of NSAs is not specifically spelled out either. Quite the opposite, NM is deemed to define the whole world order, not its parts, nor the details of the position of its participants. Moreover, it encourages to investigate entities different from the nation-state but still based on a given territory, thus focusing on the city-states, metropolitan areas, empires (Brütsch, 2013; Godehardt, 2014), and sub-state entities, aspiring for autonomy or independence (Kennedy, 2017) and regional or supranational integration as in the case of the neo-medieval empire (Zielonka, 2006).

## Spheres of Authority: Countless Authorities in a Disregulated Order

The idea of the "spheres of authority" (SOAs), was coined by James Rosenau (2003a, 2007) to frame the consequences of globalization for authority construction. The point is to picture the disaggregation of power and the crisis of public authority when the state capacity to execute its policies is weakened (Rosenau 2003b, pp. 71-72). SOAs develop through "organizational explosion" in response to the "worldwide crisis of authority" which "thoroughly undermined the prevailing distribution of global power to alter the significance of the State as a causal agent in the course of events" (Rosenau 1990, pp. 263-264). SOAs are actually new "sovereignty-free actors" (p. 36), that is, the NSAs we know today (Rosenau put there governmental agencies, international governmental organizations and political parties).

According to Rosenau (2003), "informal and non-institutional forms of authority (spheres)" emerged "to supplement, if not replace, the long-established formal and institutionalized structures of authority" (p. 294). Rosenau puts emphasis on the collective nature of those actors. They include all kinds of collectivities capable of exercising authority (Rosenau, 2003, p. 295), such as professional organizations (like industry associations or epistemic communities), business actors (MNCs), or policy regimes (like transnational issue regimes). Considering the collective nature of SOAs, there is a question whether they can act like polities (to exercise authority basing on popular legitimacy), regulate social relations, and mobilize resources. Rosenau implicitly suggests that.

There are countless SOAs: local, national, global as well as area specialized, and other at every level of community, in every realm of activity, and in every part of the world' (Rosenau, 2007, p. 89). All of them, however, are "transnational in the sense that their adherents can and do move across national boundaries in order to pursue or sustain the goals of their SOA" (Rosenau, 2007, p. 94) For Rosenau (1995), governance does not require governmental supervision or hierarchical structure as it can be successfully managed "even in the absence of established legal or political authority" (p. 15). Authority manifests "through any number of channels of *de facto* control" due to power shift from the national governments to the NSAs in the global economy (Rosenau, 1997, pp. 146-147). The key challenge here are the "authority vacuums" that emerge when "chaos is so prevalent that lines of authority are so obscure that no actor can issue directives with the hope of achieving compliance" (Rosenau, 2007, p. 91). For Rosenau the SOAs are not just a part of new emerging order but actually the only possible authority construction in the midst of disorder. Unlike Bull, however, Rosenau does not evoke any specific manifestations of this chaotic state of affairs (like the restoration of private international violence or regional integration in Bull's considerations).

Crucially, the SOAs framework is a part of Rosenau's postinternational perspective on world politics in the 21$^{st}$ century. Similarly to Bull's NM, SOAs were invented to describe the world politics after sovereignty. They constitute "the analytic units of the new ontology" (Rosenau, 1997, p. 39), created by actors capable of exercising compliance and delineating the sphere. Similarly to NM literature, SOAs link authority with actorness, although the problem of loyalty is not directly addressed; Rosenau (2007, p. 90) puts emphasis on compliance instead. The ontology of SOAs is more robust but also quite chaotic; that is not surprising since Rosenau (2007, pp. 94-96) builds his perspective in close reference to complexity theory. His ideas aptly mirror the chaos of globalized world politics. Furthermore, considering that the SOAs are supposed to be constantly in flux and do not rely on existing territorial divides, the framework contributes to the deterritorialization of authority (Rosenau, 1997, p. 89) and goes beyond the statist approach to territoriality just like NM. Consequently, SOAs picture the new geographies of the disregulated world:

"The sphere may or may not correspond to a bounded territory: those who comply may be spread around the world and have no legal relationship to one another, or they may be located in the same geographic space and have the same organizational affiliations" (Rosenau, 1997, p. 89).

Moreover, Rosenau (2007, p. 91) acknowledges the power dynamics in the emergence of SOAs, considering that the most powerful states contribute to their development (just like in the case of the jurisdictional assemblage), especially the US. Simultaneously, however, he includes the IGOs in the power structure such as International Monetary Fund, the World Bank, and the World Trade Organization (Rosenau 2007, p. 91). Those institutions contribute to the Western hegemony, so including them as entities in the power structure is necessary. On the other hand, SOAs are uncontrollable; once the mechanism boosting them is set in motion (for example, neoliberal policies or digital communication), it is hardly stoppable:

"the enormous proliferation of SOA emphasizes the severe constraints on the ability of a superpower to generate the compliance necessary for it to maintain order on a global scale or, at least, to realize its goals in myriad situations" (Rosenau, 2007, p. 91).

It is not clear whether it is possible to reverse the SOAs' development or how they would disintegrate. Moreover, it is not clear what the relationship between state and non-state authorities is supposed to look like, beyond the fact that SOAs challenge the capacity of the state authority and the exclusivity of its jurisdiction. Rosenau shows how the SOAs system works, emphasizing the direct mechanisms of authority within the SOAs and among them (deference and compliance), including their nature (formal or informal). That is lacking in the existing NM literature. On the other hand, similarly to Bull and his followers, Rosenau's does not elaborate on the details of the SOAs developments. This process is omitted with the acknowledgement given only to the external pressures of globalization as a cause, and the weakening of the states' capacity as a result. Rosenau notes only that the SOAs system relies on shared domains and governance process within, across, and beyond the state jurisdictions. In this context, "global governance refers to the patterns of SOAs in the world and not to a form of world government" (Ferguson, 2003). These patterns rely on decentralized regulatory mechanisms without much grounded structure. Like for NM, for SOAs centralization is not expected.

Due to the purpose of understanding and framing the consequences of globalization for authority construction as well as for the future of the nation-state, SOAs and NM have a lot in common. They both are grounded in the conviction that world politics after globalization is disaggregated, deterritorialized, and prone to chaos (to refer to phrases used by Rosenau). Simultaneously, the SOAs framework provides a detailed picture of the authority dynamics itself, including the close analysis of compliance and feasibility of exercising one's authority. NM is more focused on the general picture of the world order. Both ideas are used by scholars as analytical and/or conceptual frameworks. NM, similarly to SOAs, is focused on flexibility and change and therefore considered the opposite of the neat, structured and state-oriented modern order. However, SOAs frames the authority construction and order development, whereas NM broadly describes the "state of the world" and — given Hedley Bull's original formulation — logics of the post-sovereign world system. NM points to the logics constitutive to the system it describes (overlapping authority and multiple loyalty), whereas SOAs point to the proliferation of authorities in a hardly governable environment. With a proper focus on the endogenous factors for polity fragmentation, NM can be complimentary to the more narrow focus of the SOAs framework or even its more broad substitute.

## HYBRID SOVEREIGNTY: FULLY EXCLUSIVE AUTHORITY IS NEVER REACHED

Hybrid Sovereignty (HS), on the other hand, frames the diversification of state capacity in crucial areas (like security, warfare, or regulation of markets), and other forms of public-private partnership (Srivastava, 2022) Specifically, it frames:

"the overlapping relations between public and private actors in important areas of global power, such as contractors fighting international wars, corporations regulating global markets, or governments collaborating with non-governmental entities to influence foreign elections" (Srivastava, 2022, p. 1).

As a result, the NSAs participate in the co-production of sovereign capacity (Srivastava, 2022, p. 41). Crucially, the framework of HS serves unmasking the myth of full state sovereignty which recognizes public and private as two inherently different realms, labelling the private as apolitical, and assuming "sovereign power as a finished project expressed in 'the state'" (Srivastava, 2022, p. 5). As Swati Srivastava demonstrates, all kinds of state and non-state actors participate in the co-production of political, economic or moral capacity. This co-production is done through cooperation and competition, engagement, and rivalry. Consequently, the alliance of public and private authorities enables the exercise of sovereign power like in security provisions and conquest (Srivastava, 2022, p. 41). As Srivastava (2022) notes, "in the real politics of world affairs, there is no autonomous public or private; all we have is their mingling to various degrees and levels of success" (p. 7).

Free markets are as elusive and utopian as autonomous sovereigns. Hybridity is an integral feature of sovereignty in the real world, not an accident, nor an attempt to take over the state authority (Srivastava, 2022, p. 7). There are three types of public/private hybridity: contractual, institutional, and shadow (Srivastava, 2022, p. 8). Contractual hybridity relies on exercising sovereign competences through formal and publicized contracts with private actors (for example, mercenaries). Institutional hybridity enables the performance of sovereignty through institutional networks and with lobbing. Shadow hybridity does so through informal exchanges (for example, the exchange of confidential information) invisible to the public eye ((Srivastava, 2022, p. 9).

There is a crucial difference between HS and NM: HS frames the relationship between state and NSAs from the perspective of the state — the state uses capabilities developed by other actors to enhance its capacity, preserve sovereignty, and ensure its success on the world stage. NM, instead, provides a perspective crafted from the point of view of the citizens and social actors — in a sense that the development of overlapping authorities depends on multiplication of loyalties. Moreover, for HS to happen, the overlapping of different authorities needs to occur first — it would not be possible for states to use powerful NSAs if private authorities were not in place already.

The development of HS is therefore the consequence of the system of overlapping authorities and, going further, it can be explained as the result of polity fragmentation. It applies to states that choose to enhance its position relying on, for example, private contractors or rating agencies, instead of improving its legitimacy among the citizens. HS therefore tackles the problem of the ways in which statecraft uses and depends on private and/or non-governmental actors. In the perspective of NM, instead, sovereignty is being transformed or even abandoned to remain only formally, whereas public authority can still be functional and effective (however, it competes with the kinds of private authorities). Moreover, NM has been coined to describe world order architecture in the late 20th century, and — given Hedley Bull's original formulation — the logics of the post-sovereign world system. HS, instead, explains the lasting symbiotic relationship between the state and NSAs.

An approach that combines the components of NM and HS is transgovernmentalism, proposed by Anne-Marie Slaughter (2005). It relies on the assumption that the nation-state does not disappear, but is transformed into a networked and pragmatic socio-political organization. Increasing potential of NSAs does not necessarily imply the decrease in the power and the authority of states; still only states have a legal possibility to enforce its law and policies by coercive means. The emerging world order is transgovernmental: it combines the power of the state with the flexibility and pragmatism of non-state actors (Slaughter, 2005). This kind order will limit the omnipotence of the nation-state for the sake of new non-state capabilities that will be used to solve global problems. Consequently, state-non-state interactions will create differentiated heterarchical networks cutting across the state system. Moreover, national governments adopt corporate solutions to improve efficiency and control over populations. A good example can be surveillance and the development of the neoliberal security state in which NSAs are used (Hörnqvist, 2020). As a result, we face the corporatization of the state, which advances with the adoption of neoliberal governance in public administration (Voorn, van Thiel & van Genugten, 2018, pp. 481-482).

## POLYCENTRICITY: SHARING PUBLIC GOODS AND COORDINATING DISPERSED AUTHORITIES

Long-term interactions between and among state and non-state actors are crucial for the provision of public goods. They create networks whose members exercise public authority collaboratively, creating the polycentric systems of governance. A concept of polycentricity comes from public administration and governance studies. It has been proposed by Elinor Ostrom (2005). It can be defined as "a self-organizing governance system comprised of multiple governance actors, decision-making venues, and policy issues, and the relationships between them." (Morrison, Bodin, Cumming, Lubell, Seppelt, Seppelt & Weible, 2023, p. 4).

Specifically, polycentricity "connotes many centers of decision making that are formally independent of each other" (Ostrom, Tiebout & Warren 1961, pp. 831-832) but actually create an interdependent system of authorities. Competition, collaboration and conflict resolution are necessary for polycentric systems to work (Ostrom, Tiebout & Warren 1961, pp. 831-832). Effective coordination is crucial for the polycentric governance to become a system (Carlisle & Gruby, 2019, p. 928). Competition, links of collaboration, balance and representation in decision-making process have a greater importance than the number of involved authorities (Carlisle & Gruby, 2019, p. 933). "Consistent and predictable patterns of interacting behavior" (Ostrom, Tiebout & Warren 1961, pp. 831-32) are essential for polycentric governance system.

Consequently, polycentrism can be considered a transnational regime: "polycentric regimes combine distribution of power and authority with effective coordination among various centers and across spatial levels" (Pahl-Wostl, 2015, p. 215).

Polycentricity attaches pivotal importance to networks that consist of different kinds of actors and may create systems. Crucially, the idea of polycentricity is pragmatic and practical, aiming at providing practical solutions for governance and management in everyday life, especially the commons (public goods) (Smith, 2017, pp. 49-65). That includes protecting international public goods and their private equivalents as private sector is involved in their production or usage (Smith, 2017, pp. 54-57). Thinking in terms of polycentricity was inspired by the research on overlapping political units in metropolitan-area governance (Carlisle & Gruby, 2019, p. 930).

According to Elinor Ostrom (1990) the systems of commons governance "are organized in multiple layers of nested enterprises" (p. 101). The term "polycentric" happens to be used interchangeably with "nested" that refers to the overlapping of involved jurisdictions; they overlap "because they are nested at multiple jurisdictional levels (e.g., local, state, and national) and also include special-purpose governance units that cut across jurisdictions" (Carlisle & Gruby 2019, p. 928). This picture of polycentricity resembles the vision of world order offered by NM or Heterarchy. Similarly to NM, "overlapping" is a chief characteristic of polycentricity in governance. In the case of polycentricity it means:

"the layering of decision-making centers operating at multiple levels or jurisdictions when they share certain functional capacities or areas of responsibility [...]. A critical function of overlap is to facilitate the flow of information among decision-making centers, enabling them to learn which institutions employed by others have been successful [...]. (Carlisle & Gruby 2019, p. 933).

NM can be considered a particular type of polycentricity as in Andreas Faludi's vision of neo-medieval polycentrism (Faludi, 2018). Moreover, both NM and polycentricity underscore the importance of networks and networking which in the lens of NM take the shape of overlapping "concentric circles" (Zielonka, 2014). For both NM and polycentricity, overlapping of authorities and entities is crucial. However, polycentricity is focused on how governance works, including its parts (the decision-making centers), whereas NM emphasizes the basic components of order architecture, that is the overlapping of authorities and multiplication of loyalties. Unlike polycentricity, NM explicitly covers both overlapping of institutions and the overlapping of membership.

Moreover, there is the epistemic difference between polycentricity and NM: NM has been invented to describe and envision the world order after globalization for scholarly purposes. Polycentricity, instead, beyond the contribution to understanding complex governance systems, was intended to provide practical solutions for improving governance and living conditions for populations. On the other hand, however, polycentricity just like NM is not only a system of governance but also "a pervasive condition in much of the world" (Carlisle & Gruby 2019, p. 929). Hence it is imperative to help "practitioners enable and leverage the potential benefits of a polycentric governance system." (Carlisle & Gruby 2019, p. 929).

Polycentric governance combines and puts together different actors: public, private, and voluntary as they "have overlapping realms of responsibility and functional capacities." (McGinnis & Ostrom 2011, p. 15). The active involvement (both formal and informal) of private and social actors is critical for effective polycentric governance (McGinnis & Ostrom 2011, p. 15). Considering the increasing of interdependence between states as well as between public (also supranational) and private actors, polycentricity is an expected form of global cooperation in fluctuating and unpredictable international environment (p. 60) Polycentricity provides a prescription for growing heterarchy in the architecture of global governance. In a similar spirit, a "functional polycentric governance system" can be distinguished for the commons governance. Functional refers here to adaptability, fitting and capacity to embrace complexity and risk mitigation. (Carlisle & Gruby 2019, p. 929).

In a wider sense, however, polycentrism goes much further than public policy. In the study of world politics, IR included, a vision of polycentricity applies to power and ordering. In this context we can discuss heterogenous polycentricity as the potential world order beyond the nation-state (Cooper, 2000). This kind of order, similarly to Heterarchy and NM (Cerny, 2023) would be based on differentiation in state-non-state interactions, growing due to the crisis of public authority and the cross-cutting influence of non-state actors on the public sphere and national governments. Simultaneously, however, it would be better organized with coordinated. World order, established on the basis of growing heterogeneity in world politics would be called 'polycentric' because of complex relations and connections between involved actors as well as different categories of power and authority, represented by these actors in the architecture of world order with no one hegemon or center.

Moreover, polycentricity shows up in differentiation in European integration. In the European Union (EU), polycentrism is expected to ensure harmonious collaboration between differentiated entities (Zielonka, 2014). According to Zielonka, the European integration develops within functional not territorial frames since the polycentric area is expected to be deprived of hierarchical structure. Consequently, the EU becomes a networked organism consisting of "concentric circles ; polycentric governance would offer there an alternative for more territory-oriented multilevel governance (Zielonka, 2014). A drive for increased flexibility and diversity triggers changes depending on the contents of upcoming tasks and capabilities of specific entities. The model of sectoral, differentiated integration *á la carte* is reshaped into a 'network integration' of national governments, cities, regions, interest groups and social organizations (Zielonka, 2014). In this way, polycentric governance could become a remedy for the EU's governance issues, and a preventive measure against any future crises.

## HETERARCHY: WORLD POLITICS BETWEEN THE HIERARCHY AND ANARCHY

There is a question, however, how to define not only authority or sovereignty but the order in which factual hierarchies are international and transnational, and anarchies can be domestic or peripheral. This definition is provided by the fourth alternative to NM, which is the concept of Heterarchy, defined as "the predominance of cross-cutting sectoral mini- and meso- hierarchies above, below, and across states." (Cerny, 2023a, p. 3) These structures are inter-connected, autonomous, and often captured by special interests (Cerny, 2023a).

Heterarchy manifests in mechanisms, practices, and policies that undermine or transcend the anarchical logic of the state system and the hierarchical order in the domestic realm. It is a product of the dialectics of globalization and fragmentation. The supposed heterarchical order is thus a product of a dialectical interplay just like the sovereign order. However, crucial are the vertical pressures of globalization, not the horizontal (domestic/ foreign) pressures of national state-building and its maintenance, like in the reproduction of collective identities (Hardt & Negri 2000, pp. 145-146, pp. 186-189). What is a combination of hierarchical and anarchical logics in the perspective of Heterarchy, is actually close to the neomedieval description of the rivalry between 'competing universalistic claims,' as outlined by Jörg Friedrichs (2004).

Heterarchy develops at the intersection of the persisting international hierarchies and domestic anarchies whose interactions were boosted by globalization processes and neoliberal economic policies. Due to the changing construction of order and the mechanisms of aggregating power within it (including the sources necessary for that such as territory), the connections among involved actors of differentiated status (including the degree of bounding to the state), the public governance takes the shape of heterarchy. That happens due to fragmentation, decentralization, and internationalization of the state, which constitutes the precondition of heterarchy (Jones and Hameiri, 2023, p. 77). Heterarchical governance further transforms the state apparatus and, through transnational networks, affects the workings of the whole state system (Jones and Hameiri, 2023).

As a result, we deal with quasi-institutionalized, multi-layered, and multi-nodal system of global governance that aggregates power over differentiated and dispersed social structures and public/private units across the states (Cerny, 2009). The interconnections between involved actors take the shape of multi-layered and multi-nodal structural patterns. They shape the aggregated power over differentiated social structures and public/private units across states (Cerny, 2009). Similarly to Heterarchy, NM develops in settings where opposing organizational schemes are transcended: the domestic interacts with the foreign, the local with the global, the public with the private. Those interactions are enabled by socio-economic processes (for example, globalization and neoliberalization) that cut across states (Cerny, 2023a).

Heterarchical order develops thus both vertically and horizontally with diagonal links between units at different levels of governance, in different functional areas and geographical locations (Belmonte & Cerny, 2021). Increasing complexity cuts across the domestic realm, leading to the development of 'reactive states' who become *ad hoc* problem-solvers in crisis (Cerny, 2023b). Especially in the case of financial governance, the states' capacity for proactive action is limited by the so-called capitalism without capital. However, "state capacity is not simply eroded but entangled in hybrid structures and processes" (Cerny, 2023a, p. 3). Heterarchy shows us how statecraft is getting entangled in the global impacts and local anxieties.

Heterarchy conceptualizes world politics after globalization, and its basic consequence, which is socio-political fragmentation. It frames world politics in the 21$^{st}$ century and provides a paradigm to study it that is an alternative to state-centrism (Cerny, 2023a). Heterarchy, just like NM, questions the status of the nation-state as the one and only structural category of political actors. Consequently, Heterarchy, similarly to NM, de-centres and de-constructs the main black box of IR theory, that is, the nation-state. Heterarchy does so by taking into account the complexity of the power architecture in which NSAs, societies and individuals actively participate. Their contribution is significant in terms of both building the neoliberal order (as for world financial architecture or MNCs) and abusing it (as for terrorist networks or governments using non-state channels for foreign influence in the inter-state rivalry).

Heterarchy and NM are quite alike. Both picture world politics beyond the sovereign order and the de-centring of the nation-state. Both frame world order after globalization, pointing to the same qualities: heterogeneity, plurality, and de-centeredness (Belmonte & Cerny, 2021). Furthermore, they are used by scholars as analytical and/or conceptual frameworks. However, Heterarchy is a concept of world order construction, whereas NM widely describes the "state of the world," and — given Hedley Bull's original formulation — the logics of the post-sovereign world system. NM points to logics constitutive to the system it describes (overlapping authority and multiple loyalty), whereas Heterarchy points to the heterarchical, uneven structures that develop across and despite the anarchy of the state system. NM is supposed to describe a new system developing after sovereignty, whereas the purpose of Heterarchy is to elucidate the new order that develops on the basis of intersecting hierarchy and anarchy.

## CONCLUSIONS: EMBRACING POSTINTERNATIONALISM THROUGH DIFFERENT APPROACHES

This chapter reviewed and analyzed four approaches used to conceptualize postinterna-tionalism and heterogeneity of actors in world politics: New Medieval-ism (NM), Spheres of Authority (SOAs), Hybrid Sovereignty (HS) and Heterarchy. In this chapter, the point of departure was NM given that it is considered the most radical one. The chapter analyzed the assumptions and achievements of NM in International Relations (IR) theory, as coined by Hedley Bull (1977). However, the interactions among and between state NSAs can be theorized in different ways. Considering this as well as the gaps and pitfalls in the literature on NM, this chapter compares the assumptions and aims of NM with four other frameworks that paint the same phenomena, that is, the Spheres of Authority (SOAs), Hybrid Sovereignty (HS), Polycentricity and Heterarchy. This discussion is necessary to analyze NM's advantages and disadvantages in terms of how it frames the world politics in comparison to competing ideas. Interestingly, SOAs provide a more detailed picture of authority construction than NM, whereas HS, Polycentricity and Heterarchy picture the further implications of overlapping authorities and multiple loyalties.

# REFERENCES

Belmonte, R., & Cerny, P. G. (2021). *Heterarchy: Toward Paradigm Shift in World Politics*. In *The Changing Faces of Power, Journal of Political Power*, Special Issue ed. by G. Gallarotti. DOI: 10.4324/9781003200673-14

Brütsch, Ch. M. (2013). From sovereign prerogatives to metropolitan rule? the anarchical society in the urban age. *International Studies Perspectives*, 14(3), 307–324. DOI: 10.1111/j.1528-3585.2012.00496.x

Bull, H. (2002). *The Anarchical Society. A Study of Order in World Politics*. Palgrave Macmillan.

Carlisle, K., & Gruby, R. L. (2019). Polycentric systems of governance: A theoretical model for the commons. *Policy Studies Journal: the Journal of the Policy Studies Organization*, 47(4), 927–952. DOI: 10.1111/psj.12212

Cerny, P. G. (1998). Neomedievalism, civil war and the new security dilemma: Globalisation as durable disorder. *Civil Wars*, 1(1), 36–64. DOI: 10.1080/13698249808402366

Cerny, P. G. (2009). Multi-nodal politics: Globalisation is what actors make of it. *Review of International Studies*, 35(2), 421–449. DOI: 10.1017/S0260210509008584

Cerny, P. G. (2023a). Heterarchy: Toward Paradigm Shift in World Politics. In Cerny, P. G. (Ed.), *Heterarchy in World Politics* (pp. 3–15). Routledge.

Cerny, P. G. (2023b). Heterarchy in an Age of Intangibles and Financialization. In Cerny, P. G. (Ed.), *Heterarchy in World Politics* (pp. 143–154). Routledge.

Cooper, R. (2000). *The Postmodern State and the World Order*. Demos.

Doboš, B. (2020). *New Middle Ages. Geopolitics of Post-Westphalian World*. Springer Nature. DOI: 10.1007/978-3-030-58681-2

Faludi, A. (2018). *The Poverty of Territorialism. A Neo-Medieval View of Europe and European Planning*. Edward Elgar Publishing.

Ferguson, Y. H. (2003). Illusions of superpower. *Asian Journal of Political Science*, 11(2), 21–36. DOI: 10.1080/02185370308434225

Ferguson, Y. H., & Mansbach, R. W. (2007). Post-internationalism and IR theory. *Millennium*, 35(3), 529–549. DOI: 10.1177/03058298070350031001

Ferguson, Y. H., & Mansbach, R. W. (2021). In B. de Carvalho, J. Costa Lopez and H. Leira (eds.) *Afterword. Ahead to the Past*. In *Routledge Handbook of Historical International Relations* (pp. 573-582). Routledge

Friedrichs, J. (2001). The meaning of new medievalism. *European Journal of International Relations*, 7(4), 475–501. DOI: 10.1177/1354066101007004004

Friedrichs, J. (2004). The Neomedieval Renaissance: Global Governance and International Law in the New Middle Ages. In Dekker, I. F., & Werner, W. G. (Eds.), *Governance and International Legal Theory* (pp. 3–36). Springer. DOI: 10.1007/978-94-017-6192-5_1

Godehardt, N. (2014). *The Chinese Constitution of Central Asia: Regions and Intertwined Actors in International Relations*. Palgrave Macmillan. DOI: 10.1057/9781137359742

Hardt, M., & Negri, A. (2000). *Empire*. Harvard University Press.

Harrison, J. (2013). Configuring the new 'regional world': On being caught between territory and networks. *Regional Studies*, 47(1), 55–74. DOI: 10.1080/00343404.2011.644239

Hörnqvist, M. (2020). Neoliberal security provision: Between state practices and individual experience. *Punishment & Society*, 22(2), 227–246. DOI: 10.1177/1462474519875474

Jones, L., & Hameiri, S. (2023). Heterarchy and State Transformation. In Cerny, P. G. (Ed.), *Heterarchy in World Politics* (pp. 67–79). Routledge.

Kan, P. R. (2019). *The Global Challenge of Militias and Paramilitary Violence*. Springer International Publishing; Palgrave.

Kennedy, L. (2017). *Supranational Union and New Medievalism: Forging a New Scottish State*. Arktos Media Limited.

Kobrin, S. (1998). Back to the future: Neomedievalism and the postmodern digital world economy. *Journal of International Affairs*, 51(2), 361–386.

Morrison, T. H., Bodin, O., Cumming, G. S., Lubell, M., Seppelt, R., Seppelt, T., & Weible, C. M. (2023). Building blocks of polycentric governance. *Policy Studies Journal: the Journal of the Policy Studies Organization*, 51(3), 475–499. DOI: 10.1111/psj.12492

Norell, M. (2003). A new medievalism? The case of Sri Lanka. *Civil Wars*, 6(2), 121–137. DOI: 10.1080/13698240308402536

Ostrom, E. (1990). *Governing the Commons: The Evolution of Institutions for Collective Action*. Cambridge University Press. DOI: 10.1017/CBO9780511807763

Ostrom, E. (2005). *Understanding Institutional Diversity*. Princeton University Press.

Ostrom, V., Tiebout, C. M., & Warren, R. (1961). The organization of government in metropolitan areas: A theoretical inquiry. *The American Political Science Review*, 55(4), 831–842. DOI: 10.2307/1952530

Pahl-Wostl, C. (2015). *Water Governance in the Face of Global Change: From Understanding to Transformation*. Springer International Publishing. DOI: 10.1007/978-3-319-21855-7

Rosenau, J. N. (1990). *Turbulence in World Politics. A Theory of Change and Continuity*. Princeton University Press. DOI: 10.1515/9780691188522

Rosenau, J. N. (1995). Governance in the 21st Century. *Global Governance*, 1(1), 13–43. DOI: 10.1163/19426720-001-01-90000004

Rosenau, J. N. (1997). *Along the Domestic Foreign Frontier. Exploring Governance in the Turbulent World*. Cambridge University Press. DOI: 10.1017/CBO9780511549472

Rosenau, J. N. (2003a). Spheres of Authority. In Rosenau, J. N. (Ed.), *Distant Proximities: Dynamics Beyond Globalization* (pp. 293–314). Princeton University Press. DOI: 10.1515/9780691231112-016

Rosenau, J. N. (2003b). Sources and Consequences of Fragmegration. In Rosenau, J. N. (Ed.), *Distant Proximities: Dynamics Beyond Globalization* (pp. 50–78). Princeton University Press. DOI: 10.1515/9780691231112-006

Rosenau, J. N. (2007). Governing the ungovernable: the challenge of a global disaggregation of authority. *Regulation & Governance, 1*, pp. 88–97. DOI:. 00001. DOI: 10.1111/j.1748-5991.2007

Slaughter, A.-M. (2005). *A New World Order*. Princeton University Press. DOI: 10.1515/9781400825998

Smith, K. (2017). Innovating for the global commons: Multilateral collaboration in a polycentric world. *Oxford Review of Economic Policy*, 33(1), 49–65. DOI: 10.1093/oxrep/grw039

Spalińska, A. (2023). New Medievalism (Re)Appraised: Framing Heterarchy in World Politics. In Cerny, P. G. (Ed.), *Heterarchy in World Politics* (pp. 42–53). Routledge.

Télo, M. (2012). *State, Globalization and Multilateralism: The challenges of institutionalizing regionalism*. Springer Netherlands. DOI: 10.1007/978-94-007-2843-1

Voorn, B., van Thiel, S., & van Genugten, M. (2018). Debate: Corporatization as more than a recent crisis-driven development. *Public Money & Management*, 38(7), 481–482. DOI: 10.1080/09540962.2018.1527533

Wolfers, A. (1962). *Discord and Collaboration. Essays on International Politics*. The John Hopkins University Press. DOI: 10.56021/9780801806902

Zielonka, J. (2006). *Europe as Empire. The Nature of the Enlarged European Union*. Oxford University Press. DOI: 10.1093/0199292213.001.0001

Zielonka, J. (2014). *Is the EU doomed?* Polity Press.

## KEY TERMS AND DEFINITIONS

**Authority:** The concept of authority refers to public and private, domestic, and foreign, supranational, and national/local authorities. The point of departure is the public authority of the state which operates in different areas (economy, security, social welfare) that, due to the growing economic and technological interdependence, are differentiated. Considering the political organization of the world, polities are governed by their respective authorities managed by the state apparatus (with exceptions for unusual entities) within their internationally recognized exclusive jurisdictions (legally recognized and demarcated sovereign realms). There are different sources of authority: institutional, expert, delegated, principled (based on supported values), and capacity-based (competence). Both public and private actors use them.

**Heterarchy:** The prevalence of "cross-cutting sectoral mini- and meso- hierarchies above, below, and across states" in world politics (Cerny, 2023a, p. 3). These structures are inter-connected, autonomous, and often captured by special interests (Cerny, 2023a). Heterarchy manifests in mechanisms, practices, and policies that undermine or transcend the anarchical logic of the state system and the hierarchical order in the domestic realm.

**Hybrid Sovereignty:** A conception of state-non-state relationship based on the the diversification of state capacity in crucial areas (like security, warfare, or regulation of markets), and other forms of public-private partnership (Srivastava, 2022). Hybrid Sovereignty frames the relationship between state and NSAs from the perspective of the state — the state uses capabilities developed by other actors to enhance its capacity, preserve sovereignty, and ensure its success on the world stage.

**New Medievalism:** A conception of world order based on historical analogy, drawn between European Middle Ages and world politics in the era of globalization. The neo-medieval order is s a system of 'overlapping authority and multiple loyalty,' emerging as a consequence of globalization, fragmentation of polities and internationalization of power (Bull, 2002). Hedley Bull has identified several neomedieval 'trends' whose advances would lead to the emergence of NM. These trends include: the regional integration of states; the disintegration of states; the restoration of private international violence and coercion; the emergence and growing impact of transnational organizations, and the technological unification of the world (Bull, 2002, pp. 254-266).

**Non-State Actors:** Social, economic, or political actors who are not legally recognized as entitled to exercise sovereignty over the given territory. James Rosenau called them sovereignty-free actors" (Rosenau, 1990, p. 36). The category of non-state actors includes, among others, governmental agencies, international governmental organizations, political parties, non-governmental organizations, multinational corporations, organized crime or terrorist networks.

**Order:** The concept of order refers to the "pattern of activities or a set of arrangements" (Evans and Newnham, 1998, pp. 269-270). Simultaneously, it denotes the regulatory elements and 'provides a framework within which the interaction takes place" (ibidem). We can distinguish the logic and mechanisms of ordering — in postpositivist IR the concept of order is being decentered and deconstructed. Instead of "order," the "ordering" is applied as more dynamic and processual (precisely it concerns "mechanisms/practices of ordering") (Guillaume, 2007). The order involves the existence of some kind of authority and organizing rules and is closely related to the concept of rule. It encompasses rules, arrangements, and practices among the involved actors (formal and/or informal). As a result, the concept of order implies the question of who participates in the ordering and who is ordered.

**Polycentricity:** A self-organized and networked system of governance, involving multiple and heterogeneous actors, venues, and policy issues. Polycentricity attaches pivotal importance to networks that consist of different kinds of actors and create systems. In IR a vision of polycentricity applies to power and ordering, based on differentiation in state-non-state interactions, growing due to the crisis of public authority and the cross-cutting influence of non-state actors on the public sphere and national governments.

**Spheres of Authority (SOAs):** Informal and non-institutional forms of authority of collective nature that supplement or even replace the formal structures of authority. SOAs include all kinds of collectivities capable of exercising authority (Rosenau, 2003), such as professional organizations (like industry associations or epistemic communities), business actors, or policy regimes. There are countless SOAs: local, national, global as well as area specialized, and other "at every level of community, in every realm of activity, and in every part of the world" (Rosenau, 2007, p. 89).

# Chapter 5
# Anarchism and Heterarchy Rethinking Governance in a Postinternational Era:
## New Paradigms of Non-State Influence

**Adrian David Cheok**
https://orcid.org/0000-0001-6316-2339
*Nanjing University of Information Science and Technology, China*

## ABSTRACT

*This chapter explores the intersection of anarchism and heterarchical frameworks in the context of global governance, arguing that anarchistic principles provide valuable insights into the evolution of governance structures beyond the nation-state. By analyzing the theoretical underpinnings of anarchism and their applicability to heterarchical systems, this chapter illustrates how decentralized and non-hierarchical models can effectively address contemporary global challenges. It examines case studies of non-state actors and transnational movements that embody anarchistic principles, demonstrating their impact on global governance. The chapter further discusses the role of technology in facilitating anarchistic and heterarchical dynamics, shedding light on the reconfiguration of power dynamics and the challenges of legal governance in a postinternational world. Through a comprehensive analysis, this chapter contributes to the discourse on alternative governance frameworks, offering practical implications for future diplomacy and statecraft in a heterarchical global order.*

DOI: 10.4018/979-8-3693-3563-5.ch005

# INTRODUCTION

## Overview of Anarchy and Postinternationalism

Anarchy and postinternationalism stand as compelling frameworks for reimagining the complexities of global governance. Anarchy, in international relations, recalls a structureless realm, often misconstrued to mean utter chaos and disorder. Postinternationalism, on the other hand, suggests a movement beyond the confines of states as the fundamental units of global politics, proposing a mesh of interactions that cut across national boundaries and institutional confines.

Contemporary scholarship has increasingly disputed the perception of anarchy as simply a chaotic vacuum of power, highlighting instead its potential to foster non-hierarchical, cooperative coordination among states (Hirsch & van der Walt, 2010). Postinternationalism supports this perspective, offering alternative lenses to observe the interplay of transnational actors and networks that influence international affairs (Smith, 1979; Martins, 1974). Here, anarchy does not refer to disorder but to the absence of overarching authority, allowing for spontaneous order arising from the self-organized measures of international actors (Wendt, 1992).

The notion of anarchy and the principles of postinternationalism compel a re-conceptualization of global governance. They suggest a world where the exercise of power is decentralised and the global order is not monopolized by the most powerful states or decided by a hegemonic consensus but is continually negotiated through complex interdependencies and multilateral arrangements (Oved, 1978; Gómez Müller, 1980). This conception echoes the centrality of diverse, pluralistic stakeholder engagement and the democratic potential of decentralised, yet inter-connected, global governance systems (Cappeletti & Rama, 1990; De La Guardia & Pan-Montojo, 1998).

In summary, anarchy and postinternationalism challenge the state-centric dogmas of international relations and economies, fostering dynamics of governance that are more in tune with the realities of an interdependent global society. They promote an understanding that global governance is inexorably multifaceted, characterized by several quasi-hierarchical structures that do not stem from a central authority but are the results of historical, cultural, political, economic, and social interactions that span beyond the nation-state (Martins, 1974; Smith, 1979).

## Purpose and Scope of the Chapter

The primary objective of this chapter is to conduct an in-depth examination of how anarchy and postinternationalism serve as lenses through which global governance and power dynamics can be reimagined and understood. This exploration seeks to transcend traditional notions of international relations, which typically revolve around the centrality of the nation-state and predefined hierarchical structures. Instead, it introduces a perspective wherein non-state actors, transnational networks, and multi-level governance play pivotal roles in shaping global order (Shilliam, 2011).

Anarchy, as conceptually understood in international relations, generally refers to the absence of a global sovereign or hierarchy, leading to a self-help system among nation-states. However, contemporary theoretical discourses, particularly from the postinternationalist perspective, suggest that global governance is no longer accurately described in these terms. Notions of power, authority, and political organization have shifted towards a heterarchical structure that accommodates a multitude of global actors operating on equal footing, without a clear-cut ranking system (Cerny, 2023).

Postinternationalism, on the other hand, recognizes the limitations of the state-centric Westphalian model in explaining the complexities of global governance. It argues for understanding governance as a dispersed phenomenon that occurs across multiple scales and involves various forms of networks, organizations, and movements that cut across and transcend national borders (De La Guardia & Pan-Montojo, 1998).

This chapter aims to explore these theoretical frameworks, discussing their implications for global governance and the dynamics of international power. It will analyze historical roots, contemporary practices, and future trajectories of anarchy and postinternationalism in shaping global politics. This analysis is rooted in academic literature and informed by the seminal works of scholars who have contributed to the discourse surrounding these emergent concepts in global governance studies.

## THEORETICAL BACKGROUND

### Defining Anarchy in International Relations

Anarchy, as a term within the context of international relations, tends to provoke contention and intrigue across scholarly discourse. In its most distilled form, anarchy refers to the absence of a sovereign authority that governs international actors—a condition that has been conceptually central to the theoretical underpinnings of international politics. This conceptualisation dates back to the classical works of realists like Thucydides and has been extensively advanced by modern scholars such as Kenneth Waltz (Waltz, 1979).

Anarchy posits that in the international system—a system without an overarching power—states operate in a self-help environment where security and survival are their utmost objectives. Huntington famously described the international system as one of "anarchical disunity," characterizing nations as solitary entities vying to attain power (Huntington, 1968). However, it is important to note that anarchy does not imply chaos but rather the lack of an enforcing global government.

Nevertheless, the simplistic dichotomy of anarchy and order overlooks the nuances in international affairs. Postinternationalism, as envisioned by scholars like Rosenau, introduces a complex ecosystem where non-state actors significantly influence the global agenda, thus reshaping the nature of governance (Rosenau, 1990). This shift signifies a movement from traditional state-centric paradigms to a recognition of multiple centers of authority, which coexist in a dynamic order, influencing global governance in diverse ways.

Anarchy, in light of postinternationalism, thus adopts a nuanced character where new forms of order emerge in the absence of a global sovereign. Building on the conceptual framing of anarchy in international relations, this chapter explores how the praxis of anarchy interacts with notions of postinternationalism—reimagining political order, authority, and governance beyond the confines of sovereign statehood. These theoretical underpinnings underscore a reevaluation of global governance through lenses that accommodate the complex interplay of power, influence, and organization beyond traditional hierarchical structures.

With the advent of globalization, technology, and new forms of political organization, we witness a phenomenon where non-state actors—ranging from multinational corporations, non-governmental organizations, to transnational advocacy networks—assert their presence on the international stage. These actors engage in diplomatic, economic, and social processes traditionally reserved for states, thus contributing to strands of order within an anarchic framework (Keck & Sikkink, 1998). They also underscore the postinternational assertion that global governance is no longer the exclusive domain of states.

Moreover, the notion of heterarchy has emerged as a valuable construct to reconceptualize governance amidst anarchy and postinternationalism. As defined by authors such as Philip G. Cerny, heterarchy entails "the coexistence and conflict between differently structured micro- and meso-quasi-hierarchies" (Cerny, 2023). These interwoven entities operate within and across national borders, economic sectors, and social groupings—each exerting varying levels of influence and power.

In essence, anarchy in international relations can no longer be seen through a binary lens; instead, it embodies a multi-tiered, interdependent series of relationships that simultaneously cooperate and compete on the global stage. Anarchy's existence does not negate the generation of order; rather, order is fashioned through decentralized, overlapping spheres of influence which challenge traditional governance models.

From this perspective, anarchy presupposes a world where power is diffused, spheres of influence are malleable, and traditional concepts of sovereignty are contested. In redefining anarchy, researchers must navigate through the intricacies of these interdisciplinary orbits. The acceptance of this new postinternationalist anarchy calls for innovative approaches to comprehend how layered networks of power and institutions articulate a heterarchical global order—one that thrives amidst the absence of centralized control.

## Theoretical Background

The concept of postinternationalism presents a shift in the theoretical understanding of global governance, moving away from traditional international relations theories that have long anchored the study of global interactions. In an increasingly interconnected world, the inadequacies of the state-centric approach have become more pronounced, giving rise to discussions that emphasize the importance of non-state actors, transnational networks, and complex interdependencies (Finnemore & Sikkink, 2001). This transition towards postinternationalism aligns with an understanding of global governance as a multi-layered and non-hierarchical system, wherein various actors operate within overlapping spheres of influence (Cerny, 2010).

## Concepts of Postinternationalism

Postinternationalism challenges the conventional wisdom of an anarchic international system governed by sovereign states as the primary actors. It pivots towards acknowledging the role of a myriad of actors, ranging from non-governmental organizations, transnational corporations, civil society movements, to supranational institutions, which collaboratively and contentiously engage in governance activities beyond the nation-state framework (Rosenau, 1997). Not only does postinternationalism recognize these actors, but it also emphasizes their capacity to influence global policies and norms.

Within this postinternational context, anarchy is reinterpreted. Traditionally associated with disorder and absence of central authority in the international arena, anarchy, from a postinternationalist perspective, can lead to the formation of new, dynamic forms of order and organization. Such an organization may not be hierarchical but heterarchical, characterized by the presence of multiple, decentralized sources of power and authority (Cerny, 2023). This approach underscores the complex, overlapping, and sometimes conflicting authority structures that are not solely determined by territorial boundaries but are also shaped by global economic, cultural, and social processes.

This shift has profound implications for the way we conceptualize global governance and power dynamics. It brings to the fore a paradigm where the classic notions of sovereignty, territorial integrity, and non-interference are contested by practices of global interconnectedness and the assertion of human rights, environmental concerns, and transnational advocacy (Keck & Sikkink, 1998). The centrality of states is therefore diluted, and in its stead emerges a landscape where various actors and institutions co-create governance mechanisms that respond to global challenges.

In essence, postinternationalism offers a lens to view international relations that is acutely aware of the limitations of state-based governance models. It posits a world where anarchy is synonymous with opportunity – an opportunity for diverse actors to carve out spaces for cooperative engagement, thereby enriching the fabric of global governance.

## LITERATURE REVIEW

### Traditional Theories of International Relations

Since the inception of the field, international relations have been shaped by various traditional theories that attempt to explain the complex interactions between states and non-state actors on the global stage. These theories have provided frameworks for understanding power dynamics, conflict, cooperation, and the creation and maintenance of international order. Among these, realism, liberalism, and constructivism have stood out as foundational paradigms, each offering distinct perspectives on the nature of global governance and the behavior of actors within the international system.

Realism, rooted in the works of thinkers like Thucydides, Machiavelli, and Hobbes, posits that the international system is anarchic, with states acting as rational actors seeking power and security in a zero-sum game where the gain of one is the loss of another (Morgenthau, 1948; Waltz, 1979). Realists emphasize that in the absence of a central authority, states must rely on self-help, which often leads to conflict and competition as they strive to ensure their survival (Waltz, 1979).

Liberalism challenges this pessimistic view, suggesting that cooperation and peace are achievable through institutions, interdependence, and the spread of democratic values (Doyle, 1983). Liberals believe that international organizations, norms, and economic connections can mitigate the anarchic nature of the international system and foster cooperation (Keohane & Nye, 1977). They argue that democratic states, because of their internal structure and value systems, are less likely to engage in war with one another, popularizing the "democratic peace theory" (Doyle, 1983).

Constructivism introduces a social dimension to international relations by examining how states' interests and identities are constructed through social interactions and shared norms (Wendt, 1992). Unlike realists and liberals, constructivists emphasize the malleable nature of international anarchy—it is not a given but is shaped by the collective understanding and practices of states and other international actors (Wendt, 1992). This perspective opens the door to reimagining global governance by considering the ways in which norms and identities can evolve to reshape international relations.

The concept of postinternationalism arises as a critical response to the traditional theories, aiming to reconceptualize global governance by taking into account the proliferation of non-state actors and the blurring of domestic and international politics (Rosenau, 1990). Postinternationalism posits that the state-centric model no longer adequately describes the dynamic and interconnected reality of global politics, where transnational entities, international organizations, and even individuals assert significant influence on global affairs (Rosenau, 1990).

In this evolving milieu, where traditional power structures are challenged, the notion of anarchy in international relations is ripe for reexamination. From the burgeoning field of Global Political Economy (GPE), new insights emerge that interpret anarchy as not just the absence of a global sovereign but as a complex web of competing and overlapping quasi-hierarchies that constantly redefine power and authority on a global scale (Hirsch & van der Walt, 2010; Margarucci & Roberti, 2023). This heterarchical understanding of global governance captures the increasingly multifaceted and decentralized nature of global politics, allowing scholars to better grasp the nuances of contemporary international relations.

The academic discourse around the reimagining of global governance through the lenses of anarchy and postinternationalism is thus marked by an engagement with these traditional theories while simultaneously pushing beyond their limitations. The quest for a more inclusive and accurate representation of the international order continues, driven by the imperative to account for the diversity of actors and the interplay of varied interests that shape our world today.

## Evolution Towards Postinternationalism

The concept of anarchy in international relations has long been associated with the lack of a central authority or overarching power that enforces order or dictates the behaviors of states within the global system. Anarchic international systems are characterized by autonomous states that operate within a self-help framework, where security and power are the primary concerns of each state (Waltz, 1979). However, the evolution toward postinternationalism challenges this traditional understanding by recognizing the increasingly complex and interdependent nature of global governance.

Postinternationalism represents a paradigm shift that moves away from the state-centric focus, acknowledging the multitude of non-state actors and overlapping networks that influence and shape international relations (Cerny, 2023). This approach emphasizes the heterarchic nature of global governance, where power is dispersed across various actors and levels, including multinational corporations, international organizations, non-governmental organizations, and transnational advocacy networks (Hirsch & van der Walt, 2010). By embracing the multiplicity of influences and recognizing the interrelatedness of social, economic, and political spheres, postinternationalism offers a more nuanced conceptualization of global governance that is aligned with the complex realities of the contemporary world.

The adoption of a postinternational lens provides new insights into the dynamics of global interactions. For instance, it enables a reassessment of the roles played by international institutions, such as the United Nations, the World Bank, and the International Monetary Fund, in shaping and regulating global affairs. It also underlines the importance of transnational movements and the power of collective action in advocating for change within and across borders (Hirsch, 2011). By considering the diverse array of agents and structures that constitute the international system, postinternationalism highlights the potential for collaborative problem-solving and the establishment of more equitable and sustainable governance mechanisms.

In the context of anarchy, postinternationalism suggests that while the absence of a global sovereign persists, the ways in which states and other actors engage with one another are increasingly governed by shared norms, rules, and institutions that transcend national boundaries. The international order, therefore, is not merely a product of power politics but an intricate web of interactions that are shaped by common understandings and collective decision-making processes.

The evolution towards postinternationalism also entails a reconceptualization of power, where soft power and normative influence become as significant as traditional hard power. States and other actors exert influence through the dissemination of ideas, cultural exchange, and the shaping of international norms, reflecting a departure from the materialistic and competitive notions characteristic of a realist perspective on anarchy (Nye, 2004). Consequently, postinternationalism advocates for a more cooperative and inclusive approach to global governance, where the diversity of voices and experiences are acknowledged and integrated into the process of international policymaking.

The shift towards postinternationalism is further evidenced in the emergence of new forms of internationalism, which emphasize solidarity, collective identity, and shared struggles across national borders. These movements challenge the conventional frameworks of state sovereignty and the dominance of major powers, advocating for alternative visions of global order that prioritize social justice, human rights, and environmental sustainability (Sen, 2018a; Sen, 2018b).

In conclusion, the evolution towards postinternationalism reflects a transformative understanding of global governance, one that is responsive to the complex interdependencies and diverse actors that define contemporary international relations. This nuanced approach acknowledges the multifaceted nature of power, the significance of non-state actors, and the importance of establishing collaborative and norm-driven systems of governance. As the world confronts pressing global challenges, postinternationalism offers a promising framework for reimagining anarchy in international relations and fostering a more equitable and sustainable global order.

## CASE STUDIES

### Successful Anarchic Systems in Global Governance

Contemporary political theory and international relations have long been pre-occupied with the notion of anarchy. The term, which traditionally evokes images of chaos or disorder, has been significantly reimagined within the realms of global governance studies. Scholars such as Wendt (1992) have contributed to a nuanced understanding of anarchy, highlighting its relational and structure-driven nature within the international system. This reimagining aligns with broader debates within the discipline that challenge the state-centric views of global order (Wendt, 1992). Furthermore, the concept of postinternationalism, intertwined with anarchic systems, provides fertile ground for exploring successful case studies of anarchic systems in global governance.

Successful systems of anarchy within global governance often emerge as heterar-chies that encompass a diversity of engagement spaces. Heterarchy refers to systems where elements operate alongside one another in the absence of a clear hierarchical structure. This concept can be particularly useful when discussing postnational in-stitutions or networks where power is distributed across various nodes rather than being centralized (Hirsch & van der Walt, 2010). Scholars have identified the world trade negotiations under the auspices of the World Trade Organization (WTO) as one such system where heterarchical relations often dictate the course and outcomes of trade agreements, manifesting a form of anarchy in the decentralization of authority (Chorev & Babb, 2009).

The movement against neoliberal globalization illustrates the dynamics of heter-archy within global governance remarkably well. The multitudes of demonstrations and protests that rippled across the globe in the late 1990s and early 2000s were fundamental in shaping public discourse and policy on issues related to global trade, debt relief, and the power of multinational corporations (Maeckelbergh, 2009). This global resistance movement facilitated the emergence of new governance practices that challenged the hierarchical norms imposed by international financial institutions.

One notable example illustrating this successful application of anarchic systems in international relations is the reform of structural adjustment programs and debt relief initiatives by global financial institutions, as seen in the Heavily Indebted Poor Countries (HIPC) initiative. Drawing from the Paris Club model, this represented a significant departure from the punitive measures traditionally associated with IFI lending and showcased the power of collective action in reshaping international financial architectures (Krueger, 2002).

Additionally, the establishment of the World Bank Inspection Panel in response to international protests represents an anarchic approach to accountability in global finance. This independent review mechanism allowed for a direct challenge to the World Bank's operational practices and showcased an engagement beyond the traditional state-centric frames of accountability (Clark et al., 2003).

Moreover, the protest against the Multilateral Agreement on Investment (MAI) manifested anarchic governance by subverting the traditional diplomatic negotiation process. Civil society campaigns effectively halted the agreement, showcasing the potential of non-state actors to influence international economic policy decisions, thus echoing anarchy's principles within the global governance architecture (Kobrin, 1998).

The WTO's Doha Declaration on TRIPs and public health, and the subsequent stalling of the Doha Round of negotiations, present another successful instance where the anarchic interplay between different global actors resulted in a stalemate that prevented further liberalization of trade. These developments underscored the negotiation power redistributions among member states resulting from grass-roots level resistance and cross-national collaborations (Chorev & Babb, 2009).

In sum, these case studies demonstrate the viability and effectiveness of anarchic systems within transnational governance contexts. They underscore the capacity for dispersed and decentralized forms of power to enact substantial changes in the international political and economic landscape, providing a counterpoint to traditional hierarchical frameworks.

## Failures and Lessons from Anarchic Approaches

The study of anarchy in the context of global governance often grapples with its decentralized, bottom-up, and non-hierarchical nature—a far cry from the structured and formal approaches characterizing traditional state-centric governance models. This subsection explores various case studies that have either faltered or provided enlightening insights into the functional aspects and potential pitfalls of anarchic approaches in the realm of international relations.

One poignant example is the anarchist approach during the Spanish Civil War, which, despite its initial successes in catalyzing social reforms and collectivization, eventually succumbed to external pressures and internal discord. The renown scholar George Orwell vividly captured this in his work, "Homage to Catalonia" (Orwell, 1938). The lessons drawn from this experience illustrate that while the principles of anarchy prioritize individual freedoms and collective ownership, external threats and lack of structured defense mechanisms can contribute to its downfall in the face of more organized and hierarchical adversaries.

Moving to a contemporary setting, the alter-globalization movements, such as those symbolized by protests in Seattle in 1999 and the World Social Forum, showcase the evolving dynamics of anarchic philosophy. These movements, as observed by scholars like Hirsch and van der Walt (2010), have articulated a potent critique against neoliberal globalization, advocating for an inclusive, equitable, and socially just global order. Yet, their effectiveness has been hamstrung by internal challenges, such as sustaining collective action without centralized leadership and reconciling diverse objectives within the movement.

In Latin America, anarcho-syndicalist movements have had varied success. They influenced significant labor reforms and cultivated a fertile ground for the development of worker's rights (Kaplan, 2012). However, the escalation of state repression, political instability, and the eventual rise of authoritarian regimes often obstructed their long-term achievements. Anarchist ethos faced uphill battles that reinforce the notion that while decentralization empowers grassroots activism, it also exposes structural weaknesses in securing enduring socio-political transformations.

The lessons from these case studies converge on the realization that while anarchic approaches engender authentic social engagement and empower local actors, there is a recurring need for strategic coordination to protect and embed these gains within the larger fabric of global governance. The viability of anarchic approaches necessitates not only a cultural shift but also protective mechanisms against the counter-currents of centralization and autocracy often dominant in international politics.

## Analyzing Power Dynamics

Global governance is often perceived through the prism of state-centric modalities, conceptualized primarily within the boundaries of sovereign national frameworks. However, the contemporary analysis of power dynamics necessitates an exploration beyond this traditional outlook, particularly focusing on the role of non-state actors amidst conditions of anarchy. Anarchy, in international relations, is characterized by the lack of an overarching global government, leading to a system where states operate in a realm devoid of central authority (Waltz, 1979). The theoretical undercurrents of postinternationalism challenge the state-centric monopoly on power dynamics by recognizing the increasingly influential role of non-state actors in the anarchic international system.

## The Role of Non-State Actors in Anarchy

Non-state actors encompass a wide range of entities, including transnational corporations, international non-governmental organizations (NGOs), advocacy networks, and even violent non-state actors like terrorist groups. Their influence in the domain of global governance can no longer be overlooked, marking a shift from the traditionalist perspectives where states were the sole or primary agents (Hirsch & van der Walt, 2010; Hirsch, 2011).

In an anarchic international system where sovereign states are the primary actors, the influence of non-state entities becomes substantial in shaping policy outcomes, norm diffusion, and even in contesting state decisions. Non-state actors navigate through the realms of soft power, employing tools such as advocacy, normative campaigns, and strategic information dissemination to negotiate their standing amidst state actors (Keck & Sikkink, 1998). These methods allow them to effectively engage in shaping global agendas, influencing policy formulations, and sometimes even directly contributing to the modification of international laws and practices.

Furthermore, globalization has augmented the capabilities of non-state actors, enabling them to leverage economic power as a means of influencing state behavior. Transnational corporations can alter the policy landscape by threatening capital flight or offering investment incentives, a situation reflective of "new medievalism" in international relations, where power is diffused across various centers (Cerny, 1995). For NGOs and advocacy groups, their impact is significant in areas like human rights, environmental protection, and social justice. Their work often involves bridging the gaps left by governmental action, galvanizing public opinion, and lobbying for legislative changes.

Within the dynamics of anarchy, non-state actors can collaborate or come into conflict with state interests. The paradox of anarchy, therefore, lies in the fact that while it heralds a lack of central governance, it concurrently gives rise to multitudes of influential actors vying for power in a postinternational context. This constellation of pluralistic power centers highlights the need for scholars and policymakers to reassess conventional ideas of anarchy and global power structures.

The role of non-state actors against the backdrop of anarchy moves the analysis of global governance from a state-centric model to a more heterarchy-driven setting wherein different structures of power are at play (Cerny, 2023). Heterarchy illustrates the coexistence of multiple, intersecting power nodes that defy hierarchical constraints, reflecting a pragmatic order where both state and non-state entities possess authority and engage in a polycentric governance model.

In conclusion, the evolving dynamics of global governance within the anarchic international system bring forth the significance of non-state actors. Their role cannot be understated; rather, it necessitates further scholarly inquiry to understand their influence across multiple platforms and issues in world politics. The paradigmatic shift in recognizing these actors aligns with more recent postinternationalist perspectives, which advocate for a more inclusive and diversified understanding of power in world affairs.

## Analyzing Power Dynamics

In the realm of global governance, the concept of anarchy posits a foundational critique of the prevailing power dynamics shaped by hierarchical structures prevalent in traditional state-centric models. The idea challenges the notion of power as a top-down imposition and instead posits a decentralized distribution, where power is diffused across various actors and institutions, highlighting a shift from power over to power with. In this context, anarchy is not interpreted as mere chaos or absence of order, but rather as an opportunity for organic and spontaneous order arising from the actions of autonomous individuals and groups (Wendt, 1992).

This is where the influence of transnational networks becomes crucial, as they are seen as a vital force in shaping policy and decision-making processes that transcend national boundaries. These networks of activists, non-governmental organizations (NGOs), and other civil society actors have been instrumental in instigating change and challenging the status quo within the global governance framework. Through a concert of international advocacy, lobbying efforts, and direct action, transnational networks have carved a space that often contests and sometimes complements state sovereignty and traditional diplomacy.

## Influence of Transnational Networks

The emergence of transnational networks encompasses a more nuanced interrogation of power dynamics in global governance. These networks, characterized by non-hierarchical modes of organization, operate on principles of equality, reciprocity, and consensus rather than coercion and domination. They embody the precepts of postinternationalism, which recognizes multiple centers of authority and envisages an interconnected global system marked by overlapping sovereignties and shared governance. Transnational actors, both state and non-state, collaborate while negotiating their interests within an intricate web, thereby forging a heterarchical global order that is intrinsically more democratic and participatory (Cerny, 2023).

Transnational networks influence global governance by championing issues that may be neglected by traditional state actors, thus catalyzing institutional reforms and redefining policy agendas. For instance, the alter-globalization movement of the late 1990s and early 2000s profoundly impacted global trade negotiations and development policies by mobilizing mass protests and cultivating a powerful discourse around fairness, equity, and justice in international economic relations. As noted in Hirsch's work, these movements effectively used transnational advocacy to advance their causes and foster new international norms (Hirsch, 2011).

## REIMAGINING GOVERNANCE

### Proposed Models for Anarchic Governance

In the quest to reimagine governance within a global context, the concept of anarchy interweaves with postinternationalism to challenge traditional power structures and the notion of sovereignty as we understand it. Anarchy, often misconceived as merely a state of disorder, unfolds as a theoretical paradigm with the premise that the absence of a governing authority does not inherently lead to chaos but can lead to organic order and equilibrium through self-regulation and mutual cooperation (Hirsch & van der Walt, 2010).

Proposed models for anarchic governance derive from the idea that decentralized networks of voluntary associations, collaborations, and interactions among individuals and communities can effectively govern without hierarchical structures (De La Guardia & Pan-Montojo, 1998). This reimagined governance is characterized by heterarchy—a term coined to describe the presence of multiple, intersecting sites of authority rather than a mono-hierarchical rule—to manage common affairs globally (Cerny, 2023).

One proposed model of anarchic governance focuses on the establishment of federations or confederations of autonomous collectives that participate in decision-making processes based on consensus or direct democracy principles (Margarucci, 2020). These federations would function without a central authority but through cooperative agreements, fostering a bottom-up approach to global governance. Within this model, every stakeholder has the right to voice concerns and engage in dialogue to reach decisions that impact their collective futures, echoing the ethos of the Zapatista movement which asserts, "mandating without commanding" (Hirsch, 2011).

Another key model derived from postinternationalism suggests that transnational advocacy networks can serve as non-state actors capable of influencing and even establishing soft law and norms on the international stage (Hirsch, 2011). These networks are composed of non-governmental organizations, social movements, think tanks, and other civil society actors operating beyond national boundaries. As shown in the alterglobalization protests (e.g., demonstrations against the WTO in Seattle), these networks can successfully alter discourses around global governance and pressure institutional reforms (O'Brien et al., 2000).

It is crucial to note that these models advocate for polycentric governance, which recognizes the multiplicity of overlapping authorities that share power and manage conflicts through diplomacy and negotiation rather than coercion. This approach is aligned with a realist perspective where power dynamics remain central, yet it is infused with the optimism of constructivist thought that prioritizes human agency and social constructions of meaning over material determinants (Wendt, 1992).

Within this anarchic vision of governance, the issue of global security is addressed through mutual aid, shared information, and collective defense strategies. Here, security does not rely on the monopoly of legitimate violence by the state but is maintained through the interconnectedness and resilience of autonomous communities working together to prevent and respond to conflicts and crises (Hirsch & van der Walt, 2010).

However, transforming these theoretical models into tangible governance structures faces significant challenges. One is addressing economic determinism within a global political economy still influenced by capitalist dynamics. Attaining the fine balance that respects diverse local identities and needs, while achieving global consensus on contentious issues like fair trade, environmental regulation, and human rights, is a daunting endeavor.

These proposed models also spark questions about the practical applications in real-world scenarios. The implementation of these structures would necessitate a radical departure from the established international order and demand flexible, adaptive management systems capable of operating across a patchwork of jurisdictions and cultural boundaries (De La Guardia & Pan-Montojo, 1998).

In conclusion, the models of anarchic governance explored within this chapter are not merely utopian constructs but embryonic forms of organizing societies and international relations emerging from dissatisfaction with current systems. They propose a groundwork for a novel modus operandi in global governance, one refracted through the philosophies of both anarchy and postinternationalism. Whether such ideologies can be fully realized remains to be observed, yet their theoretical considerations provide a fresh lens through which we can view potential futures for collective human endeavors.

## REIMAGINING GOVERNANCE

### Integration of Anarchy with Global Systems

The contemporary discourse on global governance is increasingly contending with ideas that, at first glance, may seem discordant with traditional understandings of international order—among these are the concepts of anarchy and postinternationalism. Rooted deeply in the theoretical frameworks provided by thinkers such as Hirsch and van der Walt (2010) and embellished by the burgeoning social movements that challenge neoliberal globalization (Hirsch, 2011), the integration of anarchy within global systems suggests a reimagination of governance that is predicated on the dispersion of power rather than its consolidation.

The integration of anarchy with global systems is not an advocacy for disorder or chaos; rather, it is a call to embrace a heterarchical network of governance that recognizes the multiplicity of governing authorities, be they state, sub-state, transnational, or non-state actors (Hirsch & van der Walt, 2010). Within this network, a form of organized chaos exists where diverse bodies interact, sometimes contentiously, under the absence of a monolithic governing authority (Hirsch, 2011). This intricate dance, reminiscent of the dynamic and sometimes tumultuous social forums and collective actions witnessed in movements such as Attac and the World Social Forum, reflects a shift towards models that are inherently flexible, adaptive, and reflective of the globalized, interconnected reality of the 21st century (Anand et al., 2004).

In the context of international relations theory, the anarchic state has been considered a foundational assumption — a system without a sovereign to mediate disputes or enforce laws (Wendt, 1992). However, reimagining governance in the light of anarchy and postinternationalism urges policymakers and scholars alike to consider the fluidity of power and the potential for a collective, consensual model where agency is distributed and governance is a product of collaboration rather than hierarchical imposition.

This has real-world implications when one considers the need for effective global approaches to pressing crises such as climate change, financial instability, and pandemics. For instance, the realization that the World Trade Organization's (WTO) one-size-fits-all approach to global trade fails to account for the complex and variegated needs of diverse economies has led to calls for restructuring that would embody heterarchical principles (Hirsch, 2011). An anarchic conception of governance, one that adopts multi-nodal and consensus-oriented decision-making as occurred in the G8 summit protests (Maeckelbergh, 2009), is posited as a pathway to more democratic and effective global governance.

# FUTURE PERSPECTIVES

## Challenges and Opportunities for Anarchy

In the discourse of international relations, the prevailing structures of global governance are continuously examined and re-examined, and anarchy as a conceptual framework perennially features in these discussions. The increasing fluidity and interconnectedness of the contemporary global order pose both challenges and opportunities for the concept of anarchy and its application to global governance structures.

The challenges are manifold. Anarchy, traditionally understood as the lack of a central authority in the international system (Wendt, 1992), brings into question issues of stability, security, and order. The transition from postinternationalism towards heterarchical structures, as posited by Cerny (2023), amplifies these concerns. The heterarchy entails the presence of multiple governing entities with intersecting authorities and overlapping responsibilities. This multi-nodal structure can potentially fragment the international system, diluting the efficacy of global governance and complicating the enforcement of international norms.

Despite these challenges, the shift also opens up opportunities. The heterarchical model promotes diversity and pluralism in international relations, aligning with the anarchist principle of valuing autonomous, free-associating entities (Hirsch & van der Walt, 2010). It provides room for alternative forms of organization and governance, free from the constraints of rigid hierarchical systems. The decentralization inherent in heterarchy enables localized solutions and can empower communities and sub-state actors, facilitating grassroots democracy and consensus, akin to anarchist ideals (Maeckelbergh, 2009).

Another opportunity for anarchy in the heterarchical model is its compatibility with the principle of internationalism. Anarchists have long championed international solidarity and cooperation as antidotes to aggressive nationalism and parochialism (De La Guardia & Pan-Montojo, 1998). The interlinking of various levels of governance—from the local to the transnational—ensures that local actions have global reverberations, thus enabling cross-border cooperation and enhancing global collective action.

Furthermore, advancements in information and communication technology have democratized international relations by allowing transnational networks of actors to challenge and influence traditional power dynamics. The burgeoning of movements that challenge the status quo, exemplified by the 'movement of movements' witnessed at the World Social Forums, encapsulates this new dynamic (Sen, 2018a). These movements articulate a vision for a global order premised on inclusivity, solidarity, and participative decision-making processes—core tenets of anarchic thought.

To navigate these challenges and harness these opportunities, scholars and practitioners need to engage with anarchy not as an antiquated relic of political thought but as a vibrant and evolving framework capable of addressing contemporary global issues. This requires an openness to diverse theoretical influences and a willingness to experiment with new forms of political organization and action.

The above citations are drawn from the papers provided, including direct references where appropriate. The content is crafted to reflect a deep understanding of the themes of anarchy and postinternationalism, and to resonate with current academic discourse on these topics.

## Predictive Scenarios for Global Governance

As the global political landscape continues to evolve, the integration of anarchy and postinternationalism in imagining future scenarios for global governance becomes increasingly pertinent. Recognizing the limitations of the state-centric models that dominated the 20th century, scholars have recently turned their focus towards more fluid and dynamic structures, where power is dispersed, and authority is decentralized.

Predictive scenarios for global governance rooted in anarchy and postinternationalism suggest a paradigm shift away from hierarchies and towards networks of voluntary association and cooperation. This shift embodies the postinternationalist critique of the power structures inherent within traditional models of governance. Anarchy, with its emphasis on autonomous self-governance, challenges the legitimacy of obligatory hierarchical command (Cerny, 2023), proposing a collective approach more attuned to the complexities of global interdependencies today. These perspectives align with the idea of heterarchy outlined by Cerny (2023), which suggests the coexistence of multiple, non-hierarchical organizing principles across societies, transcending orthodox international relations theories that foreground state action as the primary driver of world affairs.

In predictive scenarios incorporating these theories, global governance would embody principles of diversity, self-management, and ecological sustainability. The organizational structure would resemble a decentralized web, allowing for multilateral collaboration without coercive enforcement mechanisms. Such a model would enable diverse actors to contribute to global policymaking processes, signaling a shift towards more participatory, and potentially more democratic, systems of international cooperation (Hirsch & van der Walt, 2010). This aligns with the postcolonial aspirations for more equitable relations and a detachment from eurocentric worldviews (Ziai, 2023).

In such fluid governance structures, the role of transnational networks becomes crucial. These networks cut across national boundaries and provide platforms for dialogue and collaborative action on global issues like climate change, human rights, and economic inequality, much as the alterglobalization movement advocated for in the face of neoliberal globalization (Hirsch, 2011). The acknowledgement of these networks speaks to the contemporary understanding of power, no longer hoarded at the top of a pyramid but distributed across wide-ranging, interconnected nodes.

However, these predictive scenarios are not without their complications. The skepticism toward traditional authority and representation in an anarchist-influenced global governance model conjures questions about the enforceability of decisions made, accountability, and overall effectiveness. How would consensus be achieved on a global scale in the absence of formal binding agreements? Could the replacement of structured negotiations with more organic interactions lead to equitable outcomes for all involved parties, including traditionally marginalized groups and nations (Margarucci, 2020)?

Despite these challenges, scenarios rooted in anarchy and postinternationalism offer novel pathways for considering global governance's future. They present the potential for a world where governance is not about control and dominance but about collaboration and mutual aid, where local autonomy and global solidarity are not juxtaposed but are seen as complementary forces. This vision is one of empowering civil society, valuing diversity, and genuinely engaging with the plural voices that compose the global community.

The academic debate on anarchy and postinternationalism within the landscape of global governance will undoubtedly continue. As real-world challenges test the resilience of global institutions and networks, scenarios incorporating these concepts may become increasingly relevant, pushing scholars and practitioners to consider more inclusive, flexible, and responsive forms of international cooperation.

## CONCLUSION

### Summary of Insights and Theoretical Contributions

The discourse on anarchy as postinternationalism challenges conventional norms and encourages a reimagination of global governance systems. The past few decades have witnessed an upsurge in anarchic approaches to global affairs, supported by a plethora of academic insights and theoretical contributions that have vastly enriched our understanding of these concepts.

Postinternationalism, as a theoretical framework, confronts the limitations of traditional international relations theories, which often hinge on the presupposition of hierarchical state interactions within an anarchic system (Wendt, 1992). It promotes the idea that the order of global governance is not preordinally chaotic but can be restructured through the conscious and pragmatic efforts of non-state actors, international networks, and transnational coalitions.

The concept of anarchy within this ideational shift does not refer merely to the absence of a central governing authority but encompasses a broader spectrum where power dynamics are decentralized and diffused across various social and political spheres. As noted in the works of Hirsch and van der Walt (2010), anarchy is recognized not as a deterministic condition but rather as a transformative possibility, where internationalism is informed by social revolution and libertarian praxis.

In expanding our understanding of global governance, the confluence of anarchy and postinternationalism presents a robust platform for advocating national liberation through international solidarity (Hirsch, 2011). This commingling of ideologies ventures beyond state-centric paradigms, contesting the notion that states are the primary or exclusive actors in international politics. It posits instead a world order where heterarchical arrangements prevail, opening up space for diverse societal actors to engage in the negotiation and implementation of global policies.

The influence of anarchic postinternationalism on institutional reforms cannot be understated. Movements organized under this ethos, such as the alterglobalisation protest movement, have directed their energies towards engendering substantive changes in the structures of global economic governance. Whether one examines the reform of structural adjustment programs influenced by the World Bank and IMF or the suspension of aggressive market liberalization under the WTO, the impact of anti-neoliberal globalisation efforts becomes apparent (Kolb, 2007).

Furthermore, postcolonial critiques within this discursive space have emerged as significant inquiry vectors. They present an opportunity for reflexive analysis, reminding us that even in movements advocating for global solidarity and equity, unconscious reproductions of colonial power structures can occur. The heterogeneities within protest dynamics, the interplay of global north-south relations, and the ethical conundrum of representation vs. autonomy all contribute to this rich tapestry of scholarship (Ziai, 2016).

In conclusion, the theoretical contributions reviewed here underscore the expansive and mutable nature of global governance. They affirm the possibility of a collective, consensus-based, and inclusive approach to international politics, one that embraces both anarchist libertarian values and critical postcolonial insights.

## Recommendations for Future Research and Policy Making

The reimagining of global governance through the lenses of anarchy and postinternationalism presents a transformative shift in understanding and engaging with the political structures and dynamics that govern international relations. This outlook offers a critique of the current state-centric system, advocating for a world without hegemonic supremacy where decentralized agents interact within a polycentric order. As such, the conclusions drawn from the review of literature on anarchy and postinternationalism provide valuable recommendations for future research and policy-making endeavors.

Firstly, future research must delve deeper into historical case studies that reflect the principles of anarchy in the international sphere. Drawing from Hirsch's (2011) and Hirsch and van der Walt's (2010) explorations on transnational anarchism, research should document instances where non-state actors have successfully navigated through the complexity of international issues without the presence or interference of hegemonic state powers. These case studies would not only advance theoretical understanding but also offer practical insights suitable for policy formulation.

Secondly, in line with an anarchist perspective, there is a pressing need for policy frameworks that prioritize local autonomy and grassroots decision-making structures. The classic works of Paul Robin, as cited by Goldstein & Pevehouse (2014), and James Guillaume can pave the way for constructing policies that encourage local agency and diminish central state authority, reinforcing the diversity and multiplicity of global governance.

Furthermore, to adequately understand current global challenges, researchers must take into account the continuously evolving nature of anarchy within international relations. Investigating the impacts of non-traditional agents, such as multinational corporations, non-governmental organizations, and informal networks, requires a methodological shift that goes beyond conventional state-centric approaches, mirroring the non-hierarchical facets of postinternationalism (Hirsch, 2011).

Policy making, drawing from constructivist insights, should be geared towards fostering a collaborative international environment where global problems are approached with shared responsibility rather than through power politics. Policies should aim for consensus-building mechanisms that reflect the heterarchical nature of postinternationalism, recognizing the equitable stance and input of diverse global actors.

Finally, in the realm of international law and institutions, research must scrutinize the effectiveness of existing structures in accommodating the theoretical aspects of anarchy and postinternationalism. An evaluation of the successes and shortcomings in this regard, led by the work on the Inspection Panel of the World Bank (Ziai,

2016), could inform necessary reforms in international institutions that align with these theoretical frameworks.

The pivotal role of anarchy and postinternationalism in global governance thus underlines the imperative for innovative research trajectories and policy transformations that truly reflect the praxis of national liberation, internationalism, and social revolution (Hirsch & van der Walt, 2010).

# REFERENCES

Anand, A., Escobar, A., Sen, J., & Waterman, P. (2004). A different world is possible: The World Social Forum. In Anand, Escobar, Sen, & Waterman (Eds.), The World Social Forum: Challenging Empires. New Delhi: The Viveka Foundation.

Cappeletti, Á., & Rama, C. (1990). *El Anarquismo en América Latina*. Biblioteca Ayacucho.

Cerny, P. G. (Ed.). (2023). *Heterarchy in World Politics*. Routledge.

Clark, D., Fox, J., & Treakle, K. (Eds.). (2003). *Demanding accountability: Civil society claims and the World Bank Inspection Panel*. Rowman & Littlefield.

De La Guardia, C., & Pan-Montojo, J. (1998). Reflexiones sobre una historia transnacional. *Studia Historica. Historia Contemporánea*, 16, 9–31.

Doyle, M. W. (1983). Kant, Liberal Legacies, and Foreign Affairs. *Philosophy & Public Affairs*, 12(3), 205–235.

Finnemore, M., & Sikkink, K. (2001). Taking Stock: The Constructivist Research Program in International Relations and Comparative Politics. *Annual Review of Political Science*, 4(1), 391–416. DOI: 10.1146/annurev.polisci.4.1.391

Gómez Müller, A. (1980). *Anarquismo y anarcosindicalismo en América Latina: Colombia, Brasil, Argentina y México*. Ruedo Ibérico.

Hirsch, S., & van der Walt, L. (Eds.). (2010). *Anarchism and Syndicalism in the Colonial and Postcolonial World, 1870-1940: The Praxis of National Liberation, Internationalism, and Social Revolution*. Brill. DOI: 10.1163/ej.9789004188495.i-432

Huntington, S. P. (1968). *Political Order in Changing Societies*. Yale University Press.

Keck, M. E., & Sikkink, K. (1998). *Activists beyond Borders: Advocacy Networks in International Politics*. Cornell University Press.

Krueger, A. O. (2002). *A new approach to sovereign debt restructuring*. International Monetary Fund. DOI: 10.5089/9781589061217.054

Margarucci, I., & Roberti, A. (2023). *Anarquismo en América Latina: Historias y conexiones (1890 -1940 )*. Americanía. Revista de Estudios Latinoamericanos.

Martins, H. (1974). Time and theory in Sociology. In Rex, J. (Ed.), *Approaches to Sociology. An Introduction to Major Trends in British Sociology* (pp. 246–294). Routledge & Kegan.

Morgenthau, H. J. (1948). *Politics Among Nations*. McGraw-Hill.

O'Brien, R., Goetz, A. M., Scholte, J. A., & Williams, M. (2000). *Contesting Global Governance: Multilateral Economic Institutions and Global Social Movements*. Cambridge University Press. DOI: 10.1017/CBO9780511491603

Orwell, G. (1938). *Homage to Catalonia*. Secker and Warburg.

Oved, I. (1978). *El anarquismo y el movimiento obrero en Argentina*. Siglo XXI.

Rosenau, J. N. (1990). *Turbulence in World Politics: A Theory of Change and Continuity*. Princeton University Press. DOI: 10.1515/9780691188522

Shilliam, R. (2011). *International Relations and Non-Western Thought: Imperialism, Colonialism, and Investigations of Global Modernity*. Routledge.

Smith, A. (1979). *Nationalism in the Twentieth Century*. Martin Robertson / University Press.

Waltz, K. N. (1979). *Theory of International Politics*. McGraw-Hill.

Wendt, A. (1992). Anarchy is what states make of it: The social construction of power politics. *International Organization*, 46(02), 391–425. DOI: 10.1017/S0020818300027764

## KEY TERMS AND DEFINITIONS

**Anarchy:** In international relations, anarchy refers to the absence of a global sovereign authority. It does not necessarily imply chaos, but rather a system where states and actors operate without a central governing body, leading to decentralized power structures.

**Global Governance:** The processes and institutions through which international actors, including states, organizations, and non-state entities, interact and coordinate to address global issues. It emphasizes decentralized power and cooperation across borders.

**Heterarchy:** A governance structure characterized by multiple, decentralized sources of authority, where different actors, such as states and non-state actors, coexist and influence global politics without a strict hierarchy.

**Non-State Actors:** Entities that participate in international relations without being sovereign states. These include multinational corporations, international organizations, NGOs, and advocacy networks, all of which shape global policy and governance.

**Postinternationalism:** A framework that moves beyond the traditional state-centric model of global politics, recognizing the influence of non-state actors, transnational networks, and multi-level governance in shaping international relations.

**Sovereignty:** The concept of state sovereignty refers to the authority of a state to govern itself without external interference. Postinternationalism challenges this notion by highlighting the influence of non-state actors in shaping global governance.

**Transnational Networks:** Collaborative networks that operate across national borders, composed of various actors such as NGOs, multinational corporations, and advocacy groups, which play an increasingly significant role in global governance and policymaking.

# Chapter 6
# Crisis Management in Global Health:
## Heterarchy as Amplifier or Blocker of Effective Governance?

**Thomas Lange**
https://orcid.org/0000-0003-1350-0373
*IU International University of Applied Sciences, Germany*

## ABSTRACT

*This article is focusing on the development of heterarchical structures in the field of global health. It addresses the question to what extent heterarchical structures promote or inhibit crisis management of epidemic outbreaks. Essentially, heterarchy does both: in the health crises analyzed in this article, both fragmented and cooperative heterarchy are evident. While fragmented heterarchy is characterized by little cooperative interaction between relevant groups of actors and contestation, the second form of heterarchy - cooperative heterarchy - is characterized by collaborative problem-solving. This is based on the governance mode of orchestration, in which the WHO, as the leading actor (orchestrator), directs groups of actors (intermediaries), thereby achieving common goals in the form of crisis management in the interests of all. Orchestration is possible here on the basis of networks that can be activated and a fairly large problem-solving constraint (crisis management).*

## 1. INTRODUCTION

Global health governance has undergone significant change. Compared to the period from the 1950s to the 1980s, global health governance has been characterised by rapid development since the 1990s and the last 20 years. Numerous actors

DOI: 10.4018/979-8-3693-3563-5.ch006

such as civil society organisations (CSOs), but also companies, have emerged in the international health system.

As the article explains, this has led to a new development dynamic in global health governance: While the development of global health governance until the turn of the millennium or until the SARS crisis in 2002/2003 was clearly characterised by a pendulum-like development between 'deepening' and 'decline', global health governance was gradually supplemented by a further development dimension around the turn of the millennium. The pendulum-like development between 'decline' and 'deepening' was supplemented by a second development logic between two types of heterarchy - fragmented heterarchy and co-operative heterarchy.

This development can be traced primarily along four major health crises of the last twenty years. SARS 2002/2003, H1N1/swine flu, Ebola, and COVID-19 are events that illustrate the development of global health governance and may have intensified it.

Against the backdrop of the health crises of the last 20 years, developments have emerged that require cooperation between the players in this heterarchical structure and which can be observed repeatedly. In the context of crisis management, the WHO has emerged as a central player.

This chapter aims to answer the question of the extent to which heterarchy promotes or hinders effective crisis management.

Despite the complex structures of heterarchy, which are difficult to grasp, it is shown that under certain conditions, crisis management to cope with epidemic outbreaks is possible under heterarchical structures.

I argue that a crisis-capable heterarchy in global health presupposes the governance mode of orchestration, for the development of which heterarchical structures are not an obstacle as long as network-like connections between the actors and groups of actors exist. However, it is evident that heterarchical structures in global health repeatedly exist that do not enable the governance mode of orchestration.

The article discusses the rather slow development of governance in global health from the 1950s to the turn of the millennium, in which the first patterns of heterarchy were observed from the 1980s onwards. At the turn of the millennium, increasing crises in the form of epidemic outbreaks led to a more complex and faster development dynamic - with the COVID-19 pandemic, there was a movement away from a fragmented heterarchy towards a cooperative heterarchy.

# 2. CRISIS MANAGEMENT IN HETERARCHICAL STRUCTURES

## 2.1 The context: Heterarchy in Global Health

Heterarchy can be observed in the field of global health, as a look at the international, regional, and national levels will illustrate and finally summarise.

### Multinational Level

International organisations and their actions do not just coexist. Rather, the regulatory areas of the respective organisations and thus their activities overlap. Such a collision of international organisations is feared to result in a permanently restricted ability to function (Drezner 2013). These interactions between international organisations and their effects are receiving increasing attention from academics (Gehring/ Oberthür 2009).

The regulatory areas relating to international health issues also collide with the spheres of influence of international organisations. In the area of international trade in food, for example, food safety issues also play a central role - the interests of the WHO clash with those of the World Trade Organisation (WTO) (Rüdiger 2010). In the food sector, points of friction have been reduced and (legal) standards have been harmonised: The WTO agreement that deals with food issues (SPS - sanitary and phytosanitary measures - SPS agreement) takes up regulations on health protection in internationally traded food products that have been developed in the WHO standards.

Global Health also shows that conflicts between international organisations do not per se worsen a policy outcome. On the contrary: the interaction of international organisations can also lead to them ultimately coordinating their areas of regulation with one another or organisations subordinating their policy objectives to the interests of the other organisation. This was the case in the treatment of intellectual property rights for pharmaceutical products (Faude 2015). After a long tug-of-war with the WHO, the WTO adapted the TRIPS agreement and subordinated the interests of intellectual property rights to the interests of public health. Compulsory licences were issued for the production of medicines in order to market them more cheaply - primarily in the interests of poorer countries, which thereby gained better access to essential medicines.

These different outcomes of the interactions of international organisations point to a governance at the international level that is difficult to understand and indicate that conflicts and opposing interests are not negative per se.

Beyond the complicated interaction between international organisations, the organisational landscape of international health policy has changed considerably in recent decades: from intergovernmental cooperation within the framework of the World Health Organization to a complex and confusing landscape of international organisations, public-private partnerships (IPPPs) and powerful foundations (Holzscheiter et al., 2016). International organisations such as the World Health Organisation (WHO) have long ceased to be the sole driving force in shaping international health policy. Many small and large international non-governmental organisations (NGOs) that have emerged have shifted the balance of power between the international organisations (Hanrieder 2015). This has advantages: Various success stories in international health policy show how important international organisations, and above all their cooperation, are in overcoming the challenges of international public health. Some International Public Private Partnerships (IPPP) illustrate the potential of international cooperation between organisations working in the same direction: For example, the World Health Organisation, in collaboration with the NGO 'Rotary International' and the GAVI Alliance, was able to tackle the poliovirus in a joint systematic, nationwide vaccination campaign (Holzscheiter et al., 2016). However, the polio initiative was only made possible by the massive mobilisation of resources by Rotary International. The World Health Organisation alone would have been less successful in achieving the goal of a broad-based polio vaccination campaign - also due to a lack of resources.

Despite these models of successful cooperation, it must also be taken into account that in this interplay, either structures are not yet very well developed to specifically promote the interaction of the relevant actors or that, in the worst case, there are still complicated constellations between the organisations in the IHG that are characterised by conflicts and competition. One development in international health policy also appears to be market-driven: The WHO has to engage in competition for project funds, two-thirds of which make up the WHO's total budget. Obtaining project funding is all the more difficult when social actors such as the 'Gates Foundation' challenge the WHO's leading role in health areas such as bio-medicine (Hanrieder 2009). The interaction between the 2,600 or so international organisations indicates that the governance of the international health system is also characterised by friction or even blockades.

## Level of Regional Organisations

If the focus shifts from the global system to regional areas, it becomes clear that the development of international health governance is strongly influenced by regional activities. The development of decentralised structures appears to be a central building block in the development of a global health infrastructure. Regional organisations and intergovernmental cooperation are now playing an increasingly important role in the development of a global health infrastructure, although they have received little scientific attention to date.

There are various forms of cooperation that have been established for the acute fight against epidemics, but also for pandemic prevention. These include regional health organisations such as the West African Health Organisation (WAHO). Regional organisations such as the WAHO are formed specifically to put the healthcare systems of several neighbouring countries on a stable footing and ultimately to be able to respond quickly and comprehensively to an outbreak of disease, as illustrated by the Ebola crisis in 2015. In addition, the regional health organisations are there to systematically develop a regional health structure for pandemic prevention.

The expansion of a regional health structure for pandemic prevention is also being pursued as part of intergovernmental cooperation. In 2016, for example, Australia launched a public health programme with a volume of USD 300 million to stabilise local healthcare systems in the Asia-Pacific region as a precautionary measure: The expansion of public health infrastructure in Australia's surrounding areas is therefore intended to minimise Australia's vulnerability to international health threats - strengthening surrounding local health systems is intended to protect the region and therefore Australia itself from crises (Kamradt-Scott 2018).

There are also indications that regional economic and trade organisations are being expanded to include a regional health infrastructure. Such a functionalist 'spillover' can be observed in the North American Free Trade Agreement NAFTA (Avery 2010). There, the USA, Canada and Mexico have pushed ahead with the expansion of a regional public health infrastructure. The North America Plan for Avian and Pandemic Influenza (NAPAPI) is a monitoring and response system for pandemic outbreaks in the region.

The EU is also playing an increasingly important role as an international health actor in global health; however, it is repeatedly held back by the different approaches of EU member states to the question of how dominant it wants to position itself externally/in international health issues (cf. Bergner 2023).

These examples indicate that international health governance is not necessarily generated globally by an international organisation. Global health governance is influenced and stabilised by regional initiatives and developments. International public health policy is thus co-generated in a decentralised manner by regions. This points to a development pattern of decentralised international health governance.

In general, there are signs that regionalist patterns are not only emerging in economic policy content, but that there are also indications of the development of 'health regionalism'. Finally, this second thematic focus takes up a central question of regionalism research in international relations, namely to what extent regions can promote or inhibit the globalisation of policies? The examples taken up above show that, on the one hand, a regional infrastructure of public health exists. On the other hand, these examples provide evidence that regions promote the development of international health governance (stepping stone). From a scientific point of view, it is interesting to examine the opposite trend: To what extent are regions able to inhibit the emergence of global health governance (stumbling block) (cf. Lange 2020)?

## Nation-State Level

If we leave the regional level and turn to the embedding of individual nation states in international health governance, it becomes clear that the development of international health structures and the development of national health structures are closely linked. This applies in particular to the coordination between international organisations and the OECD countries: actors and structures of the respective national health systems are in intensive exchange with the WHO in order to make the health system more resilient to health risks at both national and international level. Over 800 national WHO Collaborating Centres and national epidemic prevention programmes illustrate a well-developed cooperation network between national and international levels in the policy field of health. This picture is reversed when looking at individual nation states beyond the OECD world: the integration of national health structures into the international health system depends on the development of the respective nation states. In less developed countries, the often patchy healthcare systems are not only a problem in the fight against threatening diseases - a lack of political will, a weak state monopoly on the use of force or even a defensive attitude towards the international healthcare system flank a poorly or not at all developed national public healthcare system. Pakistan and Afghanistan, for example, are examples worth discussing, as international health activities to combat the polio virus are only possible there under the most unfavourable conditions - the systematic implementation of nationwide vaccinations is made considerably more difficult by a weak state (Holzscheiter 2018). As polio appears to have been virtually eradicated worldwide with the exception of these two countries, these examples show that a lack of access to a small number of nation states is already a global problem. If there is no minimal statehood, states are - sometimes even involuntarily - disconnected from the international health infrastructure. International organisations or networks of organisations therefore usually have no access to the difficult health situations of these states and are often powerless in the face of a precarious public health situation in these states.

The defensive stance of certain states therefore includes a lack of recognition of the fundamental functions of international organisations. This is a current trend that can be observed in various policy areas. The question of the extent to which this trend is reflected in international health policy and fundamental functions of the WHO are contested by states is also the subject of this thematic focus. In the area of global health, for example, there is a need for discussion and research into the extent to which the national policies of various states are increasingly casting doubt on the scientific and technical expertise of the WHO.

With this overview, the following characteristics of a heterarchical structure can be summarised in the area of global health:

- There are overlapping competences between international organisations, which can lead to conflicts within regime complexes.
- There are few superordinate and organisational relationships (hierarchies) between the actors involved in this structure.
- A high degree of fragmentation can be observed to the extent that numerous civil society organisations are active in the field of global health and are in competition with the WHO as the former central authority in global health.
- Member states engage in contestation (cf. Zürn 2018) with international organisations. In addition, WHO member states are often in conflict with each other due to their differing views and interests and can therefore slow down the effectiveness of the WHO.

## 2.2 Heterarchy and Orchestration in Global Health Governance: Conceptual Considerations for major Crises

As Chapter 2.1 shows, heterarchical structures can represent an unmanageable network in which many different actors such as states, international governmental organisations and NGOs are involved and a relationship of superordination and subordination between these actors is not/is difficult to discern.

At the same time, the question arises as to what extent heterarchy can be used to utilise governance modes for effective crisis management (Stephenson 2016). At its core, a heterarchical structure can be understood as at least three hierarchies that are interconnected in a triadic network (Stephenson 2016). These individual hierarchies can include states as well as the European Union and other regional organisations, but also the arrangement of private organisations that are arranged quasi-hierarchically (hybrid organisations). Under certain conditions, the interconnection of hierarchies can lead to effective action by all actors affected by the same problem. This can include crises of a supra-regional/global scale that can only be solved in a network: 'The combinatorial properties that result from linking three or more hierarchies together are profound precisely because they reach for a collective good that no single hierarchy could attain on ist own' (Stephenson 2016, 142). This perspective is relevant for the recent global health development with various crises that ultimately required cooperation between different groups of actors - for example, the provision of vaccinations in developing countries.

Effective crisis management in heterarchical structures is linked to various requirements. A heterarchical structure itself is not characterised by clear superordination/subordination relationships between the actors or groups of actors present, which raises the question of how leadership in crises by one or more actors is possible. Since crises are short-, medium- or long-term, it is also important how long leadership is necessary. Informal/indirect modes of governance that do not involve contractual relationships can be important here.

In this context, 'orchestration' (Abboth et al 2015) can be a suitable governance mode for effective crisis management in heterarchical structures in global health.

In orchestration, the orchestrator needs to be emphasised. This is an actor who engages an intermediary, whereby this intermediary should contribute to achieving the orchestrator's objectives. To this end, the orchestrator selects those intermediaries whose goals have a large overlap with those of the orchestrator or whose goals are at least not in too much tension with each other - otherwise these actors could not be recruited as voluntary intermediaries. Due to their legitimacy, orchestrators take on a coordinating and indirectly determining role in this relationship (Abboth et al 2015, Ansell 2023). Ultimately, orchestration differs from principal-agent relationships: In this relationship, a governance actor endows another actor with authority under a mandate or contractual relationship; however, the principal can usurp the authority in order to maintain control. In an orchestration relationship, on the other hand, an orchestrator cannot control its intermediaries - orchestration, on the other hand, will prove successful per se if the orchestrator offers support to the intermediaries (Abboth et al 2015, Ansell 2023). This leads to both the orchestrator and intermediaries achieving their goals. The support can take the form of material or administrative support. In addition, several intermediaries can also be used by the orchestrator in order to increase the impact in achieving the objectives. Orchestrators can be states, international governmental organisations, or NGOs (Abboth et al 2015, Ansell 2023).

As can be seen, the use of orchestration presupposes common goals of several actors. Orchestration can be implemented as a governance mode if the international organisation is recognised by the other actors in the network (NGOs, the EU, member states, CSOs). In the area of global health, orchestration has emerged as a governance mode, particularly during the COVID-19 crisis.

However, the development of global health shows that heterarchical structures were in place and that orchestration was not possible at the same time. Rather, this heterarchy was characterised by contestation on the part of the WHO member states and a lack of cooperation between the WHO and existing NGOs or state actors.

# 3 FROM ANARCHY TO FRAGMENTIVE HETERARCHY TO COOPERATIVE HETERARCHY

## 3.1 The Development of Global Health Governance up to the year 2000

The development of global health governance can be divided into three stages: The first stage of development is characterised by a dichotomy with the two poles of anarchy and deepening global health governance, in which the WHO and the World Bank increasingly became central authorities: From the 1950s and 1960s onwards, the idea of cooperation and thus the role of international organisations gained in importance and was supposed to banish the anarchic structure of the international system - the WHO was a directing authority of international health policy at this time. In the following four decades, the anarchic system as a whole was increasingly transformed into a Global (Health) Governance system (Hein/ Lange et al 2021, Zürn 2018): new institutions and numerous regulations made international politics more steerable. Increasingly numerous non-state actors (CSOs and business), their interests (advocacy, philanthropy and profits) and the partnerships and programmes in which they were involved made processes more confusing at the same time (Hein/ Lange et al 2021).

In the 1980s, many new civil society actors such as Civic Society Organizations (CSOs) with huge financial resources but also companies have emerged, but new organisational forms such as hybrid actors were also shaping global health governance at this time. As a result of the changed constellation of actors, the WHO changed from a central authority to a declining International Organisation.

At this time, the first form of a heterarchical order emerged, which was characterised by a lack of network-like structures, i.e. a lack of connection between the WHO and the new CSOs and companies and thus a lack of cooperation between actors. At the same time, this lack of connection meant that a hierarchical order was not formed - the lack of network-like structures led to a loss of status for the WHO as a central authority. Instead, in the initial phase, the actors were in a competitive relationship with each other (cf. Hanrieder 2009). In this respect, this second phase was characterised by a fragmented global health order (Lange et al 2023 a). Specifically, a civil society contestation of the WHO emerged in the second phase.

With the turn of the millennium, increasing crises in the form of pandemics led to a more complex and faster development dynamic - with the COVID-19 pandemic, there was a movement away from a fragmented heterarchy towards a cooperative heterarchy, whereby it can be observed that there was a pendulum movement between the two forms of heterarchy. This is discussed below along key health crises (SARS 2002/03, H1N1, Ebola in West Africa and finally COVID-19) since the year 2000.

## 3.2 The SARS crisis 2002/03 on the basis of Cooperative Heterarchy

The SARS crisis in 2002/03 illustrates an orchestration initiated by the WHO, whereby the establishment of an orchestration structure was carried out by the WHO well before the SARS 2002/03 outbreak: Prior to the SARS pandemic, the WHO increasingly drove a network with non-governmental organisations to use a broad information base for the surveillance of emerging health threats than that provided by the WHO member states (Lange et al 2023 a). This WHO-NGO network has produced numerous reports that have been categorised as 'Public Health Emergencies of International Concern' (PHEIC) (Hawkins et al 2006, Lange 2022, Ansell et al 2018). Specifically, the Global Outbreak Alert and Response Network (GOARN) represents this network. GOARN connects more than 200 countries, institutions and networks in order to facilitate the timely exchange of information and coordinate response measures. GOARN can be understood as a large information network - the WHO took on a coordinating role with the founding of GOARN - also in the SARS crisis of 2002/03 (Lange 2022, Hanrieder 2015).

At the beginning of the SARS crisis in 2002/03, the Chinese authorities communicated existing data on the outbreak of the disease to the WHO with some delay. In response, the WHO received information from NGOs in its network outside of Chinese government sources: WHO obtained information from the Global Public Health Intelligence Network (GPHIN) independently of Chinese government sources, and the information provided by the network proved to be very useful: GPHIN first pointed out atypical pneumonia in Guangdong Province, China (Lange 2022) three months before authorities reported it. Both the WHO as orchestrator was able to strengthen its role, as were its intermediaries, who demonstrated that they could use the data collected to accelerate the identification of international health threats.

It should be emphasised that the WHO has exceeded its mandate in its role as orchestrator: The International Health Regulations (IHR) of 1969, which were in force until then, did not officially provide for the WHO to access sources of information other than those provided to it by sovereign states (Lange 2022).

Due to its GOARN network initiative before the SARS crisis and especially during the SARS crisis, the WHO showed its qualities as an orchestrator, because in times of crisis (SARS 2002/03) the WHO was able to coordinate these networks as part of successful crisis management and to use the GOARN and GPHIN networks as its intermediaries for successful crisis management. The relationship between the WHO and GOARN and GPHIN illustrates the importance of networks as a basis for orchestration.

At this point in time, a cooperative heterarchy was emerging, but it was limited to links between the WHO, GOARN and GPHIN and was insular in nature at the time.

## 3.3 New Fragmented Heterarchy: H1N1 and Ebola in West Africa in 2014

The fragmented heterarchy was accompanied by other new characteristics during the H1N1 crisis and the Ebola crisis. The focus was not so much on competition with CSOs and multinational companies, but on a contestation on the part of the WHO member states to such an extent that they questioned the WHO's technical expertise. The H1N1 crisis was dominated by disagreements between the WHO and the WHO member states regarding the assessment of the severity of the virus. On the one hand, the WHO deviated from the states' assessment by declaring the second-highest pandemic alert level, and on the other hand, the WHO set the target of having 3/4 of the population vaccinated, which also led to tensions. In the context of the H1N1 crisis, the WHO sought to demonstrate its role as an increasingly independent actor in global health governance. (Lange et al. 2023 a, Garske et al 2021) In the aftermath of the H1N1 crisis, no concrete measures were taken against the WHO by nation states. Nevertheless, doubts on the side of the member states increased (cf. Lange et al 2023).

After the H1N1 influenza crisis, the fragmented heterarchy intensified again during the West African Ebola crisis. During the 2014 West African Ebola crisis, the WHO was criticised in several ways, most notably for delaying the declaration of an PHEIC by the WHO despite clear reports on the severity of the Ebola virus, which ultimately led to the spread of Ebola from Guinea to other countries, particularly Liberia and Sierra Leone (Moon 2015). The delay in alerting the WHO is thought to have contributed to the delayed response by the international community (Lange et al 2023).

In response, a process of counter-institutionalisation took place with the establishment of the United Nations Mission for Ebola Emergency Response (UNMEER) by the UN Secretary-General, which then coordinated the emergency health response in the affected countries of West Africa, thereby touching on the core mandate of the WHO (Kamradt-Scott 2016, Lange et al 2023).

During the H1N1 crisis, the fragmented heterarchy manifested itself in the form of counter-institutionalisation, which further weakened the authority of the WHO (Lange et al 2023). Counter-institutionalisation is a contestation strategy of nation states against the authority of the WHO by establishing new institutions that promise more benefits for the state (Zürn 2018). This shows that in the area of global health, counter-institutionalisation is an action strategy of the 'reactive state' (Cerny 2023).

## 3.4 SARS-CoV2: Orchestrating Crisis Management on the basis of Cooperative Heterarchy

During the COVID-19 crisis, there was a transformation from a competitive to a cooperative heterarchy. The challenge from the United States was reflected in the fundamental contestation of the competence and appropriate role of the WHO during the COVID-19 pandemic. This contestation by the Trump administration was part of a more general contestation in which other IOs, such as the WTO, were questioned by the US - this contestation dynamic culminated in the threat to withdraw from the WHO. The withdrawal of the USA also posed a challenge to the WHO's finances (Lange et al 2023 a). Contestation takes on the concrete form of a 'reactive state' at this point.

The shift from a fragmentive heterarchy to a cooperative heterarchy became apparent in the second half of the Covid-19 crisis:

After an initial reluctance of WHO to recognize the severity of SARS CoV-2 Virus, in April and May 2021 WHO developed comprehensive approaches to deal with the crisis, which included cooperation with many other actors and which serve as points of reference until today: the ACT Accelerator as a broadly formulated and supported statements on the challenges of COVID-19, COVAX as a system to guarantee access to vaccines also for the poorest countries; and finally the declaration "COVID-19 Response" at the World Health Assembly 2020: WHO demonstrated leadership with the European Union. In fact, COVAX did not reach the impact expected by WHO, but this was basically due to three long-standing problems: the conflict with the pharmaceutical industry on intellectual property rights and access to medicines and vaccines, the issue of vaccine nationalism and finally infrastructural problems in the poorest countries to develop an effective vaccination campaign at short notice (Lange et al 2023 a). Global Health Governance in the COVID-19 crisis was characterized by the network of governmental and non-governmental actors in which the WHO was involved and which it coordinated in a leading role. This is where the governance feature of orchestration becomes apparent: Orchestration leading to informal or "quasi-hierarchy", in which the WHO (together with the EU) was given a leading role.

## 4. SHIFT FROM A FRAGMENTED HETERARCHY TO A COOPERATIVE HETERARCHY

When considering the four health crises described above since the turn of the millennium, it is evident that, on the one hand, the heterarchical structures in global health governance have fundamentally remained in place. On the other hand, central features of the heterarchy have been transformed. The fragmented heterarchy has changed into a cooperative heterarchy.

It should be emphasized that along the four health crises described, there was no clear movement from fragmented heterarchy to cooperative heterarchy. Rather, this process is characterized by a pendulum-like movement between fragmented and cooperative heterarchy.

Fragmented heterarchy itself has been observable in the field of global health since the 1980s - and it was accompanied by other new characteristics during the H1N1 crisis and the Ebola crisis. The focus was less on competition with CSOs and multinationals, as in the 1980s and 1990s, and more on a contestation of the WHO by its member states.

*Table 1. Characteristics of a fragmented heterarchy and cooperative heterarchy*

| Fragmented Heterarchy | Cooperative Heterarchy |
|---|---|
| No superordinate/subordinate relationship ⇨ WHO loses function as central authority with increasing number of new actors | Networks, nodes (polycentristic structure) |
| No network-like connections between old (WHO, World Bank) and new groups of actors (CSOs, enterprises, hybrid actors) | Orchestration leading to informal or "quasi-hierarchy" ⇨ WHO becomes a network coordinating authority (orchestrator) |
| Competition between declining central authorities and new actors | Collective pressure to solve problems driven by global crises |
| "Reactive states" with contestation strategies (e.g., counter-institutionalization) | |
| ⇨ **Blocker for crises management** | ⇨ **Ampflifier for crises management** |

Source: Lange 2024

In the SARS 2002/03 crisis, the WHO showed its qualities as an orchestrator due to its initiative of the GOARN network before the SARS crisis and especially during the SARS crisis, because the WHO was able to use these networks as inter-mediaries for successful crisis management in times of crisis (SARS 2002/03). The relationship between the WHO and GOARN and GPHIN illustrates the importance of networks that make orchestration possible.

A movement from a "fragmented heterarchy" to a "cooperative heterarchy" can already be seen here. However, the cooperative heterarchy turns out to be quite unstable at this point - the H1N1 crisis as well as the Ebola crisis show a shift back from cooperative heterarchy to a fragmented heterarchy characterized by contestation (Lange et al 2023 a, Zürn 2018). This contestation dynamic is characterized by the fact that the member states question the function/role of the WHO and attack this role. In addition, fragmented heterarchy is characterized by the fact that individual networks (hierarchies) are little or not at all connected to each other. As a result, there is also no interaction between these networks, which prevents effective network governance.

The H1N1 and Ebola crises show that crises can be seen as "windows for opportunity" in which member states contest international organizations - in this case the WHO. This can be clearly seen in the actions of the member states during the Ebola crisis in West Africa: On the part of the member states, counter-institutionalization is emerging in such a way that they are disempowering the WHO by installing a new organization, the United Nations Mission for Ebola Emergency Response (UN-MEER), to coordinate the Ebola crisis. On the other hand, this became clear at the beginning of the COVID-19 crisis, when the USA withdrew from the WHO. The question arises as to whether the actions of a "reactive state" (Cerny 2023) can be identified in a policy field such as global health contestation: states not only try to adapt to international conditions in re-action, but also to counteract them in such a way that nation states try to weaken international organizations.

Along Covid 19, the development of an orchestrator heterarchy is recognizable in such a way that global health governance is evolving away from a fragmented structure towards a development in which the loose ends of the actors, hybrid actors and actor groups of global health governance come together, and connections emerge that gradually reveal a network character. The COVID-19 crisis should be emphasized as an event, as it was network-forming due to its crisis character. Based on the existing networks, the COVAX program was launched (COVAX/ COVID-19 Vaccines Global Access cooperation of important actors in the field of vaccine development/ finance), which was jointly led by the WHO and the EU.

Global Health Governance in the COVID-19 crisis was characterized by the network of governmental and non-governmental actors in which the WHO was involved and which it coordinated in a leading role. At this point, the governance characteristic of orchestration becomes apparent, whereby this orchestration is more extensive than in the SARS 2002/03 crisis: orchestration leading to informal or "quasi-hierarchy", in which the WHO (together with the EU) was given a leading role. The emergence of the governance mode of orchestration is due, on the one hand, to the collaborative problem-solving pressure driven by the global COVID-19 crisis and, on the other, to the networks that have increasingly grown in the meantime: cooperative heterarchy is suitable for implementing orchestration as a governance mode for successful crisis management due to its network character.

Overall, there are increasing signs of a governance transformation in global health governance that can best be explained by a heterarchy dichotomy. While the traditional heterarchy structure is characterized by fragmented, competitive relationships between numerous actors such as contesting states, international state organizations, civil society organizations (CSOs/NGOs) and companies, changes in the heterarchy characteristics can be observed as the crisis is overcome.

## 5. CONCLUSION

This article was addressed to the development of heterarchical structures in the field of global health. The analysis focused on epidemic outbreaks of international importance after the turn of the millennium. First, it was shown how heterarchical structures manifest themselves in the field of international health policy before the question of the extent to which heterarchical structures promote or inhibit crisis management of epidemic outbreaks was addressed. Ultimately, heterarchy has both effects: in the crises examined, both fragmented and cooperative heterarchy are evident. While fragmented heterarchy is characterized by little cooperative interaction between relevant groups of actors and contestation, the second form of heterarchy - cooperative heterarchy - is characterized by collaborative problem-solving. This is based on the governance mode of orchestration, in which the WHO, as the leading actor (orchestrator), guides groups of actors (intermediaries) to achieve common goals in the form of crisis management in the interests of all. Orchestration is possible here on the basis of existing networks and a fairly large problem-solving pressure (crisis management).

How heterarchical structures will develop in Global Health in the future depends on the problem-solving pressure of possible impending crises. If these crises are serious, a cooperative heterarchy may be important.

# REFERENCES

Abbott, K. W., Genschel, P., Snidal, D., & Zangl, B. (Eds.). (2015). *International organizations as orchestrators*. Cambridge University Press.

Abbott, K. W., Genschel, P., Snidal, D., & Zangl, B. (2015). Orchestration. International organizations as orchestrators, 3-36.

Ansell, C. (2023). *Rethinking Theories of Governance*. Edward Elgar Publishing.

Ansell, C., Sondorp, E., & Stevens, R. H. (2018). The Promise and Challenge of Global Network Governance: The Global Outbreak Alert and Response Network. *Global Governance*, 18(3), 317–337. DOI: 10.1163/19426720-01803005

Ansell, C., & Torfing, J. (Eds.). (2016). *Handbook on Theories of Governance*. Edward Elgar Publishing. DOI: 10.4337/9781782548508

Avery, D. H. (2010). The North American Plan for Avian and Pandemic Influenza: A case study of regional health security in the 21st century. *Global Health Governance*, 3(2).

Cerny, P. G. (2023). Heterarchy: Toward Paradigm Shift in World Politics. In Cherny, P. G. (Ed.), *pp*.

Drezner, D. W. (2013). The tragedy of the global institutional commons. Back to basics: State power in a contemporary world, 280, 281.

Enderlein, H., Wälti, S., & Zürn, M. (Eds.), *Handbook on Multi-level Governance*. DOI: 10.4337/9781849809047

Faude, B. (2015). *Von Konkurrenz zu Arbeitsteilung: Komplexität und Dynamik im Zusammenspiel internationaler Institutionen* (Vol. 25). Campus Verlag.

Garske, T., Legrand, J., Donnelly, C. A., Ward, H., Cauchemez, S., Fraser, C., Ferguson, N. M., & Ghani, A. C. (2009). Assessing the Severity of the Novel Influenza A/H1N1 pandemic. *British Medical Journal*, 339, 220–224. PMID: 19602714

Gehring, T., & Oberthür, S. (2009). The causal mechanisms of interaction between international institutions. *European Journal of International Relations*, 15(1), 125–156.

Hanrieder, T. (2009, September). 7 Die Weltgesundheitsorganisation unter Wettbewerbsdruck: Auswirkungen der Vermarktlichung globaler Gesundheitspolitik. In Die organisierte Welt (pp. 163-188). Nomos Verlagsgesellschaft mbH & Co. KG.

Hawkins, D., Lake, D., Nielson, D., & Tierney, M. Delegation under Anarchy 2006: States, International Organizations, and Principal-Agent Theory In: Hawkins, D, Lake D., Nielson D., Tierney M. Delegation and Agency in International Organizations, Cambridge, Cambridge University Press, pp. 3-38.

Holzscheiter, A., Bahr, T., & Pantzerhielm, L. (2016). Emerging governance architectures in global health: Do metagovernance norms explain inter-organisational convergence?.

Kamradt-Scott, A. (2016). WHO's to blame? The World Health Organization and the 2014 Ebola outbreak in West Africa. *Third World Quarterly*, 37(3), 401–418. DOI: 10.1080/01436597.2015.1112232

Kamradt-Scott, A. (2018). Securing Indo-Pacific health security: Australia's approach to regional health security. *Australian Journal of International Affairs*, 72(6), 500–519.

Kickbusch, I., & Szabo, M. M. C. 2014: A new governance space for health. In: Glob Health Action, Vol. 7. DOI: 10.3402/gha.v7.23507

Lange, T. (2020). Beyond the'asean-way'? Third-sector driven governance along sars and haze pollution. *Global Health Governance*.

Lange, T. (2021). Eine neue» Disease Surveillance «?. FEST, 57.

Lange, T. (2022). Eine neue „Disease Surveillance"? Big Data und die Gefahrenüberwachung in Global Health. In: Held, Benjamin/ van Oorschot, Frederike Ed.): Digitalisierung: Neue Technik – neue Ethik? Interdisziplinäre Auseinandersetzung mit den Folgen der digitalen Transformation. HeiBooks, Universitätsbibliothek Heidelberg, pp. 57 – 71.

Lange, T., Villarreal, P. A., & Bärnighausen, T. (2023a). Counter-contestation in global health governance: The WHO and its member states in emergency settings. *Health Policy (Amsterdam)*, 131, 104756.

Lange, T., Villarreal, P. A., & Bärnighausen, T. (2023b). The contested authority of international institutions in global health. *Health Policy (Amsterdam)*, 131, 104793.

Michael, Z. (2018). *A Theory of Global Governance: Authority, Legitimacy, and Contestation*. Oxford University Press.

Moon, S., Sridhar, D., Pate, M. A., Jha, A. K., Clinton, C., Delaunay, S., Edwin, V., Fallah, M., Fidler, D. P., Garrett, L., Goosby, E., Gostin, L. O., Heymann, D. L., Lee, K., Leung, G. M., Morrison, J. S., Saavedra, J., Tanner, M., Leigh, J. A., & Piot, P. (2015). Will Ebola change the game? Ten essential reforms before the next pandemic. The report of the Harvard-LSHTM Independent Panel on the Global Response to Ebola. *Lancet*, 386(10009), 2204–2221. DOI: 10.1016/S0140-6736(15)00946-0 PMID: 26615326

Philip, G. (Ed.). (2023). *Cerny*. Heterarchy in World Politics. Rouledge.

Risse, T., Börzel, T. A., & Draude, A. (Eds.). (2018). *The Oxford handbook of governance and limited statehood*. Oxford University Press.

Scholz, R. (2010). *Internationaler Gesundheitsschutz und Welthandel*. DUNCKER UND HUMBLOT.

Stephenson, K. (2016). Heterarchy. In *Handbook on theories of governance* (pp. 139–148). Edward Elgar Publishing.

Tine, H., & Zangl, B. (2015). *WHO Orchestrates?* Coping with Competitors in Global Health.

Zürn, M. (2010). Global governance as multi-level governance. In *Handbook on multi-level governance*. Edward Elgar Publishing.

## KEY TERMS AND DEFINITIONS

**Cooperative Heterarchy (Mode of Heterarchy 2):** Is characterized by collaborative problem-solving.

**Counter-Institutionalization:** Is a contestation strategy of nation states against the authority of an International Organization (like the WHO) by establishing new institutions that promise more benefits for the state.

**Fragmented Heterarchy (Mode of Heterarchy 1):** Is characterized by little cooperative interaction between relevant groups of actors and contestation.

**Heterarchical Structure in Global Health:** Can be summarized as (1) overlapping competences between international organizations, which can lead to conflicts within regime complexes, (2) few superordinate and organizational relationships (hierarchies) between the actors involved in this structure an (3) a high degree of fragmentation to the extent that numerous civil society organizations are active and are in competition with the WHO as a former central authority in global health.

**Heterarchical Structure:** Can be understood as at least three hierarchies that are interconnected in a triadic network.

**Orchestrator:** Is an actor who engages an intermediary, whereby this intermediary should contribute to achieving the orchestrator's objectives.

**Reactive State:** Can be identified in a policy field such as global health contestation: states not only try to adapt to international conditions in re-action, but also to counteract them in such a way that nation states try to weaken international organizations.

# Chapter 7
# From Colonialism to Heterarchy:
## New Power Dynamics in the Caribbean

**Dana-Marie Ramjit**
https://orcid.org/0000-0003-1369-8121
*St. Mary's University, Canada*

## ABSTRACT

*The Caribbean landscape is intertwined with threads of resilience, cultural richness, and a complex history marked by colonialism. The legacies of European domination continue to cast long shadows, shaping power structures and social relations across the region. Postcolonial scholarship has illuminated the enduring impact of colonialism on power dynamics, economies, and cultural identities (Parashar, & Schulz, 2021; Said, 1978; Anzaldúa, 1987). Colonial administrations established centralized control, privileging European elites, and marginalizing Indigenous and African populations. These hierarchies continue to influence land ownership patterns, political structures, and even social interactions in many Caribbean nations (Beckles, 2000; Ramjit, 2019). Heterarchy offers a compelling alternative to these entrenched power structures. Defined by anthropologists like Descola (2001) as a system that prioritizes collaboration and distributed power, heterarchy challenges the notion of a single, dominant authority.*

DOI: 10.4018/979-8-3693-3563-5.ch007

# INTRODUCTION

The Caribbean landscape is intertwined with threads of resilience, cultural richness, and a complex history marked by colonialism. The legacies of European domination continue to cast long shadows, shaping power structures and social relations across the region. Postcolonial scholarship has illuminated the enduring impact of colonialism on power dynamics, economies, and cultural identities (Parashar, & Schulz, 2021; Said, 1978; Anzaldúa, 1987). Colonial administrations established centralized control, privileging European elites, and marginalizing Indigenous and African populations. These hierarchies continue to influence land ownership patterns, political structures, and even social interactions in many Caribbean nations (Beckles, 2000; Ramjit, 2019). Heterarchy offers a compelling alternative to these entrenched power structures. Defined by anthropologists like Descola (2001) as a system that prioritizes collaboration and distributed power, heterarchy challenges the notion of a single, dominant authority. It emphasizes horizontal networks, shared decision-making, and a focus on collective well-being (Cerny, 2022). This chapter delves into the critical intersection of postcolonialism and heterarchy, proposing a framework for understanding how Caribbean societies can move beyond the rigid hierarchies imposed by their colonial past. The chapter analyzes Caribbean identity, the evolving Caribbean state, sovereignty, and role of non-state entities, which challenge Eurocentric power structures and promote and dismantle hierarchies, contributing to the evolution of legitimacy in the Caribbean. The limitations of traditional, colonial-based power structures and their continued impact on the region demonstrates the potential of heterarchy as a framework for reimagining power dynamics. The discussion further explores how various social and cultural forces in the Caribbean embody heterarchical principles, building new pathways for resilient policymaking.

## Deconstructing the Nation-State: Nationalism and Internationalism in a Postcolonial Context

The Caribbean represents a region steeped in a complex colonial past, marked by exploitation and external domination, which has stimulated a strong sense of regional identity and a desire for self-determination (Barry, et al., 2020). However, the legacies of colonialism continue to shape political and economic realities, creating challenges for governance and international cooperation. Consequently, the Caribbean offers a unique setting to examine the tensions and possibilities inherent in building strong resilient political frameworks that can address the needs and aspirations of post-colonial societies. While nationalism has undoubtedly played a crucial role in achieving independence, its emphasis on individual nations can create challenges for regional cooperation. In this context, the exploration of heterarchy as a system prioritizing collaboration and distributed authority offers an alternative approach to the limitations of traditional, state-centric power structures.

The concept of nationalism has shaped the Caribbean's fight for independence and continues to influence contemporary dynamics. Nationalism, as Breuilly (1994) outlines, revolves around three core concepts: political identity, unwavering loyalty, and self-determination. It manifests through a cultural lens, emphasizing shared nationality and citizenship, and a political lens, prioritizing state sovereignty and authority (Benoit, 2020). Nationalism posits the nation-state as the fundamental unit, often superseding other concerns.

The Caribbean journey towards independence was acutely tangled with anti-colonial nationalism. Figures like Eric Williams, the first Prime Minister of Trinidad and Tobago, famously declared, "Massa day done everywhere," signifying the dismantling of racial hierarchies imposed by colonial powers. Caribbean nationalism as championed by Williams sought to establish independent nation-states with unique national identities (Lewis, 2004). However, this narrative is not without complications. The Caribbean's history is marked by profound political tension even within the nationalist movement as there were clashes between urban elites and lower classes who championed their own distinct cultural identities, often rooted in the experiences of slavery and indentureship (Lewis, 2004). The evolution of Carnival in Trinidad and Tobago, originally a celebration of freedom amongst enslaved populations, and its transformation from a subversive act of resistance to a national spectacle highlights the ongoing negotiation of power and cultural expression within the Caribbean region (Sylvester, 2020; Gilroy, 1995).

While Caribbean nationalism played a crucial role in dismantling colonial hierarchies, it also reinforced centralized state power. This centralization is particularly evident in the face of globalization, with its emphasis on free markets and international cooperation, and the emergence of a vibrant non-state sector, which challenges state monopolies on power and resources (Ramjit, 2022). Scholars like Gellner (1983) and Hobsbawm (1983) have explored nationalism as a response to modernization and the need to defend cultural identity. However, in the Caribbean context, cultural nationalism often predated the rise of the nation-state, with enslaved populations forging distinct cultural practices that persisted after emancipation (Lewis, 2004). This suggests that Caribbean nationalism may have more complex motivations than those captured by traditional theories.

Building on the intricacies of Caribbean nationalism, Anderson's (1991) concept of the "imagined community" offers valuable insights. Nationalism fosters a sense of moral obligation among citizens, prioritizing national well-being above individual interests (Anderson, 1991). This notion is evident in the region's vibrant literary and artistic movements, like the poetry of Derek Walcott and the writings of Samuel

Selvon, which celebrated a shared sense of Caribbean identity across islands, even amidst political divisions. The Caribbean nations, formed from diverse ethnicities and colonial legacies, share a sense of belonging constructed through shared symbols, languages, and historical narratives. This "imagined community" transcends geographical boundaries and unites Caribbean people across the diaspora (Lewis, 2004). However, some argue that nationalism can be employed by governments to legitimize their actions and control narratives (Kedourie, 1960).

Classical Marxists like Lenin (1917) viewed nationalism as a tool for capitalist nations to protect domestic markets. Conversely, constructivists argue that states themselves are shaped by social interactions and evolving ideas about national identity (Wendt, 1991; Prichard, 2010). These contrasting perspectives challenge the notion of a fixed, all-powerful state and highlight the dynamic relationship between nationalism and statehood. The Caribbean's path to independence and nationhood was undeniably fueled by a unifying nationalist sentiment. However, the contemporary reality of globalization, marked by increased migration and transnational connections, exposes the limitations of state-centric power structures (Triandafyllidou, 2024). As Premdas (2011) argues, Caribbean individuals have cultivated flexible and multifaceted identities that transcend national borders. This phenomenon challenges the notion of a singular, monolithic national identity within each Caribbean nation.

Internationalism, the antithesis of nationalism's focus on individual nation-states, emphasizes interaction and cooperation between nations (During, 2024; Glossop, 2017). This rise of internationalism stemmed from a confluence of idealistic and realist perspectives (Wertheim, 2024). Idealistic theories, such as democratic peace theory posited that cooperation could foster global peace and prosperity (Rogers, 2016). Realist concerns, however, focused on the anarchic nature of the international system (Grieco, 1997). In response, international institutions like the League of Nations and the United Nations were established, reflecting a growing belief in the need for collective action to address global challenges, even amidst the perceived lack of a central authority (Karlsrud et al., 2024).

Institutionalism played a crucial role in advancing internationalism. This perspective argues that institutions, such as international law (e.g., treaties) and organizations (e.g., the World Trade Organization), can facilitate cooperation among states in several ways (Johnson, & Heiss, 2023). As Immergut (2010) highlights, institutions establish shared norms and expectations, reducing uncertainty and encouraging trust-building. They also provide a platform for dialogue and negotiation, leading to more efficient solutions to shared problems like climate change or global health crises (Roger at al., 2023). The rise of liberalism, with its emphasis on democracy, human rights, and free trade further bolstered internationalism (Moravcsik, 2001). Liberal thought posits that shared values like these create a foundation for peaceful cooperation. As the number of democratic states increased globally the potential for international cooperation also grew (Gibbins, 2023; Dunne & McDonald, 2013).

The Caribbean's engagement with internationalism is complex and evolving. With the decline of colonialism, the region embraced international institutions and cooperation to advance its development goals. Regional organizations like CARICOM (the Caribbean Community) emerged to foster economic and political integration. For instance, cooperation through CARICOM programs has helped member states improve their agricultural practices and access new markets (mention a specific program/benefit) (Ambursley & Cohen, 2024). However, internationalism also presents challenges for the Caribbean. The dominance of powerful states and the global economic order can create inequalities and limit the region's autonomy (McDougall, 2023). Furthermore, the emphasis on state sovereignty within internationalism can sometimes clash with the realities of a globalized world, where power is increasingly diffused among non-state actors (Prichard & Cerny, 2017).

The contemporary global landscape is increasingly characterized by postinternationalism (Ramjit, 2019). This perspective acknowledges the continued importance of states but argues that power is now dispersed across a wider range of actors, including non-governmental organizations, multinational corporations, and social movements (Ramjit, 2022). This dispersion of power signifies a shift from a state-centric model to one where diverse actors influence global issues (Rosenau, 2003). Furthermore, the emergence of multilayered governance, where decision-making occurs at various levels, from the local to the global, became evident (Karns, 2000). This concept of multi-nodal politics holds relevance for the Caribbean, where regional organizations like CARICOM can collaborate with local stakeholders and international institutions to address shared challenges.

While the Caribbean's journey towards self-determination and the establishment of independent states was undeniably shaped by nationalism and internationalism, the limitations of state-centric power structures become increasingly apparent in a globalized world. Heterarchy offers a compelling framework for reimagining power dynamics in the Caribbean, providing a foundation for exploring alternative models of governance that are more responsive, and empower local communities. For instance, the rise of social movements, environmental movements advocating for community-based resource management, or feminist organizations, challenge traditional power structures and promote heterarchical principles. Additionally, decentralization efforts within Caribbean nations can empower local governments and foster more participatory decision-making processes. Another area of importance is the potential of regional cooperation to address shared challenges and create a more unified Caribbean identity in a globalized world, while respecting the unique cultural and political realities of each nation.

## Navigating Hybridity: Identity, and Culture in the Postcolonial Caribbean

The Caribbean's postcolonial narrative is a story of navigating hybridity. Emerging from the legacies of Western dominance and ongoing decolonization processes, the region grapples with a multifaceted identity shaped by its colonial past (Miguel & Arias, 2020; Clegg & Seremani, 2016). This overview delves into the tensions between cultural fragmentation and creolization, exploring how the Caribbean reconfigures power structures in a postinternational world.

Central to the postcolonial framework is the dismantling of Western dominance and the marginalization of colonized populations (Condon, 2021). In the Caribbean context, this translates to a critical examination of imposed identities and a celebration of the region's rich cultural heritage. Caribbean writers like Jean Rhys, in her novel "Wide Sargasso Sea" (1966), challenge the stereotypical portrayal of the Caribbean woman by giving voice to Antoinette Cosway, a marginalized Creole figure silenced within a colonial marriage (Senel, 2014). Similarly, Said's (1978) seminal work, "Orientalism," critiques the West's misrepresentation of the "other," highlighting the Caribbean's struggle against the imposition of Western cultural norms and identities. These efforts resonate with Fanon's (1952) exploration of the psychological effects of colonialism in "Black Skin, White Masks" (1952), particularly the sense of dependency and internalized inferiority instilled in the colonized (Fanon, 1952). Caribbean thinkers like Sylvia Wynter (1995) have also emphasized the enduring impact of colonial ideologies on contemporary identity formation in the region.

The Caribbean embodies a unique form of hybridity, defying singular categorization. This concept, theorized by Bhabha (1994), transcends the binary of colonizer, and colonized. Instead, it proposes the emergence of a "third space" where identities are fluid and in constant negotiation. Cultural expressions like "creolization," a form of cultural hybridization that seeks to unite peoples, no matter the ethnic origin, further exemplify this phenomenon (Brathwaite, 1974). For instance, the vibrant music traditions of the region, like Reggae which blends African rhythms with European instrumentation and social commentary, represent a fusion of diverse cultural elements, reflecting the Caribbean's complex history of interaction and exchange (Laarmann, 2023; Guruprasad, 2014).

While Caribbean nations have achieved political independence, the legacies of colonialism continue to shape the region's social, political, and economic landscape. The adoption of the Westminster model of government, a British parliamentary system, in many Caribbean states like Jamaica and Barbados exemplifies this continuity (Smith, 2017). Furthermore, the liberal-authoritarian state model, characterized by a blend of civil liberties and bureaucratic control, reflects the tension between the aspirations of self-determination and the persistence of inherited systems (Araujo,

2023; Darby, 2004). This model, prevalent in the pre-independence period, continues to influence governance structures in some countries, manifesting in limitations on freedom of information or restrictions on civil society participation (Ramjit, 2019).

The Caribbean's cultural and ethnic diversity presents a significant challenge in forging a unified identity. While a shared history of colonialism and regional cooperation through institutions like CARICOM provide a foundation for unity, ongoing waves of migration and the forces of globalization further complicate the picture (Ledgister, 2006). The concepts of "cultural fragmentation" and "fragmegration" aptly describes this dynamic, where integration and differentiation coexist (Guruprasad, 2014; Rosenau, 2003). Large populations of East Indian and African descent, along with Indigenous communities, contribute to the region's rich cultural mosaic. Religious diversity and distinct cultural traditions across the islands underscore the complexity and fragmentation of Caribbean identity (Ledgister, 2006). Traversing these varied identities and forging a collective identity that embraces both its unique heritage and its position within a globalized world remains a central concern for the Caribbean.

The limitations of both nationalism with its emphasis on the nation-state, and traditional internationalism, which often reinforces the dominance of powerful states, become apparent in the context of the postcolonial Caribbean. Heterarchy offers a more compelling framework for navigating the region's complex future, as it moves beyond hierarchical structures, enabling more equitable participation and knowledge production (Winger, 2024; Cerny, 2023). This approach could be particularly useful in addressing issues like environmental sustainability, where regional cooperation among states, local communities, and international NGOs is crucial for effective solutions. By embracing its hybridity and advancing dialogue among these diverse actors, the Caribbean can move beyond a purely state-centric approach to governance to a more participatory configuration.

## The Caribbean Diaspora and Postcolonial Identity

The Caribbean diaspora, a vast network of people of Caribbean descent living outside the region, plays a crucial role in shaping the Caribbean's postcolonial identity and its position in the global arena. Diasporic communities serve as cultural bridges, transmitting Caribbean traditions, music, and cuisine to their host societies. For instance, the vibrant reggae scene in London, pioneered by Jamaican immigrants in the 1950s, exemplifies this cultural exchange (Harney, 1996; Gilroy, 1992). Furthermore, they contribute to the region's development through remittances, investments, and advocacy efforts (Glick Schiller & Levitt, 2004). However, the diaspora's impact can be multifaceted. While remittances provide a vital source of income for many Caribbean families, an over-reliance on remittances can hinder long-term economic development within the region (Kunz et al., 2022). For instance, brain drain and the emigration of skilled professionals, can hinder progress in sectors like healthcare and engineering (De Haas, 2010). Moreover, the experiences of the diaspora can be marked by marginalization and a sense of dislocation, grappling with issues of identity, and belonging (Ullah, 2024; Brah, 1996).

Caribbean cultural production – literature, music, art, and film – plays a critical role in decolonizing the mind and redefining identity. Walcott, in his epic poem "Omeros" (1992), explore themes of displacement, hybridity, and the complexities of Caribbean history. Kincaid's novel "Annie John" (1985) offers a poignant exploration of growing up between cultures in Antigua. Musicians like Bob Marley have become synonymous with Caribbean culture globally, promoting themes of social justice and pan-Africanism (Chang, 2003). However, the rich soundscape of the Caribbean extends far beyond reggae, encompassing genres like calypso, chutney, and more. These diverse artistic expressions challenge dominant narratives and assert the Caribbean's unique voice on the world stage.

The contemporary global landscape, characterized by increasing interconnectedness and the diffusion of power beyond the nation-state, obliges a move beyond traditional models of international relations (Cerny, 2022). The postinternational perspective holds relevance for the Caribbean, where regional cooperation and engagement with non-state actors can be crucial for addressing shared challenges. Postinternationalism acknowledges the continued importance of states but argues that power is now dispersed across a wider range of actors, including non-governmental organizations, multinational corporations, and social movements (Ramjit, 2019; Rosenau, 2003). The Caribbean's postcolonial voyage is one of continuous transformation. Grappling with the legacies of colonialism, the region is actively redefining its identity, celebrating its cultural hybridity, and forging new connections with its diaspora.

## The Evolving Caribbean State

The Caribbean's tumultuous history, marked by colonialism, slavery, and indentureship, has profoundly shaped its approach to governance. This legacy is evident in the region's diverse political systems, aptly described as a "patchwork" by Payne & Bishop (2010). For instance, the parliamentary system in many nations, with its roots in the British Westminster model, reflects the influence of its colonial past. The emergence of tutelary democracy in the late 1950s marked a significant shift in this evolution and characterized by collaboration between elected officials and appointed colonial administrators, laid the groundwork for eventual independence (Payne & Bishop, 2010). Tutelary democracy also emphasized developmental policies aimed at building infrastructure and bolstering socio-economic conditions, reflecting a nascent focus on the well-being of citizens (De Coteau, 2024). Understanding this historical evolution, particularly the transition from tutelary democracy to full independence and the ongoing debates about governance models, is crucial for analyzing the contemporary role of the Caribbean state.

## A History of Regional Integration

The Caribbean's pursuit of regional integration has been a hallmark of its evolving approach to governance. Driven by a common history and a desire for collective strength on the world stage, these efforts have unfolded alongside the development of the modern Caribbean state (Payne & Bishop, 2010). Early attempts like the West Indies Federation (1947-1962) faced challenges due to limited centralized authority and economic disparities among member states, but the spirit of regional cooperation persisted (Payne & Bishop, 2010). The Caribbean Community (CARICOM), established in 1973, represents a more developed approach to integration, fostering economic cooperation through initiatives like the removal of trade barriers between members, coordination on foreign policy, and collaboration on social development issues. While challenges remain, CARICOM serves as a testament to the Caribbean's ongoing commitment to regional unity and a stronger collective voice in the international arena.

## CARICOM: Successes and Challenges

The election of Michael Manley in Jamaica (1972) revitalized efforts at regional integration. Manley's commitment to a common market and harmonized policies led to the establishment of the Caribbean Common Market (CARICOM) (1973). This period is considered the most successful in Caribbean integration history, with CARICOM prioritizing both economic cooperation and national sovereignty (Payne & Bishop, 2010). A specific example of a successful policy during this era was the Caribbean Single Market and Economy (CSME) initiative, which aimed to create a single economic space with the free movement of goods, services, labor, and capital. CARICOM's longevity, surpassing even the European Union as the world's second-oldest regional integration organization is a significant achievement (Girvan, 2005).

Despite its successes, CARICOM continues to grapple with numerous challenges. Conflicts between regional objectives and individual foreign policies can sometimes undermine its collective bargaining power. For instance, during negotiations with the European Union over trade agreements, differences in member states' economic priorities and political alliances with external actors can complicate efforts to present a unified Caribbean front (Greene, 2024; Payne & Bishop, 2010). Economic decline and the need for external financial assistance from institutions like the International

Monetary Fund (IMF) have further highlighted limitations in state capacity within some member countries.

## The 1980s and Beyond: Re-evaluation and Reform

The 1980s and 1990s witnessed a period of re-evaluation as the Caribbean confronted a rapidly globalizing world. The West Indies Commission (1989) proposed a significant shift, advocating for a more centralized CARICOM structure modeled after the European Union, with a supranational governing body (Payne & Bishop, 2010). This proposal, however, was ultimately rejected by member states who were wary of sacrificing national sovereignty. Opting for a more incremental approach, they embraced the CSME as an alternative, reflecting a continued commitment to regional economic integration while respecting national autonomy (Payne & Bishop, 2010). The Rose Hall Declaration (2003) further reaffirmed CARICOM's character as a collection of sovereign states navigating the complexities of globalization through collaborative efforts.

## The Caribbean Political Landscape

The Caribbean's journey since independence has been far from smooth. Established democracies like Trinidad and Tobago, for instance, have faced periods of political unrest, such as the 1990 uprising triggered by economic hardship (Baptiste, 2010). The growing influence of criminal elements alongside the state underscores the fragility of security in some governments (Goujon at al., 2023). Despite this, the Caribbean's political landscape is marked by noteworthy advancements. Many nations hold regular elections and have active civil societies. This democratic foundation provides a platform for addressing challenges and pursuing reforms.

In this dynamic and diverse world, the region continues to grapple with issues arising from internal divisions, shortcomings in leadership, and the complexities of regional cooperation. The region's political systems, largely based on the Westminster model of parliamentary democracy, are also undergoing scrutiny in the face of contemporary challenges. Some argue for reforms that promote greater citizen participation, address issues like corruption, and enhance responsiveness to the needs of the people (Fanning at al., 2021).

## The Future of the Caribbean State

The Caribbean state presents a fascinating case study of navigating the legacies of colonialism, the pressures of globalization, and the aspirations of regional cooperation. From tutelary democracy to the CSME, the region's approach to governance has continuously evolved (Ayearst, 2023). As the Caribbean charts its course in the 21st century, addressing issues like limited state capacity in areas such as resource management and social service provision, fostering effective leadership, and forging a more unified regional voice will be paramount for its future success. In a world where power is diffused beyond the nation-state, regional cooperation and engagement with non-state actors will be crucial for addressing shared challenges.

## Sovereignty in a Postcolonial Landscape

The Caribbean navigates a complex landscape of sovereignty in the wake of colonialism. Scholars like Payne & Bishop (2010) argue that these challenges stem from the region's unique experience with sovereignty and the concept of a unified West Indian state, and decades of British rule forced a profound redefinition of identity as colonial ties loosened. Decolonization wasn't just about physical liberation; it was a cultural awakening, and hence, the postcolonial era saw the rise of distinct national identities on each island, each boasting its own language, culture, political systems, and social fabric (Lewis, 2004).

Initially, decolonization efforts understandably focused on achieving national liberation and establishing political power (Payne & Bishop, 2010). Sovereignty and independence became the cornerstones of West Indian statehood, evolving from a desire for cultural self determination to a strong emphasis on independent nation-states demanding unwavering national loyalty (Lewis, 2004). However, this emphasis on individual sovereignty creates a complex situation. While fiercely independent, these island nations also recognize the benefits of regional cooperation – a tension that continues to shape the Caribbean's approach to governance.

The Caribbean's quest for self-determination often mirrored European political forms, reflecting its lingering ties to the continent even after independence (Payne & Bishop, 2010). Independence granted these nations a seat at the international table – membership in the United Nations General Assembly and the ability to shape their own foreign policies. However, exercising sovereignty in a meaningful way proved challenging. The region's small size, limited economic development, and internal political divisions constrained their ability to project power on the global stage (Griffith, 2024).

Despite these constraints, Caribbean sovereignty remained a powerful symbol of equality and dignity for West Indians (Payne & Bishop, 2010). It represented a break from colonial domination and a chance to define their own futures. However, these newly independent states, still grappling with internal development, struggled to confront the growing influence of transnational forces like multinational corporations and international organizations (Payne & Bishop, 2010). Their inherent weaknesses limited their ability to assert their sovereignty in the face of these external pressures.

Understanding the concept of sovereignty is crucial when examining Caribbean politics. Clapham (1999) emphasizes the unique significance of sovereignty in the postcolonial context, considering the region's long history of exploitation, displacement, and powerlessness. Unlike their European counterparts, sovereignty for Caribbean nations wasn't just about political independence; it represented a reclamation of dignity and self-determination.

Payne and Bishop (2010) further this argument by characterizing post-colonial Caribbean politics as often prioritizing internal governance and domestic legitimacy. This focus on personalistic leadership, while crucial for building national identity, can sometimes hinder regional cooperation and compromise efforts at forging a unified voice on the international stage. The Caribbean's struggle to balance sovereignty and regional cooperation may stem, in part, from an inadequate understanding of these concepts in a postcolonial world. Decolonization dismantled formal empires, but the legacy of colonialism continues to shape how Caribbean nations define and exercise their sovereignty (Griffith, 2024).

Sovereignty itself carries diverse meanings across different ideologies. However, its definition and comprehension are critical for effective policymaking in a world increasingly defined by postinternationalism. Krasner's (2001) four-part framework for understanding sovereignty in the contemporary era is particularly insightful:

- Interdependence Sovereignty: A state's ability to regulate its borders and control the flow of goods, capital, people, and ideas.
- Domestic Sovereignty: The state's capacity to secure internal control and eliminate challenges from its citizens.
- International Legal Sovereignty: Recognition by other nations, shaping inter-state relations and interactions with international organizations.
- Westphalian Sovereignty: The state's right to set its own agendas, both domestically and internationally.

Krasner's (2001) analysis is particularly significant because sovereignty, in a democratic age, can have unintended consequences. Effective leadership demands a comprehensive understanding of how sovereignty is practiced in its various forms. Held (2003) further posits that sovereignty in the postcolonial Caribbean is complex because while states maintain legal control, effective power is increasingly influenced by non-state actors like multinational corporations and global processes. This reflects a new form of sovereignty shaped by the forces of globalization. The Caribbean's pursuit of independence, often adhering to the Westphalian ideal of absolute state control, sometimes outpaced its institutional and material capacity to effectively manage its newfound autonomy (Payne & Bishop, 2010). However, this pursuit secured international recognition and legal sovereignty, a crucial first step for the region.

Despite these achievements, many Caribbean states continue to grapple with the full exercise of sovereignty. Limited resources and internal divisions can make it difficult to exert complete control over borders, manage transnational issues, and deliver essential services to citizens (Bishop et al., 2021). The specter of climate change looms large, with rising sea levels and intensifying weather patterns posing a long-term existential threat to some island nations (Nurse & McLean, 2011). Additionally, the region's historical dependence on tourism and a few primary commodities leaves it vulnerable to fluctuations in global markets (Connell, 2007). These multifaceted challenges expose the limitations of traditional, centralized governance models that often struggle to foster the innovation and collaboration needed for effective solutions.

This situation underscores the need for the Caribbean to reassess its approach to sovereignty considering contemporary challenges. While the ideal of Westphalian sovereignty may hold historical significance, the realities of globalization and interdependence require a more multifaceted understanding. The Caribbean cannot achieve its goals by clinging to a rigid understanding of Westphalian sovereignty. The concept of postinternationalism acknowledges the limitations of the nation-state and emphasizes the importance of collaboration among diverse actors at various levels (Rosenau, 2003). By embracing this framework, the Caribbean can navigate the complexities of a globalized world and secure its interests more effectively.

## Weathering Storms: Challenges and Opportunities in the Caribbean

The traditional Westphalian model of sovereignty, emphasizing absolute state control, faces increasing scrutiny in the face of the interdependencies fostered by globalization (Rosenau, 1998). This is particularly true for the Caribbean's island nations. Resource-constrained and intertwined through economic ties and shared vulnerabilities, these states can no longer operate as isolated entities (Nurse, 2001). Consequently, a paradigm shift towards multilateralism is necessary. Regional unity must be pursued while safeguarding distinct national interests (Mahon, 2013). Striking this balance will be crucial for the Caribbean's progress in the 21st century.

The concept of sovereignty in the Caribbean is further complicated by the burgeoning influence of non-state actors on the regional stage (Rosenau, 1998). Civil society organizations (CSOs) offer invaluable expertise and resources, contributing to social development, environmental protection, and disaster relief efforts (Hewitt, 2015). However, their effectiveness can be hampered by resource constraints and a lack of formal enforcement power (Ramjit, 2019). On the other hand, transnational criminal organizations (TCOs) exploit vulnerabilities in the region, fueling human trafficking, drug cartels, and money laundering activities. These illicit activities not only erode state authority but also hinder broader development efforts (Hignett, 2021). This complex scenario demands a collaborative approach. Caribbean states must find ways to collaborate strategically with CSOs, leveraging their expertise while simultaneously strengthening their own institutional capacities to address resource limitations. Concurrently, robust regional and international cooperation is crucial to combat the influence of TCOs and disrupt their criminal networks.

Transnationalism, the interwoven web of actors and issues that transcends borders, is another defining characteristic of the contemporary Caribbean (Rosenau, 1998; Weatherby et al., 2017). This is evident in the proliferation of regional and international NGOs actively addressing critical issues such as poverty, human rights, and environmental sustainability (Tedeschi et al., 2020). The ubiquity of these transnational actors underscores the limitations of unilateral state action in tackling these complex challenges. This interconnected reality compels a shift towards heterarchical governance models. Heterarchy, characterized by distributed power and horizontal collaboration, fosters a more inclusive approach where states, NGOs, and civil society can work together to achieve common goals (Descola, 2001). By employing the expertise and resources of diverse actors, heterarchy offers a promising framework for navigating the interwoven challenges faced by the Caribbean in the 21st century.

The concept of fragmegration, introduced by Rosenau (1998), offers a valuable lens through which to view the Caribbean's multifaceted challenges. Fragmegration captures the concurrent processes of globalization and localization, highlighting the region's susceptibility to external economic fluctuations, environmental threats like climate change, and the flow of ideas and technology (Rosenau, 2003). However, these same forces can exacerbate existing internal cleavages based on national identity and historical rivalries, potentially hindering collective action (Campos & Timini, 2023). This underscores the need for embracing the benefits of globalization, such as increased trade and access to resources, while fostering regional unity and strengthening national resilience to external shocks.

Security in the Caribbean has transcended the traditional focus on territorial defense. The region now faces a multifaceted security landscape, encompassing transnational crime networks, cybersecurity vulnerabilities, and public health emergencies (Ellis, 2023). These complex and interconnected threats demand a shift towards a postinternational approach to security (Rosenau, 2003). The postinternational framework acknowledges the limitations of the nation-state in addressing these transborder challenges. It emphasizes collaboration among diverse actors operating at various levels of governance (Ramjit, 2022). This multi-stakeholder approach encompasses fostering regional cooperation through organizations like CARICOM, engaging with international organizations, and leveraging the expertise of civil society organizations working on issues like public health preparedness. By exploiting the collective strengths of these diverse actors, a postinternational approach offers a more effective framework for ensuring comprehensive security in the Caribbean.

## Toward a Heterarchical Approach

The multifaceted challenges confronting the Caribbean in the 21st century demand innovative approaches to policymaking and governance. A heterarchical system, characterized by distributed power and horizontal collaboration among diverse actors, offers a promising framework for navigating this complex landscape (Thompson, 2007). This stands in stark contrast to the traditional, top-down Westminster model prevalent in many Caribbean nations. The Westminster model, with its inherently hierarchical structure and limited avenues for participation, often struggles to address the region's interconnected and rapidly evolving challenges (Sabatier & Jenkins-Smith, 1993; Weible & Sabatier, 2017).

Heterarchy, on the other hand, fosters a more inclusive and adaptable approach to governance. By decentralizing power and encouraging collaboration between state and non-state actors, such as civil society organizations and the private sector, heterarchy can harness a wider range of knowledge and expertise (Dekker & Kuchař, 2021). This collaborative approach can lead to the development of more contextually relevant and effective solutions to the region's challenges.

The limitations of the Westminster model become evident when considering its inherent challenges in integrating diverse expertise and resources into policymaking processes. Its centralized decision-making structure often fails to create space for meaningful contributions from non-state actors, leading to policy inertia and a lack of responsiveness to the multifaceted needs of the population (Weible & Sabatier, 2017). Furthermore, the entrenched two-party system can stifle innovation and prioritize the interests of a narrow political base, potentially neglecting broader societal concerns (Sabatier & Jenkins-Smith, 1993). This can lead to policies that fail to adequately address the complex challenges faced by the Caribbean in the 21st century.

Heterarchy, derived from the Greek words heteros (different) and arche (rule), literally translates to different rule (Miura, 2014; Aligica & Tarko, 2013). Anthropologists like Philippe Descola (2001) define it as a system characterized by three essential features:

1. Distributed Power - Power is not concentrated in a single entity but dispersed across various actors and institutions.
2. Horizontal Networks - Collaboration and decision-making occur through horizontal networks rather than top-down hierarchies.

3.  Shared Goals - The emphasis lies on collective well-being and achieving shared goals, rather than individual or institutional dominance.

A heterarchical approach promotes a more inclusive and collaborative policymaking process. For instance, network governance, a key aspect of heterarchy, emphasizes communication and collaboration among diverse actors within a policy subsystem (Cerny, 2022). This approach recognizes the interconnectedness of challenges faced by the contemporary Caribbean, such as climate change, disaster preparedness, and economic development. Collaboration among state and non-state actors through network governance allows for the pooling of resources and expertise to develop more effective and comprehensive solutions (Edwards et al., 2021).

The diverse landscape of non-state actors in the Caribbean plays a critical role in addressing the region's challenges. NGOs offer valuable expertise in critical areas like social development, environmental protection, and disaster relief (Youssef, 2024; McCormick, 2023; Rahman & Tasnim, 2023). However, their effectiveness can be hampered by resource constraints and a lack of formal decision-making authority within traditional, top-down governance structures. A heterarchical approach offers a framework for overcoming these limitations. By emphasizing joint problem-solving and collaboration between state and non-state actors, heterarchy allows governments to leverage the expertise and resources of NGOs. This collaborative approach can lead to the development of more effective and comprehensive solutions to complex challenges (Weible & Sabatier, 2017). For example, NGOs can provide valuable insights and local knowledge during policy formulation, while the government can offer resources and legitimacy to support NGO-led initiatives.

## The Path Forward

Transitioning from the Westminster model to a heterarchical system in the Caribbean is not without its challenges. The legacy of colonialism often translates to entrenched power structures, where dominant actors may resist a dilution of their influence (Griffith, 2024). Implementing heterarchy requires careful navigation of these power dynamics and addressing concerns about potential loss of control. While non-state actors brim with expertise in critical areas, they may lack the resources and training necessary for complex policy discussions and effective participation in governance (Ramjit, 2019). Building capacity within these groups through training programs and resource allocation is crucial for their meaningful engagement in a heterarchical system. Distributing power across diverse actors also raises concerns about accountability (Thompson, 2007). Mechanisms for transparent decision-making and monitoring outcomes need to be established within a heterarchical framework. This could involve participatory budgeting processes and the creation of independent oversight bodies. These challenges highlight the need for careful institutional design and capacity building efforts when transitioning towards a heterarchical governance model in the Caribbean. Addressing these challenges will be crucial for ensuring the effectiveness and legitimacy of heterarchy as a framework for tackling the complex challenges faced by the region. The Caribbean's journey forward compels a redefinition of sovereignty in a globalized context alongside a multi-pronged approach that incorporates the following:

## 1. Institutional Reform

Institutional reforms are deliberate alterations to the formal and informal rules that govern human interactions within an organization or society (Acemoglu et al., 2001). The quality of institutions is a significant factor influencing income differences across countries (Rodrik et al., 2004). Countries with strong institutions, characterized by characteristics like rule of law, political stability, and limited corruption, tend to experience higher levels of economic growth and development while governments with excessive spending, political instability, and weak rule of law can hinder economic progress (Zhao et al., 2021). Reforming political institutions through alternative electoral systems and fostering a culture of collaboration between government and civil society can promote greater participation and inclusivity in policymaking.

## 2. Capacity Building

State capacity is a fundamental component of economic and institutional development. To enhance bureaucratic quality, states must understand the collective nature of bureaucracies, engage deeply with the contextual specificity and contingency inherent in policy implementation, and prioritize measurement and reform efforts focused on actual performance rather than hypothetical capacity (Williams, 2020). Additionally, investing in training for negotiation, conflict resolution, and network management for both state and non-state actors can significantly enhance collaborative governance.

## 3. *Transparency and Accountability*

System redesign is driven by the shift towards networked governance and a decentralized state, characterized by institutional freedom from bureaucracy, de-professionalization of public sector workers, an increase in managers, and the redefinition of citizens as consumers (Ozga, 2020). These reforms have profound political implications, as political legitimacy is essential for the sustainability of the welfare state. Welfare state organizations rely on active political processes to generate legitimacy and ensure political accountability (Higgins & Larner, 2010). Open communication among actors and opportunities for public input and oversight are critical mechanisms to ensure transparency and accountability in decision-making processes.

A crucial element for strengthening heterarchical governance in the Caribbean lies in co-production, the joint production of knowledge and solutions between state and non-state actors (Ostrom, 1972). This approach fosters collaborative research and policy analysis, ensuring non-state actors contribute their ground-level expertise from the very beginning. Co-production aligns perfectly with heterarchy's goals, as it guarantees diverse perspectives are included, leading to solutions that directly address real-world needs (Aligica & Tarko, 2013). Governments, alongside international donors, can invest in training programs for NGOs and CSOs, empowering them to effectively participate in policy discussions. Establishing formal platforms for dialogue and collaboration is essential. These platforms can foster trust, transparency, and hold all stakeholders accountable for achieving shared goals. Ultimately, co-production within a heterarchical framework can lead to enhanced policymaking, increased ownership of solutions, and improved legitimacy for governance processes in the Caribbean.

## CONCLUSION

This chapter calls for a paradigm shift in governance within the Caribbean, advocating for a transition from the Westminster model towards a heterarchical system. This heterarchical approach, characterized by distributed power and collaborative decision-making, necessitates a fundamental restructuring of power dynamics and a commitment to collaboration across sectors.

Success in this endeavor hinges on a multi-pronged strategy. First, governments must embrace a more inclusive model of governance, actively fostering a culture of trust and collaboration with non-state actor. This may involve establishing formal platforms for dialogue and co-production. Second, non-state actors must actively seek to build their capacity to effectively engage in complex policy discussions. Building strong leadership within these organizations, developing effective communication and negotiation skills, and fostering collaboration among themselves are all crucial elements for enhancing their collective voice and influence.

Overcoming these challenges will allow the Caribbean to harness the collective wisdom and resources of its diverse stakeholders. This collaborative approach, grounded in heterarchy and co-production, has the potential to foster a more responsive, effective, and ultimately, more democratic approach to policymaking.

By empowering citizens, NGOs, and the private sector to play a more active role in shaping the region's future, this framework can lead to the development of more equitable and sustainable solutions to the complex challenges facing the Caribbean in the 21st century.

# REFERENCES

Acemoglu, D., Johnson, S., & Robinson, J. A. (2001). The Colonial Origins of Comparative Development: An Empirical investigation. *˜the œAmerican. The American Economic Review*, 91(5), 1369–1401. DOI: 10.1257/aer.91.5.1369

Agostini, L. (2012, August 28). *Trinidad and Tobago Guardian*. Retrieved from Independent, but are we truly developed?: https://www.guardian.co.tt/columnist/2012-08-28/independent-are-we-truly-developed

Aho, E. (2017). *Shrinking space for civil society: challenges for implementing the 2030 agenda*. Retrieved from http://www.forumsyd.org: http://www.forumsyd.org/PageFiles/8150/PO150943_Rapport_5maj_web.pdf

Alexander, G. (2017, July 2). *Marlene fired again*. Retrieved from guardian.co.tt: https://www.guardian.co.tt/news/2017-07-02/marlene-fired-again

Ali, M., Miller, K., & Ponce de Leon, R. (2017). Family planning and Zika virus: Need for renewed and cohesive efforts to ensure availability of intrauterine contraception in Latin America and the Caribbean. *The European Journal of Contraception & Reproductive Health Care*, 102-106(2), 102–106. Advance online publication. DOI: 10.1080/13625187.2017.1288902 PMID: 28256913

Aligica, P. D., & Tarko, V. (2013). Co-Production, Polycentricity, and Value Heterogeneity: The Ostroms' Public Choice Institutionalism Revisited. *The American Political Science Review*, 107(4), 726–741. DOI: 10.1017/S0003055413000427

Aljazeera. (2017, May 17). *Caribbean to Caliphate: why are young Muslims from the Caribbean island of Trinidad and Tobago being drawn to the conflicts in Syria and Iraq?* Retrieved from aljazeera.com: https://www.aljazeera.com/programmes/peopleandpower/2017/05/caribbean-caliphate-170517073332147.html

Alleyne, G. (2017, February 17). *The role of civil society as advocates and watchdogs in NCD prevention and control in the Caribbean*. Retrieved from healthycaribbean.org: https://www.healthycaribbean.org/wp-content/uploads/2017/02/2017-03-The-role-of-civil-society-as-advocastes-and-watchdogs.pdf

Alvare, B. (2010). Babylon makes the rules: compliance, fear, and self-discipline in the quest for official NGO status. *Political and Legal Anthropology*, 178-200. DOI: 10.1111/j.1555-2934.2010.01110.x

Ambursley, F., & Cohen, R. (2024). Crisis in the Caribbean: internal transformations and external constraints. In *Routledge eBooks* (pp.26). https://doi.org/DOI: 10.4324/9781032703480-1

Anderson, B. (1991). *Imagined communities: reflections on the origin and spread of nationalism*. Verso.

Anderson, C. (2010). Presenting and evaluating qualitative research. *American Journal of Pharmaceutical Education*, 74–141. http://www.ajpe.org/doi/pdf/10 .5688/aj7408141 PMID: 21179252

Ansell, C., & Trondal, J. (2017). Governing turbulence. *EUSA fifteenth biennial conference*. Miami.

Ansell, C., Trondal, J., & Morten, O. (2017). *Governance in Turbulent Times*. Oxford University.

Araujo, A. L. (2023). How Britain Underdeveloped the Caribbean: A Reparation Response to Europe's Legacy of Plunder and Poverty, by Hilary McD. Beckles. *NWIG, New West Indian Guide/NWIG, 97*(1–2), 216–217. https://doi.org/DOI: 10.1163/22134360-09701002

Astrov, A. (2002). Pondering dramatic endings, probing possible beginnings; or doing politics as usual? *Journal of International Relations and Development*, 63–76. http://eds.a.ebscohost.com.ezp.waldenulibrary.org/eds/pdfviewer/pdfviewer?vid=1 &sid=61db2c8a-030d-4c5c-abb1-c51dd43fe9f7%40sessionmgr4006

Awad, I. (2017). *The multiple levels of governance of international migration: understanding disparities and disorder*. Retrieved from Cambridge.org: https://www .cambridge.org/core/services/aop-cambridge-core/content/view/E714B022BC70D 8B07E2320351B31F9AA/S2398772317000368a.pdf/multiple_levels_of _governance_of_international_migration_understanding_disparities_and_disorder .pdf

Ayearst, M. (2023). *The British West Indies*. https://doi.org/DOI: 10.4324/9781003362043

Balbis, J. (2003). *NGOs, governance and development in Latin America and the Caribbean*. UNESCO. Retrieved from http://digital-library.unesco.org/shs/ most/gsdl/cgi-bin/library?e=d-000-00---0most--00-0-0--0prompt-10---4------0-11 --1-en-50---20-about---00031-001-1-0utfZz-8-00&a=d&c=most&cl=CL5.9&d= HASH01000b50ae2385471f29df53

Bandola-Gill, J., Arthur, M., & Leng, R. I. (2023). What is co-production? Conceptualising and understanding co-production of knowledge and policy across different theoretical perspectives. *Evidence & Policy, 19*(2), 275 298. https://doi.org/DOI: 10.1332/174426421X16420955772641

Barkanov, B. (2016, June 14). *Institutionalism*. Retrieved from Encyclopaedia Britannica: https://www.britannica.com/topic/institutionalism

Barry, T., Gahman, L., Greenidge, A., & Mohamed, A. (2020). Wrestling with race and colonialism in Caribbean agriculture: Toward a (food) sovereign and (gender) just future. *Geoforum*, 109, 106–110. DOI: 10.1016/j.geoforum.2019.12.018

Bellamy, R. (2017). A European republic of sovereign states: Sovereignty, republicanism and the European Union. *European Journal of Political Theory*, 16(2), 188–209. DOI: 10.1177/1474885116654389

Benoit, O. (2020). Ressentiment, nationalism and the emergence of political culture in Grenada. In *Edward Elgar Publishing eBooks*. https://doi.org/DOI: 10.4337/9781789903447.00016

Bhabha, H. (1994). *The location of culture*. Routledge.

Bishop, M. L., Byron-Reid, J., Corbett, J., & Veenendaal, W. (2021). Secession, Territorial Integrity and (Non)-Sovereignty: Why do Some Separatist Movements in the Caribbean Succeed and Others Fail? *Ethnopolitics, 21*(5), 538 560. DOI: 10.1080/17449057.2021.1975414

Boodram, K. (2015, July 11). *NGOs: health card a danger to treating HIV/AIDS in T&T*. Retrieved from Trinidad and Tobago Guardian: http://www.trinidadexpress.com/20150711/news/ngos-health-card-a-danger-to-treating-hivaids-in-tt

Boodram, K. (2017, Januray 6). *Civil society presents unified voice, offers suggestions*. Retrieved from trinidadexpress.com: http://www.trinidadexpress.com/20170106/news/civil-society-presents-unified-voice-offers-suggestions

Brathwaite, K. (1974). *Contradictory omens : cultural diversity and integration in the Caribbean*. http://ci.nii.ac.jp/ncid/BA55331113

Braveboy, M. (2017, January 18). *Crippling murder rate continues in Trinidad in2017*. Retrieved from Caribbean News Now: http://www.caribbeannewsnow.com/headline-Crippling-murder-rate-continues-in-Trinidad-in-2017-33219.html

Brent Edwards Jr, D., Caravaca, A., & Moschetti, C., M. (2021). Network governance and new philanthropy in Latin America and the Caribbean: Reconfiguration of the state. *British Journal of Sociology of Education*, 42(8), 1210–1226.

Campos, R., & Timini, J. (2023). Latin America and the Caribbean: Trade relations in the face of global geopolitical fragmentation risks. *Economic Bulletin*, 2023(2023/Q1, Q1). Advance online publication. DOI: 10.53479/29631

Caribbean News Now. (2014, July 26). *Civil society identifies sustainable development priorities for Trinidad and Tobago*. Retrieved from http://www.caribbeannewsnow .com/headline-Civil-society-identifies-sustainable-development-priorities-for -Trinidad-and-Tobago-22169.html

Cerny, P. G. (2023). Capitalism, democracy and world politics in the 21st century. *European Review of International Studies*, 10(2), 205–213. DOI: 10.1163/21967415-10020016

Clapham, C. (1999). Sovereignty and the third world state. *Political Studies*, 47(3), 522–537. DOI: 10.1111/1467-9248.00215

Condon, S. (2021). Caribbean migrations: The legacies of colonialism. *Ethnic and Racial Studies*, 45(3), 524–526. DOI: 10.1080/01419870.2021.1926525

CrimeWriter. (2019). *Crime Statistics*. Retrieved from TT Crime: https://ttcrime .com/crime-statistics/

Daily Express. (2011, March 22). *Massa day done?* Retrieved from http://www .trinidadexpress.com/commentaries/Massa-Day-done-118412154.html

Davies, C. (2013). *Caribbean Spaces: escapes from twighlight zones*. University of Illinois. DOI: 10.5406/illinois/9780252038020.001.0001

Davies, T. (2013, January 24). *NGOs: A long and turbulent history*. Retrieved from The Global Journal: https://www.theglobaljournal.net/article/view/981/

De Coteau, D. (2024). Massa Day Done or 'Same Old Khaki Pants?' Contextualising Caribbean Political Corruption. In *Black Fins White Sharks: Unmasking the Genealogy of Caribbean Political Corruption* (pp. 1–33). https://doi.org/DOI: 10.1007/978-3-031-47479-8_1

Dekker, E., & Kuchař, P. (2021). Heterarchy. In *Springer eBooks* (pp. 1 6). https:// doi.org/DOI: 10.1007/978-1-4614-7883-6_640-2

Department of Foreign Affairs & Trade. A. (2014). *Trinidad and Tobago Country Brief*. Retrieved from Australian Government Department of Foerign Affairs and Trade: http://dfat.gov.au/geo/trinidad-tobago/pages/trinidad-and-tobago-country -brief.aspx

Desch, M. C., Dominguez, J. I., & Serbin, A. (1998). *From pirates to drug lords: the post-cold war Caribbean security environment*. State University of New York Press.

During, S. (2024). The Global South and internationalism. In *Routledge eBooks* (pp. 71 80). https://doi.org/DOI: 10.4324/9781003255871-9

Ellis, R. E. (2023). Security challenges in the Caribbean: threats, migration, and international cooperation (By Institute of Caribbean Studies & Peruvian Army Center for Strategic Studies). https://ceeep.mil.pe/wp-content/uploads/2023/07/PDF-Security-Challenges-in the-Caribbean-Threats-Migration-and-International-Cooperation-R-Evan-Ellis-60930 Jul-23.pdfFanning

Fanon, F. (1952). *Black skin white masks.* Grove Press.

Ferguson, Y., & Mansbach, R. (2007). Post internationalism and IR theory. *Millennium*, 35(3), 529–550. DOI: 10.1177/03058298070350031001

Gibbins, J. (2023). J. S. Mill, liberalism, and progress. In *Routledge eBooks* (pp. 91 109). https://doi.org/DOI: 10.4324/9781032671581-6

Gilroy, P. (1995). *The Black Atlantic: Double Consciousness and Modernity.* Harvard University Press.

Girvan, N. (2005). Whither CMSE? *Journal of Caribbean International Relations*, 13-34. Retrieved from https://www.scribd.com/document/13902381/Norman-Girvan-Whither-CSME

Glossop, R. (2017). Meaning of the 21st century: From internationalism to globalism. *Comparative Civilizations Review*, (76), 15. http://scholarsarchive.byu.edu/cgi/viewcontent.cgi?article=2011&context=ccr

Gonzales, E. (2017, June 2). *Alexandrov complains of unfair treatment for Tobago autopsies.* Retrieved from newsday.co.tt: https://www.newsday.co.tt/news/0,244503.html

Gottsche, D. (2017). Postimperialism, postcolonialism and beyond: Toward a periodization of cultural discourse about colonial legacies. *Journal of European Studies*, 47(2), 111–128. DOI: 10.1177/0047244117700070

Goujon, M., & Wagner, L. (2023). Fragility of small island developing states. In *Edward Elgar Publishing eBooks*(pp. 299–315). https://doi.org/DOI: 10.4337/9781800883475.00023

Gov.tt. (2014, September). *UWI and Canadian NGO to research private security in the Caribbean and Latin America.* Retrieved from Gov.tt: http://www.news.gov.tt/content/uwi-and-canadian-ngo-research-private-security-caribbean-and-latin-america-0#.WWOw2Ijyvic

Gov.uk. (2017). *Oversees business risk - Trinidad and Tobago.* Retrieved from https://www.gov.uk/government/publications/overseas-business-risk-trinidad-tobago/overseas-business-risk-trinidad-tobago

Gramsci, A. (1971). *Selections from the prison notebooks*. International Publishers.

Granderson, A. (2011). Enabling multi-faceted measures of success for protected area management in Trinidad and Tobago. *Evaluation and Program Planning*, 34(3), 185–195. DOI: 10.1016/j.evalprogplan.2011.02.010 PMID: 21555042

Greene, E. (2024). Reflections on the future of the Caribbean Community through the mirror of functional co-operation. *The Round Table, 113*(1), 15 28. https://doi.org/DOI: 10.1080/00358533.2024.2307777

Grenade, W. (2013). *Governance in the Caribbean: challenges and prospects.* Retrieved from http://www.commonwealthgovernance.org/assets/uploads/2012/10/Governance-in-the-Caribbean.pdf

Grieco, J. (1997). Realist international theory and the study of world politics. In Ikenberry, J., & Doyle, M. (Eds.), *New thinking in international relations theory* (pp. 163–201). Westview.

Griffith, I. L. (2024). *Challenged Sovereignty: The Impact of Drugs, Crime, Terrorism, and Cyber Threats in the Caribbean*. University of Illinois Press. https://www.jstor.org/stable/10.5406/jj.9827024

Guruprasad, S. (2014). *The creole identity in the Caribbean postcolonial society: a study of Selvon's A Brighter Sun*. Retrieved from http://www.ijims.com

Guy, S. (2009). What is global and what is local? A theoretical discussion around globalization. *Parsons Journal for Information Mapping*. Retrieved from http://piim.newschool.edu/journal/issues/2009/02/pdfs/ParsonsJournalForInformationMapping_Guy-JeanSebastian.pdf

Harney, S., & Harney, C. (1996). *Nationalism and Identity: Culture and the imagination in a Caribbean diaspora.* https://www.amazon.com/Nationalism-Identity-Imagination Caribbean-Diaspora-ebook/dp/B00844WMKU

Harrinanan, S. (2017, January 13). *NGO, Chamber in launch*. Retrieved from Trinidad and Tobago Newsday: https://www.newsday.co.tt/news/0,238385.html

Heileman, S., Leotaud, N., McConney, P., Moreno, M. P., Phillips, T., & Toro, C. (2021). Challenges to implementing regional ocean governance in the wider Caribbean region. *Frontiers in Marine Science*, 8, 667273. Advance online publication. DOI: 10.3389/fmars.2021.667273

Higgins, V., & Larner, W. (2010). Calculating the social. In *Palgrave Macmillan UK eBooks*. https://doi.org/DOI: 10.1057/9780230289673

Higman, B. (2001). *A concise history of the Caribbean*. Cambridge University.

Hignett, K. (2021). Transnational organized crime and the global village. In *Routledge eBooks* (pp. 305–317). https://doi.org/DOI: 10.4324/9781003044703-22

Hirst, P., & Thompson, G. (2002). The future of globalization: cooperation and conflict. *Nordic International Studies Association*, 247-265. DOI: 10.1177/0010836702037003671

Hobbs, H. H. (2000). *Pondering postinternationalism*. State University of New York.

Immergut, E. (2010, January 26). *Institution/Institutionalism*. Retrieved from https://www.sowi.hu-berlin.de/de/lehrbereiche/comppol/pubb/pdfs/Immergut2011.pdf

Johnson, T., & Heiss, A. (2023). Liberal institutionalism. In *Routledge eBooks* (pp. 120 132). https://doi.org/DOI: 10.4324/9781003266365-12

Karlsrud, J., Hofmann, S., & Reykers, Y. (2024). Is liberal internationalism worth saving? Ad hoc coalitions and their consequences for international security. *Policy Brief*, 1 / 2024. https://www.nupi.no/content/pdf_preview/28165/file/NUPI_Policy_Brief_1_202 Karlsrud%20mfl.pdf

Kedourie, E. (1960). *Nationalism*. Praeger.

Keohane, R. (2002). *Power and governance in a partially globalized world*. Routledge.

Keohane, R., & Nye, J. (1998, September/October). *Power and interdependence in the information age*. Retrieved from Foreign Affairs: https://www.foreignaffairs.com/articles/1998-09-01/power-and-interdependence-information-age

Kirton, M. (2010). *Political culture of democracy in Trinidad and Tobago*. Retrieved from Vanderbilt University: https://www.vanderbilt.edu/lapop/trinidad-tobago/2010-political-culture.pdf

Krasner, S. (2001, July). *Abiding sovereignty*. Retrieved from https://maihold.org/mediapool/113/1132142/data/Krasner.pdf

Krasner, S. (2001, November). *Think again: sovereignty*. Retrieved from Foreign Policy: https://foreignpolicy.com/2009/11/20/think-again-sovereignty/

Kuhn, T. (1963). *The function of dogma in scientific research*. Basic Books.

Laarmann, M. (2023). Hybrid Aesthetics and Social Reality: Reading Caribbean Literature in the postcolonial Present. In *De Gruyter eBooks* (pp. 119 136). https://doi.org/DOI: 10.1515/9783110798494-008

Ledgister, F. (2006). *Democracy in the Caribbean: postcolonial experience*. Retrieved from Academia.edu: https://www.academia.edu/428522/Democracy_in_the_Caribbean_Post Colonial_Experience

Lewis, D. (1994). Nongovernmental organizations and Caribbean development. *The Annals of the American Academy of Political and Social Science*, 533(1), 125–138. DOI: 10.1177/0002716294533001009

Lewis, G. (2004). *Main currents in Caribbean thought* (2nd ed.). University of Nebraska Press.

Maguire, E., Johnson, D., Kuhns, J., & Apostolos, R. (2017). The effects of community policing on fear of crime and perceived safety: Findings from a pilot project in Trinidad and Tobago. *Policing and Society*, 1–20. DOI: 10.1080/10439463.2017.1294177

Marx, K., & Engels, F. (1977). *Collected Works* (Vol. 9). Lawrence and Wishart.

Maull, H. (2011). *World politics in turbulence*. Retrieved from library.fes.de: https://library.fes.de/pdf-files/ipg/ipg-2011-1/2011-1__03_a_maull.pdf

McCormick, J. (2023). The role of environmental NGOs in international regimes. In *Routledge eBooks* (pp. 52–71). https://doi.org/DOI: 10.4324/9781003421368-4

McCoy, J., & Knight, A. (2017). Homegrown violent extremism in Trinidad and Tobago. *Studies in Conflict and Terrorism*, 40(4), 267–299. Advance online publication. DOI: 10.1080/1057610X.2016.1206734

McDougall, H. (2023). Colonial internationalism and the governmentality of empire, 1893 1982. *International Affairs*, 99(2), 843–844. DOI: 10.1093/ia/iiad004

McNair, B. (2017). *An introduction to political communication* (6th ed.). Routledge. DOI: 10.4324/9781315750293

Middelbeek, L., Kolle, K., & Verrest, H. (2016). Built to last? Local climate change adaptation and governance in the Caribbean – The case of an informal urban settlement in Trinidad and Tobago. *Urban Climate*, 8, 138–154. DOI: 10.1016/j.uclim.2013.12.003

Miguel, Y. M., & Arias, S. (2020). Between colonialism and coloniality. In *Routledge eBooks* (pp. 1–39). https://doi.org/DOI: 10.4324/9781315107189-1

Milhaupt, C., & Pargendler, M. (2017). Governance challenges of listed state owned enterprises around the world: national experiences and a framework for reform. *Law Working Paper N° 352/2017*. Curtis J. Milhaupt & Mariana Pargendler 2017.

Ministry of Attorney General and Legal Affairs. (1976). *The Constitution of the Republic of Trinidad and Tobago*. Retrieved from Ministry of attorney general and legal affairs: http://rgd.legalaffairs.gov.tt/laws2/Constitution.pdf

Ministry of Finance. (2011, October). *Medium term policy framework 2011-2014 - Ministry of finance*. Retrieved from finance.gov.tt: https://www.finance.gov.tt/wp -content/uploads/2013/11/Medium-Term-Policy-Framework-2011-14.pdf

Ministry of Social Development and Family Services. (2017). *Nongovernmental organization unit*. Retrieved from https://www.social.gov.tt/divisions/nongovernmental -organization-n-g-o-unit/

Minto-Coy, I., Cowell, N., & McLeod, M. (2016). Breaking the barriers: Entrepreneurship, enterprise, competitivenes and growth in the Caribbean. *Social and Economic Studies*, 1–13. DOI: 10.1080/08985626.2015.1088727

Miura, S. (2014, December 1). Heterarchy. *Social Science, Power Structures & Organizations*. Encyclopedia Britannica. https://www.britannica.com/topic/heterarchy

Moravcsik, A. (2001, April). *Liberal international relations theory: a social scientific assessment*. Retrieved from Weatherhead Center for International Affairs, Harvard University: https://wcfia.harvard.edu/files/wcfia/files/607_moravscik.pdf

Moreno, A., Bourillon, L., Flores, E., & Fulton, S. (2017). Fostering fisheries management efficiency through collaboration networks: The case of the Kanan Kay Alliance in the Mexican Caribbean. *Bulletin of Marine Science*, 93(1), 233–247. DOI: 10.5343/bms.2015.1085

One Caribbean Health. (2016, July 28). *Trinidad and Tobago: civil society rises to the NCD challenge*. Retrieved from onecaribbeahealth.org: http://onecaribbeanhealth .org/trinidad-and-tobago-civil-society-rises-to-the-ncd-challenge/

Open Government Partnership. (2014). *OGP annual report 2014*. Retrieved from https://www.opengovpartnership.org/stories/ogp-annual-report-2014

Ozga, J. (2019). The politics of accountability. *Journal of Educational Change*, 21(1), 19–35. DOI: 10.1007/s10833-019-09354-2

Parashar, S., & Schulz, M. (2021). Colonial legacies, postcolonial 'selfhood' and the (un)doing of Africa. *Third World Quarterly*, 42(5), 867–881. DOI: 10.1080/01436597.2021.1903313

Parliament, Trinidad and Tobago. (2017, July 12). *Evolution of a nation: Trinidad and Tobago at fifty*. Retrieved from ttparliament.org: http://www.ttparliament.org/ documents/2183.pdf

Pawelz, J. (2016). *Violent gangs as social actors in a world of socio-economic inequality. The case of Trinidad and Tobago.* Retrieved from German Institute of Global and Area Studies: https://www.giga-hamburg.de/en/event/violent-gangs-as-social-actors-in-a-world-of-socio-economic-inequality

Payne, A., & Bishop, M. (2010, January 29). *Caribbean regional governance and the sovereignty/statehood problem.* Retrieved from Center for International Governance Innovation: https://www.cigionline.org/publications/caribbean-regional-governance-and-sovereigntystatehood-problem

Perrone, D. (2009, July). *Latin American & Caribbean NGOs: facing challenges for greater participation at the United Nations Economic and Social Council.* Retrieved from http://csonet.org/content/documents/LAC.pdf

Pierre, J., & Galaz, V. (2017). Superconnected, compex and ultrafast: governance of hyperfunctionality in financial markets. *Complexity, Governance & Networks*, 12-28. doi:DOI: 10.20377/cgn-55

Pineda, A. (2013, May 1). *NGOs and development in Latin American and the Caribbean: A case study of Haiti.* Retrieved from University of New Orleans: http://scholarworks.uno.edu/cgi/viewcontent.cgi?article=1047&context=honors_theses

Powers, M. (2014, November 23). *Hazel Brown to step down as NGO head.* Retrieved from Trinidad and Tobago Guardian: https://www.guardian.co.tt/news/2014-11-23/hazel-brown-step-down-ngo%E2%80%88head

Premdas, R. (2011). Identity, ethnicity and the Caribbean homeland in an era of globalization. *Social Identities*, 17(6), 811–832. DOI: 10.1080/13504630.2011.606676

Prichard, A. (2010). *Rethinking anarchy and the state in IR theory: the contributions of classical anarchism.* Retrieved from University of Bristol: https://www.bristol.ac.uk/media-library/sites/spais/migrated/documents/prichard0310.pdf

Rahman, S., & Tasnim, F. (2023). The role of NGOs in ensuring local governance in Bangladesh: From the perception of other actors of governance. *Asia-Pacific Journal of Regional Science*, 7(3), 1007–1034. DOI: 10.1007/s41685-023-00283-w

Ramadan, A., & Fregonese, S. (2017). Hybrid sovereignty and the state of exception in the Palestinian refugee camps in Lebanon. *Annals of the American Association of Geographers*, 107(4), 2469–4460. DOI: 10.1080/24694452.2016.1270189

Ramdass, A. (2019, March 1). *Amnesty for Venezuelans in Trinidad.* Retrieved from Daily Express: https://www.trinidadexpress.com/news/local/amnesty-for-venezuelans-in-t-t/article_8127756c-3bc7-11e9-b487-e3592eda812c.html

Ramos, M. (1989). Some ethical implications of qualitative research. *Research in Nursing & Health*, 12(1), 57–63. DOI: 10.1002/nur.4770120109 PMID: 2922491

Rampersad, S., & Julien, J. (2017, June 25). *Speaker under fire from UNC*. Retrieved from guardian.co.tt: https://www.guardian.co.tt/news/2017-06-24/speaker-under-fire-unc

Raphael, C. (2015, January 18). *Accept the disabled*. Retrieved from Trinidad and Tobago Guardian: https://www.guardian.co.tt/news/2015-01-18/accept-disabled

Raphael, J. (2017, August 1). *NGOs must focus on relationships, accountability to survive*. Retrieved from guardian.co.tt: https://www.guardian.co.tt/news/2017-08-01/ngos-must-focus-relationships-accountability-survive

Rawlins, G. (2017, June 15). *Civil society's overlooked role in natural resource governance*. Retrieved from tteiti.org/tt: http://www.tteiti.org.tt/civil-societys-overlooked-role-in-natural-resource-governance/

Research, B. M. I. (2017). *Local elections deliver little change in political climate*. Latin American Monitor.

Rodrik, D., Subramanian, A., & Trebbi, F. (2004). Institutions Rule: the primacy of institutions over geography and integration in economic development. *Journal of Economic Growth, 9*(2), 131–165. Rhys, J. (1966). *Wide Sargasso Sea*. New York: Norton.DOI: 10.1023/B:JOEG.0000031425.72248.85

Roger, C., Snidal, D., & Vabulas, F. (2023). The importance of rational institutionalism in the analysis of informal international institutions. *International Politics*. Advance online publication. DOI: 10.1057/s41311-023-00483-3

Rogers, D. (2009). *Postinternationalism and small arms control: theory, politics, security*. Ashgate.

Rosenau, J. N. (1990). *Turbulence in world politics: a theory of change and continuity*. Princeton University Press. DOI: 10.1515/9780691188522

Rosenau, J. N. (2003). *Dynamics beyond globalization*. Princeton University Press.

Said, E. (1978). *Orientalism*. Ramdom House.

Saint Ville, A., Hickey, G., & Phillip, L. (2017). How do stakeholder interactions influence national food security policy in the Caribbean? The case of Saint Lucia. *Food Policy*, 68, 53–64. DOI: 10.1016/j.foodpol.2017.01.002

Senel, N. (2014). A postcolonial reading of Wide Sargasso Sea by Jean Rhys. *Journal of Language & Literacy Education*, 38–45. DOI: 10.12973/jlle.11.246

Senior, O. (1994). *Gardening in the tropics*. McClelland & Stewart.

Seremani, T., & Clegg, S. (2016). Postcolonialism, organization and management theory: The rold of epistemological third spaces. *Journal of Management Inquiry*, 25(2), 171–183. DOI: 10.1177/1056492615589973

SOFRECO. (2009). *Mapping of non state actors in Trinidad and Tobago*. Retrieved from Mapping of non state actors in Trinidad and Tobago: https://www.eeas.europa .eu/archives/delegations/trinidad/documents/1__final_report20131007_01_en.pdf

Stalin, J. (2013). *Marxism and the national question*. Prism Key.

Stouck, J. (2005, December). *Gardening in the diaspora: place and identity in Olive Senior's poetry*. Retrieved from https://malcolmliteratureresource.wordpress.com/ 2012/10/22/gardening-in-the-tropics-journal-essay/

Strange, S. (1996). *The retreat of the state: the diffusion of power in the world economy*. DOI: 10.1017/CBO9780511559143

Strongman, L. (2014, October 3). *Postcolonialism and international development studies: a dialectic exchange*. DOI: 10.1080/01436597.2014.946248

Superville, J. (2017, August 12). *Alexandrov: Our forensic pathology systems outdated*. Retrieved from newsday.co.tt: https://www.newsday.co.tt/news/0,247612.html

Sylvester, M. A. (2020). Narratives of resistance in Trinidad's Calypso and Soca music. *Cultural and Pedagogical Inquiry*, 11(3), 105–116. DOI: 10.18733/cpi29507

Tack, C. (2016, June 16). *Hulsie calls for more state support for NGOs*. Retrieved from newsday.co.tt: https://www.newsday.co.tt/news/0,229278.html

Tarrow, S. (2010). Dynamics of diffusion: mechanisms, institutions, and scale shift. In Givan, R., Roberts, K., & Soule, S. (Eds.), *The diffusion of social movements: actors, mechanisms, and political effects* (pp. 204–220). Cambridge University Press. DOI: 10.1017/CBO9780511761638.012

Tedeschi, M., Vorobeva, E., & Jauhiainen, J. S. (2020). Transnationalism: Current debates and new perspectives. *GeoJournal*, 87(2), 603–619. DOI: 10.1007/s10708-020-10271-8

The Silver Lining Foundation. (2013). *US Embassy awards $9400USD to The Silver Lining Foundation*. Retrieved from https://www.silverliningtt.com/us-embassy-grant/

Transparency International. (2016). *Corruption perceptions index 2016*. Retrieved from https://www.transparency.org/news/feature/corruption_perceptions_index _2016

Triandafyllidou, A. (2024). Migration and globalization: dynamics and contradictions. In *Edward Elgar Publishing eBooks* (pp. 1–23). https://doi.org/DOI: 10.4337/9781800887657.00007

Trinidad and Tobago News. (2003, January 8). *Trinidad and Tobago emancipation day*. Retrieved from trinidadanadtobagonews.com: http://www.trinidadand tobagonews.com/forum/webbbs_config.pl?md=read;id=1171

Trinidad and Tobago Newsday. (2016, September 30). *Civil society wants transparent governance*. Retrieved from newsday.co.tt: https://www.newsday.co.tt/news/0,233921.html

Trommer, S., & Teivainen, T. (2017). Representation beyond the state: Towards transnational democratic nonstate politics. *Globalizations*, 14(1), 17–31. DOI: 10.1080/14747731.2016.1160599

Ullah, A. K. M. A. (2024). Struggles for identity formation: Second-generation South Asian diaspora overseas. *South Asian Diaspora*, 1, 16. DOI: 10.1080/19438192.2024.2328465

Walcott, D. (1981). *The Fortunate Traveller*. Farrar, Strauss & Giroux.

Walcott, D. (2007). *Selected Poems*. Farrar, Straus and Giroux.

Weatherby, J., Arceneaux, C., Leithner, A., Reed, I., Timms, B., & Zhang, S. (2017). *The other world: issues and politics in the developing world* (10th ed.). Routledge. DOI: 10.4324/9781315543383

Webster, C. (2017). Political turbulence and business as usual: Tourism's future. *Journal of Tourism Futures*, 4-7(1), 4–7. Advance online publication. DOI: 10.1108/JTF-11-2016-0045

Weible, M., & Sabatier, P. (2017). *Theories of the policy process* (4th ed.). Westview.

Wendt, A. (1991). *Anarcy is what states make of it: the social construction of power politics*. Cambridge University.

Wertheim, S. (2024). Internationalism/Isolationism: Concepts of American Global Power. In *Springer eBooks* (pp. 49–88). https://doi.org/DOI: 10.1007/978-3-031-49677-6_3

Wight, C. (2006). *Agents, structures and nternational relations: politics as ontology*. Cambridge University. DOI: 10.1017/CBO9780511491764

Williams, M. J. (2020). Beyond state capacity: Bureaucratic performance, policy implementation and reform. *Journal of Institutional Economics*, 17(2), 339–357. DOI: 10.1017/S1744137420000478

Williams, P., & Chrisman, L. (1988). Can the subaltern speak? In Spivak, G. (Ed.), *Colonial discourse and postcolonial theory* (pp. 66–111). Columbia University.

Winger, K. (2024). Power from Below in Premodern Societies: The Dynamics of Political Complexity in the Archaeological RecordT. L. Thurston and Manuel Fernández-Götz (eds.): Power from Below in Premodern Societies: The Dynamics of Political Complexity in the Archaeological Record. CambridgeUniversity Press, Cambridge, 2021. 320 pp. ISBN: 9781316515396. *Norwegian Archaeological Review*, 1 2. https://doi.org/DOI: 10.1080/00293652.2024.2324800

Worrel, A. (2016, December 31). *Economic challenges in2017*. Retrieved from guardian.co.tt: https://www.guardian.co.tt/business/2016-12-30/economic-challenges-2017

Worth, O. (2017). *Hegemony, international political economy and post-communist Russia*. Routledge. DOI: 10.4324/9781315253459

Youssef, A. B. (2024). The role of NGOs in climate policies: The case of Tunisia. *Journal of Economic Behavior & Organization, 220*, 388 401. https://doi.org/DOI: 10.1016/j.jebo.2024.02.016

## KEY TERMS AND DEFINITIONS

**Eurocentric:** A perspective that views European culture, history, and experiences as the center or norm in global affairs, often prioritizing European ideas and values.

**Heterarchy:** A social or organizational structure where power is shared among multiple individuals or groups, without a strict hierarchy or centralized authority. Unlike a hierarchical structure with a clear chain of command, heterarchy allows for a more decentralized and flexible distribution of power.

**Hybridity:** Refers to the process of mixing or blending distinct cultural, social, or genetic elements, often resulting from the interaction and exchange between individuals or groups from diverse backgrounds.

**Internationalism:** A counterbalance to nationalism, which emphasizes the primacy of the nation-state. While nationalism focuses on national interests, internationalism emphasizes the importance of global cooperation and interdependence.

**Nationalism:** A belief in the unity of a nation, often based on shared language, culture, or history, inspiring patriotism, civic-mindedness.

**Postinternationalism:** A theoretical framework that challenges the traditional concepts of sovereignty, nation-states, and international relations. Postinternationalism emphasizes the role of globalization, interdependence, and non-state actors, highlightinh a new, more complex, and interconnected world order.

**Sovereignty:** The supreme authority of a state within its own territory. Sovereignty implies the right of a state to govern itself without interference from other nations.

# Chapter 8
# Navigating Regionalism in a Heterarchical Global Order:
## A Comprehensive Analysis of the EU's Empowerment in Global Investment Governance

**Dealan Riga**

*University of Liege, Belgium*

## ABSTRACT

*This chapter argues that the European Union (EU) has gained empowerment through the fragmentation of the Common Commercial Policy (CCP), particularly focusing on investment governance. It highlights how the EU has utilized this altered policy landscape to enhance Brussels' capabilities in addressing investment issues. The argument posits that the CCP has become heterarchical due to politicization and geopoliticization, leading to a discussion on how the EU has navigated this new landscape to bolster its competencies in investment governance. Firstly, the chapter examines the adoption of an Investment Screening Mechanism (ISM), asserting its significance in shaping a Brussels-oriented perspective on investment-related risks. Secondly, it underscores the EU's revised approach to multilateral investment agreements, shifting from a state-centric demand for investment facilitation to a Brussels-centric framing of investment protection.*

DOI: 10.4018/979-8-3693-3563-5.ch008

## INTRODUCTION

Investment governance has long been one of the most challenging topics in global affairs, given its crucial role in the global economic system. While the TRIMs agreement highlights its importance in the world policy agenda, its limited scope poses significant challenges in advocating for a comprehensive global investment framework. The failure of the Multilateral Agreement on Investment (AMI) provides key insights into the difficulties of achieving global consensus, leaving the world ill-prepared for investment governance at a time when shifting geo-economic realities enable new stakeholders to enter the global Foreign Direct Investment (FDI) arena. The absence of a comprehensive multilateral framework generates a renewed call for establishing a level playing field in investment governance. Yet, few, if any, global attempts to regulate investment are close to being signed, and the heterarchical set up of global affairs exacerbates this state of play (Cerny, 2022). In the end, despite the growing fragmentation of world politics and the transnational aspects of investment policy, the state appears to remain the most salient unit of analysis for investment regulation.

Against this background, this chapter asserts that the increasing significance of FDI regulation calls for a fresh approach to multilateral regulation, where regions assert themselves as central players in global affairs. Drawing from European studies, it contends that the European Union, empowered in these specific matters, has adeptly navigated the fragmentation of the investment governance landscape resulting from politicization and geopoliticization. With the emergence of new stakeholders advocating various interests, both private and public, Brussels has positioned itself at the nexus of this fragmentation process. In doing so, it incorporates these emerging voices into a revamped framework for investment governance, one rooted in EU priorities rather than purely national interests. Consequently, the EU emerges as a novel leader in shaping FDI regulation preferences, often superseding individual states.

To illustrate this trend, this chapter scrutinizes the way the EU has transitioned from state-driven investment liberalization to the creation of its own global approach to investment. It first delves into the adoption of an Investment Screening Mechanism (ISM). While the state remains the salient unit for its implementation, the chapter argues that the ISM is pivotal in shaping a Brussels-based perspective on investment-related risks. Furthermore, the EU gains greater discretionary power in influencing state approaches to investment. Recent developments suggest that this trend is poised to continue, with Brussels emerging as a key component in the European framework of economic security. Secondly, the chapter emphasizes the renewed approach to multilateral investment agreements proposed by the EU. The EU was previously constrained in its actions to ensure investment facilitation, as requested by member states. Nevertheless, it has managed to partly shift this dynamic and is hedging towards a greater capacity to promote its own multilateral agenda in global affairs. Not only does the EU establish its own perspective on investment governance stakes, but it also promotes this view on the global stage through both bilateral and multilateral means.

This chapter is structured into two sections. The first section provides an overview of the European Union's journey toward investment governance since gaining competency in this specific sector. It also introduces the concept of politicization and geopoliticization, and the fragmented landscape emerging from these processes. The second section delves into the European integration of the investment governance debate. It first scrutinizes the way the ISM enables the EU to disseminate a common understanding of investment stakes. Then, it emphasizes the bilateral and multilateral efforts of the regional organization toward the promotion of its own investment governance agenda. The conclusion reflect on broader theoretical implication of the findings in term of regional organization role in world affairs. It then outline the research agenda derived from this analysis for both European studies and Global Political Economy.

# 1. SECTION 1: EVOLVING EU INVESTMENT GOVERNANCE: FROM MULTILATERAL SUPPORT TO LEADERSHIP IMPERATIVES

## 1.1 The EU Competency in FDI: Balancing CCP Exclusive Competency and Member States Reluctances

The EU's investment journey began with the implementation of the Lisbon Treaty in 2009, which included the amendment of Article 207 TFEU to designate Foreign Direct Investment (FDI) as part of the Common Commercial Policy (CCP), an exclusive competency of the Commission (EU, 2012). While this competency could have been utilized through Article 67 TFUE previously, Meunier (2014) and Basedow (2017, 2020) demonstrate how the inclusion of investment chapters in free trade agreements (FTAs) only became possible after the transfer of competence over FDI policy into the CCP by the 2009 Treaty of Lisbon.

At the outset, the Commission's utilization of this competency was highly dependent on member states' priorities. They wielded significant discretionary power over the process, with the mandatory adoption of a Council mandate. Back in 2010, member states displayed little support for the implementation of EU competence in FDI, thus limiting the scope of the negotiating mandate to investment facilitation purposes (Bungenberg, 2011; Vlasiuk Nibe et al., 2024; Reinisch, 2013). Furthermore, the Council considered only FDI as part of EU competences, not investment as a whole. As an illustration, for the launch of the Comprehensive Agreement on Investment (CAI), the Council, by providing the negotiation mandate to the Commission in 2013, clearly stated: "The Representatives of the Governments of the Member States, meeting within the Council, adopted the draft Decision authorising the European Commission to negotiate on behalf of the Member States, the provisions of an investment agreement with the People's Republic of China *that fall within the competences of the Member State*" (COEU, 2013, 5).

Despite uncertainty regarding the scope of EU competency, the Commission established its view on FDI in 2010. In doing so, it maneuvered its policy goals on behalf of states' preferences to combine the FDI-led growth model and the export-led growth model (Regan & Brassis, 2021; Bohle & Regan, 2021; Vlasiuk Nibe et al., 2024). Accordingly, the Commission's framing of investment priorities was strongly directed toward the neoliberal consensus of that time claiming that: "FDI represents an important source of productivity gains and plays a crucial role in establishing and organizing businesses and jobs at home and abroad. Through FDI, companies build the global supply chains that are part of the modern international economy" (EC, 2010, 3). Consequently, the Commission's own interpretation of its competency remains sets FDI as key elements of competitiveness, economic growth, and innovation (EC, 2010). Few years later, in the wake of the economic crisis turmoil, FDI was framed as a key component of EU economic recovery, and its liberalization became a clear policy goal. As late as 2015, Cecilia Malmström stated that: "As the world's largest source and destination of FDI, the EU is a major beneficiary of an open world economic system and is committed to ensuring that markets remain open" (EP, 2015).

Accordingly, from 2010 to 2015, the EU's approach to FDI was closely scrutinized by member states, and the EU followed a similar logic by integrating FDI liberalization as a key component for EU growth and competitiveness. With this in mind, the EU Commission obtained Council mandates to negotiate investment-related issues within major global partnership agreements such as the Transatlantic Trade and Investment Partnership (TTIP), Comprehensive Economic and Trade Agreement (CETA), and Comprehensive Agreement on Investment (CAI). All of these agreements followed the same framework, integrating concerns revolving around investment facilitation by providing investors with a higher degree of certainty when investing.

## 1.2 Paramount Neo-Liberal Approach Meets Public and Private Reluctance: EU in the Wake of Politicization and Geopoliticization

Between 2015 and 2020, EU attempts to further ensure investment liberalization have faced two distinct backlashes: politicization and geopoliticization. Both factors come into play within the specific context of EU mega-regional agreement negotiations (TTIP and CETA). Nevertheless, as presented below, the global diffusion of power emerging from globalization plays a significant role in fuelling the fragmentation processes enabled by these backlashes.

The first backlash has been captured by the concept of politicization in EU trade negotiations. From a theoretical standpoint, politicization arises when institutions gain authority beyond nation-states, as exemplified by the EU (Zürn et al., 2021; De Bièvre & Poletti, 2020; De Wilde, 2011). Accordingly, Politicization of international institutions is defined as "growing public awareness of international institutions and increased public mobilization of competing political preferences regarding institutions' policies or procedures" (Zürn et al., 2021, p. 71). Early works on the concept emphasize the rise of public awareness, particularly in the cases of the TTIP and CETA treaties, leading to greater public attention to trade policy debates (De Bièvre & Poletti, 2020; De Ville & Gheyle, 2024; Hurrelmann & Wendler, 2024). In both cases, public opinion materialized in protests all over Europe, with thousands of people gathering in Brussels to demonstrate their reluctance toward these agreements (Dunia, 2019; Roederer-Rynning, 2017). The Wallonian veto attempt over the ratification process further fuelled political debate, exacerbating the situation in the case of CETA (Huysseune & Paquin, 2023; Crespy & Rone, 2022)

The politicization of EU trade policy appears to reflect public apprehension towards mega-regional agreements. However, despite the prominence of public opinion, politicization is a multifaceted process that incorporates both private and public interests. A prime example is the mobilization of European farmers, who have been vigorous in condemning the impact of such agreements on European meat producers. These private and public interests influence EU decision-making through protests and by leveraging the openness of the European Parliament to their concerns (Migliorati & Vignoli, 2022; Braun & Grande, 2021). While Wallonia underscores the multi-level dimension of the process, the significance of the European Parliament also suggests a horizontal redistribution of power among institutions affected by politicization. Ultimately, politicization has disrupted existing hierarchies within EU decision-making, leading to a profound fragmentation where public and private interests intersect across states and institutions to advance their agendas. Thus, politicization could be viewed as a fragmegrative process (Rosenau, 2000), wherein the fragmentation of decision-making processes initiated by heightened public awareness enables the integration of new forms of private-public alliances into the European decision-making arena. Indeed, politicization underscores how new stakeholders polarize decision-making while also organizing around new policy preferences on a transnational scale.

The second challenge to EU framing on investment, paralleling politicization, is the geopoliticization of EU trade policy. This concept captures the inclusion of a strategically oriented approach to trade in response to external pressure (Christou & Damro, 2024; Siles-Brügge & Strange, 2020; Bauerle Danzman & Meunier, 2024). Accordingly, geopoliticization is defined as "the discursive construction of an issue as a geopolitical problem, whereby policy instruments come to be used to win over allies, overcome foes, and restructure the global balance of power" (Meunier and Nicolaidis, 2019, p. 107). While the concept is still in an early defining stage, it contributes to the academic consensus that the EU is adapting to the overall "weaponization" of world trade policy (Hopewell, 2022; Llano et al., 2021; Narlikar, 2022). Accordingly, sources of geopoliticization parallel those of the politicization of trade policy on the one hand and are inherited from systemic pressure and 'geoeconomics' on the other.

Among these external pressures, China holds significant attention from the European Union, particularly regarding investment governance. From 2010 to 2016, Chinese FDI flows to Europe surged along an exponential trajectory (Hanemann & Huotari, 2017). While the CAI was supposed to address these dynamics, the pace of negotiations did not keep up with the rapid evolution of economic realities. Concern gradually escalated in the EU decision-making arena, eventually reaching a tipping point in 2015-2016 (Riga, 2022; Vlasiuk Nibe et al., 2024; Meunier, 2014). During this period, Chinese acquisitions such as Kuka Robotics, alongside the launch of Made in China 2025[1], underscored the risks associated with Chinese investment amid a global technological race (Godement, 2021). The private sector became more cautious regarding Chinese investment and its potential long-term impacts on competition (Business Europe, 2016). However, geopoliticization is not solely about China; another example is the private sector's calls for greater scrutiny from the EU regarding risks to the European steel industry due to the Trump administration's tariffs on this sector (Eurofer, 2019).

While the private sector plays a central role in concerns about geopoliticization, public support for human rights has been pivotal in the European Parliament's call for a more assertive approach to China. Similarly to politicization, external pressures reach various stakeholders whose preferences aggregate into new policy agendas integrated into the European institutional structure. However, unlike politicization, geopoliticization does not typically manifest in social mobilization or protest; instead, stakeholders' concerns are expressed primarily through lobbying, the form and organization of which may vary. Consequently, geopoliticization might be more challenging to identify due to the inherent informality of lobbying. Nonetheless, several indicators may suggest the occurrence of such lobbying. For instance, in their position paper on the decision to grant market economy status to China, ETUC and BusinessEurope mention that: "The EU should therefore maintain effective trade defence instruments that take the real market situation in China into account. (...) The EU should engage in dialogue with China through all available channels and aim for a balanced long-term solution" (BusinessEurope, 2016, p. 1). Similarly, many lobbyists have advocated for a greater strategic approach by the EU in ensuring a level global playing field (BASF, 2024, p. 4; Basedow, 2021; Woolcock, 2011).

*Figure 1. The heterarchical set up of the CCP*

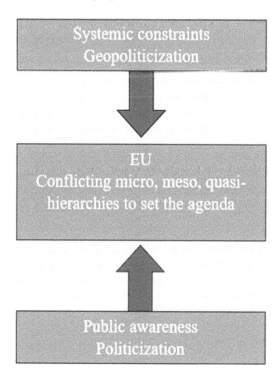

In light of these two processes, this chapter argues that EU trade policy-making has reached an unprecedented level of fragmentation, where global, local, private, or public interests aggregate around distinct agendas. However, these policy preferences have integrated the European decisional arena, offering a window of opportunity for the EU to foster its own regulation over investment policy. A such the EU posit itself at the crossroad of multiple stakes surround by a galaxy of vested interests, which this chapter argue could only be capture by the concept of Heterarchy (Cerny, 2022).

Indeed, contemporary approaches to EU decision-making can only be understood by emphasizing the conflict between quasi "micro- and meso- quasi-hierarchies" that intersect within EU decision-making (Cerny, 2022, p. 2). Graph 1 summarizes this logic.

## 2. SECTION 2: SCRUTINIZING CCP IN A HETERARCHICAL SET UP

The confluence of increasing public awareness and systemic constraints demands a renewed approach to EU trade policy. This chapter contends that the EU has responded reactively to this dynamic by striving for greater integration of the debate within its decision-making arena. The European Parliament has displayed openness to pressure, notably by amplifying calls for heightened scrutiny of the spillover effects of free trade and global unfair practices. It has played a pivotal role in highlighting the risks associated with granting China Market Economy Status, particularly regarding safeguarding the single market against dumping. Meanwhile, the Council of the European Union has adopted a more tempered stance toward liberalization, reflecting the experiences of individual member states amidst these processes. Notably, the Commission's approach to trade risks has also evolved. As early as 2017, in his State of the Union speech, Jean-Claude Juncker declared: "Let me say once and for all: we are not naïve free traders. Europe must always defend its strategic interests. This is why today we are proposing a new EU framework for investment screening. It is a political responsibility to know what is going on in our own backyard so that we can protect our collective security if needed" (EC, 2017a, P3). Graph 2 summarizes the impact of politicization and geopoliticization on the Union.

*Figure 2. EU institutions porousness to politicization and geopoliticization*

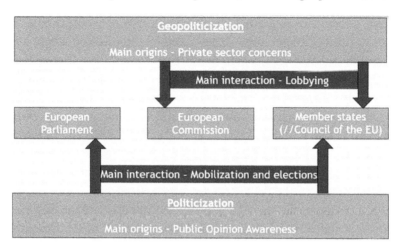

Beyond discourse, this section delves into the practical engagement of the EU with the fragmentation of the CCP. Focusing on investment issues, it assesses how the EU has adopted a new agenda on economic matters. This seems necessary as the presented heterarchical setup of the system makes sense of complexity and sheds light on the variety of vested interests within the system. However, by doing so, it introduces a higher degree of uncertainty toward policy output into the system. Therefore, it is imperative to attempt to make sense of heterarchy by scrutinizing the practical changes it implies. Accordingly, this chapter emphasizes two trends emerging from the EU's response to politicization and geopoliticization. Firstly, it fosters a shared understanding of investment stakes through a renewed political framework facilitated by specific tools such as investment screening mechanisms. Secondly, it applies this framework beyond its borders to actively pursue its own investment regulation agenda in world affairs. In essence, the EU's integration of the heterarchical setup draws on two distinct mechanisms: harmonization and representation.

## 2.1 Investment Screening Mechanism: A Shared Understanding of Investment Related Risks

In February 2017, France, Germany, and Italy sent a joint letter to the Commission calling for investment review at the EU level, followed by a Proposal for a Union Act on the screening of FDIs in strategic sectors by the Parliament in March 2017 (Vlasiuk Nibe et al, 2024). Thus, Jean Claude Juncker's announcement of 'a less naïve EU' directly stems from the requests made by states and the Parliament for a European approach to FDI screening. This dynamic might also suggest that the Parliament was more directly impacted or at least inclined to convey the change in investment governance requested. Furthermore, it is noteworthy that since the early phases of the discussion, states have called for coordinated action within the single market rather than a state-centered response. Nevertheless, during these early processes, some states remained cautious into granting the European Commission autonomous investment screening capabilities (Chan & Meunier, 2022). Additionally, competency issues regarding investment were still ongoing, with few efforts made to clarify the inclusion of FDI in Article 207 of the TFEU (EC, 2012). Intriguingly, a few months after the launch of the Commission's staff work for ISM, the European Union Court of Justice (CJEU) clarified this status. It stated that FDI was an exclusive competence of the CCP but also emphasized that ISDS and portfolio investment remain under the shared competence of the EU and the member states. This implies that states remain key stakeholders on behalf of the Commission in the negotiation of investment treaties, as most of them include ISDS (EP, 2022). Nevertheless, the judgement empowers the Commission for the establishment of the investment screening mechanism, as it is designed to deal with FDI. Accordingly, it was only in 2017, in the wake of geopoliticization and politicization, that the EU's competencies in terms of FDI were clarified and understood clearly.

Despite this juridical clarification, the ISM proposal as accepted in 2019 is still highly dependent on member states as they are the main unit for implementation (Chaisse, 2012). The regulation establishes a system for cooperation and exchange of information on investments from non-EU countries that may affect security or public order, ensuring that the EU is better equipped to protect its own interests (EP, 2022). While EU interests are advanced, states are responsible for the notification, indicating they have the lead in making use of the framework. Thus, the definition of EU interests remains in state hands, suggesting that ISM couldn't be considered as inducing a high discretionary power of the Commission into state investment preferences. Furthermore, success remains to be seen as, currently, three member states still don't have an ISM (EP, 2022). Since its implementation, the mechanism has resulted in more than 400 cases being screened by the Commission; in the most recent available period (11 October 2020 – 30 June 2021), 265 cases were notified to the Commission (EP, 2022). Twenty percent of these cases were deemed to be a possible cause for concern, and in eight cases (three percent of the total), the Commission adopted formal opinions with information or recommendations to member states (EP, 2022; OECD, 2022). ISM is still in its early stage, and its efficiency remains to be discussed in the longer term; however, it already comes quite clearly that the EU has not replaced the state in the screening of investment. From this outlook, ISM should rather be considered as an attempt to promote a common framework harmonizing state approach to FDI.

Nevertheless, this chapter argues that ISM is a gamechanger empowering the EU for investment regulation. Sure, the Union does not have the last word in choosing which investments could or couldn't reach the single market, yet it has become the one to define what the risks related to investment are (Chaisse, 2012). Back in 2017, since the early stages of the project on what the ISM should stand for, the Commission claimed that one of the main objectives is to create: "a cooperation mechanism where Member States and the Commission are able to exchange information and raise concerns related to specific investment" (EC, 2017b, 1). Accordingly, from the outset, the Commission sought to play a role in harmonizing state practices rather than substituting for them in terms of investment preferences. With this in mind, the novelty of ISM doesn't rely on the screening effort, which was already existing in certain member states, but rather on the establishment of a European Commission group of experts dedicated to this framework, which "should discuss, in particular, issues related to the screening of foreign direct investments, share best practices and lessons learned, and exchange views on trends and issues of common concern related to foreign direct" (EC, 2019, 4). Through this group, the Commission has gained expertise and leverage to set its own framing of which sectors should be considered at risk and, more broadly, what could be defined as risk-related to an investment. Not only has the Commission managed to harmonize state practices in terms of investment screening, but it has also positioned itself as the authority to foster a shared definition of what is to be screened.

It is noteworthy that Covid-19 and the Ukraine war have further fueled systemic constraints, intensifying the process of geopoliticization. Accordingly, the harmonization efforts of the Commission should be understood as an ongoing process that requires continuous effort. As an illustration, the Commission proposed an improved framework for the ISM as one of the pillars of the European Economic Security Strategy (EESC) (EC, 2023). It is too early to assess the potential of this review in terms of harmonization; however, the inclusion of ISM in a broader economic security framework is meaningful in terms of Commission empowerment. While CCP is an exclusive competency, security is not. Scholars have already emphasized how the EU utilizes geopoliticization to incorporate concerns traditionally tied to national security into its framework (Chan & Meunier, 2022; Bauerle Danzman & Meunier, 2023; 2024). This chapter does not seek to discuss whether the EU gains security competencies in the wake of geopoliticization. Yet, the inclusion of a review of investment screening into the economic security framework suggests that harmonization efforts are progressing swiftly. In the same vein, the Economic Security package might include further development for the screening of outbound investment (EC, 2023). If implemented, such a proposal would be another cornerstone in the EU toolbox to frame a harmonized view of investor behavior, another step toward a European definition of investment governance.

To sum up, ISM represents a European response to both private and public calls for greater caution in European markets towards FDI. States remain the key stakeholders in the implementation process. Nevertheless, the Commission gains leverage in framing investment-related risks with a dedicated group of experts overseeing which sectors are most important to protect. Accordingly, the Commission expands its capabilities to harmonize state approaches, practices, and understanding of investment stakes, positioning itself as the authority for investment regulation within the single market. In essence, CCP fragmentation prompts new calls for EU regulation, and the EU's response enables it to gain greater prominence in the sector. Spillover effects are expected in the long term as the Commission's efforts to foster its own view of investment regulation continue. Additionally, ISM has been presented with another key objective: to encourage international cooperation on investment screening, including sharing experiences, best practices, and information on issues of common concern (EC, 2017b). Thus, ISM is also linked to another aspect of the EU's investment leadership efforts, which will be further explored through the analysis of renewed EU economic diplomacy.

## 2.2 An Economic Diplomacy Shifting From Investment Liberalization to Investment Defence

Despite renewed stance to investment screening, the EU has always make clear that it remains committed to an open world following a rule-based order (Danzman & Meunier, 2023; Young, 2019; Jacobs et al., 2023). Even when addressing its economic security, the EU recalls that: "The EU is one of the most attractive destinations for global companies and for investment. Our economies thrive on open and rules-based trade and investment, on secure cross-border connectivity and collaboration on research and innovation" (EC, 2023, 2). Arguably, EU efforts toward bilateral and multilateral means to secure a greater playing field in investment governance haven't been undermined by geopoliticization and politicization. Nevertheless, there is a noticeable change in the way it has been leading its economic diplomacy toward the promotion of its own investment agenda. The most prominent example has been the launch of the "Open Strategic Autonomy" (OSA) policy (Juncos & Vanhoonacker, 2024), which is officially defined as: "Open strategic autonomy emphasizes the EU's ability to make its own choices and shape the world around it through leadership and engagement, reflecting its strategic interests and values" (EC, 2021, p. 4)

This Policy relies on three pillars that articulate a renewed approach of the EU to economic diplomacy. One of them relies on assertiveness and rule-based cooperation (EC, 2021). According to this analysis, this pillar encompasses two means of actions: a defensive toolbox and its promotion worldwide. Regarding the building of a defensive toolbox, EU has adopted an anti-subsidy regulation[2], an anti-coercion instrument[3] and International procurement instrument[4]. These tools enable the Union to enforce defensive measures aimed at ensuring fair competition within the internal market (Bauerle Danzman & Meunier, 2024). Combined with the ISM, the EU witnesses a significant enhancement of its defensive capabilities amidst ongoing politicization and geopoliticization. While the scope of these instruments extends beyond investment policy, they underscore how the fragmentation of the CCP has empowered the EU in various aspects related to it. This highlights the profound impact of politicization and geopoliticization within the EU, which has solidified its position as the leading authority in trade defence matters.

Nevertheless, the OSA policy extends beyond this innovative toolbox, as the EU has revitalized its economic diplomacy to promote these tools worldwide. This aspect of the OSA policy is encapsulated in the concept of a "De-risking strategy," which, according to Ursula Von der Leyen, "is about managing risks, addressing excessive dependencies, and increasing resilience. It is about learning the lessons from both the global COVID-19 pandemic and Russia's energy blackmail" (Von der Leyen quoted in, EC, 2023, 1). The specific reference to the pandemic and Russia serves as a reminder that De-risking is a response to both ongoing geopoliticization, which imposes greater external constraints and calls for increased responsibility within the EU, and politicization, which heightens public awareness of security risks and post-pandemic recovery needs. De-risking has gradually become a guiding principle of EU trade diplomacy as the EU seeks to further institutionalize this framework with like-minded partners to establish these tools as global standards. One example is the EU's coordination within the G7. Economic security framed through de-risking was central to the discussions at the 2023 Hiroshima summit (COEU, 2023b). The summit focused on establishing a global agenda to ensure a level playing field in trade and investment matters amidst the backdrop of geopolitical and geoeconomic disruptions. Charles Michel, President of the European Council, emphasized that "Open trade is in the European DNA. That's why we are working to build an open, rules-based multilateral trading system. Our goal must be to ensure a global level playing field. Trade policy plays a key role in advancing our partners' green and digital transitions, human rights, and labor conditions" (COEU, 2023c, 1). Not only does the EU discuss its standards with its partners, but it also sits at the negotiation table to incorporate them into a global project to build an open and rules-based multilateral trading system. While the EU gains competency in innovative defence tool development, it also represents member states in shaping global standards based on these tools.

In parallel to its multilateral efforts, the EU has been proactively upgrading and developing its partnerships across the globe to incorporate a risk management-oriented approach to trade and investment. For example, the EU-Japan bilateral talks, EU-Singapore agreement, and EU-India under negotiation agreements all include an investment protection component (Gehrke, 2020; Duchatel, 2023). Within these agreements, the EU's framework aims to foster a common understanding of investment-related risks. It is noteworthy to emphasize that the mere discussion of investment protection is a new concept for the EU. Previously, a neoliberal stance towards investment facilitation predominated, but this has shifted with the de-risking approach, where partnerships are established to ensure investment protection. As a result, the EU has not only become a key authority for investment agreements, but it has also broadened the scope of these agreements from facilitation to protection (Makarenko & Chernikova, 2020). Whereas facilitation was driven by state preferences in terms of accessing third markets, protection now relies on EU knowledge and framing. Consequently, the EU has gained autonomy in both framing and representing European investment standards. Nevertheless, it is important to note that the OSA policy did not generate a U-turn in EU trading preferences. Whether under the facilitation or protection paradigm, the main objective remains to ensure a level global playing field. Instead, OSA represents a shift in the means of action, wherein the EU has positioned itself as the primary authority.

Therefore, the EU's empowerment relies on both new capabilities to ensure a level playing field within the single market through defensive measures and a new economic diplomacy aimed at promoting its own investment agenda. It has become the primary authority for investment regulation within Europe and is also recognized as such by third parties. However, this claim must be nuanced, as the EU's empowerment does not mean that states have disappeared from decision-making. Firstly, Commission negotiations still depend on a Council mandate, where state preferences can influence the Commission's priorities. Secondly, these agreement negotiations still require state ratification for entry into force, giving states a veto power. This means that states are not passive actors, yet the relative success of the Commission in promoting its agenda confirms that politicization and geopoliticization processes have also impacted state preferences towards a Brussels-centric approach to investment politics. The trends presented in this chapter are ongoing, and their outcomes remain uncertain. While the EU has been able to aggregate some preferences into its renewed approach, further politicization could bring unexpected shifts in the hierarchy of these preferences. For example, large protests have taken place following the ratification of the EU-Mercosur agreements, leaving the outcomes for its entry into force unpredictable. Similarly, the Comprehensive Agreement on Investment with China is still pending in the European backyard. In this specific case, the fragmentation of the CCP has led to conflicting voices within the EU's decision-making process. As a reminder, the CAI was initially accepted by the European Commission before being frozen by the EU Parliament (Godement,

2021; Burnay et al., 2022). Thus, the fragmentation of the CCP could also lead to blockages within the decision-making process.

Accordingly, the policy outcomes of the presented shift remain to be seen in the coming years. However, the argument that the EU empowers itself thanks to CCP fragmentation remains valid. Regardless of the efficiency of these new defensive toolboxes or the impact of de-risking-oriented economic diplomacy, they represent something new in the way the EU deals with trade and investment. Brussels has elevated its speeches and practices to a higher level of authority than ever before in this sector. By integrating private and public concerns, it has gained new competencies and seeks to continue this trend. In this regard, the new global gateway strategy, where the EU itself proposes to become a global investor in developing markets, could be interpreted as another attempt to strengthen this authority. While the outcomes remain to be discussed, the shift is evident, and the EU is aligning its entire trade policy to further integrate CCP fragmentation.

## CONCLUSION

This chapter delves into the implications of heterarchy for regional organizations through the case study of European Union investment governance. It demonstrates that the fragmentation of the CCP generated by politicization and geopoliticization has created a window of opportunity for the EU to expand its competencies. Indeed, systemic constraints and public opinion awareness have fostered new stakeholders whose preferences are aggregated within EU decision-making processes. Accordingly, the chapter scrutinizes how the EU responds to these requests by leveraging this opportunity to expand its competencies over investment. Firstly, the EU has managed to become the key authority for framing investment-related risks. Secondly, the EU has pursued proactive policymaking to address these risks from Brussels. While the effectiveness of the renewed toolbox remains to be seen, the EU's capabilities to attempt such policies mark a real change in how investment governance is perceived as a Brussels-based concern in Europe. This hypothesis challenges two expectations from the academic field.

Firstly, Global Political Economy and concepts such as Heterarchy have often overlooked the indirect impact of power reconfigurations within the system. As heterarchy posits, conflicts across micro-, meso-, and quasi-hierarchies are ongoing, casting uncertainty on policy outputs. However, as observed in EU investment governance, these conflicts have shifted from the national to the regional sphere, implying that regardless of the outcome, the EU will emerge as the guiding authority. While the internal power configuration is dynamic, as suggested by heterarchy, few if any elements suggest that states could successfully counterbalance this process. Thus, the heterarchical setup of the CCP strengthens the European Union. This implies that making sense of complexity could also involve understanding the winners and losers of transnational conflicts captured under heterarchy. Also, further studies are needed to assess the role of states in a heterarchical system. This chapter tends to portray a negative image as the EU gains prominence in investment regulation at the expense of states. However, states remain consistent stakeholders throughout the process; the EU has not replaced them but has gained leverage over them. Nevertheless, when considering the security implications inherent in the focus on "economic security," we may be skeptical that this hypothesis holds true. In essence, does heterarchy empower regional settings beyond trade and investment-related issues? This question warrants further exploration.

Secondly, the chapter scrutinizes the empowerment of the European Union, which opens the Pandora's box of EU global actorness. While politicization and geopoliticization are acknowledged as fueling a shift in the way the EU deals with its trade policy, few authors attempt to make sense of this in terms of global actorness. This seems problematic, as CCP fragmentation has enabled the EU to reshape its economic diplomacy through new means under the concept of Open Strategic Autonomy and De-risking. As EU actorness essentially relies on EU-exclusive trade competency or normative power, it is time to develop new concepts that capture the changes initiated by both politicization and geopoliticization. In essence, could the EU emerge as a consistent geo-economic actor in world affairs? This question prompts further exploration and conceptual development.

Ultimately, this chapter initiates a broader discussion regarding the impact of Brussels-led investment governance on global affairs. Consequently, EU studies and global political economy must scrutinize ongoing shifts and reveal their key features. While this chapter aids in understanding the impact of CCP fragmentation, it fails to address how stakeholders aggregate into the EU policy agenda. Although it provides some insight with lobbying and protests, further research is necessary to identify key stakeholders in the process. In essence, it emphasizes the need for greater consideration of strategically positioned agents driving the integration process. Similarly, additional research is required to comprehend the EU's empowerment in terms of global investment governance. While a Brussels-based agenda is being implemented and promoted, this article suggests few considerations about how this might hinder or enhance global investment regulation. In a time where WTO reform lags, defining the capabilities of regions, or at least the EU, to foster new multilateral solutions is crucial. Should the EU be the primary force fostering real global investment regulation, or is it simply a new stakeholder contributing to the diffusion of global power?

# REFERENCES

Basedow, J. R. (2017). *The EU in the global investment regime: commission entrepreneurship, incremental institutional change and business lethargy.* Routledge. DOI: 10.4324/9781315112282

Basedow, R. (2019). Business lobbying in international investment policy-making in Europe. In Dialer, D., & Richter, M. (Eds.), *Lobbying in the European Union: Strategies, dynamics and trends* (pp. 389–400). DOI: 10.1007/978-3-319-98800-9_28

Basedow, R. (2020). The EU's International Investment Policy ten years on: The Policy-Making Implications of Unintended Competence Transfers. *Journal of Common Market Studies*, 59(3), 643–660. DOI: 10.1111/jcms.13124

BASF (2024). BASF priorities for a competitive Europe. Available at: file:///C:/Users/u233569/Downloads/BASF-Priorities-for-a-Competitive-Europe.pdf

Bauerle Danzman, S., & Meunier, S. (2023). Naïve no more: Foreign direct investment screening in the European Union. *Global Policy*, 14(S3), 40–53. DOI: 10.1111/1758-5899.13215

Bauerle Danzman, S., & Meunier, S. (2024). The EU's Geoeconomic Turn: From Policy Laggard to Institutional Innovator. *Journal of Common Market Studies*, 62(4), 1–19. DOI: 10.1111/jcms.13599

Bohle, D., & Regan, A. (2021). The comparative political economy of growth models: Explaining the continuity of FDI-led growth in Ireland and Hungary. *Politics & Society*, 49(1), 75–106. DOI: 10.1177/0032329220985723

Braun, D., & Grande, E. (2021). Politicizing Europe in elections to the European Parliament (1994–2019): The crucial role of mainstream parties. *Journal of Common Market Studies*, 59(5), 1124–1141. DOI: 10.1111/jcms.13168

Bungenberg, M. (2011). The division of competences between the EU and its member states in the area of investment politics. In Bungenberg, M., & Griebel, J. (Eds.), *Hindelang Steffen. International investment law and EU law* (pp. 29–42). Springer. DOI: 10.1007/978-3-642-14855-2_2

Burnay, M., & Raube, K. (2022). Obstacles, Opportunities, and Red Lines in the European Union: Past and Future of the CAI in Times of (Geo)-Politicisation. *The Journal of World Investment & Trade*, 23(4), 675–699. DOI: 10.1163/22119000-12340265

BusinessEurope. (2016). ETUC – BusinessEurope joint declaration on China's Market Economy Status. Position Paper. Available at: https://www.businesseurope.eu/publications/etuc-businesseurope-joint-declaration-chinas-market-economy-status

Cerny, P. G. (Ed.). (2022). *Heterarchy in world politics*. Routledge. DOI: 10.4324/9781003352617

Chaisse, J. (2012). Promises and Pitfalls of the European Union Policy on Foreign Investment—How will the New EU Competence on FDI affect the Emerging Global Regime? *Journal of International Economic Law*, 15(1), 51–84. DOI: 10.1093/jiel/jgs001

Chan, Z. T., & Meunier, S. (2022). Behind the screen: Understanding national support for a foreign investment screening mechanism in the European Union. *The Review of International Organizations*, 17(3), 513–541. DOI: 10.1007/s11558-021-09436-y PMID: 35719695

Christou, A., & Damro, C. (2024). Frames and Issue Linkage: EU Trade Policy in the Geoeconomic Turn. *Journal of Common Market Studies*, 62(4), 1–17. DOI: 10.1111/jcms.13598

Council of the European Union. (2013). 3266th meeting of the Council of the European Union (foreign affairs) held in Luxembourg on 18 October 2013. Press release – 14845/13. Available at: https://data.consilium.europa.eu/doc/document/ST-15105-2013-INIT/en/pdf

Council of The European Union. (2016). Regulation (EU) 2016/1037 on protection against subsidised imports from countries not members of the European Union. OJ L 176/55 – 30.06.2016. available at: https://eur-lex.europa.eu/legal-content/EN/TXT/PDF/?uri=CELEX:32016R1037

Council of the European Union. (2022). Regulation 2022/1031 on the access of third-country economic operators, goods and services to the Union's public procurement and concession markets and procedures supporting negotiations on access of Union economic operators, goods and services to the public procurement and concession markets of third countries (International Procurement Instrument – IPI). OJ L 171/1 – 30.06.2022. Available at: https://eur-lex.europa.eu/legal-content/EN/TXT/PDF/?uri=CELEX:32022R1031

Council of The European Union. (2023). Regulation (EU) 2023/2675 on the protection of the Union and its Member States from economic coercion by third countries. OJ L – 07.12.2023. available at: https://eur-lex.europa.eu/legal-content/EN/TXT/PDF/?uri=OJ:L_202302675

Council of the European Union. (2023b). G7 Hiroshima Leaders' Communiqué. Press release – 20.05.2023. available at: https://www.consilium.europa.eu/en/press/press-releases/2023/05/20/g7-hiroshima-leaders-communique/

Council of the European Union. (2023c). Remarks by President Charles Michel before the G7 summit in Hiroshima. Remarks by President Charles Michel before the G7 summit in Hiroshima. Press Release – 19.05.2023. available at: https://www.consilium.europa.eu/en/press/press-releases/2023/05/19/remarks-by-president-charles-michel-before-the-g7-summit-in-hiroshima/

Crespy, A., & Rone, J. (2022). Conflicts of sovereignty over EU trade policy: A new constitutional settlement? *Comparative European Politics*, 20(3), 314–335. DOI: 10.1057/s41295-022-00272-x

De Bièvre, D., & Poletti, A. (2020). Towards explaining varying degrees of politicization of EU trade agreement negotiations. *Politics and Governance*, 8(1), 243–253. DOI: 10.17645/pag.v8i1.2686

De Ville, F., & Gheyle, N. (2024). How TTIP split the social-democrats: Reacting to the politicisation of EU trade policy in the European parliament. *Journal of European Public Policy*, 31(1), 54–78. DOI: 10.1080/13501763.2023.2223226

De Wilde, P. (2011). No polity for old politics? A framework for analyzing the politicization of European integration. *Journal of European Integration*, 33(5), 559–575. DOI: 10.1080/07036337.2010.546849

Duchatel M. (2023). Economic Security: the Missing Link in EU-Japan Cooperation. *Institut Montaigne policy paper,* available at: file:///C:/Users/u233569/Downloads/Institut_Montaigne_policy_paper_economic_security_the_missing_link_in_eu_japan_cooperation.pdf

Duina, F. (2019). Why the excitement? Values, identities, and the politicization of EU trade policy with North America. *Journal of European Public Policy*, 26(12), 1866–1882. DOI: 10.1080/13501763.2019.1678056

Eurofer (2019). Eurofer on the global forum on steel excess capacity. Position paper. New EUROFER document

European Commission. (2010). Communication of European Commission: Towards a comprehensive European international investment policy. COM(2010)243. Available at: https://eur-lex.europa.eu/LexUriServ/LexUriServ.do?uri=COM:2010:0343:FIN:EN:PDF

European Commission. (2017a). President Jean Claude Juncker's State of the Union Adress 2017. Speech 17/3165, available at https://ec.europa.eu/commission/presscorner/detail/en/SPEECH_17_3165

European Commission. (2017b). Proposal for establishing a framework for screening of foreign direct investments into the European Union. COM(2017) 487. Available at: https://eur-lex.europa.eu/legal-content/EN/TXT/HTML/?uri=CELEX:52017PC0487&rid=4

European Commission. (2021). Communication – Trade Policy review – An Open Sustainable and Assertive Trade Policy. Com(2021)66, available at: https://eur-lex.europa.eu/resource.html?uri=cellar:5bf4e9d0-71d2-11eb-9ac9-01aa75ed71a1.0001.02/DOC_1&format=PDF

European Commission. (2023). Joint Communication on "European Economic Security Strategy". JOIN(2023) 20, available at https://eur-lex.europa.eu/legal content/EN/TXT/PDF/?uri=CELEX:52023JC0020

European Commission. (2023). President von der Leyen calls for a rebalanced trade relation with China in "Summit of choices". Press release – 08.12.2023. available at: https://ec.europa.eu/commission/presscorner/detail/en/ac_23_6446

European Parliament. (2015). Answer given by Ms Malmström on behalf of the Commission. Parliamentary question E-009974/2014. Available at: https://www.europarl.europa.eu/doceo/document/E-8-2014-009974-ASW_EN.html

European Parliament. (2022). EU international investment policy: Looking ahead. EPRS Brief (PE 729.276). Available at: https://www.europarl.europa.eu/RegData/etudes/BRIE/2022/729276/EPRS_BRI(2022)729276_EN.pdf

European Parliament and European Council. (2019). Regulation (EU) establishing a framework for the screening of foreign direct investments into the Union. OJ L 79 1/1 – 21.03.2019. Available at: https://eur-lex.europa.eu/legal-content/EN/TXT/PDF/?uri=CELEX:32019R0452

European Union (2012). Consolidated Version of the Treaty on the functioning of the European Union. OJ C 326/47 – 26. at: eur-lex.europa.eu/legal-content/EN/TXT/PDF/?uri=CELEX:12012E/TXTDOI: 10.2012. Available

Gehrke, T. (2020). After Covid-19: Economic security in EU-Asia connectivity. *Asia Europe Journal*, 18(1), 239–243. DOI: 10.1007/s10308-020-00579-y PMID: 32837473

Godement, F. (2022). The EU-China Comprehensive Agreement on Investment: Context and Content. *Asia Europe Journal*, 20(1), 59–64. DOI: 10.1007/s10308-021-00622-6

Hanemann, T. & Huotari M. (2017). Record flows and growing imbalances: Chinese investment in Europe in 2016. Merics research paper on China. Available at: MPOC_03_Update_COFDI.indd (merics.org)

Hopewell, K. (2022). Beyond US-China Rivalry: Rule Breaking, Economic Coercion, and the Weaponization of Trade. In: Shaffer H. *Governing the interface of U.S.-China Trade relations*. 58-63

Hurrelmann, A., & Wendler, F. (2024). How does politicisation affect the ratification of mixed EU trade agreements? The case of CETA. *Journal of European Public Policy*, 31(1), 157–181. DOI: 10.1080/13501763.2023.2202196

Huysseune, M., & Paquin, S. (2023). Paradiplomacy and the European Union's trade treaty negotiations: The role of Wallonia and Brussels. *Territory, Politics, Governance*, •••, 1–20. DOI: 10.1080/21622671.2023.2181207

Jacobs, T., Gheyle, N., De Ville, F., & Orbie, J. (2023). The hegemonic politics of 'strategic autonomy' and 'resilience': COVID-19 and the dislocation of EU trade policy. *Journal of Common Market Studies*, 61(1), 3–19. DOI: 10.1111/jcms.13348 PMID: 35936871

Llano, C., Pérez, J., El Khatabi, F., & Steinberg, F. (2021). Weaponized trade policy: The impact of US tariffs on the European automobile sector. *Economic Systems Research*, 33(3), 287–315. DOI: 10.1080/09535314.2020.1804330

Makarenko, A., & Chernikova, L. (2020). "New Generation" EU Free Trade Agreements: A Combination of Traditional and Innovative Mechanisms. In: Kovalchuk J. *Post-Industrial Society: The Choice Between Innovation and Tradition*, 109-122.

Meunier, S. (2014). Divide and conquer? China and the cacophony of foreign investment rules in the EU. *Journal of European Public Policy*, 21(7), 996–1016. DOI: 10.1080/13501763.2014.912145

Mcunier, S., & Nicolaidis, K. (2019). The geopoliticization of European trade and investment policy. *J. Common Mkt.Stud.*, 57, 103.

Migliorati, M., & Vignoli, V. (2022). When politicization meets ideology: the European Parliament and free trade agreements. *Italian Political Science Review/ Rivista Italiana Di Scienza Politica,* 52(3), 346-361.

Narlikar, A. (2022). Trade governance: the politics of prosperity, development and weaponization. In: Rüland J. & Carrapatoso A. *Handbook on Global Governance and Regionalism* (pp. 334-349). Edward Elgar Publishing.

OECD. (2022). Framework for screening foreign direct investment into the EU: Assessing effectiveness and efficiency. OECD report. Available at: https://www.oecd.org/daf/inv/investment-policy/oecd-eu-fdi-screening-assessment.pdf

Regan, A., & Brazys, S. (2021). Celtic phoenix or leprechaun economics? The politics of an FDI-led growth model in Europe. In Johnston, A., & Regan, A. (Eds.), *Is the European Union Capable of Integrating Diverse Models of Capitalism?* (pp. 79–94). Routledge. DOI: 10.4324/9781003158455-6

Reinisch, A. (2013). The scope of investor-state dispute settlement in international investment agreements. *Asia Pacific Law Review*, 21(1), 3–26. DOI: 10.1080/10192557.2013.11788264

Riga, D. (2022). Socialization through Interregional Relations: EU's Normative Power in its Dialogue with China. In: *The Twelfth International Convention of Asia Scholars (ICAS 12)*. Amsterdam University Press. 583-593

Roederer-Rynning, C. (2017). Parliamentary assertion and deep integration: The European parliament in the CETA and TTIP negotiations. *Cambridge Review of International Affairs*, 30(5-6), 507–526. DOI: 10.1080/09557571.2018.1461808

Rosenau, J. N. (2000). The governance of fragmegration: Neither a world republic nor a global interstate system. *Studia Diplomatica*, 15-39.

Siles-Brügge, G., & Strange, M. (2020). National autonomy or transnational solidarity? Using multiple geographic frames to politicize EU trade policy. *Politics and Governance*, 8(1), 277–289.

Vlasiuk Nibe, A., Meunier, S., & Roederer-Rynning, C. (2024). Pre-emptive depoliticisation: The European Commission and the EU foreign investment screening regulation. *Journal of European Public Policy*, 31(1), 182–211. DOI: 10.1080/13501763.2023.2258153

Woolcock, S. (2011). *European Union economic diplomacy: The role of the EU in external economic relations*. Ashgate.

Young, A. R. (2019). Two wrongs make a right? The politicization of trade policy and European trade strategy. *Journal of European Public Policy*, 26(12), 1883–1899. DOI: 10.1080/13501763.2019.1678055

Zürn, M., Binder, M., & Ecker-Ehrhardt, M. (2012). International authority and its politicization. *International Theory*, 4(1), 69–106. DOI: 10.1017/S1752971912000012

## KEY TERMS AND DEFINITIONS

**EU Empowerment:** Reflects how the EU's actorness is enhanced by new developments within the regional organization. This empowerment can refer to the acquisition of new competencies, changes in its internal structure that improve efficiency, or the introduction of new tools to ensure greater consistency.

**Geopoliticization:** Is defined as the integration of strategic objectives into trade policy. It refers to the EU's geo-economic shift, often described as part of the global weaponization of trade interdependence. In essence, geopoliticization could be seen as the development of an EU economic statecraft.

**Global Investment Governance:** Cannot be confined to a single shared definition. For the purposes of this article, it will be considered as the global negotiation process aimed at establishing common rules for investment regulation. In this context, stakeholders in global investment governance may include private actors, regions, states, or international organizations (IOs).

**Global Politics:** Is a response to the classical framing of international politics. While both deal with world affairs, international politics emphasizes the nation-state, whereas global politics considers the state as one unit of analysis among others, including transnational actors.

**Heterarchy:** Is a concept that defines system structure by combining both hierarchy and anarchy. According to Heterarchy world politics is structure of various nodes which hierarchies vary across time and issues.

**Politicization:** Is defined as the growing public awareness of trade agreements or any trade-related issues. Accordingly, politicization is a bottom-up process in which public opinion plays a key role in mobilizing the political arena, either in support of or opposition to a specific economic decision.

**Regionalism:** Is a research field that studies the proliferation of cooperative frameworks among states on a regional basis. While the EU often serves as a common unit of analysis, regionalism is a broad field that embraces comparative approaches to reveal key features of the diverse regional frameworks.

# ENDNOTES

[1]    Made in China 2025 is a national development programme enacted by Beijing in 2015. It seeks to promote Chinese champions, in particular technological firms, for internal consumption and world competition.

[2]    The anti-subsidy regulation empowers the EU to sanctions goods that are subsidied by a non-EU country when it enters the single market. The main principle being: 'A countervailing duty may be imposed to offset any subsidy granted, directly or indirectly, for the manufacture, production, export or transport of any product whose release for free circulation in the Union causes injury (COEU, 2016,4)'.

[3]    The anti-coercion instrument empowers the EU to respond to non-EU state coercion by sanctions. As presented in 2023: 'This Regulation establishes a framework for the Union to respond to economic coercion with the objective of deterring economic coercion or obtaining the cessation of economic coercion, whilst enabling the Union, as a last resort, to counteract economic coercion through Union response measures'. (COEU, 2023, 7)

[4]    The international procurement instrument empowers the EU to prevent the access of third countries on the single market public procurement. As presented in 2023: 'This Regulation provides for the possibility for the Commission to impose IPI measures in relation to such third-country measures or practices to restrict the access of economic operators, goods or services from third countries to Union public procurement procedures' (COEU, 2022, 6).

# Chapter 9
# From a State–Centric System to a Cosmopolitan International System:
## Exploring Political Participation and the West Philippine Sea Issue in a Decentralized World

**Aileen Joy Adion Pactao**
https://orcid.org/0009-0007-7276-042X
*Palawan State University, Philippines*

## ABSTRACT

*Globalization has been transforming the nature and characteristics of the present state-centric international system. Specifically, the process of fragmentation, decentralization, and internationalization associated with the promotion of neoliberal globalization altered the role of the state from being the only proactive player in the international arena to becoming more and more reactive. The proliferation of different specialized regimes into areas previously controlled and dominated by the state (e.g., trade law, environmental law, and human rights), international institutions sanctioned by intergovernmental organizations undermining the Westphalian constitutional concepts of state sovereignty, and the prevalence of internet governance and cybersecurity concerns reflect the emergence of post-internationalism and heterarchical governance as an alternative.*

DOI: 10.4018/979-8-3693-3563-5.ch009

## INTRODUCTION

Globalization has been transforming the nature and characteristics of the international system (Ip, 2010; Brown, 2014) which is traditionally perceived as state-centric or a system of states where all actions and institutions are under their control. Due to increasing [varied] manifestations challenging and dismantling or deconstructing this classic perception of the international system, several scholars (Abbott & Snidal, 2009; Ramjit, 2023) argued that post-internationalism and heterarchical governance will be better alternatives because they enhance actors' resilience against international crises or challenges and there are diversified channels of cooperation that reduce dependencies on single actors or institutions (Abbott & Snidal, 2009; Ramjit, 2023). Particularly, this change is currently manifested by the proliferation of different specialized regimes into areas previously controlled and dominated by the state (e.g., trade law, environmental law, and human rights), international institutions sanctioned by intergovernmental organizations undermining the Westphalian constitutional concepts of state sovereignty (Ip, 2010; Brown, 2014), and the prevalence of internet governance and cybersecurity concerns.

Despite these seemingly undeniable manifestations of post-internationalism and heterarchy, some scholars (e.g., Cox, 1991; Slaughter, 2004) are still uncertain and antagonistic as to the implications. They argued that heterarchical governance may lead to further fragmentation and inefficiency since there will be overlapping institutions and competing interests among various players that may hinder effective institutional implementation. Also, it might reinforce existing power imbalances, where powerful states and groups exert dominant influence over decision-making processes, leaving less powerful actors marginalized and voiceless (Cox, 1991; Slaughter, 2004). These qualms strengthen the assertions of realism, a classic International Relations (IR) theory, that states are and will remain primary actors in an anarchic international system and that their behavior is significantly defined by self-interest and the pursuit of power to survive.

The 'anarchic' nature[1] of the international system forces the states to pursue security[2] and power maximization[3] and will persist as they are fundamental facilitators of international relations. Moreover, liberalism affirms the centrality of states in the [anarchic] international system – they are viewed as important players; however, their behavior is not solely defined by power calculations. Instead, states can and should cooperate with one another in addressing common threats or challenges and advance shared goals through diplomatic processes, international organizations, and other means of cooperation. While these conventional IR theories still hold their respective truth in the international system, contemporary realities manifest a new landscape. This centrality resulted in an overburdened state like the Philippines. Specifically, the Philippines is presently struggling to meet its different responsibilities effectively as shown by its high debt levels, inflation, high unemployment and underemployment rates, inequality, social unrest, bureaucratic inefficiency, corruption, dependency on foreign aid, and some signs of service delivery failures (e.g., policy inconsistencies, nepotism). These limitations of the seemingly overburdened state necessitate the recognition of the advantage of the existing institutions and structures that advance sustainability.

Particularly, in the 21st century, multi-nodal and heterarchic'[4] world politics is increasingly taking over the center stage of the international system. Hence, it denotes a paradigm shift away from "competing classic International Relations (IR) theories" which include realism, liberalism, and constructivism that specifically and consistently argue on the centrality and fundamentality of the state as the central actor in the international system. Further, it is argued that the growing numbers of nonstate actors undermine the relevance of the state or the notion of national sovereignty (Ansell & Trondal, 2017; Bellamy, 2017; Abbott & Snidal, 2009) which resulted in multicentrism – a system where states coexist with other and many actors. This system seems to be an endearing feature of the post-international world. Following Rosenau's (1990) theory of post-internationalism, the international system is experiencing changing orientations and shifting authority among diverse actors; the anarchic structure that sustains and facilitates international relations seems to be unsettling now and experiencing inevitable 'restructuring'. Also, the emergence of internet and digital platforms, facilitating instant communication and mobilization across borders, undermines the traditional control states have over information. Hence, it makes the country's national security vulnerable to the cybersecurity attack from state and non-state actors, such as hackers and terrorist organizations.

This paper aims to examine whether or not there is a declining role of the state or just a mere refashioning or rebranding of the state's role in an evolving international environment influenced by globalization [and interdependence] through analyzing the available secondary literature (or body of knowledge) buttressed with the utilization of various international realities or events. Specifically, the exploration focuses on (a) demystifying the three essential concepts – anarchy, hierarchy, and heterarchy, (b) navigating the state-centric system and the cosmopolitical international system, and (c) implications of post-internationalism and heterarchical governance to contemporary international relations. This includes also the assessment of the effects of this seemingly alternative international system that may hinder or facilitate the effectiveness of ASEAN as a non-hierarchical structure in addressing the West Philippine Sea issue and the digital political participation in the Philippines. By taking these matters into account, useful policy lessons can be drawn that may facilitate better relationships, cooperation, and coordination between international actors despite the limitations and negative implications of this so-called alternative.

## Demystifying the Three Concepts: Anarchy, Hierarchy, and Heterarchy

The complete understanding of anarchy, hierarchy, and heterarchy is fundamental for examining different forms of governance and social structures.

Anarchy is defined as a system characterized by having no central authority which imposes limits on the pursuit of interests by the state (Oye, 1985; Wendt, 1992); hence, can anytime trigger the occurrence of a war. It is further claimed that an anarchic international system has no overarching hierarchical order (Cerny, 2023) where states may compete or cooperate with one another in order to survive. As a result, relationships in an anarchic environment are defined by concert and war, arms control and arms races, trade agreements and trade wars, financial aid and economic crisis, and monetary stabilization and competitive currency devaluation. At times, states compete with one another because they cannot completely surrender control over a supranational sovereign; yet, at other times, they do realize common goals through cooperation under anarchy. These viewpoints are associated with realism wherein its later spinoff is "neorealism" (Waltz, 1979 in Wendt, 1992). It argues that states are inherently set up in a hierarchical mode domestically – they are analytically unique, bureaucratically ordered, and endogenously sovereign units leading to a perception of "hierarchy-within-anarchy" (Cerny, 2023).

Hierarchy, in contrast to anarchy, represents a structured system where entities are organized according to rank, authority, power, or status. It facilitates a clear line of command, authority, and responsibility which can result in efficiency and coordination. However, it can lead to power imbalances, lack of innovation and participatory mechanisms, and inequality.

Heterarchy is the less familiar concept among the three. It is a system of organization where elements are not hierarchical but, co-equal (flat structure). With the advent of globalization, societal elements are significantly being homogenized[5] facilitated through the hegemony of neoliberal ideology (Cerny, 2020 in Cerny 2023), socio-cultural convergence, economic interconnectedness, liberal institutionalism, technological intensification and innovation, and the emergence of a so-called "flat world" (Friedman, 2005). Heterarchical manifestations are cited by various theorists (e.g., Schotte, 2000; Root, 2013; Spalinska, 2023; Rosenau, 1990; Hameiri & Jones, 2023; Macdonald & Macdonald, 2020; Belmonte, 2023) as cited by Cerny (2023) such as functional differentiation," "multiscalarity", "deterritorialization," disparate "landscapes", "neomedievalism", "fragmegration", "state transformation", or a "pluralist world order".

*Table 1. Comparative analysis of these three concepts*

| Concepts | Anarchy | Hierarchy | Heterarchy |
|---|---|---|---|
| *Distribution of Authority* | Decentralized | Centralized | Flexible & Context-dependent |
| *Decision-making* | Voluntary & Autonomous | Top-down approach | Collaborative & participatory |
| **Order & Structure** | No formal structure | Rigid and ranked | Flexible & network-like |

These three fundamental concepts in political science and international relations vary in terms of how they characterize the *distribution of authority, decision-making process, and order and structure*. Particularly, anarchy is a decentralized system where states can voluntarily do their preferences and wants and, since they are equally sovereign with one another, the system has no formal structure. On the other hand, hierarchy is a centralized system with a top-down decision-making process, and has a formal structure that is ranked and determined according to certain standards. Heterarchy is a context-based and flexible system that facilitates collaborative and participatory decision-making processes and has a flexible and network-like structure and order. This is viewed to be responsive and dynamic [see Table 1].

Generally, demystifying these concepts first allows us to navigate whether or not there has been a paradigm shift from a traditional state-centric system to a cosmopolitical system. This is an interesting focus of contemporary discussions as the state itself, in this globalized era, has become a globalizing agent facilitating its own disaggregation (Cerny, 1997; Genschel & Seelkopf, 2015).

## Navigating Two Worlds: State-centric System and the Cosmopolitical International System

The mainstream International Relations (IR) theories (e.g., realism, neorealism, constructivism, liberalism, and neoliberalism) view states as transhistorical actors - unitary, territorially bounded, exercising exclusive sovereign. This has been very prevalent in the late 19th century until a few decades after World War II (Jones & Hameiri, 2023). In this state-centric system, state sovereignty, territorial integrity, and the principle of non-intervention govern the interactions and conflicts between states. They are posited as sovereign entities that possess ultimate authority within their borders, responsible for conducting foreign policy, represent their people's interests on the global stage, and ensuring national security. They act based on their [respective] national interests – weighing opportunities and rationally maximizing their power and security[6]. Despite the emergence of non-state actors (e.g., multinational corporations, international organizations, and transnational advocacy networks), the state remains the predominant actor demonstrating significant influence over global affairs.

This changed since the late 1970s when the classic 'state centric' system has been transformed by processes of *fragmentation, decentralization, and internationalization* associated with the promotion of neoliberal globalization. States are no longer the only 'proactive' players but tend to be more and more 'reactive'. Their state capacity became entangled in these hybrid structures and processes facilitated by globalization (Cerny, 2023). The transformation, in this sense, was a necessary condition for the processes characterized as heterarchy to emerge. Further, it underscores that the modern politics demands a new perspective that takes into account the dynamic changes in the international system (Ramjit, 2023) often manifested as concerns or struggles.

Global issues identified by Ramjit (2023) as "turbulence" (e.g., climate change, global terrorism, financial instability, migration, failed states, humanitarian crises and conflicts, pandemics, nuclear weapon) [are argued to have] revealed the declining relevance, impact, and appeal of the states as the traditional unit actors of the international system. Particularly, there has been an undeniable dissatisfaction with the effectiveness of the state to address a range of critical policy concerns (Belmonte & Cerny, 2021); thus, instead of states, individuals are now active players as technology mobilized them to acquire vast data needed to make politically sound decisions.

Change has become the defining fate of the international system. For the proponents of post-internationalism and heterarchical governance, the phenomenon of globalization has eroded the sovereignty of states and resulted in the increasing proliferation of non-state actors (e.g., multi-national corporations, non-governmental organizations, and other networks) as alternatives operating within the traditional territories or areas of states. State transformation became an essential prerequisite for the emergence of heterarchical system (Jones & Hameiri, 2023) and the dialectic of fragmentation and globalization (Cerny & Prichard, 2018 in Ramjit, 2023) caught states and the interstate system in 'heterarchical' process centered on the 'disaggregation of state' (Slaughter, 2004). The policymaking processes and bureaucratic institutions are now embedded in distinct issue-contexts and sectors than centripetal state structures, governance became fragmented along with "regime complexes" (Alter & Raustiala 2018), and the context "functional differentiation." Simply, state actors and structures have less and less "state capacity" to act as "unit actors" in world politics because globalization disperses political power among an increasingly complex structure of societal forces and levels of governance that transform the traditional anarchic and state-centric global political system (Cerny, 2010) in which domestic politics and international relations intersect.

*For example*, the Association of Southeast Asian Nations (ASEAN) is characterized by a non-hierarchical structure since the decision-making power is distributed among its member states rather than concentrated in a central authority. Through this system, cooperative and consensual approach to regional issues, manifesting mutual respect, non-interference, and collective decision-making are evident. Each member country retains sovereignty and engages as an equal platform contributing to a flexible and dynamic political arena. This heterarchical nature of ASEAN allows it to address various political, cultural, and economic contexts of the members effectively, facilitating regional stability and integration while respecting national autonomy.

Another relevant context is the notion of *digital political participation*. The presence of digital platforms complements the decentralized and non-hierarchical nature of heterarchical governance. Particularly, social media platforms and other digital tools enable people to engage directly with policymakers, share their perspective, and influence decision-making processes. This nature and level of participation denotes democratization or trickling down of political engagement, providing a space for grassroots movements and marginalized communities to be heard on a larger scale. With this, digital political participation enhances collaboration and integration. Moreover, this digital connectivity promotes the heterarchical principles of inclusivity and consensus-building because people are empowered to share information and ideas across borders.

However, this also poses challenges, such as the need to address digital divides, misinformation, and varying levels of internet freedom among member states. Further, in the Philippines, widespread utilization of social media platforms transformed how campaigns are done and how citizens engage with candidates and political issues. These platforms provide a decentralized and inclusive form of participation, where voters can access information, engage in discussions, and express their views without the traditional barriers of geography and socio-economic status. On the other hand, the political candidates invest on these digital tools to connect with a broader audience, engage directly with voters, and mobilize support.

These mentioned contexts are just some of the visible manifestations of heterarchical governance. Nevertheless, there are still reasonable arguments to retain a focus on state power in today's context. First, despite that state capacity appears to be weaker today than the postwar period, for Cerny (2023), it is misleading to assert that states are "vulnerable and impotent," because it will distort the reality and put state managers off the hook. He argued that we must note that it is these people [state managers] who have promoted and enabled globalization and thus conspire in their own transformation. States, simply, retain the most important functions that other groups cannot perform.

# Implications of Post-internationalism and Heterarchical Governance

Post-internationalism and heterarchical governance have profound implications – shaping how global and regional politics are conducted. These two big concepts (characterized by distributed power and non-hierarchical decision-making) facilitate greater cooperation and adaptability among diverse actors, including states, non-governmental organizations, and transnational entities. The contemporary context of the global system, embraced by different issues that are no longer within the control of the states, calls for heterarchical governance approaches. In this section, the *author* highlights a few implications of post-internationalism and heterarchical governance based on contemporary dealings of the Philippines.

## West Philippine Sea and ASEAN

The West Philippine Sea is one of the most talked territorial issues in Southeast Asia. Due to the resources available (e.g., rich fishing grounds and potentially contain gas and oil deposits) and strategic location (Gacal, 2013), China, Malaysia, Vietnam, Brunei, Taiwan, Indonesia, and the Philippines are asserting their respective rights for fishing, oil exploration and gas deposits, and ownership of the islands for almost three decades. These contradicting claims over the past decades led to harassment and detention of fishermen, military skirmishes, change in the foreign policy landscape, a series of diplomatic talks, travel bans, and even strains on economic relations.

This territorial issue necessitates heterarchical approaches as this matter is not just an exclusive concern of a single state. Because of this, multilateral treaties like the United Nations Convention on the Law of the Sea (UNCLOS), bilateral and multilateral dialogues like the ASEAN-China negotiations on the Code of Conduct, and joint development proposals are the diverse approaches to settling the conflict and governing this issue. Hence, heterarchical framework present opportunities for cooperative resource management, environmental protection, and enhanced regional stability.

Furthermore, because the issue rests on the overlapping claims of the involved countries driven by historical, legal, and economic factors, traditional state-centric approaches to governance are being challenged. The Association of Southeast Asian Nations (ASEAN), in this regard, plays an important role in the heterarchical governance of the West Philippine Sea by facilitating cooperation and dialogue between member states and external powers. There are efforts to mediate and promote stability (e.g., China negotiations on the Code of Conduct (COC) in the South China Sea). Despite the inevitable differences in terms of the national interests of its member states, the organization serves as a multilateral mechanism for engagement, underscoring the importance of cooperation and dialogue in addressing this complex maritime concern.

Particularly, the heterarchical governance in the West Philippine Sea is reflected by the involvement and interaction of multiple actors, including states, international organizations, NGOs describing a decentralized governance. Within the heterarchical governance nature of ASEAN, addressing the West Philippine Sea issue requires a delicate balance between diplomatic efforts and interests. By guaranteeing that members have equal standing in terms of decision-making, ASEAN facilitates a platform where members voice their perspectives and standpoints about the issue hence a consensus-based decision-making (e.g., Declaration on the Conduct of Parties in the South China Sea). It provides a space for a more nuanced and inclusive dialogue, which is significant given the complex geopolitical dynamics of this territorial issue.

However, the heterarchical model also reflects challenges in dealing with the dispute. The requirement for consensus in various decision-making processes slows down diplomatic actions making it difficult to present a united front against the China's aggressiveness. Also, the varying national interests and degrees of economic and political influence from China complicates efforts to have a cohesive regional strategy. Nonetheless, ASEAN's role in this issue remains vital. By leveraging its heterarchical governance, the regional organization can continue to facilitate diplomatic efforts, foster mutual understanding, and introduce reasonable solutions to protect and uphold regional peace and stability.

## Political Participation in a Decentralized Network

The design of the internet as a decentralized network is supposed to empower the *demos* to freely associate and share ideas and information. However, it becomes a convenient platform for economic giants to earn more, for the vulnerable *demos* to become more vulnerable, and for opportunistic politicians to benefit a lot, particularly, during elections. Specifically, this situation characterizes communicative capitalism.

According to Dean (2014), communicative capitalism is "a form of late capitalism in which 'values' heralded as crucial to democracy materialize in networked communication technologies. Specifically, the expansion, intensification, and interconnection of global communications facilitate the ideals of access, inclusion, discussion, and participation." In this system, the expropriation and exploitation of communicative processes reflect capitalist productivity. Communication serves as the capital hence, it is seized, privatized, and monetized. As such, it does not depend on commodity-thing, rather it directly exploits the social relations at heart.

The social field of communicative capitalism involves division, inequality, and competition thus, it is not an arena of rational deliberation and democratic decision-making (Dean, 2014). It is an information environment where number matters more than the content, where civilized and legitimate discourses are defeated by highly emotional, divisive, and polarized thinking, where 'how many' takes the place of 'how come and why', and where correlation displaces causation (Dean, 2014). In this sense, democracy is just a marketing slogan of this digital capitalism and information seems a commodity. As a consequence, with the advent of technology, disinformation has become a serious matter of concern. It has been well-sheltered and furthered in platforms where the *demos* are more vulnerable to deceit and manipulation hence, jeopardizing their belief system and political engagement. Their data are being collected by numerous social media sites (likely owned by Facebook or Google) (Lamdan, 2019), and their behavior is being manipulated by corporate algorithms seeking profits and political power. And, because anyone can be a content creator, anyone can have the opportunity to earn out of whatever social media engagement. This reality follows Metcalfe's Law which states that "the value of communication networks is proportional to the square of the number of its users." This implies that the more people are using it, the more valuable it is. As such, the platform rewards the spread of information regardless of its validity and reliability; it incentivizes users to spread lies with no [considerable] punishment system to those who exploit content for personal gain.

Significantly, since content or information has a corresponding [monetary] value, the *demos* who exist in an economically hierarchical and pyramidal society (a capitalist society) compete to earn or gain. Political discourses become money-driven and are fueled by emotions, deception, manipulation, and hatred. The *demos* are divided and conquered by opportunistic politicians and business or tech giants who strategically and systematically invested resources and efforts to realize economic and electoral ambitions through 'extraction' from the vulnerability of the *demos*.

Some of the *demos* who are already vulnerable due to their socioeconomic circumstances, which results in their rational ignorance, become more vulnerable due to their inevitable exposure to disinformation – false content - that heavily shapes or alters their preferences, belief system, and even political stances. Their economic struggle puts them into a more 'helpless' situation where deceit and manipulation prevail; this susceptibility becomes an opportunity by those who have access to the capital (*communication*) and machinery (e.g., digital platforms) to gain or extract benefits. For example, Public Relations (PR) firms are hired that spread lies on behalf of corporate and political clients (Silverman et al., 2020).

The status of the Filipino *demos* in this situation is called as 'double vulnerability'. To argue on this, the following instances revealed the vulnerabilities of the country's democracy to disinformation: *(a) Polarized Political Discourses and (2) Electoral Realities in the Philippines.*

*Polarized Political Discourses.* A well-informed citizenry is argued to be a prerequisite of thriving democracy because they have the ability to facilitate healthy political discourses which can deliver many advantages to society. Thus, a healthy political discourse is a vital component of a well-functioning democracy. Furthermore, meaningful political discourse is characterized as the honest, constructive, respectful, inclusive, and evidence-based exchange of ideas or dialogue between and among the *demos*. It serves as their platform to make their sentiments be heard, discussed and carried out in the discussion table.

However, the capitalist structure of society is one of the barriers that hinder some *demos* from taking their part actively. Other limitations can be associated with the *demos'* cognitive biases where they tend to focus on data that fit their existing beliefs and discount evidence that conflicts with them, and some deal with emotionally engaging information even to the extent of discounting evidence that is more systematic and robust. Also, changes in the media over recent decades led to a novel news landscape that weakens traditional journalism and, through social media, removed filters on access to the public realm. Every *demos* now acts as a content creator or reporter who increasingly focuses on 'clickbait', and has very limited resources for knowledgeable reporting. With this, it can be argued that while the presence of social media may have democratized political participation in public debate, it has also amplified the creation and dissemination of lies or false content, extreme voices, conspiracy theories, and abuse. Simply, political discourses become polarized. *Demos* have the greater tendency to believe 'facts' from one's own side while disregarding those from the other side; and a willingness to demonize rather than respect those with different views.

Regrettably, the democratization of discourses due to the advent of information technology (which is supposedly advantageous) privileges the Philippine *demos* to utilize communicative abundance in cyberspace as a tool to advance their causes and silence the critics. In this sense, communicative capitalism pointed out that communication is not facilitated for the purpose of sincere political discourses but to gain or earn. Manufactured facts, theories, judgments, opinions, fantasies, jokes, and lies circulate indiscriminately. Communicative production is for circulation more than use (getting attention not furthering understanding); it works because it capitalizes on rational ignorance disguised as political awareness (Dean, 2014). Noting this, again, while social media democratizes, it defeats and disregards the purpose of political discourses. People now create a fantasy that when they are expressing opinions online [regardless of the content], it constitutes a democratic potential. Indeed, communicative abundance is a double-edged sword.

Not only the Philippine *demos*, elected people can also escape from their responsibility and accountability by contributing to the circulation of social media content thereby shaping information consumption that can affect people's opinions and participation (Dean 2014). This communicative abundance narrows down spaces for reliable articles or news while providing more room for soundbites, scandalous comments, gossip, and unverified news. Political participation, in this sense, is a function of falsehood and deceit. It is no longer based on the veracity of the content, but by how long these data are being consumed and disseminated. Also, noting that competition, division, and inequality are prevalent in the social field of communicative capitalism, those who have an upper hand in this resource will exploit those who have minimal to no access to these platforms hence, influencing how they decide and what will be their decision. Clearly, this is not an arena we can view in terms of a public sphere of rational deliberation and democratic decision-making, instead, this is a situation where numbers are more significant than content. Disinformation becomes a tool for a government to shape domestic and international opinion and make it favorable for itself. And, it fuels hate speech against the marginalized and excluded and undermines shared humanity.

The second contributing factor boils down to the traditional divide between the privileged class of society and powerless, disenfranchised segments of society that are often accused of being "*bobotante.*" This label discounts the fact that these people barely have access to information resources and platforms hence, some are not able to participate, if not truly participate (Untalan, 2018). Because of this, despite that people have now become very political compared to before, the practice of politics becomes alienating. The use of derogatory terms by the Philippine *demos* and even the mainstream to discredit the claims of the *demos* they oppose widens the gaps between them and leaves no space for meaningful discourse. The real issue does not solely lie in the unequal access to information resources and platforms but also to finger pointing "who is who" during crucial political decision-making. The polarization of public opinion has become the defining element of today's democratic society.

For example, in the case of Die-Hard Duterte Supporters (DDS), the political hardliners, who support President Duterte despite controversy after controversy, viewed his politics as a necessary evil and that, it is the only way to enact meaningful change in the country (Rappler, 2021). They have their own media arms that provide news content wherein the main goal is to secure high engagements among digital users to market their preferred candidate. They only consume what news they have produced and often ridicule or label mainstream news and reporters as biased, paid, and insulting. The good news for them is only those that reflect the good deeds of the person that they are supporting. Because of these mechanisms, the Duterte Administration was successful in undermining the credibility of the mainstream media, hence, people looked for an alternative, that is a less regulated platform – social media. The mainstream media was maligned by producing and spreading narratives that are often labeled as "fake news" or alternative truths. Former President Duterte presented the critical mainstream media as a willing and convenient arm of the political elites. Through the consistent launch of a rapid-fire salvo of insults and expletives against the "biased" and "bayaran" (paid-hacked) media, President Duterte successfully marshaled public support among Filipino social media users to fight and abandon them (Divinagracia, n.d.).

Moreover, social media had an important role in the 2022 Philippine national elections characterized by "disinformation narratives of authoritarian nostalgia, strongman leadership, conspiracy theory, and democratic disillusionment", which furthered support for President Bongbong Marcos Jr. and undermined other candidates (Arugay & Baquisal, 2022). Generally, the presence of online platforms has dramatically expanded and simplified access to information and debates, while doing the same for the potential means of participation. It has significantly altered political mobilization - both in the positive and negative sense. It may have furthered the platforms for the *demos'* engagement, but it has also been used to divide them by spreading hate speech, lies, and conspiracy theories. Fueled by anonymity online, public debate has become uncivilized, personal, emotional, and harsher in recent years. Those who argue differently are no longer recognized and respected; those who confirm and support are welcomed and embraced. Personal attacks and insults have replaced reasoned argument and debate.

*Electoral Realities in the Philippines.* After years of utilizing only the traditional platforms of political participation, people have slowly innovated and improved them by expanding the physical world of electoral campaigns to virtual platforms. Social media have democratized political participation in the Philippines because the *demos* who are normally marginalized from political discourses and limitedly accessed public information were now given opportunities through the accessibility of social networking sites such as Facebook and Twitter (Untalan, 2018).

This role of social media in electoral participation was highly evident during the 2016 elections which can be labeled as the "first social media election' (Buenaobra 2016) and the recent 2022 elections (Arugay & Baquisal, 2022). There are more than 41 million active Facebook users between the ages of 18 and 65 in the country and Facebook has been the most utilized platform during elections. It became the lifeline of information (or misinformation) (Buenaobra, 2016). Moreover, in a survey conducted in 2020, Filipinos rank first globally in internet usage with an average daily screen time of 10 hours and almost 50% of adults use the internet. More importantly, a third of the 61 million-strong Philippine electorates are from the 18-35 age bracket, where perhaps the majority of social media users actually belong. Thus, with respect to the numbers, they have the power to define the interplay of social media and democracy since they are within a volatile and divisive political battle.

Additionally, social media platforms discredited traditional campaign strategies by rendering them insufficient, dividing voters between "them" and "us," and manipulating the content of political discourses. The presence of technologies intensified the interconnections of communications which are reflected through moving beyond physical borders. Under this system, economics dominates politics – and with this domination comes different forms of ruthlessness. Disinformation is deliberately and strategically incentivized by those who have ulterior motives (e.g., political elites, corporate elites). Deceit, lies, manipulation, hatred, and conspiracy theories have characterized the discourses. These forms of content gain more attention and engagement as they are sensational, emotional, and monetized. Because of this, unfortunately, the country is sliding into a full-blown authoritarianism that rests on falsehood and deception. Those in power lie, cheat, and steal through unwitting consent as people would blindly and unquestioningly adhere to whatever these people would say despite how little truth there is. These powerful individuals can sway the vulnerable *demos* to produce more falsehoods for them to either drum up support for otherwise unpopular policies, destroy or silence opponents, or even both (Eusebio, 2022).

As reflected, disinformation thrives in a politically demobilized society, that is, a society in which the *demos* pay no attention to the operations of the government. It seems that every apathetic citizen is a silent enlistee in the cause of inverted totalitarianism and communicative capitalism. However, it must be noted that this 'apathy' is not just an outcome of whatever culture but also, a political response banking on distrust and frustrations. Inverted totalitarianism evolves from "a continuing and increasingly unequal struggle between an unrealized democracy and an antidemocracy that dares not speak its name" (Wolin, 2008). Despite the familiar elements of a democratic system such as popular elections, free political parties, the three branches of government, and a bill of rights, however, these go otherwise – the operations are different from the formal structure. As a consequence, the combination of widespread disinformation and growing political polarization becomes a grave threat to the Philippines' already fragile democracy.

Generally, while heterarchical governance or structure is considered a good alternative to status quo, taking into account its inherent limitations can guide us on how to favorably maximize its utilities or benefits.

## Policy Implications

Based on the insights drawn from the discussion, the following are the possible implications to existing policies:

Revisiting traditional IR approaches and accommodating possible alternatives (e.g., frameworks and approaches) can better assist policymakers, think tanks, diplomats, cultural agents and other crucial actors on how to address global challenges and issues and facilitate further international cooperation and solidarity to attain a more just and sustainable world. Heterarchical approaches (e.g., decentralized decision-making, efficiency and optimization, flexibility, autonomy, innovation, and resilience) promise various advantages that the status quo can no longer avail.

Exploring post-internationalism and heterarchy as contemporary alternative approaches and their responses to classic IR approaches sufficiently inform contemporary engagements of states and better the landscape of world politics. Further, the scrutinization of the issue offers new insights and lenses that can be used on how to make sense of various international events expanding beyond the classic boxes of International Relations (IR).

## CONCLUSION

The 21st century is characterized by a multi-nodal and heterarchic' world politics increasingly taking over the center stage of the international system. It denotes a paradigm shift away from "competing classic International Relations (IR) theories" that specifically and consistently argue on the centrality and fundamentality of the state as the central actor in the international system. As an alternative, heterarchical structure allows reengineering of the system in dynamic and complex conditions defined by different global issues that are no longer exclusive within the control of states. It improves the flexibility of governance hence allowing overall effectiveness.

While it offers a promising future, it is better to take into account the possible limitations associated with it in order to maximize the benefits it can provide.

# REFERENCES

Abbott, K. W., & Snidal, D. (2009). The Governance Triangle: Regulatory Standards Institutions and the Shadow of the State. In *The Politics of Global Regulation* (pp. 44–88). Princeton University Press. DOI: 10.2307/j.ctt7rgmj.6

Alter, K. J. & Raustiala, K. (2018). The Rise of International Regime Complexity, *Annual Review of Law and Social Science*, 14 (1), pp. 18.2–18.21.

Ansell, C. & Trondal, J. (2017). Governing Turbulence: An Organizational Institutional Agenda.

Arugay, A. & Baquisal, J. (2022). Mobilized and Polarized: Social Media and Disinformation

Arugay, A. A., & Baquisal, J. K. A.Narratives in the. (2022). Philippine Elections. *Pacific Affairs*, 95(3), 549–573. DOI: 10.5509/2022953549

Bellamy, R. (2017). A European republic of sovereign states: Sovereignty, republicanism and the European Union. *European Journal of Political Theory*, 16(2), 188–209. DOI: 10.1177/1474885116654389

Belmonte, R., & Cerny, P. G. (2021). Heterarchy: Toward Paradigm Shift in World Politics. *Journal of Political Power*, 14(1), 235–257. DOI: 10.1080/2158379X.2021.1879574

Brown, M. M. (2014). The future of the nation state. World Economic Forum. Retrieved from: https://www.weforum.org/agenda/2014/11/the-future-of-the-nation-state/

Buenaobra, M. (2016). *Social Media: A Game Changer in Philippine Elections*. The Asia Foundation, April 27.

Cerny, P. G. (1997). Paradoxes of the Competition State: The Dynamics of Political Globalization [Spring.]. *Government and Opposition*, 32(2), 251–274. DOI: 10.1111/j.1477-7053.1997.tb00161.x

Cerny, P. G. (2010). *Rethinking world politics: a theory of transnational neopluralism*. Oxford University Press. DOI: 10.1093/acprof:oso/9780199733699.001.0001

Cerny, P. G. (2023). Heterarchy in World Politics. In *"Innovations in International Affairs"*. Routledge: Taylor & Francis Group.

Cox, R. W. (1981). Social Forces, States and World Orders: Beyond International Relations Theory. *Millennium*, 10(2), 126–155. DOI: 10.1177/03058298810100020501

Dean, J. (2014). Communicative Capitalism and Class Struggle. Journal for Digital Cultures. Retrieved from: https://spheres-journal.org/contribution/communicative-capitalism-and-class-struggle/

Divinagracia, A. (n.d.). Rodrigo Duterte's Toolbox of Media Co-optation: The mainstream media vs. illiberal democracy in social media. Retrieved from: https://kyotoreview.org/issue-27/dutertes-toolbox-of-media-co-optation-mainstream-media-vs-illiberal-democracy-in-social-media/

Eusebio, G. (2022). Fake news and internet propaganda, and the Philippine elections: 2022.

Friedman, T. L. (2005). *The world is flat: a brief history of the 21st century* (1st ed.). Farrar, Straus and Giroux.

Gacal, F. (2013). Territorial Disputes in Spratly: An Assessment of the Philippine Initiatives. US Army War College, 1-42.

Genschel, P., & Seelkopf, L. (2015). The Competition State. In Leibfried, S. (Eds.), *The Oxford handbook of transformations of the state* (pp. 1–23). Oxford University Press.

Ip, E. C. (2010). Globalization and the future of the law of the sovereign state. *International Journal of Constitutional Law*, 8(3), 636–655. DOI: 10.1093/icon/moq033

Jones, L., & Hameiri, S. (2023). Heterarchy and State Transformation. In *"Heterarchy in World Politics"* edited by Philip G. Cerny (2023). Routledge: Taylor & Francis Group.

Lamdan, S. (2019). *Librarianship at the crossroads of ICE surveillance*. In the Library with the Lead Pipe.

Oye, K. (1985). Explaining Cooperation under Anarchy: Hypotheses and Strategies. *World Politics*, 38(1), 1–24. DOI: 10.2307/2010349

Ramjit, D. (2023). From Post-internationalism to Heterarchy: Turbulence and Distance Proximities in a World of Globalization and Fragmentation. In *"Heterarchy in World Politics"* edited by Philip G. Cerny (2023). Routledge: Taylor & Francis Group.

Rappler. (2021). #TunayNaPagbabago: Kuwentong Ex-DDS. Retrieved from: https://www.rappler.com/nation/elections/video-stories-former-duterte-supporters/

Rappler. Retrieved from: https://www.rappler.com/technology/features/analysis-fake-news-internet-propaganda-2022-philippine-elections/

Rosenau, J. N. (1990). *Turbulence in world politics: a theory of change and continuity.* Princeton University Press. DOI: 10.1515/9780691188522

Silverman, C., Lytvynenko, J., & Kung, W. (2020, January 7). Disinformation for hire: How a new breed of PR firms is selling lies online. BuzzFeed News. https://www.buzzfeednews.com/article/craigsilverman/disinformation-for-hire-black-pr-firms

Slaughter, A. M. (2004). *A New World Order.* Princeton University Press.

Untalan, C. (2018). The Curious Case of the Duterte Presidency: Turning the Demos Against Democracy? *Development.* Advance online publication. DOI: 10.1057/s41301-018-0149-6

Wendt, A. (1992, Spring). Anarchy is what states make of it: The social construction of power politics. *International Organization*, 46(2), 391–42. DOI: 10.1017/S0020818300027764

Wendt, A. (1992). Anarchy is what states make of it: The social construction of power politics. *International Organization*, 46(2), 391–425.

Wolin, S. (2008). *Democracy Incorporated: Managed Democracy and the Specter of Inverted Totalitarianism.* Princeton University Press Princeton and Oxford.

## KEY TERMS AND DEFINITIONS

**Anarchy:** A "self-help" system in which all state actors are considered equally sovereign, without a central governing authority. This lack of overarching governing power is the defining characteristic of the traditional international system.

**Cosmopolitanism:** A vision of a single global community that emphasizes global citizenship. It encourages individuals to think and act beyond local or national boundaries, fostering global responsibility, cooperation, and interconnectedness.

**Decentralized World:** A pluralistic global order where power and decision-making are distributed across various actors, including international organizations, states, corporations, and individuals. In this system, global issues are addressed through collective efforts among diverse stakeholders at different levels.

**Double Vulnerability:** *In this chapter*, it refers to a situation where an individual or group struggles two distinct sources of vulnerability (socio-economic injustices in the physical world, coupled with unequal access to digital platforms that facilitate quality political discourse in the virtual realm) that intersect, compounding the challenges they face.

**Fragmentation:** The breakdown of economic, political, and social structures into smaller, often independent units or groups. This process is often viewed as an outcome or implication of globalization, as political, economic, and social aspects are dispersed into multiple, sometimes competing, streams rather than being concentrated.

**Globalization:** The phenomenon that drives the transition from a state-centric system to one characterized by heterarchical governance and post-internationalism, where authority and influence are distributed more widely across various actors. It facilitates the free flow of goods and services, ideas and culture, capital, and even the movement of people from one place to another.

**Heterarchy:** An alternative to both anarchical and hierarchical systems, characterized by a flat structure. In a heterarchical world order, actors are co-equal in terms of authority and power, leading to decision-making that emphasizes collaboration, flexibility, and adaptability.

**Hierarchy:** A system in which actors are governed by a single authority, with positions ranked in a structured order of power and influence.

**Internationalization:** The process by which institutions, businesses, and governments expand their influence and operations across national borders, increasing engagement in global networks.

**Political Participation:** The various ways or mechanisms in which individuals engage in political processes and activities to influence decision-making and governance.

**Post-Internationalism:** A framework in international relations that argues for the decline of the state-centric system due to the rise of non-state actors and transnational networks. This shift suggests that national sovereignty is declining or blurring as global governance, involving both state and non-state actors, evolves and power diffusion beyond traditional nation-states occurs.

**West Philippine Sea:** A territorial issue in Southeast Asia involving multiple countries, including the Philippines, China, Malaysia, Vietnam, Brunei, Taiwan, and Indonesia. This dispute centers around sovereignty and rights over maritime areas and resources.


## ENDNOTES

[1] *Anarchy* means there is no overarching authority to enforce rules or resolve disputes; states are equally sovereign to one another.

[2] Defensive realism asserts that states pursue security maximization to survive in an anarchic international environment.

3    Offensive realism claims that states seek power maximization to survive in an anarchic international environment.

4    Heterarchy, according to Cerny (2023), is *"the coexistence and conflict between differently structured micro- and meso quasi-hierarchies that compete and overlap not only across borders but also across economic-financial sectors and social groupings."*

5    Globalization is viewed as a structurally homogenizing process that requires new form of intergovernmental cooperation or global governance (Cerny, 2023).

6    This perspective is foundational in realism which perceives the anarchical international system as a competitive arena where states must explore threats and opportunities to survive and thrive.

# Chapter 10
# Crisis of Authority and the Cybernetic Politics of African International Organizations:
## The ECOWAS and Its Institutional Circuits of Heterarchical Entanglement

**Nene Lomotey Kuditchar**
https://orcid.org/0000-0002-2453-0917
*University of Ghana, Ghana*

## ABSTRACT

*This chapter examines how African inter-state relations are shaped by the crisis management initiatives of African International Organizations using the case of the Economic Community of West African States. It leverages the insights of cybernetic politics and heterarchy to decentre the dominant heuristic of hierarchy in the framing of intra-African international politics given that it hardly accommodates transactions beyond a one-dimensional understanding of power by. The chapter demonstrates how ECOWAS member states use the logic of cybernetic politics and heterachy to acquire flexibility and speed to pragmatically manage multiple episodes of authority crisis in West Africa.*

DOI: 10.4018/979-8-3693-3563-5.ch010

# INTRODUCTION

This chapter examines how African inter-state relations are (re)configured by the crisis management initiatives of African International Organizations (AIOs). It focuses on the Economic Community of West African States (ECOWAS) by mapping the heterarchical contours of cybernetic politics enacted by its member states to manage crises of authority. This chapter is theoretically motivated by the need for a framework of international politics curated with the peculiarities of Africa in mind. This imperative requires decentering the dominant heuristic of hierarchy in the framing of intra-African politics to pave the way for a nuanced audit and comprehension of the continent's experiences in the light of its aspirations. Without suggesting that the heuristic of hierarchy is irrelevant in any quest to decode African political realities, it is worth noting that it is reductionist, for it can hardly accommodate transactions beyond a one-dimensional understanding of power manifesting as coercive, dominant-dominated relationships, the essence of hard-wired bureaucratic systems. More often than not, scholars contemplating AIOs, enamoured with the experiences of the European Union (EU) as enacted in the context of its relatively 'fit-for-its-purpose' hierarchically arrayed formal institutions, consciously or unconsciously use Brussels as the benchmark to interrogate and assess differently configured African institutions and experiences. Given the status of the EU as the world's most efficiently organized International Organization relative to AIOs, such assessments always yield predictable pessimistic conclusions designating African actors as subpar, passive, and strategically naive. Such conclusions, as such, suffer from confirmation bias and a "soft bigotry of low expectations" (Peachey, 2009), the essence of Afro-pessimism in scholarly circles. This chapter seeks to cure the analytical limitations of hierarchy with the notions of cybernetic politics and heterarchy. Cybernetic politics studies the circulation of information and how actors pick and act on strategic imperatives implied or communicated to gain agency and control over their domains. In other words, cybernetic politics examines how actors decode and react to external stimuli to avoid being overtaken by unanticipated events. Heterarchy is a mode of interaction between multiple centres (of hierarchy) embedded in a horizontally decentralized system of interdependent power relations. The subsequent sections of this chapter are as follows: a review of literature on AIOs in the context of William H. Sewell, Jr.'s "three temporalities", theoretical framework crafted from a fusion of crisis, cognitive politics and heterachy, the methodology of historical institutionalism and the method of historical sociology, discussion, and a conclusion.

## Literature Review: Temporal Fallacies in the Epistemic Framing of AIOs-A Sketch

The ideational basis and strategic orientation of AIOs are framed by a series of 19th-century Pan-African conferences that took place in the West (Oloruntoba, 2020; Aniche, 2020; Sherwood, 2012). Of the lot, the 5th 1945 Manchester Pan-African Congress had the most profound conceptual impact on the future configuration of AIOs. It marked a shift from a tradition of anti-racism agitations to nationalism. Indeed, a communique issued at the end of the meeting demanded unconditional independence for colonized African people. Among others, the conferees served notice that if European governments ignored the demand for autonomy, Africans would fight for it by resorting to force as a last resort (Varela, 2017, p. 82).

The sequel to the Manchester Congress was the November 1958 Accra All African People's Conference (AAPC), the first in a series of such meetings, the last of which was convened in Cario, Egypt 1961. The AAPC was convened for political parties and anticolonial activists (Sherwood, 2021; Shepperson, 2008). In a resolution issued at the end of the meeting, the conferees reiterated the demand made at Manchester for the granting of unconditional independence to colonized Africans and called on independent African states (eight at the time) to actively seek to form regional integration groups as a step toward the eventual establishment of a Pan African Commonwealth (International Organization, 1962, pp. 430-431; University of California Press, 1959).

The Accra AAPC was preceded by the April Conference of Independent African States (CIAS) in the same year (Johnson, 1962). The first such meeting in African history, it can be understood within the context of European imperialist schemes as a rally by African governments at the time to set a long-term agenda to undo the cartographic legacies of the 1884/85 Berlin Conference, which accelerated European scramble for and the partition of Africa (Michalopoulos & Papaioannou, 2016) and set up unviable state systems engineered to advance imperialism (Robinson, 1988; Mommsen, 1988; Breytenbach, 2019). The Accra CIAS kicked off a series of such meetings, with the last episode convened in Addis Ababa, Ethiopia, paving the way for the establishment of a "Provisional General Secretariat" that operationalized decisions taken by the conferees pending the adoption of the Charter to set up the agreed upon Organization of African Unity (OAU) (Organization of African Unity, 1965, p. 12).

The OAU's Charter came into effect on September 13, 1963, after 2/3 of its signatories had deposited their instruments of ratification with Ethiopia (United Nations Treaty Collection, 1963). At the 1999 OAU "Fourth Extraordinary Session of The Assembly of Heads of State and Government" convened in Libya, its member states, in what came to be known as the "Sirte Declaration", among others, undertook to dissolve the OAU and replace it with the African Union (AU) (African Union Common Repository, 1999, p. 3). Subsequently, at a 2000 Summit in Lome, Togo, African governments adopted the Constitutive Act of the AU and its implementation plan in another summit in Lusaka, Zambia, in 2001. The AU convened the first session of its Assembly of Heads of State and Governments in Durban, South Africa, in 2002 (Maluwa, 2012).

A survey of assessments by observers of the OAU/AU and the motley of their initiatives indicates that most observers perceive AIOs as outright failures. However, close reading and an audit of the ontological and epistemic basis of the designation of AIOs as failed initiatives shows that (un)conscious infatuation with the status and stature of the EU led to impatience or lack of empathy, causing observers to lose sight of that fact that statement of policy intent is one thing and the politics of implementation is another and that more often than not policy intent and implementation are mediated by the logic of objective contextual pressures beyond the control of policy actors (Mueller, 2020; Brady et al., 2014; Shimamoto, 2021; Chollete & Harrison, 2021; Andrews, 2021).

William Sewell (1990, pp. 2-3) refers to research endeavours which pay scant attention to objective contextual logics as burdened by the limitations of "teleological explanation": "the attribution of the cause of a historical event neither to the actions and reactions that constitute the happening, nor to concrete and specifiable conditions that shape or constrain the actions and reactions, but rather to abstract transhistorical processes leading to some future historical state". He notes that research conclusions not rooted in contextual dynamics are fallacies because they seek to explain current tendencies, in the manner of linear thinking, with reference to a-historical abstract outcomes or anticipated developments in the future and, as such, do not take into account the imprint of contingent events on reality.

Sewell's teleological fallacy is evident in scholarly contemplations on AIOs. George B. N. Ayittey (2016), for instance, referred to the OAU as "an irrelevant dinosaur" which served as "the den of unrepentant despots". Further, the establishment of the AU, which he suggests was based on the template of the EU, "has achieved spectacularly little in its decade and a half of existence" at the time that he wrote, noting that it was off to a false start given that it was burdened by debt with its integrity (assuming it had any) threatened by "intrigue" and machinations of sabotage". Given these, among others, he called for the AU to be disbanded and, in its place, an African Confederation with strict rules of admission and a decentralized power system established (Ayittey, 2010, pp. 93;95;96).

Kofi Oteng Kufour (2005), of the same ontological tangent as Ayittey but from the perspective of New Institutional Economics, notes that the dissolution and collapse (he conflated the two words) of the OAU resulted from, among others, its members shying away from taking up the cost for running it and the inter-institutional rivalry between the OAU and its sub-regional units. Indeed, Kufour stressed that the OAU became irrelevant since subregional organizations provided better public goods for their members. Just as Ayittey, he overserved that unconditional admission of governments into the OAU generated a "tragedy of the regional commons", a disruptive development amplified by bureaucratic inertia emanating from cumbersome decision-making processes. Also, Wafula Okumu (2009) attributed the institutional inertia of the AU to factors such as its mimicry of the OAU, its bloated, inept staff, and the fact that it draws on the EU model and relies on it for financial support and inspiration. He also highlights a disconnect between African people and the AU as an essential factor in institutional paralysis. Aleck Humphrey Che-Mponda (1987) concurs with Okumu's observation of the void between the AU and African people. He noted that the main problem of the OAU was a mistake in the structure of its Charter in the form of assigning decision-making privileges to government leaders rather than ordinary Africans. Using the example of Morrocco's departure from the OAU in 1984 (it joined the AU in 2017 (de Larramendi & Tomé-Alonso, 2017)), he argued that governments have arrogantly abused the decision-making powers conferred on them by the Charter in ways that contradict the quest for a people-centred Pan-Africanism.

According to Percy S. Mistry (2000), in what he says is the result of his objective and impartial reflection, AIOs are nothing more than artefacts forged by a "visceral rather than rational, rhetorical rather than real" commitment to integration. He adds that AIOs are bogged down by principles rooted in "lofty transcontinental ambitions, evocative of political slogans, a plethora of treaties and regional institutions, high-minded principles and protectionist proclivities". Consequently, Africa's quest for economic integration is out of sync with the continent's mundane conditions and peoples. He points out that the tendencies he identified as the essence of AIOs result from African governments jealously preserving borders inherited from the days of European imperialism while at the same time aspiring to integrate economically.

While acknowledging the fact that AIOs, unlike similar initiatives in other parts of the world, have nothing to show given the existence of numerous regional integration groups and the stark absence of developed countries on the continent, Jude Uwakwe Eke and Kelechi Johnmary Ani (2017) drawing on (neo) functionalist insights suggest that poverty, conflict, boarders and the disruptive interventions of world powers have hampered initiatives by AIOs to improve the lot of African people. The said external disruptive interventions are designated by Dot Keet (2002, p.5) as "counter pressures and persuasions", which she notes undermine the strategic aims and objectives of African unity in the quest for collective self-reliance and self-sustaining state-led development.

There is no denying that the sketched perspectives approximate the experiences of AIOs but do not account for contextual factors that may have generated the tendencies observed. The insights reflect the decontextualized expectations of the authors rather than insights derived from efforts to ascertain how the undercurrents of Africa's historical evolution may account for the AIO traits observed. Sewell (1990, pp. 16-18) emphasizes the importance of this imperative with his "evenemential concept of temporality" which pays attention to the capacity of path-dependent events to shape the underlying structures of tendencies such that events occurring at earlier points in time either enable or constrain tendencies occurring at later periods. Evenemential temporality, which pays heed to the structuring effects of contingent/conjunctural events, upholds the conviction of a non-linear "causal dependence of later occurrences on prior occurrences and assumes that social causality is temporally heterogeneous, not temporally uniform". This chapter, therefore, considers the traits of AIOs as sediments of path-dependent tendencies (that were) active in Africa's historical evolution with the intent to interrogate them as such.

## Eclectic Theoretical Framework: Crisis of Authority and the Heterachy of Cybernetic Politics

"Crisis" is an elusive concept that defies standard definition (Hay, 1999). However, this paper adopts Antonio Gramsci's conceptualization expressed in the definition: "The crisis consists precisely in the fact that the old is dying and the new cannot be born; in this interregnum, a great variety of morbid symptoms appear" (Babic, 2020, p. 773). As it relates to authority, the Gramscian notion of crisis refers to tendencies occurring somewhere on the two extremes of the spectrum of cohesive and disrupted authority systems. While the extreme of cohesive authority is marked by political stability anchored on stable hierarchical structures of power, that of disrupted authority, akin to anarchy, is not and, as such, characterized by multiple, autonomous actors with no overarching governance structures (Lake, 1996; Kinna & Prichard, 2019; Onuf & Klink, 1989). The space between the two extremes, "the interregnum", has features of both stable hierarchical authority structures and unstable autonomous, decentralized systems; it is a zone of moderated anarchy without macro structures of authority (Holmes, 2011). As noted, the structure of the interregnum depicts the logic of heterachy: dynamic networked horizontal transactions between multiple units of autonomous hierarchically arrayed authority regimes (Cumming, 2016). In times of acute volatility and heightened uncertainty, heterarchical relations tend to be characterized by "distributed intelligence": the forging of compact tactical alliances and the sharing of information. Further, given the disparate regimes of organization and the co-existence of contradictory values enacted in disparate authority regimes, heterarchies tend to be spontaneous, flexible and adaptable regimes across multiple domains of transaction (Stark,2001, pp. 27-28).

Distributed intelligence and its ancillary features of spontaneity, flexibility and adaptability across multiple domains of transactions reflect tendencies of "cybernetic politics": how actors react to (spontaneous conjunctural) stimuli to gain agency over or govern outcomes (Kasianiuk, 2018; Yolles, 2003; Bryen, 1971). The cybernetic politics of distributed intelligence as it relates to an interregnum, with its "morbid symptoms" of turbulence, has to do with the management of contingencies[REMOVED CITATION FIELD]: the governance of conjunctural events which test the power of actors and requires prompt attention (McCormick, 1993; Borja, 2016;Schedler, 2007). In this respect, cybernetic politics is the art of "steering" through "conditions of 'storms, currents, waves, and sandbanks'" (Bates, 2020, p. 122).

The theoretical framework's relevance to this chapter is that, first, the experiences of AIOs have been impacted by the crisis of authority attending state formation in Africa; second, AIOs are heterarchical systems of distributed intelligence pragmatically steering the quest for African Unity.

## Methodology and Method: Historical institutionalism and Historical Sociology

This chapter is oriented by historical institutionalism: the philosophy that the temporal dynamics of events, in terms of inception and sequence, etch path-dependent effects on the structure and substance of institutions and mediate the governance of socio-political transactions. The occurrence of past events which stamp the present with their effects marks critical juncture moments in history (Capoccia & Kelemen, 2007). Historical institutionalism anticipates that the inception of path-dependent occurrences, which may be locked-in, i.e. difficult to reverse once set in motion, can affect behaviours in anticipated or unanticipated ways and generating efficient or inefficient outcomes (Fioretos, 2011; Liebowitz & Margolis, 1995). Further, how actors react to occurrences may lead to new historical paths, given their (future) aspirations and anxieties (Gáspár, 2011).

The method of historical sociology frames this chapter's arguments. It is an interdisciplinary approach based on a fusion of methods of inquiry from sociology and history in the quest for insights into how past occurrences shape experiences in the present and over time. The method seeks to reveal how perceptible occurrences (the empirical domain) are shaped by latent structures (Steinmetz, 1998; Bhambra, 2010). This chapter investigates how the historical sociology of state formation in Africa impacted the experiences of AIOs using the ECOWAS as a case study.

## The Historical Institutionalism of AIOs in the (Re)Configuration of Ambivalent African States-The ECOWAS in Perspective

African states crystallized in crisis and ambivalence in the context of the Cold War, aided by the convergence of two critical juncture events. First, the victory of Allied states over the Axis powers during WWII enabled the operationalization of the 1941 "Atlantic Charter", which set out the post-WWII aspirations of the USA and the UK for a new global order devoid of the scramble for territorial acquisitions and colonial domains (Stone, 1942). The terms of the Atlantic Charter were subsequently incorporated into the Charter of the UN upon its constitution in October 1945 (Verheul, 2021; Kilian, 2019). Specifically, people's right to self-determination is provisioned in Article 1, paragraph 2 of the UN Charter (Cristescu, 1981, p. 1) and reinforced by the 1960 UN General Assembly Resolutions 1514 and 1541 (Clapham, 1996, p. 17). These developments coincided with the 1945 5th Pan-African Congress, which catalyzed the transformation of proto-nationalism (legal, non-violent negotiations for colonial reforms) into militant nationalism in Africa (Nathan, 2001; Mazrui & Michael, 1984). The path-dependent impulses of the aspirations of the UN Charter and its Resolutions, while converging with the path creation of nationalistic fervours and initiatives of Africans, unleashed pressures which colonial powers such as Apartheid South Africa, Portugal and France, unwilling to let go of their African colonies, could not withstand (Reis, 2013; McNamara, 1989; Ndlovu et al., 2019). In 1960, designated as "the Year of Africa" (The New York Times, 2020), and as such a critical juncture era, 17 colonies gained independence, followed by 18 in 1961 and 13 more into the early 1970s (Hargreaves, 1996).

However, even though the newly minted states in Africa were legally structured with the Westphalian model of European states (Warner, 2001), they lacked the de facto attributes one would theoretically expect such states to possess; they were nominal leviathans (Hopkins, 2000; Jackson & Roberg, 1986; Jackson, 1986; Fowler & Bunck, 1996; Geertz, 2004). For example, African states were cartographic certainties with clearly defined and internationally accepted borders, but their spatial integrity, primarily evident in capitals, was contested by secessionists (Schomerus et al., 2019; Herbst, 2000). Secessionism implied that governments' spatial authority did not cover their territory's entire legal expanse (Storey, 2017; Mampilly, 2003). Further, African states had what Peter Ekeh (1975) referred to as "two publics": African states had populations (e.g. Nigerians, Togolese) but no citizens since people felt relatively more attached to particularistic (e.g. ethnic) groups for identity (Green, 2017) and actively sought to emotionally and materially detach from states (Animashaun, 2009; Melber et al., 2023). In addition, even though African militaries, in theory, are established as insurance against external threats, they were empirically ethno-praetorian guards (recruited from the ethnic groups of presidents) to protect governments from internal threats e.g. rebellions (Harkness, 2022; Welch, 1986).

The preceding set up centripetal pressures, amplified by the hardened colonial legacies of "divide and conquer" implemented through British policies of "indirect rule" engineered to reconfigure African traditional institutions as conduits of exploitation and structural violence (Lange et al., 2021), the establishment of "warrant chiefs" in African polities with decentralized power and imposing minority groups over majority populations as governors on behalf of colonial administrators (Müller-Crepon et al., 2021; Ali et al., 2015) and "direct rule" enacted by France, Belgium and Portugal to merge with their African colonies (Kamalu, 2019; Betts, 2005). African states at independence ware thus trapped in a crisis of authority and its ancillary of coups (Christopher, 1997; Wiking, 1993).

Meanwhile, the "Year of Africa" coincided with the Cold War and its rivalrous politics and hence defined the global parameter which shaped the embryonic pockets of sovereign regimes established on the continent. The Cold War rivalry between the Soviet Union and the USA enacted a worldwide straightforward bipolar conflict system demonstrated by the US-led North Atlantic Treaty Organization and the Soviet-anchored Warsaw Treaty Organization (Rapkin et al., 1979). However, in Africa, the conflict dynamics of the Cold War revolved around the tri-polar Washington-Moscow-Beijing system of rivalry, which came into being after the Sino-Soviet split of the early 1960s (Lüthi, 2008; Scalapino, 1964; Wills, 2024; Jersild, 2018; Friedman, 2015; Olympio, 1961; Reynolds, 2015). The said worldwide ideological rivalry, which panned out as a quest for global leadership, made the five permanent members of the UN Security Council, expected to be the guardians and guarantors of the UN's aspirations, the agents of political stability and instability in Africa (Ryder et al., 2020; Sinclair, 2019; Schmidt, 2013; Cawthra, 2016; Adebajo, 2011; Davidson & Munslow, 1990; Englebert, 2000): to the extent that the permanent 5, by protecting their client states ensured a semblance of political stability (Kunert, 1978; Bonnier & Hedenskog, 2020), they were also active entrepreneurs of destabilizing proxy wars (Tafotie & Idahosa, 2016; Lawrence, 2004).

The critical juncture events of the 1st CIAS and the 1st AAPC set up path-dependent and path-creation currents, leading to the establishment of the OAU. To be sure, the movement from the CIAS/AAPC to the OAU was not linear. It was characterized by disagreements on the pace of unification. Leaders such as Tanzania's Julius Nyerere and Nigeria's Abubakar Tafa Balewa opposed the single-minded quest by Ghana's Kwame Nkrumah urging African states to immediately surrender their sovereignty to establish a fully integrated continent (Nkrumah, 1963; The New York Times, 1964; Hirschmann, 1975). These differences crystallized around rival blocs. While the Casablanca Group (constituted by Ghana, Guinea, Mali, Libya, Egypt, Morocco and Algeria) supported Nkrumah's agenda, the Monrovia Group (made up of Nigeria, Tunisia, Ethiopia, Liberia, Sudan, Togo, and Somalia) opted for a moderate, incremental approach without any explicit quest for a comprehensively united Africa. Further, the Brazzaville Group (comprised of the Francophone states of Senegal and the Ivory Coast) saw close ties with France as more critical than African unity. After several failed attempts to broker a rapprochement between the rival blocs (Wallerstein, 1974, p. 20), Guniea's Sekou Toure, a vital member of the Casablanca bloc and Ethiopia's Haile Selassie succeeded in convincing the rival groups to dissolve in the name of unity (Červenka, 1977, pp. 1-2). The Casablanca bloc acceded to a proposal by Ture and Haile Selasi to accommodate the preferences of the Monrovia and Brazzaville blocs as enshrined in the OAU Charter's principle of "uti possidetis juris": the "inalienable right to independent existence" (Abraham, 2007; Mnyongani, 2008; Shawt, M. N, 1997, p. 103; The Organization of African Unity, 1963, p. 4). The norm of "uti possidetis juris" defined the OAU as a sovereignty-preserving continental union and captures its essence as a heterarchical institution anchored on its Assembly of Heads of State and Government with each member having one vote (The Organization of African Unity, 1963, p. 5). In return, the Monrovia and Brazzaville blocs agreed to align with the Casablanca bloc's initiative to support anticolonial armed groups across the continent. For this, the OAU set up the "African Liberation Committee" (Wallerstein, 1974, p. 20). It is evident that the OAU took off as a compromise institution, a "katechon organization" engineered (Bates, 2020) to keep the disruptions of rivalry in check.

Designating the OAU as a "katechon organization" is not so much about its tangible institutions or material capabilities. It is about its essence as a Pan-African "meta institution": "an institution of institutions, i.e. the normative undercurrents of institutions which set priorities cutting across specific institutions. Meta institutions are noncoercive and enact co-creation through formal and informal interactions. Meta-institutions "pulsate": their substance and form expand or contract in line with the disparate interests of actors. Pulsation generates conflicts, given that their macro logic may be out of sync with actors' heterogeneous interests and aspirations. Nevertheless, pulsation has an inbuilt capacity to deescalate disputes by serving as a confidence troubleshooting regime which provides clues for the scope for informal or formal adjustments (Grigorievna et al., 2019, p. 145; Gjaltema et al., 2020).

Meta-institutions, as sketched, enhances the ability of autonomous, interdependent actors to (i) interactively learn about causal processes and capacity for action in challenging environments; (ii) develop coordinating strategies among disparate social forces over multiple spatiotemporal horizons and action domains; and (iii). stabilize actor expectations, and codes of conduct, and create a shared worldview for collective action. Meta-institutions, therefore, enable co-creation through learning by enacting solidarity-based "power-with" relationships (Jessop, 2022; Torfing et al., 2012; Strokosch & Osborne, 2020). Claude Ake, as far back as 1965, perceived the

Pan-African meta-institutional logic of AIOs in what he described as "psychologi-cal unity" facilitating national "institutional uniformity…by focusing the attention of African governments on common problems and pressuring them into adopting certain standard solutions to these problems" (Ake, 1965, pp. 532;539). Subregional AIOs are, in effect, a heterachy of sovereignties embedded in the meta-institution of Pan-Africanism, with their sub-regional units being secondary "katechon insti-tutions". The following section demonstrates how the preceding manifests in the ECOWAS experience.

## The Conversion of the ECOWAS into "ECOWAS" (Economic Community for West African Stability)

The ECOWAS is one of 8 regional pillars of the AU, with the African diaspora being the 9th (The African Union Commission and New Zealand Ministry of Foreign Affairs and Trade/Manatū Aorere, 2014, pp. 18-20). 15 West African Heads of State and Government constituted the ECOWAS in May 28 1975, in Lagos, Nigeria, with the primary quest for "collective self-sufficiency" (ECOWAS/ CEDEAO, 2024) through the promotion of "cooperation and development in all fields of economic activity" and incrementally removing obstacles which hinder same. The 1975 ECOWAS Treaty set up the "Authority of Heads of State and Government" as a principal governing organ (ECOWAS/CEDEAO, 1975).

In just over a decade of its establishment, the ECOWAS, confronted by a series of interlinked uncivil wars, reconfigured as an economic bloc to a broker of political stability in the form of the establishment and near-simultaneous deployment of the ECOMOG (Economic Community of West African States Monitoring Group), to intervene in interlinked insurrections in Liberia and Serra Leone (1989 to 1997) and the ECOMIL (ECOWAS Mission in Liberia) after the second implosion of Liberia from 1999-2003 (see Aboagye, 2018, pp. 69-100;265-281; 233-238).

The said reconfiguration without precedent in the annals of AIOs, was riddled with acute contradictions which, without the meta-institution of Pan-Africanism, may not have been resolved. To be sure, the ECOWAS had two protocols which had not been operationalized at the time of Liberia's implosion: the 1978 Protocol on Non-Aggression and the 1981 Protocol on Mutual Assistance in Defence, which provisioned for an "Allied Armed Forces of the Community" to respond to external and not internal threats to peace (ECOWAS Commission, 2018, pp. 11-12; Obi, 2009, p. 121). Against this backdrop, Nigeria set up an ECOWAS "Standing Medi-ation Committee" (SMC) constituted by Gambia, Ghana, Mali, Nigeria and Togo. Against opposition by the Francophone group of the ECOWAS (Aboagye, 2018, p. 234), and in an act which turned out to be legally invalid, the SMC subsequently set up the ECOMOG, dominated and bankrolled by Nigeria to impose a cease-fire beyond its original mandate of facilitating mediation.

Even though the ECOMOG restored normalcy and enabled elections in 1997, the ensuing democratic order could not hold, and Liberia plunged again into violence in 1999. The ECOWAS then set up and deployed the ECOMIL (ECOWAS Mission in Liberia) to keep the belligerents apart before the arrival of the United Nations Mission in Liberia, essentially made up of ECOMOG soldiers, to restore peace, which it did in 2003 after the conclusion of a "Comprehensive Peace Agreement" in Accra, Ghana (Obi, 2009, pp. 121; 124; Walraven, 1999, pp. 25-26). Unlike the initial ECOMOG deployment, the ECOMIL initiative was characterized by less acrimony and broad consensus due to an institutional restructuring of the ECOWAS. Among others, the revised ECOWAS Treaty provided a regional security protocol and adopted a doctrine of preventive diplomacy and mediation (ECOWAS Commission, 1993, p. 36; 2018, p. 5).

Meanwhile, in 1997, the ECOWAS expanded the ECOMOG (ECOMOG II) mandate beyond Liberia into neighbouring Sierra Leone to restore a democratically elected government toppled in a coup d état. In 1998, ECOMOG II, primarily sponsored by Nigeria, successfully reinstated the ousted government. Nevertheless, the departure of ECOMOG II created room for rebel groups to resume their belligerence. Eventually, the United Nations Peacekeeping in Sierra Leone, made up of ECOMOG II troops, was constituted, and in 1999, it successfully executed its mandate and restored order (Obi, 2009, p. 126).

In 1999, the ECOWAS deployed ECOMOG in Guinea Bissau to end hostilities between the instigators of a coup d état and government troops backed by Senegal and Guinea. Ultimately, the protagonists agreed to the 1998 "Abuja Peace Agreement" (United Nations, 1998), which they subsequently broke by resuming hostilities. In the meantime, in 2012, the ECOWAS set up the ECOMIB (ECOWAS Mission in Guinea Bissau) to reform the military of Guinea Bissau. In 2016, the ECOWAS brokered another peace accord, the "Agreement on the Resolution of the Political Crisis in Guinea Bissau", paving the way for elections with a controversial outcome (ACCORD, 2019). At this stage, it is worth noting that the deployment of the ECOMOG into Guinea Bissau, just like the episodes of Liberia and Serra Leone, was not effected within the remit of the revised ECOWAS Treaty. Further, unlike the Liberian and Serra Leonean operations, Nigeria, due to fatigue and apprehensions by Francophone states that it has regional hegemonic ambitions, did not contribute troops but instead took on a mediatory role (Obi, 2009, pp. 127-128).

On two occasions, 2003 and 2011, the ECOWAS sought to intervene in La Côte d'Ivoire after an elections dispute (Schiel et al., 2017). The 2003 violence had ethnic and religious undertones (Badmus, 2017; Miran-Guyon, 2006), and after stalled efforts to commit the conflicting actors to peace, the ECOWAS set up the

ECOFORCE (ECOWAS Forces) to keep the belligerents apart while it explored other avenues for peace. There was a breakthrough in 2003 when the belligerents committed to the "Linas-Marcoussis Agreement", brokered by the ECOWAS and international third parties, set the terms for a government of national reconciliation (United Nations Digital Library, 2003).

In 2011, the ECOWAS received an invitation from the then-presidential candidate Alassane Ouattara of Côte d'Ivoire, embroiled in a 2010 election dispute with the then-sitting president Laurent Gbagbo. Even though polling results indicated that Gbagbo had lost elections conducted, he refused to concede defeat and relinquish power to Ouattara, widely perceived to be the winner. The ECOWAS, urged on by the United States and the African Union, affirmed Ouattara as the election winner, issued an ultimatum to Gbagbo to do what was needed, and offered to escort him into exile. However, should Gbagbo fail to relinquish power, the ECOWAS served notice that it "would be left with no alternative" than to use "legitimate force" to enforce the democratic will of the Ivorian electorate (Gagnon, 2013, p. 55). Ultimately, Gbagbo was evicted from office by loyalists of Ouattara, who paved the way for his induction as president. Julie Dubé Gagnon (2013, p.52) noted that the ECOWAS's threat to use force to evict Gbagbo from office had no basis in law. She argued that the ECOWAS ultimatum, which encoded a "pro-democratic intervention" intent, contravened the UN Charter because it had no authorization from the Security Council.

Gagnon's argument foregrounds the 2012 ECOWAS-organized AFISMA (African-led International Support Mission to Mali) initiative to combat insurgent groups in Northern Mali (Akanji, 2019). At the time of AFISMA's deployment, the ECOWAS had imposed sanctions on Mali after a coup d'etat and was activating its Standby Force (the ECOBRIG) to stem the advance of insurgent groups on Mali's capital. Being a component of the continent-wide African Standby Force established under Chapter VIII of the United Nations Charter and regulated by Article 7(e) of the Constitutive Act of the African Union (AU), the ECOWAS could not unilaterally deploy the ECOBRIG without UN Security Council (UNSC) authorization sought through the AU. The UNSC's authorization of ECOWAS's intention to deploy the ECOBRIG (United Nations, 2012) led to the establishment of the AFISMA, subsequently transformed, by way of name change, into MINUSMA (United Nations Multidimensional Integrated Stabilization Mission in Mali) in 2013 (African Union, 2013).

In 2016, the ECOWAS authorized the deployment of the ECOMIG (the ECOWAS Military Intervention in the Gambia) at the request of Adama Barrow, widely believed to be the winner in an election with the then-sitting President Yahya Jammeh, who refused to step down. The ECOWAS gave Jammeh up to January 19, 2017, to hand over power or it would dislodge him by force of arms. Jammeh acceded, and the ECOWAS deposed him in "Operation Restore Democracy" (Hartmann, 2017). It is worth noting that the ECOMIG had the unanimous support of the UNSC with Resolution 2337 mandating it to exhaust all avenues to resolve the crisis before opting for a military intervention. The ECOWAS acted against Resolution 2337 and opted for military intervention as a first resort (United Nations Digital Library, 2017).

On January 28 2024, for the first time in its history, three member states of the ECOWAS: Burkina Faso, Mali and Niger (BFMN, hereafter), issued a joint statement announcing their withdrawal from the group. The BFMN noted that the ECOWAS, a stooge of foreign powers, has become a threat to the sovereignty of its members by deviating from its foundational principles. They were also outraged by what they said was the ECOWAS's obsession with sanctions and its insensitivity to the threat they face from terrorists. The issue of sanctions had to do with punitive measures the ECOWAS imposed after the coup de états in Mali (2020 and 2021), Burkina Faso (2022) and Niger (2023). ECOWAS's decision to use its Standby Force as a last resort to reinstate president Mohamed Bazoum, deposed in a coup d état on July 26 2023 (Al Jazeera, 2023), was the proximate trigger which caused the BFMN to act the way they did. 11 ECOWAS member states pledged to support the intervention (Mednick, 2023). The BFMN subsequently concluded a collective defence pact called "Alliance of Sahel States" (ASS) and served notice that it considers an ECOWAS intervention in any of its member states as an act of war (Al Jazeera, 2024).

In response to the decision of the BFMN, the ECOWAS convened an Extraordinary Summit and issued a communique which, while emphasizing the group's "zero tolerance" coup de états, lifted the sanctions it had imposed on the ASS group and the Gambian junta and called on them to reconsider their decision to part ways. The communique mandated the ECOWAS Commission to engage the three in a spirit of reconciliation, announced the activation of the ECOWAS Standby Force to fight against militant groups actively and called on the ECOWAS Commission to organize a meeting of "Ministers of Finance and Defence" to recommend strategies to raise funds and procure equipment for the Standby Force (ECOWAS Commission, 2024, p. 9-10).

## The ECOWAS and the Heterarchy of its Institutional Praxis

By way of reiteration, the pragmatic art of transforming the ECOWAS (Economic Community of West African States), a regional broker of economic cooperation to 'ECOWAS' (Economic Community of West African Stability), into a political fixer of authority crisis, reflects the essence of cybernetic politics: actors "steering" through turmoil. To the extent that the "steering" of the ECOWAS is riddled with conflict, it can be designated as a 'tension-filled hive of sovereign states' or, better still, a heterarchy of sovereign states entangled in centrifugal and centripetal pressures but whose identity is dynamically framed by how it governs crisis of authority. The ECOWAS had to proactively transform its core remit as a regional broker of economic cooperation to a political fixer of broken-down authority systems, given the exigency of having to constantly respond to a motley of contingent events promptly. Beginning with the Liberian implosion and up to its rapprochement with the BFMN, the ECOWAS, over 35 years, had to simultaneously and in rapid succession and without the guidance of institutions or precedent, intervene in the internal affairs of its member states caught in the abyss of crisis. That its member states can contemplate and execute such initiatives even in a context of dissensus is due to the enabling flexible logic of heterarchy enacted by the decentralized format of "power-with", which facilitates the prosecution of ad hoc networked horizontal transactions of multiple sovereign units. The same flexible logic of heterarchy enhanced the ease with which different (coalitions) states mobilized to execute the imperatives of the ECOWAS even without legal backing, as in the cases of Libera, Serra Leone and Guinea Bissau.

This said, the tendency of the ECOWAS to act beyond the remit of (its) international law should not be seen as a disregard for legal discipline but rather (as exemplified by the case of Gambia) an indicator of the group to opt for pragmatism when human security is at risk. As evidenced by the 1994 Rwandan genocide (see Anyidoho, 2021, pp. 54;60), International Organizations tend to defer to the sanctity of international law rather than protect human security. The ECOWAS acting pragmatically without recourse to (its) international law against the backdrop of "acute volatility and heightened uncertainty" (as in the case with the exit of Niger, Burkina Faso and Mali) is in tandem with the theoretical anticipations of cybernetic politics within the context of heterarchy where the imperative of managing contingent events with speed and spontaneity motivates actors to promptly engineer regimes of "distributed intelligence" by forging of ad hoc tactical alliances and the sharing of information to "steer" out of disorder. Steering out of disorder without recourse to law has obvious challenges, such as coordination problems and predictability. Nevertheless, the power of meta-institutions (such as Pan-Africanism) to coordinate the actions of disparate actors neutralizes the said dangers; it enables joint initiatives even in the context of dissensus on strategy. Hence, the ECOWAS, by steering without absolute recourse to international law, has learned, the hard way, the dynamics of interactions among its member states, the scope for interdependent actions and how to frame coordination in challenging situations. It has also learned to develop customized strategies to coordinate actions among social forces with different interests across multiple spatiotemporal horizons and action domains. The preceding has stabilized and crystalized the expectations of its member states on codes of conduct and created a shared worldview for individual and collective action amid contingent events. Therefore, it is no surprise that Ouattara (Côte d'Ivoire) and Barrow (the Gambia) expressed faith in ECOWAS amid instability.

Further, the ECOWAS's peace enforcement initiatives as rooted in Pan-Africanism "pulsate" (see meta-institutions supra) since its endeavours are mediated by anxiety (e.g. the perception that Nigeria's hegemonic ambitions by Francophone) and dissensus between Francophone and Anglophone states. However, the inbuilt capacity of pulsation to deescalate conflicts triggered by the ECOWAS's illegal actions is evidenced by the invitation extended by Ouattara of Côte d'Ivoire (the leading Francophone state in West Africa) for the intervention of ECOWAS to protect his country's democracy and also break ranks with other Francophone states and align with the Anglophone group against BFMN, also of the Francophone community. At the end of it all, the rallying meta-institutional power of Pan-African, enabled by informal and formal adjustments, prevailed over sectional differences.

The meta-institution and the path dependence of ECOWAS initiatives, namely the ECOMOG (19990-1998), the ECOWAS Standing Mediation Committee (1991), and ECOMOG II (1998) provided a normative template for the African Peace and Security Architecture (APSA) adopted in 2001 as an institution of the AU. Article 13 of the "Protocol Relating to the Establishment of the Peace and Security Council of the African Union" establishes an "African Standby Force" mandated to, among others, intervene "in a Member State in respect of grave circumstances or at the request of a Member State in order to restore peace and security" (African Union, n.d., p. 19). Article 13 draws its strength from Article 4 (h) and (j) of the AU's Constitutive Act, which gives it "the right…to intervene in a Member State…in respect of grave circumstances" (African Union, n.d., p. 17). Article 4 (h) and (j) make the Constitutive Act of the AU the first accord in the history of international law, with the mandate to militarily intercede in a third country for humanitarian reasons (Aneme, 2008). By serving as the barricade against the chaos that will ensue from a total meltdown of West African authority systems and undermine human security, the ECOWAS, with all its crudeness in tow, has shown Africa (and indeed the rest of the world) how to go about it as a regional katechon.

## CONCLUSION

This chapter sought to decentre the hierarchy heuristic in the study of AIOs using the experiences of the ECOWAS. Guided by the notional compass of cybernetic politics and heterarchy, the chapter demonstrated that a net assessment of the ensemble of transactions of the ECOWAS shows that the regional group has effectively assuaged episodes of crisis of authority in West Africa. Without the guidance of lessons instructed by precedent or institutional remit, the ECOWAS embarked on initiatives and gained experiences that counted as proof of concept in managing humanitarian crises. Using unconventional and pragmatic strategies such as conditional adherence to (its) international law, flexibility and spontaneity in responding to crises and mobilizing different state coalitions to respond to crises, the ECOWAS provided the conceptual template for the AU's humanitarian interventionist policy as enshrined in its Constitutive Act, the only such accord in international law. The ECOWAS response to crisis of authority (critical juncture events) in West Africa, etched a path-dependent process of norm development, which the AU emulated. The experiences of the ECOWAS from the perspective of cybernetic politics and heterarchy expose the analytical limitations of the hierarchy heuristic, which, given its one-dimensional understanding of power relations, can not accommodate transactions not arrayed in a top-down, dominant-dominated format. It also exposes the limited perspectives of scholars who, impressed with the stature and efficiency of the hard-wired hierarchical institutional orders of the EU, tend to dismiss the theoretical and empirical relevance of AIOs as scholarly backburners.

# REFERENCES

Aboagye, F. B. (2018). *ECOMOG: A Sub-Regional Experience in Conflict Resolution, Management and Peacekeeping in Liberia* (2nd ed.). Ulinzi Africa Resources.

Abraham, G. (2007). "Lines Upon Maps": Africa and The Sanctity of African Boundaries. *African Journal of International and Comparative Law*, 61-84.

ACCORD. (2019, September 2). *ECOWAS's Efforts at Resolving Guinea-Bissau's Protracted Political Crisis, 2015-2019.* Retrieved from ACCORD: https://www.accord.org.za/conflict-trends/ecowass-efforts-at-resolving-guinea-bissaus-protracted-political-crisis-2015-2019/

Adebajo, A. (2011). *UN Peacekeeping in Africa: From the Suez Crisis to the Sudan Conflicts.* Lynne Rienner Publishers. DOI: 10.1515/9781626376007

African Union. (2013, July 10). *AFISMA Transfers its Authority to MINUSMA.* Retrieved from African Union: https://www.peaceau.org/en/article/afisma-transfers-its-authority-to-minusma

African Union. (n.d.). *Constitutive Act of the African Union.* Retrieved from African Union: https://au.int/sites/default/files/pages/34873-file-constitutiveact_en.pdf

African Union. (n.d.). *Protocol Relating to the Establishment of the Peace and Security Council of the African Union.* Retrieved from African Union: https://au.int/en/treaties/protocol-relating-establishment-peace-and-security-council-african-union

African Union Common Repository. (1999, September 9). *Sirte Declaration.* Retrieved from African Union Common Repository: https://archives.au.int/handle/123456789/10157

Akanji, O. O. (2019). Sub-regional Security Challenge: ECOWAS and the War on Terrorism in West Africa. *Insight on Africa*, 94–112.

Ake, C. (1965). Pan-Africanism and African Governments. *The Review of Politics*, 27(4), 532–542. DOI: 10.1017/S0034670500005775

Al Jazeera. (2023, August 18). *ECOWAS Defence Chiefs Agree 'D-day' for Niger Military Intervention.* Retrieved from Al Jazeera: https://www.aljazeera.com/news/2023/8/18/ecowas-defence-chiefs-agree-d-day-for-niger-military-intervention

Al Jazeera. (2024, January 28). *Niger, Mali, Burkina Faso Announce Withdrawal from ECOWAS: The Three Nations, Led by Military Governments, Accused the Regional Bloc of Becoming a Threat to Member States.* Retrieved from Al Jazeera: https://www.aljazeera.com/news/2024/1/28/niger-mali-burkina-faso-announce -withdrawal-from-ecowas

Ali, M., Fjeldstad, O.-H., Jiang, B., & Shifaz, A. B. (2015, December). Colonial Legacy, State-building and the Salience of Ethnicity in Sub-Saharan Africa. *CMI Working Paper.WP 2015:16.* Bergen: CMI (Chr. Michelsen Institute).

Andrews, M. (2021, November). *Getting Real About Unknowns in Complex Policy Work.* Retrieved from RISE Working Paper Series.: https://doi.org/DOI: 10.35489/ BSG-RISE-WP_2021/083

Aneme, G. A. (2008). The African Standby Force: Major Issues Under 'Mission Scenario Six' . *Political Perspectives*, 1-22.

Aniche, E. T. (2020). Pan-Africanism and Regionalism in Africa: The Journey So Far. In Oloruntoba, S. O. (Ed.), *Pan Africanism, Regional Integration and Development in Africa* (pp. 17–38). Palgrave Macmillan. DOI: 10.1007/978-3-030-34296-8_2

Animashaun, M. A. (2009). State Failure, Crisis of Governance and Disengagement from the State in Africa. *Africa Development. Afrique et Developpement*, 34(3-4), 47–63. DOI. 10.4314/ad.v34i3-4.63527

Anyidoho, H. K. (2021). *Guns Over Kigali.* Sub-Saharan Publishers.

Ayittey, G. B. (2010). The United States of Africa: A Revisit. *The Annals of the American Academy of Political and Social Science*, 632(1), 86–102. DOI: 10.1177/0002716210378988

Ayittey, G. B. (2016, July 10). *Disband the African Union: African Leaders Should Admit that a Caricature of the European Union Can't Possibly Work for Africa.* Retrieved from Foreign Policy: https://foreignpolicy.com/2016/07/10/disband-the -african-union/

Babic, M. (2020). Let's Talk About the Interregnum: Gramsci and the Crisis of the Liberal World Order. *International Affairs*, 96(3), 767–786. DOI: 10.1093/ia/iiz254

Badmus, I. A. (2017). Even the Stones are Burning: Explaining the Ethnic Dimensions of the Civil War in La Côte d'Ivoire. *Journal of Social Sciences*, 45–57.

Bates, D. (2020). The Political Theology of Entropy: A Katechon for the Cybernetic Age. *History of the Human Sciences*, 33(1), 109–127. DOI: 10.1177/0952695119864237

Betts, R. (2005). *Assimilation and Association in French Colonial Theory*. University of Nebraska Press.

Bhambra, G. K. (2010). Historical Sociology, International Relations and Connected Histories. *Cambridge Review of International Affairs*, 23(1), 127–143. DOI: 10.1080/09557570903433639

Bonnier, E., & Hedenskog, J. (2020, December). *The United States and Russia in Africa: A Survey of US and Russian Political, Economic, and Military-security Relations with Africa. FOI-R--5039--SE*. Stockholm, Sweden: Swedish Defence Agency.

Borja, A. L. (2016). Virtù, Fortuna, and Statecraft: A Dialectical Analysis of Machiavelli. *Kritike: An OnlineJournal of Philosophy*, 192–21.

Brady, M. P., Duffy, M. L., & Hazelkor, M. (2014). Policy and Systems Change: Planning for Unintended Consequences. *The Clearing House: A Journal of Educational Strategies, Issues and Ideas*, 87(3), 102–109. DOI: 10.1080/00098655.2014.891882

Breytenbach, W. J. (2019). *The Making and Unmaking of Modern Boundaries in Africa: From Berlin to Kigali. 2019 Border Management Workshop*. Security Institute for Governance and Leadership in Africa.

Bryen, S. D. (1971). *The Application of Cybernetic Analysis to the Study of International Politics*. Springer Dordrecht. DOI: 10.1007/978-94-010-3005-2

Capoccia, G., & Kelemen, R. D. (2007). The Study of Critical Junctures: Theory, Narrative and Counterfactuals in Historical Institutionalism. *World Politics*, 59(3), 341–369. DOI: 10.1017/S0043887100020852

Cawthra, G. (2016). *Peacekeeping Interventions in Africa: "War is Peace, Freedom is Slavery, Ignorance is Strength."*. Friedrich-Ebert-Stiftung.

Červenka, Z. (1977). *The Unfinished Quest for Unity: Africa and the OAU*. Julian Friedmann Publishers Ltd.

Che-Mponda, A. H. (1987). Charter of the Organization of African Unity and the Problems of African Unity. *African Study Monographs*, 53–63.

Christopher, A. (1997). 'Nation-states', 'Quasi-states', and 'Collapsed-states' in Contemporary Africa. *GeoJournal*, 43(1), 91–97. DOI: 10.1023/A:1006833519243

Clapham, C. (1996). *Africa and the International System: The Politics of State Survival*. Cambridge University Press. DOI: 10.1017/CBO9780511549823

Collette, L., & Harrison, S. G. (2021). Unintended Consequences: Ambiguity Neglect and Policy Ineffectiveness. *Eastern Economic Journal*, 47(2), 206–226. DOI: 10.1057/s41302-021-00187-7 PMID: 33551514

Cristescu, A. (1981). *The Right to Self-Determination: Historical and Current Development on the Basis of United Nations Instruments*. United Nations.

Cumming, G. S. (2016). Heterarchies: Reconciling Networks and Hierarchies. *Trends in Ecology & Evolution*, 31(8), 622–632. Advance online publication. DOI: 10.1016/j.tree.2016.04.009 PMID: 27233444

Davidson, B., & Munslow, B. (1990). The Crisis of the Nation-State in Africa. *Review of African Political Economy*, 17(49), 9–21. DOI: 10.1080/03056249008703872

de Larramendi, M. H., & Tomé-Alonso, B. (2017). The Return of Morocco to the African Union. *Panorama*, 229-232.

ECOWAS/CEDEAO. (2024). *About ECOWAS*. Retrieved from ECOWAS/CEDEAO: https://www.ecowas.int/about-ecowas/ ECOWAS/CEDEAO.

*Treaty*. (1975, May 28). Retrieved from The 1975 Treaty of The Economic Community Of West African States: https://www.ecowas.int/publication/treaty/#:~:text=The%20Economic%20Community%20of%20West,in%201975%20in%20Lagos%2C%20Nigeria

ECOWAS Commission. (1993, July 24). Economic Community of West African States (ECOWAS): Revised Treaty. Abuja: Economic Community of West African States.

ECOWAS Commission. (2018). *ECOWAS Mediation Guidelines*. ECOWAS Commission/Crisis Management Initiative.

ECOWAS Commission. (2024, February 24). *Extraordinary Summit of The ECOWAS Authority of Heads of State and Government on The Political, Peace and Security Situation in The Region*. Retrieved from ECOWAS Commission: chrome-extension://efaidnbmnnnibpcajpcglclefindmkaj/https://www.ecowas.int/wp-content/uploads/2024/02/EXT-ORD-SUMMIT-FINAL-COMMUNIQUE-ENGLISH-_240225_160529.pdf

Eke, J. U., & Ani, K. J. (2017). Africa and the Challenges of Regional Integration. *Journal of African Union Studies*, 63-80.

Ekeh, P. (1975). Colonialism and the Two Publics in Africa: A Theoretical Statement. *Comparative Studies in Society and History*, 17(1), 91–112. DOI: 10.1017/S0010417500007659

Englebert, P. (2000). Pre-Colonial Institutions, Postcolonial States, and Economic Development in Tropical Africa. *Political Research Quarterly*, 53(1), 7–36. DOI: 10.1177/106591290005300101

Fioretos, O. (2011). Historical Institutionalism in International Relations. *International Organization*, 65(2), 367–399. DOI: 10.1017/S0020818311000002

Fowler, M. R., & Bunck, J. M. (1996). What Constitutes the Sovereign State? *Review of International Studies*, 22(4), 381–404. DOI: 10.1017/S0260210500118637

Friedman, J. (2015). *Shadow Cold War: The Sino-Soviet Competition for the Third World*. The University of North Carolina Press. DOI: 10.5149/northcarolina/9781469623764.001.0001

Gagnon, J. D. (2013). ECOWAS's Right t s Right to Intervene in Côte D'Ivoire to Install Alassane Ouattara as President-Elect . *Notre Dame Journal of International & Comparative Law*, 51-72.

Gáspár, T. (2011). Path Dependency and Path Creation in a Strategic Perspective. *Journal of Futures Studies*, 93–108.

Geertz, C. (2004). What Is a State If It is Not a Sovereign?: Reflections on Politics in Complicated Places. *Current Anthropology*, 45(5), 577–593. DOI: 10.1086/423972

Gjaltema, J., Biesbroek, R., & Termeer, K. (2020). From Government to Governance...to Meta-governance: A Systematic Literature Review. *Public Management Review*, 22(12), 1760–1780. DOI: 10.1080/14719037.2019.1648697

Green, E. D. (2017). Ethnicity, National Identity and the State: Evidence from Sub-Saharan Africa. *British Journal of Political Science*, 757–779.

Grigorievna, A. P., Nikolaevna, J. N., & Sverdlikova, A. (2019). Meta-institutions as a Product of Institutional Dynamics and Institutional Reformation. *Post Mordern Openings*, 137-154.

Hargreaves, J. D. (1996). *Decolonization in Africa*. Routledge.

Harkness, K. A. (2016). The Ethnic Army and the State: Explaining Coup Traps and Difficulties of Democratization in Africa. *The Journal of Conflict Resolution*, 60(4), 587–616. DOI: 10.1177/0022002714545332

Harkness, K. A. (2022). The Ethnic Stacking in Africa Data Set: When Leaders Use Ascriptive Identity to Build Military Loyalty. *Conflict Management and Peace Science*, 39(5), 609–632. DOI: 10.1177/07388942211044999

Hartmann, C. (2017). ECOWAS and the Restoration of Democracy in the Gambia. *Africa Spectrum*, 52(1), 85–99. DOI: 10.1177/000203971705200104

Hay, C. (1999). Crisis and the Structural Transformation of the State: Interrogating the Process of Change. *British Journal of Politics and International Relations*, 1(3), 317–344. DOI: 10.1111/1467-856X.00018

Herbst, J. (2000). *States and Power in Africa: Comparative Lessons in Authority and Control*. Princeton University Press.

Hirschmann, D. (1975). Balewa's Nigeria and Nkrumah's Ghana. *The South African Journal of African Affairs*, 71–77.

Holmes, M. (2011). Something Old, Something New, Something Borrowed: Representations of Anarchy in International Relations Theory. *International Relations of the Asia-Pacific*, 11(2), 279–308. DOI: 10.1093/irap/lcr005

Hopkins, A. (2000). Quasi-states, Weak States and the Partition of Africa. *Review of International Studies*, 26(2), 311–320. DOI: 10.1017/S0260210500003119

International Organization. (1962). All-African People's Conferences. *International Organization*, 429 - 434.

Jackson, A. (2010). The Impact of the Cold War and the New Srambles for Africa. *Journal of Southern African Studies*, 36(1), 229–239. DOI: 10.1080/03057071003607469

Jackson, R. H. (1986). Negative Sovereignty in Sub-Saharan Africa. *Review of International Studies*, 12(4), 247–264. DOI: 10.1017/S0260210500113828

Jackson, R. H., & Rosberg, C. G. (1986). Sovereignty and Underdevelopment: Juridical Statehood in the African Crisis. *The Journal of Modern African Studies*, 24(1), 1–31. DOI: 10.1017/S0022278X0000673X

Jersild, A. (2018). Sino-Soviet Relations, Decolonization, and the Global Cold War. *Kritika: Explorations in Russian and Eurasian History*, 217-224.

Jessop, B. (2022). Governance and Metagovernance: On Reflexivity, Requisite Variety, and Requisite Irony in Participatory Governance. In Heinelt, H., Getimis, P., Kafkalas, G., & Smith, R. (Eds.), *Participatory Governance in Multi-Level Context: Concepts and Experience* (pp. 33–56). VS Verlag für Sozialwissenschaften.

Johnson, C. A. (1962). Conferences of Independent African States. *International Organization*, 16(2), 426–429. DOI: 10.1017/S0020818300011152

Kamalu, N. C. (2019). British, French, Belgian, and Portuguese Models of Colonial Rule and Economic Development in Africa. *Annals of Global History*, 37-47.

Kasianiuk, K. (2018). A System-cybernetic Approach to the Study of Political Power. Introductory Remarks. *Kybernetes*, 47(6), 1262–1276. DOI: 10.1108/K-04-2017-0145

Keet, D. (2002). *The New Partnership for Africa's Development (NEPAD) and the African Union: Unity and Integration Within Africa or Integration of Africa into the Global Economy?* Cape Town: Alternative Information and Development Center (AIDC).

Kilian, P. (2019). Self-determination of Peoples in the Charter of the United Nations. *Revista de Estudos Constitucionais, Hermenêutica e Teoria do Direito (RECHTD)*, 341-353.

Kinna, R., & Prichard, A. (2019). Anarchism and Non-domination. *Journal of Political Ideologies*, 24(3), 221–240. DOI: 10.1080/13569317.2019.1633100

Kufuor, K. O. (2005). The Collapse of the Organization of African Unity: Lessons from Economics and Law. *Journal of African Law*, 49(2), 132–144. DOI: 10.1017/S0021855305000112

Kunert, D. (1978). The Role of the Super Powers in Africa. *The South African Journal of African Affairs*, 129–133.

Lake, D. A. (1996). Anarchy, Hierarchy, and the Variety of International Relations. *International Organization*, 50(1), 1–33. DOI: 10.1017/S002081830000165X

Lange, M., Jeong, T., & Amasyali, E. (2021). The Colonial Origins of Ethinc Warfare: Re-examining the Impact of Communalizing Colonial Policies in the British and French Empires. *International Journal of Comparative Sociology*, 62(2), 141–165. DOI: 10.1177/00207152211023793 PMID: 35228760

Lawrence, M. A. (2004). Hot Wars in Cold War Africa. *Reviews in American History*, 32(1), 114–121. DOI: 10.1353/rah.2004.0007

Liebowitz, S., & Margolis, S. E. (1995). Path Dependence, Lock-in, and History. *Journal of Law Economics and Organization*, 205–226.

Lüthi, L. M. (2008). *The Sino-Soviet Split: Cold War in the Communist World*. Princeton University Press.

Maluwa, T. (2012). The Transition from the Organisation of African Unity to the African Union. In Yusuf, A. A., & Ouguergouz, F. (Eds.), *The African Union: Legal and Institutional Framework. A Manual on the Pan-African Organization* (pp. 25–52). Martinus Nijhoff Publishers. DOI: 10.1163/9789004227729_004

Mampilly, Z. (2003). Pacellized Sovereignty: The State, Non-state Actors, and the Politics of Conflict in Africa. *Ufahamu*, 15-62.

Mazrui, A., & Michael, T. (1984). *Nationalism and the New States of Africa.* Heinemann.

McCormick, J. P. (1993). Addressing the Political Exception: Machiavelli's "Accidents" and the Mixed Regime. *The American Political Science Review*, 87(4), 888–900. DOI: 10.2307/2938821

McNamara, F. T. (1989). *France in Black Africa.* National Defense University. DOI: 10.21236/ADA229583

Mednick, S. (2023, August 19). *11 Nations of West Africa Commit to a Military Deployment to Restore the Ousted President of Niger.* Retrieved from The Associated Press: https://apnews.com/article/niger-coup-extremists-c4c4024bdd7cd8b7354a448411388137

Melber, H., Bjarnesen, J., Lanzano, C., & Mususa, P. (2023). Citizenship Matters: Explorations into the Citizen-State Relationship in Africa. *Forum for Development Studies*, 50(1), 35–58. DOI: 10.1080/08039410.2022.2145992

Michalopoulos, S., & Papaioannou, E. (2016). The Long-Run Effects of the Scramble for Africa. *The American Economic Review*, 106(7), 1802–1848. DOI: 10.1257/aer.20131311

Miran-Guyon, M. (2006). The Political Economy of Civil Islam in Côte d'Ivoire. In Bestandsaufnahume, E. (Ed.), *Plitical Islam in West Africa* (pp. 82–113). Lit Verlag.

Mistry, P. S. (2000). Africa's Record of Regional Cooperation and Integration. *African Affairs*, 99(397), 553–573. DOI: 10.1093/afraf/99.397.553

Mnyongani, F. D. (2008). Between a Rock and a Hard Place: The Right to Self-determination Versus Uti Possidetis in Africa. *The Comparative and International Law Journal of Southern Africa*, 463–479.

Mommsen, W. J. (1988). Bismark, the Concert of Europe, and the Future of West Africa, 1883-1885. In Forster, S., Mommsen, W., & Robinson, R. (Eds.), *Bismarck, Europe and Africa: The Berlin Africa Conference, 1884–1885, and the Onset of Partition* (pp. 151–170). Oxford University Press.

Mueller, B. (2020). Why Public Policies Fail: Policymaking Under Complexity. *Economía*, 21(2), 311–323. DOI: 10.1016/j.econ.2019.11.002

Müller-Crepon, C., Hunziker, P., & Cederman, L.-E. (2021). Roads to Rule, Roads to Rebel: Relational State Capacity and Conflict in Africa. *The Journal of Conflict Resolution*, 65(2-3), 563–590. DOI: 10.1177/0022002720963674 PMID: 33487734

Nathan, R. (2001). African Redemption: Black Nationalism, and End of Empire in Africa. *Exchange*, 30(2), 125–144. DOI: 10.1163/157254301X00084

Ndlovu, S., Houston, G., & Magubane, B. (2019). The South African Liberation Struggle. In Temu, A. J. (Ed.), *J. d. Tembe, Southern African Liberation Struggles Contemporaneous Documents:1960–1994* (pp. 101–112). Mkuki na Nyota Publishers Ltd.

Nkrumah, K. (1963). *Africa Must Unite*. Panaf Books.

Obi, C. I. (2009). Economic Community of West African States on the Ground: Comparing Peacekeeping in Liberia, Sierra Leone, Guinea Bissau, and Côte d'Ivoire. *African Security*, 2(2-3), 119–135. DOI: 10.1080/19362200903361945

Okumu, W. (2009). The African Union: Pitfalls and Prospects for Uniting Africa. *Journal of International Affairs*, 93–111.

Oloruntoba, S. O. (2020). Pan-Africanism, Regional Integration and Development in Africa. In Oloruntoba, S. O. (Ed.), *Pan Africanism, Regional Integration and Development in Africa* (pp. 1–14). Palgrave Macmillan. DOI: 10.1007/978-3-030-34296-8_1

Olympio, S. (1961, October). African Problems and the Cold War. *Foreign Affairs*, 40(1), 50–57. DOI: 10.2307/20029532

Onuf, N., & Klink, F. F. (1989). Anarchy, Authority, Rule. *International Studies Quarterly*, 33(2), 149–173. DOI: 10.2307/2600535

Organization of African Unity. (1965, May 22-25). *Resolutions Adopted by the First Conference of Independent African Heads of State and Governments Held in Addis Ababa, Ethiopia, from 22 to May 25 1963*. Retrieved from African Union Common Repository: https://au.int/sites/default/files/decisions/32247-1963_cias_plen_2 -3_cias_res_1-2_e.pdf

Peachey, A. (2009, May 2). *Conspicuously Politically Incorrect: The Soft Bigotry of Low Expectations*. Retrieved April 5, 2024, from https://www.nzcpr.com/ conspicuously-politically-incorrect-the-soft-bigotry-of-low-expectations/

Rapkin, D. P., Thompson, W. R., & Christopherson, J. A. (1979). Bipolarity and Bipolarization in the Cold War Era: Conceptualization, Measurement, and Validation. *The Journal of Conflict Resolution*, 23(2), 261–295. DOI: 10.1177/002200277902300203

Reis, B. C. (2013). Portugal and the UN: A Rogue State Resisting the Norm of Decolonization (1956–1974). *Portuguese Studies*, 251-276.

Reynolds, J. T. (2015). *Sovereignty and Struggle: Africa and Africans in the Era of the Cold War, 1945-1994*. Oxford University Press.

Robinson, R. (1988). The Conference in Berlin and the Future of Africa, 1884-1885. In Forster, S., Mommsen, W., & Robinson, R. (Eds.), *Bismarck, Europe and Africa: The Berlin Africa Conference, 1884–1885, and the Onset of Partition* (pp. 1–32). Oxford University Press.

Ryder, H., Baisch, A., & Eguegu, O. (2020, September 19). *Decolonizing the United Nations Means Abolishing the Permanent Five: The Inequalities of the Past Can't Set the Rules of the Present*. Retrieved from Foreign Policy: https://foreignpolicy .com/2020/09/17/decolonizing-united-nations-means-abolish-permanent-five -security-council/

Scalapino, R. A. (1964, July). Sino-Soviet Competition in Africa. *Foreign Affairs*, 42(4), 640–654. DOI: 10.2307/20029719

Schedler, A. (2007). Mapping Contingency. In Shapiro, I., & Sonu, B. (Eds.), *Political Contingency: Studying the Unexpected, the Accidental, and the Unforeseen* (pp. 54–78). New York University Press.

Schiel, R., Faulkner, C., & Powell, J. (2017). Mutiny in Côte d'Ivoire. *Africa Spectrum*, 52(2), 103–115. DOI: 10.1177/000203971705200205

Schmidt, E. (2013). *Foreign intervention in Africa: From the Cold War to the War on Terror*. Cambridge University. DOI: 10.1017/CBO9781139021371

Schomerus, M., Englebert, P., & Vries, L. d. (2019). Africa's Secessionism: A Breakdance of Aspiration, Grievance, Performance and Disenchantment. In *L. d. Vires, P. E. Englebert, & M. Schomerus, Secessionism in African Politics* (pp. 1–20). Palgrave Macmillan. DOI: 10.1007/978-3-319-90206-7_1

Sewell, W. H. (1990, October). *"Three Temporalities: Toward a Sociology of the Event"*. Retrieved from University of Michigan: https://deepblue.lib.umich.edu/ bitstream/handle/2027.42/51215/448.pdf

Shaw, M. N. (1997). The Heritage of States: The Principle of Uti Possidetis Juris Today. *The British Year Book of International Law*, 75-154.

Shepperson, G. (2008). The Fifth Pan-African Conference, 1945 and the All African Peoples Congress, 1958. *Contributions in Black Studies*, 35-66.

Sherwood, M. (2012). Pan-African Conferences, 1900-1953: What Did 'Pan-Africanism' Mean? *The Journal of Pan African Studies*, 106-126.

Sherwood, M. (2021). The All African People's Congress (AAPC) was called by Kwame Nkrumah-- and George Padmore. *Contemporary Journal of African Studies*, 63-68.

Shimamoto, M. (2021). Unintended Consequences of Government Policy. *Japanese Research in Business History*, 38(0), 1–5. DOI: 10.5029/jrbh.38.1

Sinclair, G. F. (2019). A Battlefield Transformed the United Nations and the Struggle over Postcolonial Statehood. In *J. v. Bernstorff, & P. Dann, The Battle for International Law: South-North Perspectives on Decolonization Era* (pp. 257–277). Oxford University Press. DOI: 10.1093/oso/9780198849636.003.0012

Stark, D. (2001). Heterarchy: Exploiting Ambiguity and Organizing Diversity. *Brazilian Journal of Political Economy*, 22-41.

Steinmetz, G. (1998). Critical Realism and Historical Sociology. A Review Article. *Comparative Studies in Society and History*, 40(1), 170–186. DOI: 10.1017/S0010417598980069

Stone, J. (1942). Peace Planning and Atlantic Charter. *The Australian Quarterly*, 14(2), 5–22. DOI: 10.2307/20631017

Storey, D. (2017). States, Territory and Sovereignty. *Geography (Sheffield, England)*, 102(3), 116–121. DOI: 10.1080/00167487.2017.12094021

Strokosch, K., & Osborne, S. P. (2020). Co-experience, Co-production and Co-governance: An Ecosystem Approach to the Analysis of Value Creation. *Policy and Politics*, 48(3), 425–442. DOI: 10.1332/030557320X15857337955214

Tafotie, J., & Idahosa, S. (2016). Conflicts in Africa and Major Powers: Proxy Wars, Zone of Influence, or Provocating Instability. *Вестник РУДН, серия «Международные отношения», сентябрь*, 451-460.

The African Union Commission and New Zealand Ministry of Foreign Affairs and Trade/Manatū Aorere. (2014). *African Union Handbook 2021*. The African Union Commission and New Zealand Ministry of Foreign Affairs and Trade/Manatū Aorere.

The New York Times. (1964, July 21). *Nyerere, at Cairo, Assails Nkrumah; Tangangikan Says Ghanaian Only Preaches Unity*. Retrieved from The New York Times: https://www.nytimes.com/1964/07/21/archives/nyerere-atcairo-assails-nkrumah-tangangikan-says-ghanaian-only.html

The New York Times. (2020, June 2). *A Continent Remade: Reflections on 1960, the Year of Africa*. Retrieved from The New York Times: https://www.nytimes.com/interactive/2020/02/06/world/africa/africa-independence-year.html#:~:text=The%20year%20was%201960.,for%20this%20project%20was%20born

The Organization of African Unity. (1963, May 25). *OAU Charter*. Retrieved from African Union: https://au.int/sites/default/files/treaties/7759-file-oau_charter_1963.pdf

Torfing, J., Peters, G. B., Pierre, J., & Sørensen, E. (2012). *Interactive Governance: Advancing the Paradigm*. Oxford University Press. DOI: 10.1093/acprof:oso/9780199596751.001.0001

United Nations. (1998, November 3). *Agreement between the Government of Guinea-Bissau and the Self-proclaimed Military junta*. Retrieved from United Nations: https://peacemaker.un.org/guatemala-abujaagreement98

United Nations. (2012, December 20). *Security Council Resolution 2085 (2012)*. Retrieved from United Nations: https://www.refworld.org/legal/resolution/unsc/2012/en/89613

United Nations Digital Library. (2003, March 26). *Report of the Secretary-General on Côte d'Ivoire*. Retrieved from United Nations Digital Library: https://digitallibrary.un.org/record/491307?ln=en&v=pdf#files

United Nations Digital Library. (2017, January 19). *Resolution 2337 (2017) / adopted by the Security Council at its 7866th meeting on January 19 2017*. Retrieved from United Nations Digital Library: https://digitallibrary.un.org/record/856865?ln=en&v=pdf

United Nations Treaty Collection. (1963, May 25). *No. 6947. Charter of the Organization of African Unity. Done at Addis Ababa onMay251963*. Retrieved from United Nations Treaty Collection: https://treaties.un.org/doc/Publication/UNTS/Volume%20479/volume-479-I-6947-English.pdf

University of California Press. (1959). Resolutions of the All Africans People's Conference. *Current History*, 41-46.

Varela, C. (2017). Africa Finds Voice in the Halls of Manchester. *History in the Making*, 55-87.

Verheul, J. (2021). The Atlantic Charter: Genesis of the Transatlantic World Order. *Atlantisch Perspectief*, 42-46.

Wallerstein, I. (1974). The Role of the Organization of African Unity in Contemporary African Politics. In Y. El-Ayouty, & H. C. Brooks, Africa and International Organization (pp. 18–28). Martinus Nijhofj. DOI: 10.1007/978-94-010-2050-3_3

Walraven, K. v. (1999, January). Containing Conflict in the Economic Community of West African States. The Hague: Clingendael .

Warner, C. M. (2001). The Rise of the State System in Africa. *Review of International Studies*, 27(5), 65–89. DOI: 10.1017/S0260210501008038

Welch, J. C.Jr. (1986). Ethnic Factors in African Armies. *Ethnic and Racial Studies*, 9(3), 321–333. DOI: 10.1080/01419870.1986.9993536

Wiking, S. (1993). *Military Coups in Sub-Saharan Africa: How to Justify Illegal Assumptions of Power*. Scandinavian Institute of African Studies.

Wills, M. (2024). *A Messy Divorce: The Sino-Soviet Split*. Retrieved from J Stor Daily: https://daily.jstor.org/a-messy-divorce-the-sino-soviet-split/

Yolles, M. (2003). The Political Cybernetics of Organizations. *Kybernetes*, 32(9/10), 1253–1282. DOI: 10.1108/03684920310493242

## KEY TERMS AND DEFINITIONS

**African International Organizations:** Transnational institutions created and nurtured in Africa.

**Authority:** Legitimate power or right to (un)make public decisions, and enforce compliance in line with legally sanctioned due processes.

**Crisis:** An unstable political condition characterized by the convergence and/or divergence of actor interests and initiatives.

**Cybernetic Politics:** The pursuit and navigation of actor interests in contexts of unprecedented crisis and unpredictability; the governance of contingent events.

**ECOWAS:** The Economic Community of West African States.

**Entanglement:** Actors enmeshed in complex settings with difficult disengagement options.

**Heterarchical:** Horizontally structured transactions enacted by formally unranked autonomous actors.

**Institutional Circuits:** Permanent/ad hoc formal and informal transactional networks of public agencies.

# Conclusion

The chapters in *Postinternationalism and the Rise of Heterarchy* collectively underscore the critical need to re-evaluate and redefine traditional frameworks of governance and international relations. As we navigate through the complexities of a rapidly changing global order, the concepts of postinternationalism and heterarchy offer fresh perspectives that challenge the long-held supremacy of the nation-state as the sole arbiter of power and influence in the world.

The book begins by laying the theoretical foundations of postinternationalism, where Dana-Marie Ramjit opens with a thought-provoking exploration of how global interconnectedness, spurred by technological advancements, has blurred the once-clear boundaries of nation-states. As power increasingly diffuses across non-state actors, technological platforms, and transnational movements, the state finds itself not as the dominant force it once was, but rather as one of many players in an intricate web of global governance.

The shift from a state-centric system to one characterized by polycontexturality and heterarchy is vividly illustrated by the diverse case studies and analyses presented by authors such as Philip Cerny, Richard Weiner, and Aleksandra Spalińska. They delve deep into the dynamics of emerging governance systems, highlighting how heterarchical structures provide both opportunities and challenges for contemporary political actors. From examining the reactive nature of states in a heterarchical world to mapping out the deeper complexities of governance beyond polycentrism, the contributors highlight the inadequacies of traditional hierarchical models in addressing the multidimensional issues of the 21st century.

As demonstrated by the contributions of Adrian Cheok and Thomas Lange, the heterarchical framework is not limited to the realm of political theory but extends into practical domains such as global health and crisis management. Their insights reveal how non-state actors, particularly those driven by anarchistic principles, play a pivotal role in global governance, challenging the conventional wisdom of centralized control. Furthermore, the discussion on crisis management in global health emphasizes how heterarchical structures can either amplify or block effective governance, offering nuanced perspectives on collaborative problem-solving in the face of global threats.

The chapters on the Caribbean and African contexts, by Dana-Marie Ramjit and Nene Kuditchar, further extend the book's analysis to regions historically defined by colonialism and centralized power structures. These chapters underscore the profound influence of heterarchical dynamics on postcolonial states, where the legacy of colonialism continues to shape contemporary governance structures. In these contexts, heterarchy emerges as a compelling alternative to entrenched hierarchies, fostering collaboration and distributed power in ways that challenge traditional authority.

From the European Union's navigation of investment governance to the decentralization of political participation in the West Philippine Sea, the contributors illustrate how heterarchical governance is becoming a defining feature of modern international relations. Dealan Riga's examination of the EU and Aileen Joy Pactao's analysis of political participation in the West Philippine Sea provide practical examples of how heterarchical dynamics are reshaping regional and global power structures. These case studies highlight the practical implications of heterarchy in specific geopolitical contexts, demonstrating its ability to facilitate flexibility and adaptability in response to global challenges.

In conclusion, *Postinternationalism and the Rise of Heterarchy* serves as both a theoretical exploration and a practical guide for understanding the emerging global order. The concept of heterarchy, as explored throughout this volume, invites us to reconsider our assumptions about power, authority, and governance in an increasingly complex and interconnected world. It is evident that as globalization, technology, and transnational movements continue to shape international relations, the role of the nation-state will continue to evolve, giving way to new forms of governance that better reflect the realities of the 21st century. This book provides an essential resource for scholars, policymakers, and students seeking to understand and navigate this transition, offering insights that are both timely and crucial for addressing the challenges of our time.

# Compilation of References

Abbott, K. W., Genschel, P., Snidal, D., & Zangl, B. (2015). Orchestration. International organizations as orchestrators, 3-36.

Abbott, K. W., Genschel, P., Snidal, D., & Zangl, B. (Eds.). (2015). *International organizations as orchestrators*. Cambridge University Press.

Abbott, K. W., & Snidal, D. (2009). The Governance Triangle: Regulatory Standards Institutions and the Shadow of the State. In *The Politics of Global Regulation* (pp. 44–88). Princeton University Press. DOI: 10.2307/j.ctt7rgmj.6

Aboagye, F. B. (2018). *ECOMOG: A Sub-Regional Experience in Conflict Resolution, Management and Peacekeeping in Liberia* (2nd ed.). Ulinzi Africa Resources.

Abraham, G. (2007). "Lines Upon Maps": Africa and The Sanctity of African Boundaries. *African Journal of International and Comparative Law*, 61-84.

ACCORD. (2019, September 2). *ECOWAS's Efforts at Resolving Guinea-Bissau's Protracted Political Crisis, 2015-2019*. Retrieved from ACCORD: https://www.accord.org.za/conflict-trends/ecowass-efforts-at-resolving-guinea-bissaus-protracted-political-crisis-2015-2019/

Acemoglu, D., Johnson, S., & Robinson, J. A. (2001). The Colonial Origins of Comparative Development: An Empirical investigation. ˜the œAmerican. *The American Economic Review*, 91(5), 1369–1401. DOI: 10.1257/aer.91.5.1369

Acharya, A. (2017). After Liberal hegemony: The advent of a multiplex world order. *Ethics & International Affairs*, 31(3), 271–285. DOI: 10.1017/S089267941700020X

Adebajo, A. (2011). *UN Peacekeeping in Africa: From the Suez Crisis to the Sudan Conflicts*. Lynne Rienner Publishers. DOI: 10.1515/9781626376007

African Union Common Repository. (1999, September 9). *Sirte Declaration*. Retrieved from African Union Common Repository: https://archives.au.int/handle/123456789/10157

African Union. (2013, July 10). *AFISMA Transfers its Authority to MINUSMA.* Retrieved from African Union: https://www.peaceau.org/en/article/afisma-transfers-its-authority-to-minusma

African Union. (n.d.). *Constitutive Act of the African Union.* Retrieved from African Union: https://au.int/sites/default/files/pages/34873-file-constitutiveact_en.pdf

African Union. (n.d.). *Protocol Relating to the Establishment of the Peace and Security Council of the African Union.* Retrieved from African Union: https://au.int/en/treaties/protocol-relating-establishment-peace-and-security-council-african-union

Agostini, L. (2012, August 28). *Trinidad and Tobago Guardian.* Retrieved from Independent, but are we truly developed?: https://www.guardian.co.tt/columnist/2012-08-28/independent-are-we-truly-developed

Aho, E. (2017). *Shrinking space for civil society: challenges for implementing the 2030 agenda.* Retrieved from http://www.forumsyd.org: http://www.forumsyd.org/PageFiles/8150/PO150943_Rapport_5maj_web.pdf

Akanji, O. O. (2019). Sub-regional Security Challenge: ECOWAS and the War on Terrorism in West Africa. *Insight on Africa*, 94–112.

Ake, C. (1965). Pan-Africanism and African Governments. *The Review of Politics*, 27(4), 532–542. DOI: 10.1017/S0034670500005775

Al Jazeera. (2023, August 18). *ECOWAS Defence Chiefs Agree 'D-day' for Niger Military Intervention.* Retrieved from Al Jazeera: https://www.aljazeera.com/news/2023/8/18/ecowas-defence-chiefs-agree-d-day-for-niger-military-intervention

Al Jazeera. (2024, January 28). *Niger, Mali, Burkina Faso Announce Withdrawal from ECOWAS: The Three Nations, Led by Military Governments, Accused the Regional Bloc of Becoming a Threat to Member States.* Retrieved from Al Jazeera: https://www.aljazeera.com/news/2024/1/28/niger-mali-burkina-faso-announce-withdrawal-from-ecowas

Albert, M., Buzan, B., & Zürn, M. (Eds.). (2013). *Bringing Sociology to International Relations: World Politics as Differentiation Theory.* Cambridge University Press. DOI: 10.1017/CBO9781139856041

Alexander, G. (2017, July 2). *Marlene fired again.* Retrieved from guardian.co.tt: https://www.guardian.co.tt/news/2017-07-02/marlene-fired-again

Ali, M., Fjeldstad, O.-H., Jiang, B., & Shifaz, A. B. (2015, December). Colonial Legacy, State-building and the Salience of Ethnicity in Sub-Saharan Africa. *CMI Working Paper.WP 2015:16.* Bergen: CMI (Chr. Michelsen Institute).

Aligica, P. D., & Tarko, V. (2013). Co-Production, Polycentricity, and Value Heterogeneity: The Ostroms' Public Choice Institutionalism Revisited. *The American Political Science Review*, 107(4), 726–741. DOI: 10.1017/S0003055413000427

Aligica, P. D., & Tarko, V. (2014). Institutional Resilience and Economic Systems: Lessons from Elinor Ostrom's Work. *Comparative Economic Studies*, 56(1), 52–76. DOI: 10.1057/ces.2013.29

Ali, M., Miller, K., & Ponce de Leon, R. (2017). Family planning and Zika virus: Need for renewed and cohesive efforts to ensure availability of intrauterine contraception in Latin America and the Caribbean. *The European Journal of Contraception & Reproductive Health Care*, 102-106(2), 102–106. Advance online publication. DOI: 10.1080/13625187.2017.1288902 PMID: 28256913

Aljazeera. (2017, May 17). *Caribbean to Caliphate: why are young Muslims from the Caribbean island of Trinidad and Tobago being drawn to the conflicts in Syria and Iraq?* Retrieved from aljazeera.com: https://www.aljazeera.com/programmes/peopleandpower/2017/05/caribbean-caliphate-170517073332147.html

Alleyne, G. (2017, February 17). *The role of civil society as advocates and watchdogs in NCD prevention and control in the Caribbean.* Retrieved from healthycaribbean.org: https://www.healthycaribbean.org/wp-content/uploads/2017/02/2017-03-The-role-of-civil-society-as-advocastes-and-watchdogs.pdf

Alter, K. J. & Raustiala, K. (2018). The Rise of International Regime Complexity, *Annual Review of Law and Social Science*, 14 (1), pp. 18.2–18.21.

Alvare, B. (2010). Babylon makes the rules: compliance, fear, and self-discipline in the quest for official NGO status. *Political and Legal Anthropology*, 178-200. DOI: 10.1111/j.1555-2934.2010.01110.x

Amable, B. (2016). Institutional Complementarities in the Dynamic Comparative Analysis.'. *Journal of Institutional Economics*, 12(1), 79–103. DOI: 10.1017/S1744137415000211

Ambursley, F., & Cohen, R. (2024). Crisis in the Caribbean: internal transformations and external constraints. In *Routledge eBooks* (pp.26). https://doi.org/DOI: 10.4324/9781032703480-1

Anand, A., Escobar, A., Sen, J., & Waterman, P. (2004). A different world is possible: The World Social Forum. In Anand, Escobar, Sen, & Waterman (Eds.), The World Social Forum: Challenging Empires. New Delhi: The Viveka Foundation.

Andaya, B. (2017). Glocalization and the Marketing of Christianity in Early Modern Southeast Asia. *Religions*, 8(1), 7. DOI: 10.3390/rel8010007

Anderson, B. (1991). *Imagined communities: reflections on the origin and spread of nationalism*. Verso.

Anderson, C. (2010). Presenting and evaluating qualitative research. *American Journal of Pharmaceutical Education*, 74–141. http://www.ajpe.org/doi/pdf/10.5688/aj7408141 PMID: 21179252

Andrews, M. (2021, November). *Getting Real About Unknowns in Complex Policy Work*. Retrieved from RISE Working Paper Series.: https://doi.org/DOI: 10.35489/BSG-RISE-WP_2021/083

Aneme, G. A. (2008). The African Standby Force: Major Issues Under 'Mission Scenario Six' . *Political Perspectives*, 1-22.

Aniche, E. T. (2020). Pan-Africanism and Regionalism in Africa: The Journey So Far. In Oloruntoba, S. O. (Ed.), *Pan Africanism, Regional Integration and Development in Africa* (pp. 17–38). Palgrave Macmillan. DOI: 10.1007/978-3-030-34296-8_2

Animashaun, M. A. (2009). State Failure, Crisis of Governance and Disengagement from the State in Africa. *Africa Development. Afrique et Developpement*, 34(3-4), 47–63. DOI: 10.4314/ad.v34i3-4.63527

Ansell, C. & Trondal, J. (2017). Governing Turbulence: An Organizational Institutional Agenda.

Ansell, C., & Trondal, J. (2017). Governing turbulence. *EUSA fifteenth biennial conference*. Miami.

Ansell, C. (2006). Network Institutionalism. In Rhodes, R. A. W. (Ed.), *The Oxford Handbook of Political Institutions*. Oxford University Press.

Ansell, C. (2023). *Rethinking Theories of Governance*. Edward Elgar Publishing.

Ansell, C., Sondorp, E., & Stevens, R. H. (2018). The Promise and Challenge of Global Network Governance: The Global Outbreak Alert and Response Network. *Global Governance*, 18(3), 317–337. DOI: 10.1163/19426720-01803005

Ansell, C., & Torfing, J. (Eds.). (2016). *Handbook on Theories of Governance*. Edward Elgar Publishing. DOI: 10.4337/9781782548508

Ansell, C., Trondal, J., & Morten, O. (2017). *Governance in Turbulent Times*. Oxford University.

Anyidoho, H. K. (2021). *Guns Over Kigali*. Sub-Saharan Publishers.

Araujo, A. L. (2023). How Britain Underdeveloped the Caribbean: A Reparation Response to Europe's Legacy of Plunder and Poverty, by Hilary McD. Beckles. *NWIG, New West Indian Guide/NWIG, 97*(1–2), 216–217. https://doi.org/DOI: 10.1163/22134360-09701002

Archibugi, D. (2008). *The Global Commonwealth of Citizens: Toward Cosmopolitan Democracy*. Princeton University Press.

Arugay, A. & Baquisal, J. (2022). Mobilized and Polarized: Social Media and Disinformation

Arugay, A. A., & Baquisal, J. K. A.Narratives in the. (2022). Philippine Elections. *Pacific Affairs*, 95(3), 549–573. DOI: 10.5509/2022953549

Astrov, A. (2002). Pondering dramatic endings, probing possible beginnings; or doing politics as usual? *Journal of International Relations and Development*, 63–76. http://eds.a.ebscohost.com.ezp.waldenulibrary.org/eds/pdfviewer/pdfviewer?vid=1&sid=61db2c8a-030d-4c5c-abb1-c51dd43fe9f7%40sessionmgr4006

Avdagic, S. Rhodes, M. & Visser, J., (Eds.). (2011). *Social Pacts in Europe" Emergence, Evolution and Institutionalization*. Oxford University Press

Avery, D. H. (2010). The North American Plan for Avian and Pandemic Influenza: A case study of regional health security in the 21st century. *Global Health Governance*, 3(2).

Awad, I. (2017). *The multiple levels of governance of international migration: understanding disparities and disorder*. Retrieved from Cambridge.org: https://www.cambridge.org/core/services/aop-cambridge-core/content/view/E714B022BC70D8B07E2320351B31F9AA/S2398772317000368a.pdf/multiple_levels_of_governance_of_international_migration_understanding_disparities_and_disorder.pdf

Ayearst, M. (2023). *The British West Indies*. https://doi.org/DOI: 10.4324/9781003362043

Ayittey, G. B. (2016, July 10). *Disband the African Union: African Leaders Should Admit that a Caricature of the European Union Can't Possibly Work for Africa*. Retrieved from Foreign Policy: https://foreignpolicy.com/2016/07/10/disband-the-african-union/

Ayittey, G. B. (2010). The United States of Africa: A Revisit. *The Annals of the American Academy of Political and Social Science*, 632(1), 86–102. DOI: 10.1177/0002716210378988

Babic, M. (2020). Let's Talk About the Interregnum: Gramsci and the Crisis of the Liberal World Order. *International Affairs*, 96(3), 767–786. DOI: 10.1093/ia/iiz254

Baccaro, L., Blyth, M., & Pontusson, J. (Eds.). (2022). *Diminishing Returns: The New Politics of Growth and Stagnation.* Oxford University Press. DOI: 10.1093/oso/9780197607855.001.0001

Bäckstrand, K. (2006). Multi-stakeholder Partnerships for Sustainable Development. *European Environment*, 16(5), 290–293. DOI: 10.1002/eet.425

Badie, B., & Birnbaum, P. (1983). *The Sociology of the State* (Chicago, Ilinois: University of Chicago Press)

Badmus, I. A. (2017). Even the Stones are Burning: Explaining the Ethnic Dimensions of the Civil War in La Côte d'Ivoire. *Journal of Social Sciences*, 45–57.

Balbis, J. (2003). *NGOs, governance and development in Latin America and the Caribbean.* UNESCO. Retrieved from http://digital-library.unesco.org/shs/most/gsdl/cgi-bin/library?e=d-000-00---0most--00-0-0--0prompt-10---4------0-11--1-en-50---20-about---00031-001-1-0utfZz-8-00&a=d&c=most&cl=CL5.9&d=HASH01000b50ae2385471f29df53

Bandola-Gill, J., Arthur, M., & Leng, R. I. (2023). What is co-production? Conceptualising and understanding co-production of knowledge and policy across different theoretical perspectives. *Evidence & Policy, 19*(2), 275 298. https://doi.org/DOI: 10.1332/174426421X16420955772641

Barkanov, B. (2016, June 14). *Institutionalism.* Retrieved from Encyclopaedia Britannica: https://www.britannica.com/topic/institutionalism

Barker, S. E. (Ed.). (1962). *Social Contract: Essays by Locke, Hume and Rousseau.* Oxford University Press.

Barry, T., Gahman, L., Greenidge, A., & Mohamed, A. (2020). Wrestling with race and colonialism in Caribbean agriculture: Toward a (food) sovereign and (gender) just future. *Geoforum*, 109, 106–110. DOI: 10.1016/j.geoforum.2019.12.018

Bartmanski, D. (2021). "Imbricated -A Conceptual Morphology of Contextuality," *Sozialraum.de.* Special Issue/ 2021 ISSN 1868-2596. https://www.sozialraum.de/imbricated-a-conceptual-morphology-of-contextuality

Basedow, J. R. (2017). *The EU in the global investment regime: commission entrepreneurship, incremental institutional change and business lethargy.* Routledge. DOI: 10.4324/9781315112282

Basedow, R. (2019). Business lobbying in international investment policy-making in Europe. In Dialer, D., & Richter, M. (Eds.), *Lobbying in the European Union: Strategies, dynamics and trends* (pp. 389–400). DOI: 10.1007/978-3-319-98800-9_28

Basedow, R. (2020). The EU's International Investment Policy ten years on: The Policy-Making Implications of Unintended Competence Transfers. *Journal of Common Market Studies*, 59(3), 643–660. DOI: 10.1111/jcms.13124

BASF (2024). BASF priorities for a competitive Europe. Available at: file:///C:/Users/u233569/Downloads/BASF-Priorities-for-a-Competitive-Europe.pdf

Bates, D. (2020). The Political Theology of Entropy: A Katechon for the Cybernetic Age. *History of the Human Sciences*, 33(1), 109–127. DOI: 10.1177/0952695119864237

Bauerle Danzman, S., & Meunier, S. (2023). Naïve no more: Foreign direct investment screening in the European Union. *Global Policy*, 14(S3), 40–53. DOI: 10.1111/1758-5899.13215

Bauerle Danzman, S., & Meunier, S. (2024). The EU's Geoeconomic Turn: From Policy Laggard to Institutional Innovator. *Journal of Common Market Studies*, 62(4), 1–19. DOI: 10.1111/jcms.13599

Bauman, Z. (2000/2010). *Liquid Modernity*. Polity Press.

Beck, U. (1992). *Risk Society: Towards a New Modernity. Theory, Culture and Society*, 1st Edition. Sage.

Beeson, M., & Bell, S. (2009, Spring). The G-20 and International Economic Governance: Hegemony, Collectivism, or Both? *Global Governance*, 15(1), 67–86. DOI: 10.1163/19426720-01501005

Bellamy, R. (2017). A European republic of sovereign states: Sovereignty, republicanism and the European Union. *European Journal of Political Theory*, 16(2), 188–209. DOI: 10.1177/1474885116654389

Belmonte, R., & Cerny, P. G. (2021). *Heterarchy: Toward Paradigm Shift in World Politics*. In *The Changing Faces of Power, Journal of Political Power*, Special Issue ed. by G. Gallarotti. DOI: 10.4324/9781003200673-14

Belmonte, R., & Cerny, P. G. (2021). Heterarchy: Toward Paradigm Shift in World Politics. *Journal of Political Power*, 14(1), 235–257. DOI: 10.1080/2158379X.2021.1879574

Bendix, R. (1964). *Nation-Building and Citizenship*. Anchor Books.

Benoit, O. (2020). Ressentiment, nationalism and the emergence of political culture in Grenada. In *Edward Elgar Publishing eBooks*. https://doi.org/DOI: 10.4337/9781789903447.00016

Berger, P., & Luckmann, T. (1966). *The Social Construction of Reality*. Doubleday.

Betts, R. (2005). *Assimilation and Association in French Colonial Theory*. University of Nebraska Press.

Bhabha, H. (1994). *The location of culture*. Routledge.

Bhambra, G. K. (2010). Historical Sociology, International Relations and Connected Histories. *Cambridge Review of International Affairs*, 23(1), 127–143. DOI: 10.1080/09557570903433639

Bianchi, C., Nasi, G., & Rivenbark, W. C. (2021). Implementing collaborative governance: models, experiences, and challenges. *Public Management Review, 23*(11), 1581 1589. https://doi.org/DOI: 10.1080/14719037.2021.1878777

Bilmes, L., & Stiglitz, J. (2008). *The Three Trillion Dollar War: The True Cost of the Iraq Conflict*. Norton.

Bishop, M. L., Byron-Reid, J., Corbett, J., & Veenendaal, W. (2021). Secession, Territorial Integrity and (Non)-Sovereignty: Why do Some Separatist Movements in the Caribbean Succeed and Others Fail? *Ethnopolitics, 21*(5), 538 560. DOI: 10.1080/17449057.2021.1975414

Black, J. (2008). Constructing and Contesting Legitimation and Accountability in Polycentric Regulatory Regimes. *Regulation & Governance*, 2(2), 137–164. DOI: 10.1111/j.1748-5991.2008.00034.x

Bohle, D., & Regan, A. (2021). The comparative political economy of growth models: Explaining the continuity of FDI-led growth in Ireland and Hungary. *Politics & Society*, 49(1), 75–106. DOI: 10.1177/0032329220985723

Bonnier, E., & Hedenskog, J. (2020, December). *The United States and Russia in Africa: A Survey of US and Russian Political, Economic, and Military-security Relations with Africa. FOI-R--5039--SE*. Stockholm, Sweden: Swedish Defence Agency.

Boodram, K. (2015, July 11). *NGOs: health card a danger to treating HIV/AIDS in T&T*. Retrieved from Trinidad and Tobago Guardian: http://www.trinidadexpress.com/20150711/news/ngos-health-card-a-danger-to-treating-hivaids-in-tt

Boodram, K. (2017, Januray 6). *Civil society presents unified voice, offers suggestions*. Retrieved from trinidadexpress.com: http://www.trinidadexpress.com/20170106/news/civil-society-presents-unified-voice-offers-suggestions

Borja, A. L. (2016). Virtù, Fortuna, and Statecraft: A Dialectical Analysis of Machiavelli. *Kritike: An OnlineJournal of Philosophy*, 192–21.

Boyer, R., & Saillard, Y. (Eds.). (2002). *Regulation Theory: The State of the Art* Shread, C., Trans.). Routledge.

Brady, M. P., Duffy, M. L., & Hazelkor, M. (2014). Policy and Systems Change: Planning for Unintended Consequences. *The Clearing House: A Journal of Educational Strategies, Issues and Ideas*, 87(3), 102–109. DOI: 10.1080/00098655.2014.891882

Braithwaite, J. (2008). *Regulatory Capitalism: How it Works, Ideas for Making It Work Better*. Edward Elgar. DOI: 10.4337/9781848441262

Brathwaite, K. (1974). *Contradictory omens : cultural diversity and integration in the Caribbean*. http://ci.nii.ac.jp/ncid/BA55331113

Braun, D., & Grande, E. (2021). Politicizing Europe in elections to the European Parliament (1994–2019): The crucial role of mainstream parties. *Journal of Common Market Studies*, 59(5), 1124–1141. DOI: 10.1111/jcms.13168

Braveboy, M. (2017, January 18). *Crippling murder rate continues in Trinidad in 2017*. Retrieved from Caribbean News Now: http://www.caribbeannewsnow.com/headline-Crippling-murder-rate-continues-in-Trinidad-in-2017-33219.html

Brenner, N. (2004). *New State Spaces: Urban Governance and the Rescaling of Statehood*. Oxford University Press. DOI: 10.1093/acprof:oso/9780199270057.001.0001

Brenner, N., Jessop, B., Jones, M., & MacLeod, G. (Eds.). (2003). *State/Space: A Reader*. Blackwell. DOI: 10.1002/9780470755686

Brent Edwards Jr, D., Caravaca, A., & Moschetti, C., M. (2021). Network governance and new philanthropy in Latin America and the Caribbean: Reconfiguration of the state. *British Journal of Sociology of Education*, 42(8), 1210–1226.

Breytenbach, W. J. (2019). *The Making and Unmaking of Modern Boundaries in Africa: From Berlin to Kigali. 2019 Border Management Workshop*. Security Institute for Governance and Leadership in Africa.

Brown, M. M. (2014). The future of the nation state. World Economic Forum. Retrieved from: https://www.weforum.org/agenda/2014/11/the-future-of-the-nation-state/

Brütsch, Ch. M. (2013). From sovereign prerogatives to metropolitan rule? the anarchical society in the urban age. *International Studies Perspectives*, 14(3), 307–324. DOI: 10.1111/j.1528-3585.2012.00496.x

Bryen, S. D. (1971). *The Application of Cybernetic Analysis to the Study of International Politics*. Springer Dordrecht. DOI: 10.1007/978-94-010-3005-2

Buenaobra, M. (2016). *Social Media: A Game Changer in Philippine Elections*. The Asia Foundation, April 27.

Bull, H. (2002). *The Anarchical Society. A Study of Order in World Politics*. Palgrave Macmillan.

Bungenberg, M. (2011). The division of competences between the EU and its member states in the area of investment politics. In Bungenberg, M., & Griebel, J. (Eds.), *Hindelang Steffen. International investment law and EU law* (pp. 29–42). Springer. DOI: 10.1007/978-3-642-14855-2_2

Burchell, G., Gordon, C., & Miller, P. (Eds.). (1991). *The Foucault Effect: Studies in Governmentality*. University of Chicago Press. DOI: 10.7208/chicago/9780226028811.001.0001

Burnay, M., & Raube, K. (2022). Obstacles, Opportunities, and Red Lines in the European Union: Past and Future of the CAI in Times of (Geo)-Politicisation. *The Journal of World Investment & Trade*, 23(4), 675–699. DOI: 10.1163/22119000-12340265

BusinessEurope. (2016). ETUC – BusinessEurope joint declaration on China's Market Economy Status. Position Paper. Available at: https://www.businesseurope.eu/publications/etuc-businesseurope-joint-declaration-chinas-market-economy-status

Byrne, D. (1998). *Complexity Theory and the Social Sciences: An Introduction*. Routledge.

Campos, R., & Timini, J. (2023). Latin America and the Caribbean: Trade relations in the face of global geopolitical fragmentation risks. *Economic Bulletin*, 2023(2023/Q1, Q1). Advance online publication. DOI: 10.53479/29631

Capoccia, G., & Kelemen, R. D. (2007). The Study of Critical Junctures: Theory, Narrative and Counterfactuals in Historical Institutionalism. *World Politics*, 59(3), 341–369. DOI: 10.1017/S0043887100020852

Cappeletti, Á., & Rama, C. (1990). *El Anarquismo en América Latina*. Biblioteca Ayacucho.

Caribbean News Now. (2014, July 26). *Civil society identifies sustainable development priorities for Trinidad and Tobago*. Retrieved from http://www.caribbeannewsnow.com/headline-Civil-society-identifies-sustainable-development-priorities-for-Trinidad-and-Tobago-22169.html

Carlisle, K., & Gruby, R. L. (2019). Polycentric systems of governance: A theoretical model for the commons. *Policy Studies Journal: the Journal of the Policy Studies Organization*, 47(4), 927–952. DOI: 10.1111/psj.12212

Catá-Backer, L. (2012). *The Structure of Global Law: Fracture, Fluidity, Permeability, Polycentrism*. CPE Working Paper n. 2012-7/ Penn State Law Research Paper 15-20

Cawthra, G. (2016). *Peacekeeping Interventions in Africa: "War is Peace, Freedom is Slavery, Ignorance is Strength."*. Friedrich-Ebert-Stiftung.

Cerny, P. G. (2000b). 'Restructuring the Political Arena: Globalization and the Paradoxes of the Competition State,' in Randall D. Germain, ed., *Globalization and Its Critics: Perspectives from Political Economy* (London: Macmillan), pp. 117-138 DOI: 10.1007/978-1-137-07588-8_4

Cerny, P. G. (2006). 'Dilemmas of Operationalizing Hegemony', in Mark Haugaard and Howard H. Lentner, eds., H*gemony and Power: Consensus and Coercion in Contemporary Politics* (Lanham, MD: Lexington Books on behalf of the International Political Science Association, Research Committee No. 36 [Political Power]), pp. 67-87

Cerny, P. G. (2012). 'The New Security Dilemma Revisited', paper presented at the annual convention of the International Studies Association, San Diego, California, 1-4 April

Cerny, P. G. (2023). Heterarchy in World Politics. In *"Innovations in International Affairs"*. Routledge: Taylor & Francis Group.

Cerny, P. (2013). Functional Differentiation, Globalization, and Transnational Neopluralism. In Albert, M., Buzan, B., & Zürn, M. (Eds.), *Bringing Sociology into International Relations* (pp. 205–227).

Cerny, P. G. (1990). *The Changing Architecture of Politics: Structure, Agency and the Future of the State*. Sage.

Cerny, P. G. (1997, Spring). Paradoxes of the Competition State: The Dynamics of Political Globilization. *Government and Opposition*, 32(2), 251–274. DOI: 10.1111/j.1477-7053.1997.tb00161.x

Cerny, P. G. (1998). Neomedievalism, civil war and the new security dilemma: Globalisation as durable disorder. *Civil Wars*, 1(1), 36–64. DOI: 10.1080/13698249808402366

Cerny, P. G. (2000a). Globalization and the Disarticulation of Political Power: Toward a New Middle Ages? In Goverde, H., Cerny, P. G., Haugaard, M., & Lentner, H. H. (Eds.), *Power in Contemporary Politics: Theories, Practices, Globalizations* (pp. 170–186). Sage. DOI: 10.4135/9781446219935.n9

Cerny, P. G. (2009a, May). Some Pitfalls of Democratisation: Thoughts on the 2008 *Millennium* Conference. *Millennium*, 37(3), 763–786. DOI: 10.1177/03058298809103243

Cerny, P. G. (2009b, April). Multi-nodal Politics: Globalisation is What States Make of It. *Review of International Studies*, 35(2), 421–449. DOI: 10.1017/S0260210509008584

Cerny, P. G. (2010). *Rethinking World Politics: A Theory of Transnational Neopluralism*. Oxford University Press. DOI: 10.1093/acprof:oso/9780199733699.001.0001

Cerny, P. G. (2011, May). "Saving Capitalism from the Capitalists?" Financial Regulation after the Crash. *St. Antony's International Review*, 7(1), 11–29.

Cerny, P. G. (2023). Capitalism, democracy and world politics in the 21st century. *European Review of International Studies*, 10(2), 205–213. DOI: 10.1163/21967415-10020016

Cerny, P. G. (2023). *Heterarchy in World Politics*. Routledge.

Cerny, P. G. (2023). Heterarchy: Toward Paradigm Shift in World Politics. In Cherny, P. G. (Ed.), *pp*.

Cerny, P. G. (Ed.). (2022). *Heterarchy in world politics*. Routledge. DOI: 10.4324/9781003352617

Červenka, Z. (1977). *The Unfinished Quest for Unity: Africa and the OAU*. Julian Friedmann Publishers Ltd.

Chaisse, J. (2012). Promises and Pitfalls of the European Union Policy on Foreign Investment—How will the New EU Competence on FDI affect the Emerging Global Regime? *Journal of International Economic Law*, 15(1), 51–84. DOI: 10.1093/jiel/jgs001

Chan, Z. T., & Meunier, S. (2022). Behind the screen: Understanding national support for a foreign investment screening mechanism in the European Union. *The Review of International Organizations*, 17(3), 513–541. DOI: 10.1007/s11558-021-09436-y PMID: 35719695

Che-Mponda, A. H. (1987). Charter of the Organization of African Unity and the Problems of African Unity. *African Study Monographs*, 53–63.

Chen, P. (2010). *Economic Complexity and Economic Illusion: Essays on Market Instability and Macro Vitality*. Routledge.

Chen, P. (2023). "Interview," *Commentaries.Newsletter of The World Economic Association.*, 3(2), 8–11.

Christopher, A. (1997). 'Nation-states', 'Quasi-states', and 'Collapsed-states' in Contemporary Africa. *GeoJournal*, 43(1), 91–97. DOI: 10.1023/A:1006833519243

Christou, A., & Damro, C. (2024). Frames and Issue Linkage: EU Trade Policy in the Geoeconomic Turn. *Journal of Common Market Studies*, 62(4), 1–17. DOI: 10.1111/jcms.13598

Clapham, C. (1996). *Africa and the International System: The Politics of State Survival*. Cambridge University Press. DOI: 10.1017/CBO9780511549823

Clapham, C. (1999). Sovereignty and the third world state. *Political Studies*, 47(3), 522–537. DOI: 10.1111/1467-9248.00215

Clark, D., Fox, J., & Treakle, K. (Eds.). (2003). *Demanding accountability: Civil society claims and the World Bank Inspection Panel*. Rowman & Littlefield.

Collette, L., & Harrison, S. G. (2021). Unintended Consequences: Ambiguity Neglect and Policy Ineffectiveness. *Eastern Economic Journal*, 47(2), 206–226. DOI: 10.1057/s41302-021-00187-7 PMID: 33551514

Condon, S. (2021). Caribbean migrations: The legacies of colonialism. *Ethnic and Racial Studies*, 45(3), 524–526. DOI: 10.1080/01419870.2021.1926525

Cooper, R. (2000). *The Postmodern State and the World Order*. Demos.

Council of the European Union. (2013). 3266th meeting of the Council of the European Union (foreign affairs) held in Luxembourg on 18 October 2013. Press release – 14845/13. Available at: https://data.consilium.europa.eu/doc/document/ST-15105-2013-INIT/en/pdf

Council of The European Union. (2016). Regulation (EU) 2016/1037 on protection against subsidised imports from countries not members of the European Union. OJ L 176/55 – 30.06.2016. available at: https://eur-lex.europa.eu/legal-content/EN/TXT/PDF/?uri=CELEX:32016R1037

Council of the European Union. (2022). Regulation 2022/1031 on the access of third-country economic operators, goods and services to the Union's public procurement and concession markets and procedures supporting negotiations on access of Union economic operators, goods and services to the public procurement and concession markets of third countries (International Procurement Instrument – IPI). OJ L 171/1 – 30.06.2022. Available at: https://eur-lex.europa.eu/legal-content/EN/TXT/PDF/?uri=CELEX:32022R1031

Council of The European Union. (2023). Regulation (EU) 2023/2675 on the protection of the Union and its Member States from economic coercion by third countries. OJ L – 07.12.2023. available at: https://eur-lex.europa.eu/legal-content/EN/TXT/PDF/?uri=OJ:L_202302675

Council of the European Union. (2023b). G7 Hiroshima Leaders' Communiqué. Press release – 20.05.2023. available at: https://www.consilium.europa.eu/en/press/press-releases/2023/05/20/g7-hiroshima-leaders-communique/

Council of the European Union. (2023c). Remarks by President Charles Michel before the G7 summit in Hiroshima. Remarks by President Charles Michel before the G7 summit in Hiroshima. Press Release – 19.05.2023. available at: https://www.consilium.europa.eu/en/press/press-releases/2023/05/19/remarks-by-president-charles-michel-before-the-g7-summit-in-hiroshima/

Cox, R. W. (1981). Social Forces, States and World Orders: Beyond International Relations Theory. *Millennium*, 10(2), 126–155. DOI: 10.1177/03058298810100020501

Crespy, A., & Rone, J. (2022). Conflicts of sovereignty over EU trade policy: A new constitutional settlement? *Comparative European Politics*, 20(3), 314–335. DOI: 10.1057/s41295-022-00272-x

CrimeWriter. (2019). *Crime Statistics*. Retrieved from TT Crime: https://ttcrime.com/crime-statistics/

Cristescu, A. (1981). *The Right to Self-Determination: Historical and Current Development on the Basis of United Nations Instruments*. United Nations.

Crocker, D. (2008). *Ethics of Economic Development: Agency, Capability and Deliberative Democracy*. Cambridge University Press.

Crouch, C. (2005). Dialogue on 'Institutional Complementarity and Political Economy,'. *Socio-economic Review*, 3(2), 359–382. DOI: 10.1093/SER/mwi015

Crumley, C. (2015). Heterarchy. In Kosslyn, S. (Ed.), *Emerging Trends in the Social and Behavioral Sciences* (pp. 1–14). John Wiley and Sons. DOI: 10.1002/9781118900772.etrds0158

Cumming, G. S. (2016). Heterarchies: Reconciling Networks and Hierarchies. *Trends in Ecology & Evolution*, 31(8), 622–632. Advance online publication. DOI: 10.1016/j.tree.2016.04.009 PMID: 27233444

Curry, D. (2012). The Structure-Agency Paradox of New Forms of Non-Binding Governance: Actor Networks, Multi-Level Governance and Canadian and EU Lessons. Working Paper for 2012 84th Annual Conference of the Canadian Political Science Association, 13–15 June 2012, University of Alberta.

Curry, D. (2018). Multi-Level Governance in British Columbia. British Columbia, Canada. Retrieved from https://www.researchgate.net/publication/320085647 _Multilevel_Governance_of_Sustai ability_Transitions_in_Canada_Policy_Alignment_Innovation_and_Evaluation

Daily Express. (2011, March 22). *Massa day done?* Retrieved from http://www .trinidadexpress.com/commentaries/Massa-Day-done-118412154.html

Davidson, B., & Munslow, B. (1990). The Crisis of the Nation-State in Africa. *Review of African Political Economy*, 17(49), 9–21. DOI: 10.1080/03056249008703872

Davies, T. (2013, January 24). *NGOs: A long and turbulent history*. Retrieved from The Global Journal: https://www.theglobaljournal.net/article/view/981/

Davies, C. (2013). *Caribbean Spaces: escapes from twighlight zones*. University of Illinois. DOI: 10.5406/illinois/9780252038020.001.0001

De Bièvre, D., & Poletti, A. (2020). Towards explaining varying degrees of politicization of EU trade agreement negotiations. *Politics and Governance*, 8(1), 243–253. DOI: 10.17645/pag.v8i1.2686

De Coteau, D. (2024). Massa Day Done or 'Same Old Khaki Pants?' Contextualising Caribbean Political Corruption. In *Black Fins White Sharks: Unmasking the Genealogy of Caribbean Political Corruption* (pp. 1–33). https://doi.org/DOI: 10.1007/978-3-031-47479-8_1

De La Guardia, C., & Pan-Montojo, J. (1998). Reflexiones sobre una historia transnacional. *Studia Historica. Historia Contemporánea*, 16, 9–31.

de Larosière, J. (2009). *The High-Level Group on Financial Supervision in the EU*, chaired by Jacques de Larosière (Brussels, 25 February 2009), https://ec.europa.eu/ internal_market/finances/docs/de_larosiere_report_en.pdf

de Larramendi, M. H., & Tomé-Alonso, B. (2017). The Return of Morocco to the African Union. *Panorama*, 229-232.

De Ville, F., & Gheyle, N. (2024). How TTIP split the social-democrats: Reacting to the politicisation of EU trade policy in the European parliament. *Journal of European Public Policy*, 31(1), 54–78. DOI: 10.1080/13501763.2023.2223226

De Wilde, P. (2011). No polity for old politics? A framework for analyzing the politicization of European integration. *Journal of European Integration*, 33(5), 559–575. DOI: 10.1080/07036337.2010.546849

Dean, J. (2014). Communicative Capitalism and Class Struggle. Journal for Digital Cultures. Retrieved from: https://spheres-journal.org/contribution/communicative -capitalism-and-class-struggle/

Dekker, E., & Kuchař, P. (2021). Heterarchy. In *Springer eBooks* (pp. 1 6). https:// doi.org/DOI: 10.1007/978-1-4614-7883-6_640-2

DeLanda, M. (2016). *Assemblage Theory*. Edinburgh University Press. DOI: 10.1515/9781474413640

Department of Foreign Affairs & Trade. A. (2014). *Trinidad and Tobago Country Brief*. Retrieved from Australian Government Department of Foerign Affairs and Trade: http://dfat.gov.au/geo/trinidad-tobago/pages/trinidad-and-tobago-country -brief.aspx

Desch, M. C., Dominguez, J. I., & Serbin, A. (1998). *From pirates to drug lords: the post-cold war Caribbean security environment*. State University of New York Press.

Divinagracia, A. (n.d.). Rodrigo Duterte's Toolbox of Media Co-optation: The mainstream media vs. illiberal democracy in social media. Retrieved from: https:// kyotoreview.org/issue-27/dutertes-toolbox-of-media-co-optation-mainstream-media -vs-illiberal-democracy-in-social-media/

Doboš, B. (2020). *New Middle Ages. Geopolitics of Post-Westphalian World*. Springer Nature. DOI: 10.1007/978-3-030-58681-2

Doyle, M. W. (1983). Kant, Liberal Legacies, and Foreign Affairs. *Philosophy & Public Affairs*, 12(3), 205–235.

Drezner, D. W. (2013). The tragedy of the global institutional commons. Back to basics: State power in a contemporary world, 280, 281.

Duchatel M. (2023). Economic Security: the Missing Link in EU-Japan Cooperation. *Institut Montaigne policy paper*, available at: file:///C:/Users/u233569/Downloads/ Institut_Montaigne_policy_paper_economic_security_the_missing_link_in_eu_ja- pan_cooperation.pdf

Duina, F. (2019). Why the excitement? Values, identities, and the politicization of EU trade policy with North America. *Journal of European Public Policy*, 26(12), 1866–1882. DOI: 10.1080/13501763.2019.1678056

Duit, A., & Galaz, V. (2008). Governance and Complexity: Emerging Issues in Governance Theory. *Governance: An International Journal of Policy, Administration and Institutions*, 21(3), 311–335. DOI: 10.1111/j.1468-0491.2008.00402.x

Dukes, R. (2014). *The Labour Constitution: The Enduring Idea of Labour Law*. Oxford University Press. DOI: 10.1093/acprof:oso/9780199601691.001.0001

During, S. (2024). The Global South and internationalism. In *Routledge eBooks* (pp. 71 80). https://doi.org/DOI: 10.4324/9781003255871-9

Dybvig, P. (2022) *Multiple Equilibria*. Nobel Lecture in Economic Sciences, 8 December 2022.

ECOWAS Commission. (1993, July 24). Economic Community of West African States (ECOWAS): Revised Treaty. Abuja: Economic Community of West African States.

ECOWAS Commission. (2018). *ECOWAS Mediation Guidelines*. ECOWAS Commission/Crisis Management Initiative.

ECOWAS Commission. (2024, February 24). *Extraordinary Summit of The ECOWAS Authority of Heads of State and Government on The Political, Peace and Security Situation in The Region*. Retrieved from ECOWAS Commission: chrome-extension://efaidnbmnnnibpcajpcglclefindmkaj/https://www.ecowas.int/wp-content/uploads/2024/02/EXT-ORD-SUMMIT-FINAL-COMMUNIQUE-ENGLISH-_240225_160529.pdf

ECOWAS/CEDEAO. (2024). *About ECOWAS*. Retrieved from ECOWAS/CEDEAO: https://www.ecowas.int/about-ecowas/ ECOWAS/CEDEAO.

Edwards, M. (2004). *Civil Society*. Polity Press.

Eke, J. U., & Ani, K. J. (2017). Africa and the Challenges of Regional Integration. *Journal of African Union Studies*, 63-80.

Ekeh, P. (1975). Colonialism and the Two Publics in Africa: A Theoretical Statement. *Comparative Studies in Society and History*, 17(1), 91–112. DOI: 10.1017/S0010417500007659

Ellis, R. E. (2023). Security challenges in the Caribbean: threats, migration, and international cooperation (By Institute of Caribbean Studies & Peruvian Army Center for Strategic Studies). https://ceeep.mil.pe/wp-content/uploads/2023/07/ PDF-Security-Challenges-in the-Caribbean-Threats-Migration-and-International-Cooperation-R-Evan-Ellis-60930 Jul-23.pdfFanning

Enderlein, H., Wälti, S., & Zürn, M. (Eds.), *Handbook on Multi-level Governance*. DOI: 10.4337/9781849809047

Englebert, P. (2000). Pre-Colonial Institutions, Postcolonial States, and Economic Development in Tropical Africa. *Political Research Quarterly*, 53(1), 7–36. DOI: 10.1177/106591290005300101

Eurofer (2019). Eurofer on the global forum on steel excess capacity. Position paper. New EUROFER document

European Commission. (2010). Communication of European Commission: Towards a comprehensive European international investment policy. COM(2010)243. Available at: https://eur-lex.europa.eu/LexUriServ/LexUriServ.do?uri=COM:2010: 0343:FIN:EN:PDF

European Commission. (2017a). President Jean Claude Juncker's State of the Union Adress 2017. Speech 17/3165, available at https://ec.europa.eu/commission/ presscorner/detail/en/SPEECH_17_3165

European Commission. (2017b). Proposal for establishing a framework for screening of foreign direct investments into the European Union. COM(2017) 487. Available at: https://eur-lex.europa.eu/legal-content/EN/TXT/HTML/?uri=CELEX: 52017PC0487&rid=4

European Commission. (2021). Communication – Trade Policy review – An Open Sustainable and Assertive Trade Policy. Com(2021)66, available at: https://eur-lex .europa.eu/resource.html?uri=cellar:5bf4e9d0-71d2-11eb-9ac9-01aa75ed71a1.0001 .02/DOC_1&format=PDF

European Commission. (2023). Joint Communication on "European Economic Security Strategy". JOIN(2023) 20, available at https://eur-lex.europa.eu/legal content/ EN/TXT/PDF/?uri=CELEX:52023JC0020

European Commission. (2023). President von der Leyen calls for a rebalanced trade relation with China in "Summit of choices". Press release – 08.12.2023. available at: https://ec.europa.eu/commission/presscorner/detail/en/ac_23_6446

European Parliament and European Council. (2019). Regulation (EU) establishing a framework for the screening of foreign direct investments into the Union. OJ L 79 1/1 – 21.03.2019. Available at: https://eur-lex.europa.eu/legal-content/EN/TXT/PDF/?uri=CELEX:32019R0452

European Parliament. (2015). Answer given by Ms Malmström on behalf of the Commission. Parliamentary question E-009974/2014. Available at: https://www.europarl.europa.eu/doceo/document/E-8-2014-009974-ASW_EN.html

European Parliament. (2022). EU international investment policy: Looking ahead. EPRS Brief (PE 729.276). Available at: https://www.europarl.europa.eu/RegData/etudes/BRIE/2022/729276/EPRS_BRI(2022)729276_EN.pdf

European Union (2012). Consolidated Version of the Treaty on the functioning of the European Union. OJ C 326/47 – 26. at: eur-lex.europa.eu/legal-content/EN/TXT/PDF/?uri=CELEX:12012E/TXTDOI: 10.2012. Available

Eusebio, G. (2022). Fake news and internet propaganda, and the Philippine elections: 2022.

Evans, M. G. (2005). *Policy Transfer in Global Perspective*. Ashgate.

*Experiments with Global Ideas* (London and New York: Routledge)

Falk, R. (1987). The Global Promise of Social Movements: Explorations at the Edge of Time. *Alternatives*, 12(2), 173–196. DOI: 10.1177/030437548701200202

Faludi, A. (2018). *The Poverty of Territorialism. A Neo-Medieval View of Europe and European Planning*. Edward Elgar Publishing.

Fanon, F. (1952). *Black skin white masks*. Grove Press.

Faude, B. (2015). *Von Konkurrenz zu Arbeitsteilung: Komplexität und Dynamik im Zusammenspiel internationaler Institutionen* (Vol. 25). Campus Verlag.

Ferguson, Y. H., & Mansbach, R. W. (2021). In B. de Carvalho, J. Costa Lopez and H. Leira (eds.) *Afterword. Ahead to the Past*. In *Routledge Handbook of Historical International Relations* (pp. 573-582). Routledge

Ferguson, Y. H. (2003). Illusions of superpower. *Asian Journal of Political Science*, 11(2), 21–36. DOI: 10.1080/02185370308434225

Ferguson, Y., & Mansbach, R. (2007). Post internationalism and IR theory. *Millennium*, 35(3), 529–550. DOI: 10.1177/03058298070350031001

Finnemore, M., & Sikkink, K. (2001). Taking Stock: The Constructivist Research Program in International Relations and Comparative Politics. *Annual Review of Political Science*, 4(1), 391–416. DOI: 10.1146/annurev.polisci.4.1.391

Fioretos, O. (2011). Historical Institutionalism in International Relations. *International Organization*, 65(2), 367–399. DOI: 10.1017/S0020818311000002

Fischer-Lescano, A., & Teubner, G. (2012). Critical Systems Theory. *Philosophy and Social Criticism*, 38(1), 3–23. DOI: 10.1177/0191453711421600

Forst, R. (2002). *Contexts of Justice* (Farrell, J., Trans.). University of California Press.

Forst, R. (2018). *Normativity and Power* (Cronin, C., Trans.). Oxford University Press.

Foucault, M. (2007). *Security, Territory, Population: Lectures at the Collège de France, 1977-1978* (French edition 2004). (Burchell, G., Trans.). Palgrave Macmillan.

Foucault, M. (2008). *The Birth of Biopolitics: Lectures at the Collège de France, 1978-1979* (French edition 2004). (Burchell, G., Trans.). Palgrave Macmillan.

Fowler, M. R., & Bunck, J. M. (1996). What Constitutes the Sovereign State? *Review of International Studies*, 22(4), 381–404. DOI: 10.1017/S0260210500118637

Francot-Timmermans, L., & Christodoulidis, E. (2011). The normative turn in Teubner's systems theory of law. *Rechtsfilosophie & Rechtstheorie, 40*, 187.

Friedman, J. (2015). *Shadow Cold War: The Sino-Soviet Competition for the Third World*. The University of North Carolina Press. DOI: 10.5149/northcarolina/9781469623764.001.0001

Friedman, T. L. (2005). *The world is flat: a brief history of the 21st century* (1st ed.). Farrar, Straus and Giroux.

Friedrichs, J. (2001). The meaning of new medievalism. *European Journal of International Relations*, 7(4), 475–501. DOI: 10.1177/1354066101007004004

Friedrichs, J. (2004). The Neomedieval Renaissance: Global Governance and International Law in the New Middle Ages. In Dekker, I. F., & Werner, W. G. (Eds.), *Governance and International Legal Theory* (pp. 3–36). Springer. DOI: 10.1007/978-94-017-6192-5_1

Fukuyama, F. (2004). *State-Building: Governance and World Order in the 21st Century*. Cornell University Press.

Gacal, F. (2013). Territorial Disputes in Spratly: An Assessment of the Philippine Initiatives. US Army War College, 1-42.

Gagnon, J. D. (2013). ECOWAS's Right t s Right to Intervene in Côte D'Ivoire to Install Alassane Ouattara as President-Elect . *Notre Dame Journal of International & Comparative Law*, 51-72.

Galbraith, J. K. (2024), "Entropy, the Theory of Value, and the Future of Humanity," Economic Democracy Initiative. Rubric 7., https://www.postneoliberalism.org/articles/entropy-the-theory-of-value-and-the-future-of-humanity

Galbraith, J. K., & Chen, J. (2025). *Entropy Economics: The Living Basis of Value and Production*. University of Chicago Press.

Gallarotti, G. M. (2000, January). The Advent of the Prosperous Society: The Rise of the Guardian State and Structural Change in the World Economy. *Review of International Political Economy*, 7(1), 1–52. DOI: 10.1080/096922900347036

Gallarotti, G. M. (2009 forthcoming). *The Power Curse: Influence and Illusion in World Politics*. Lynne Rienner. DOI: 10.1515/9781685854355

Garske, T., Legrand, J., Donnelly, C. A., Ward, H., Cauchemez, S., Fraser, C., Ferguson, N. M., & Ghani, A. C. (2009). Assessing the Severity of the Novel Influenza A/H1N1 pandemic. *British Medical Journal*, 339, 220–224. PMID: 19602714

Gáspár, T. (2011). Path Dependency and Path Creation in a Strategic Perspective. *Journal of Futures Studies*, 93–108.

Geertz, C. (2004). What Is a State If It is Not a Sovereign?: Reflections on Politics in Complicated Places. *Current Anthropology*, 45(5), 577–593. DOI: 10.1086/423972

Gehring, T., & Oberthür, S. (2009). The causal mechanisms of interaction between international institutions. *European Journal of International Relations*, 15(1), 125–156.

Gehrke, T. (2020). After Covid-19: Economic security in EU-Asia connectivity. *Asia Europe Journal*, 18(1), 239–243. DOI: 10.1007/s10308-020-00579-y PMID: 32837473

Genschel, P., & Seelkopf, L. (2015). The Competition State. In Leibfried, S. (Eds.), *The Oxford handbook of transformations of the state* (pp. 1–23). Oxford University Press.

Gibbins, J. (2023). J. S. Mill, liberalism, and progress. In *Routledge eBooks* (pp. 91 109). https://doi.org/DOI: 10.4324/9781032671581-6

Gill, S. (2003). *Power and Resistance in the New World Order*. Palgrave Macmillan.

Gilroy, P. (1995). *The Black Atlantic: Double Consciousness and Modernity*. Harvard University Press.

Girvan, N. (2005). Whither CMSE? *Journal of Caribbean International Relations*, 13-34. Retrieved from https://www.scribd.com/document/13902381/Norman-Girvan -Whither-CSME

Gjaltema, J., Biesbroek, R., & Termeer, K. (2020). From Government to Governance…to Meta-governance: A Systematic Literature Review. *Public Management Review*, 22(12), 1760–1780. DOI: 10.1080/14719037.2019.1648697

Gleckman, H. (2018). *MultiStakeholder Governance: A Global Challenge*. Routledge. DOI: 10.4324/9781315144740

Glossop, R. (2017). Meaning of the 21st century: From internationalism to globalism. *Comparative Civilizations Review*, (76), 15. http://scholarsarchive.byu.edu/ cgi/viewcontent.cgi?article=2011&context=ccr

Godehardt, N. (2014). *The Chinese Constitution of Central Asia: Regions and Intertwined Actors in International Relations*. Palgrave Macmillan. DOI: 10.1057/9781137359742

Godement, F. (2022). The EU-China Comprehensive Agreement on Investment: Context and Content. *Asia Europe Journal*, 20(1), 59–64. DOI: 10.1007/s10308-021-00622-6

Goldoni, M., & Wilkinson, M. (2016). The Material Constitution. *The Modern Law Review*, 18(4), 1–31.

Goldstein, J. S. (2011). *Winning the War on War: The Decline of Armed Conflict Worldwide*. Dutton.

Gómez Müller, A. (1980). *Anarquismo y anarcosindicalismo en América Latina: Colombia, Brasil, Argentina y México*. Ruedo Ibérico.

Gonzales, E. (2017, June 2). *Alexandrov complains of unfair treatment for Tobago autopsies*. Retrieved from newsday.co.tt: https://www.newsday.co.tt/news/0,244503 .html

Gordon, S. (2017). *Online communities as agents of change and social movements*. IGI Global. DOI: 10.4018/978-1-5225-2495-3

Gottsche, D. (2017). Postimperialism, postcolonialism and beyond: Toward a periodization of cultural discourse about colonial legacies. *Journal of European Studies*, 47(2), 111–128. DOI: 10.1177/0047244117700070

Goujon, M., & Wagner, L. (2023). Fragility of small island developing states. In *Edward Elgar Publishing eBooks*(pp. 299–315). https://doi.org/DOI: 10.4337/9781800883475.00023

Gov.tt. (2014, September). *UWI and Canadian NGO to research private security in the Caribbean and Latin America*. Retrieved from Gov.tt: http://www.news.gov .tt/content/uwi-and-canadian-ngo-research-private-security-caribbean-and-latin -america-0#.WWOw2Ijyvic

Gov.uk. (2017). *Oversees business risk - Trinidad and Tobago*. Retrieved from https:// www.gov.uk/government/publications/overseas-business-risk-trinidad-tobago/ overseas-business-risk-trinidad-tobago

Gramsci, A. (1971). *Selections from the prison notebooks*. International Publishers.

Granderson, A. (2011). Enabling multi-faceted measures of success for protected area management in Trinidad and Tobago. *Evaluation and Program Planning*, 34(3), 185–195. DOI: 10.1016/j.evalprogplan.2011.02.010 PMID: 21555042

Greene, E. (2024). Reflections on the future of the Caribbean Community through the mirror of functional co-operation. *The Round Table, 113*(1), 15 28. https://doi .org/DOI: 10.1080/00358533.2024.2307777

Green, E. D. (2017). Ethnicity, National Identity and the State: Evidence from Sub-Saharan Africa. *British Journal of Political Science*, 757–779.

Grenade, W. (2013). *Governance in the Caribbean: challenges and prospects*. Retrieved from http://www.commonwealthgovernance.org/assets/uploads/2012/10/ Governance-in-the-Caribbean.pdf

Grieco, J. (1997). Realist international theory and the study of world politics. In Ikenberry, J., & Doyle, M. (Eds.), *New thinking in international relations theory* (pp. 163–201). Westview.

Griffith, I. L. (2024). *Challenged Sovereignty: The Impact of Drugs, Crime, Terrorism, and Cyber Threats in the Caribbean*. University of Illinois Press. https:// www.jstor.org/stable/10.5406/jj.9827024

Grigorievna, A. P., Nikolaevna, J. N., & Sverdlikova, A. (2019). Meta-institutions as a Product of Institutional Dynamics and Institutional Reformation. *Post Mordern Openinings*, 137-154.

Guazzone, L., & Pioppi, D. (2022). *The Arab State and neo-liberal globalization. the restructuring of state power in the Middle East*. (pp. 1–400). http://ci.nii.ac.jp/ ncid/BB13295258

Gunningham, N. (2012). Regulatory Reform and Reflexive Regulation: Beyond Command and Control. In T. Dedeurwaerdere, T. & Siebenhüner, B. (Eds.) *Reflexive Governance for Global Public Goods*. MIT Press. DOI: 10.7551/mitpress/9780262017244.003.0103

Günther, G. (1980). Life as Polycontexturality. In *Beitrage zur Grandlegung einer operationsfuhien Dalekth* (Vol. 3). Felix Meiner Verlag.

Guruprasad, S. (2014). *The creole identity in the Caribbean postcolonial society: a study of Selvon's A Brighter Sun*. Retrieved from http://www.ijims.com

Guy, S. (2009). What is global and what is local? A theoretical discussion around globalization. *Parsons Journal for Information Mapping*. Retrieved from http://piim.newschool.edu/journal/issues/2009/02/pdfs/ParsonsJournalForInformationM pping_Guy-JeanSebastian.pdf

Guy, S. (2009). What is global and what is local? A theoretical discussion around globalization. *Parsons Journal for Information Mapping*. Retrieved from http://piim .newschool.edu/journal/issues/2009/02/pdfs/ParsonsJournalForInformationMapping _Guy-JeanSebastian.pdf

Habermas, J. (1985). Law as Medium and Law as Institution. In Teubner, G. (Ed.), *Dilemmas of Law in the Welfare State* (pp. 203–220). DeGruyter.

Habermas, J. (1989). Der Philosoph als wahrer Rechtslehrer: Rudolf Wiethölter. *Kritische Justiz*, 22(2), 138–196. DOI: 10.5771/0023-4834-1989-2-138

Hall, P. A., & Soskice, D. (Eds.). (2013). *Varieties of Capitalism: The Institutional Foundtions of Comparative Advantage*. Oxford University Press.

Hanemann, T. & Huotari M. (2017). Record flows and growing imbalances: Chinese investment in Europe in 2016. Merics research paper on China. Available at: MPOC_03_Update_COFDI.indd (merics.org)

Hanrieder, T. (2009, September). 7 Die Weltgesundheitsorganisation unter Wettbewerbsdruck: Auswirkungen der Vermarktlichung globaler Gesundheitspolitik. In Die organisierte Welt (pp. 163-188). Nomos Verlagsgesellschaft mbH & Co. KG.

Hardt, M., & Negri, A. (2000). *Empire*. Harvard University Press.

Hargreaves, J. D. (1996). *Decolonization in Africa*. Routledge.

Harkness, K. A. (2016). The Ethnic Army and the State: Explaining Coup Traps and Difficulties of Democratization in Africa. *The Journal of Conflict Resolution*, 60(4), 587–616. DOI: 10.1177/0022002714545332

Harkness, K. A. (2022). The Ethnic Stacking in Africa Data Set: When Leaders Use Ascriptive Identity to Build Military Loyalty. *Conflict Management and Peace Science*, 39(5), 609–632. DOI: 10.1177/07388942211044999

Harney, S., & Harney, C. (1996). *Nationalism and Identity: Culture and the imagination in a Caribbean diaspora*. https://www.amazon.com/Nationalism-Identity-Imagination Caribbean-Diaspora-ebook/dp/B00844WMKU

Harrinanan, S. (2017, January 13). *NGO, Chamber in launch*. Retrieved from Trinidad and Tobago Newsday: https://www.newsday.co.tt/news/0,238385.html

Harrison, J. (2013). Configuring the new 'regional world': On being caught between territory and networks. *Regional Studies*, 47(1), 55–74. DOI: 10.1080/00343404.2011.644239

Hartmann, C. (2017). ECOWAS and the Restoration of Democracy in the Gambia. *Africa Spectrum*, 52(1), 85–99. DOI: 10.1177/000203971705200104

Hartse, G. (2021). *The Habermas-Luhmann Debate*. Columbia University Press.

Harvey, D., & Reed, M. (1996). Social Science as the Study of Complex Systems. In Kiel, L. D., & Elliott, E. (Eds.), *Chaos Theory in the Social Sciences: Foundations and Applications*. University of Michigan Press.

Hasker, W. (1999). *The Emergent Self*. Cornell University Press.

Hawkins, D., Lake, D., Nielson, D., & Tierney, M. Delegation under Anarchy 2006: States, International Organizations, and Principal-Agent Theory In: Hawkins, D, Lake D., Nielson D., Tierney M. Delegation and Agency in International Organizations, Cambridge, Cambridge University Press, pp. 3-38.

Hay, C. (1999). Crisis and the Structural Transformation of the State: Interrogating the Process of Change. *British Journal of Politics and International Relations*, 1(3), 317–344. DOI: 10.1111/1467-856X.00018

Heath, J. (2001). *Communicative Action and Rational Choice*. MIT Press. DOI: 10.7551/mitpress/1955.001.0001

Heileman, S., Leotaud, N., McConney, P., Moreno, M. P., Phillips, T., & Toro, C. (2021). Challenges to implementing regional ocean governance in the wider Caribbean region. *Frontiers in Marine Science*, 8, 667273. Advance online publication. DOI: 10.3389/fmars.2021.667273

Helberger, N. (2020). The Political Power of Platforms: How Current Attempts to Regulate Misinformation Amplify Opinion Power. *Digital Journalism (Abingdon, England)*, 8(6), 842–854. DOI: 10.1080/21670811.2020.1773888

Held, D. (1995). *Democracy and the Global Order: From the Modern State to Cosmopolitan Governance*. Polity Press.

Henning, C. (2009). Networks of Power in the CAP System of the EU-15 and EU-27. *Journal of Public Policy*, 29(2), 153–177. DOI: 10.1017/S0143814X09001056

Herbst, J. (2000). *States and Power in Africa: Comparative Lessons in Authority and Control*. Princeton University Press.

Higgins, V., & Larner, W. (2010). Calculating the social. In *Palgrave Macmillan UK eBooks*. https://doi.org/DOI: 10.1057/9780230289673

Higman, B. (2001). *A concise history of the Caribbean*. Cambridge University.

Hignett, K. (2021). Transnational organized crime and the global village. In *Routledge eBooks* (pp. 305–317). https://doi.org/DOI: 10.4324/9781003044703-22

Hinsley, F. H. (1966). *Sovereignty*. Watts.

Hirschmann, D. (1975). Balewa's Nigeria and Nkrumah's Ghana. *The South African Journal of African Affairs*, 71–77.

Hirsch, S., & van der Walt, L. (Eds.). (2010). *Anarchism and Syndicalism in the Colonial and Postcolonial World, 1870-1940: The Praxis of National Liberation, Internationalism, and Social Revolution*. Brill. DOI: 10.1163/ej.9789004188495.i-432

Hirst, P., & Thompson, G. (2002). The future of globalization: cooperation and conflict. *Nordic International Studies Association*, 247-265. DOI: 10.1177/0010836702037003671

Hobbs, H. (Ed.). (2000). *Pondering Postinternationalism; A Paradigm for the 21st Century*. SUNY Press.

Hobbs, H. H. (2000). *Pondering postinternationalism*. State University of New York.

Hofstadter, D. (1979). *Godel, Escher, Bach: An Eternal Golden Braid*. Basic Books.

Holmes, M. (2011). Something Old, Something New, Something Borrowed: Representations of Anarchy in International Relations Theory. *International Relations of the Asia-Pacific*, 11(2), 279–308. DOI: 10.1093/irap/lcr005

Holzscheiter, A., Bahr, T., & Pantzerhielm, L. (2016). Emerging governance architectures in global health: Do metagovernance norms explain inter-organisational convergence?.

Hopewell, K. (2022). Beyond US-China Rivalry: Rule Breaking, Economic Coercion, and the Weaponization of Trade. In: Shaffer H. *Governing the interface of U.S.-China Trade relations*. 58-63

Hopkins, A. (2000). Quasi-states, Weak States and the Partition of Africa. *Review of International Studies*, 26(2), 311–320. DOI: 10.1017/S0260210500003119

Hörnqvist, M. (2020). Neoliberal security provision: Between state practices and individual experience. *Punishment & Society*, 22(2), 227–246. DOI: 10.1177/1462474519875474

Huntington, S. P. (1968). *Political Order in Changing Societies*. Yale University Press.

Hurrell, A. (2007). *On Global Order: Power, Values and the Constitution of International Society*. Oxford University Press. DOI: 10.1093/acprof:oso/9780199233106.001.0001

Hurrelmann, A., & Wendler, F. (2024). How does politicisation affect the ratification of mixed EU trade agreements? The case of CETA. *Journal of European Public Policy*, 31(1), 157–181. DOI: 10.1080/13501763.2023.2202196

Hutchins, E. (1994). *Cognition in the Wild*. MIT Press.

Huysseune, M., & Paquin, S. (2023). Paradiplomacy and the European Union's trade treaty negotiations: The role of Wallonia and Brussels. *Territory, Politics, Governance*, ●●●, 1–20. DOI: 10.1080/21622671.2023.2181207

Immergut, E. (2010, January 26). *Institution/Institutionalism*. Retrieved from https://www.sowi.hu-berlin.de/de/lehrbereiche/comppol/pubb/pdfs/Immergut2011.pdf

International Organization. (1962). All-African People's Conferences. *International Organization*, 429 - 434.

Ip, E. C. (2010). Globalization and the future of the law of the sovereign state. *International Journal of Constitutional Law*, 8(3), 636–655. DOI: 10.1093/icon/moq033

Jackson, A. (2010). The Impact of the Cold War and the New Srambles for Africa. *Journal of Southern African Studies*, 36(1), 229–239. DOI: 10.1080/03057071003607469

Jackson, R. H. (1986). Negative Sovereignty in Sub-Saharan Africa. *Review of International Studies*, 12(4), 247–264. DOI: 10.1017/S0260210500113828

Jackson, R. H., & Rosberg, C. G. (1986). Sovereignty and Underdevelopment: Juridical Statehood in the African Crisis. *The Journal of Modern African Studies*, 24(1), 1–31. DOI: 10.1017/S0022278X0000673X

Jacobs, T., Gheyle, N., De Ville, F., & Orbie, J. (2023). The hegemonic politics of 'strategic autonomy'and 'resilience': COVID-19 and the dislocation of EU trade policy. *Journal of Common Market Studies*, 61(1), 3–19. DOI: 10.1111/jcms.13348 PMID: 35936871

James, A. (1986). *Sovereign Statehood: The Basis of International Society*. Allen & Unwin.

Jenkins-Smith, H., & Sabatier, P. (1994). Evaluating the Advocacy Coalition Framework. *Journal of Public Policy*, 14(2), 175–203. Retrieved May 5, 2021, from https://www.jstor.org/stable/4007571. DOI: 10.1017/S0143814X00007431

Jersild, A. (2018). Sino-Soviet Relations, Decolonization, and the Global Cold War. *Kritika: Explorations in Russian and Eurasian History*, 217-224.

Jessop, B. (2020). The Governance of Complexity and the Complexity of Governance. In B. Jessop, *Putting Civil Society in Its Place: Governance, Metagovernance and Subjectivity* (chapter 2). Policy Press. DOI: 10.1017/9781108675635

Jessop, B. (2022). Governance and Metagovernance: On Reflexivity, Requisite Variety, and Requisite Irony in Participatory Governance. In Heinelt, H., Getimis, P., Kafkalas, G., & Smith, R. (Eds.), *Participatory Governance in Multi-Level Context: Concepts and Experience* (pp. 33–56). VS Verlag für Sozialwissenschaften.

Johnson, T., & Heiss, A. (2023). Liberal institutionalism. In *Routledge eBooks* (pp. 120 132). https://doi.org/DOI: 10.4324/9781003266365-12

Johnson, C. A. (1962). Conferences of Independent African States. *International Organization*, 16(2), 426–429. DOI: 10.1017/S0020818300011152

Jones, L., & Hameiri, S. (2023). Heterarchy and State Transformation. In *"Heterarchy in World Politics"* edited by Philip G. Cerny (2023). Routledge: Taylor & Francis Group.

Kamalu, N. C. (2019). British, French, Belgian, and Portuguese Models of Colonial Rule and Economic Development in Africa. *Annals of Global History*, 37-47.

Kamradt-Scott, A. (2016). WHO's to blame? The World Health Organization and the 2014 Ebola outbreak in West Africa. *Third World Quarterly*, 37(3), 401–418. DOI: 10.1080/01436597.2015.1112232

Kamradt-Scott, A. (2018). Securing Indo-Pacific health security: Australia's approach to regional health security. *Australian Journal of International Affairs*, 72(6), 500–519.

Kan, P. R. (2019). *The Global Challenge of Militias and Paramilitary Violence.* Springer International Publishing; Palgrave.

Kaplan, R. D. (2012). *Monsoon: The Indian Ocean and the Future of American Power.* Random House.

Kapucu, N., & Hu, Q. (2020). Network governance. In *Routledge eBooks.* DOI: 10.4324/9781351056540

Karlsrud, J., Hofmann, S., & Reykers, Y. (2024). Is liberal internationalism worth saving? Ad hoc coalitions and their consequences for international security. *Policy Brief*, 1 / 2024. https://www.nupi.no/content/pdf_preview/28165/file/NUPI_Policy _Brief_1_202 Karlsrud%20mfl.pdf

Karns, M., Mingst, K., & Stiles, K. (2015). *International Organizations.* Lynne Rienner.

Kasianiuk, K. (2018). A System-cybernetic Approach to the Study of Political Power. Introductory Remarks. *Kybernetes*, 47(6), 1262–1276. DOI: 10.1108/K-04-2017-0145

Keck, M. E., & Sikkink, K. (1998). *Activists beyond Borders: Advocacy Networks in International Politics.* Cornell University Press.

Kedourie, E. (1960). *Nationalism.* Praeger.

Keet, D. (2002). *The New Partnership for Africa's Development (NEPAD) and the African Union: Unity and Integration Within Africa or Integration of Africa into the Global Economy?* Cape Town: Alternative Information and Development Center (AIDC).

Kelsen, H. (1945). *General Theory of Law and the State* (Wedberg, A., Trans.). Harvard University Press.

Kennedy, L. (2017). *Supranational Union and New Medievalism: Forging a New Scottish State.* Arktos Media Limited.

Kennedy, P. (1987). *The Rise and Fall of the Great Powers: Economic Change and Military Conflict from 1500 to 2000.* Random House.

Keohane, R., & Nye, J. (1998, September/October). *Power and interdependence in the information age.* Retrieved from Foreign Affairs: https://www.foreignaffairs .com/articles/1998-09-01/power-and-interdependence-information-age

Keohane, R. (2002). *Power and governance in a partially globalized world.* Routledge.

Keohane, R. O., & Nye, J. S.Jr. (1977). *Power and Interdependence: World Politics in Transition.* Little, Brown.

Kibbler, J. (2011). Cognitive disequilibrium. *Encyclopedia of Child Behaviour and Development*, 380-380. DOI: 10.1007/SpringerReference_179877

Kickbusch, I., & Szabo, M. M. C. 2014: A new governance space for health. In: Glob Health Action, Vol. 7. DOI: 10.3402/gha.v7.23507

Kilian, P. (2019). Self-determination of Peoples in the Charter of the United Nations. *Revista de Estudos Constitucionais, Hermenêutica e Teoria do Direito (RECHTD)*, 341-353.

Kim, R. E. (2020). Is Global Governance Fragmented? Polycentricity or Complexity? The Art of the Network Approach. *International Studies Review*, 22(4), 903–931. DOI: 10.1093/isr/viz052

Kinna, R., & Prichard, A. (2019). Anarchism and Non-domination. *Journal of Political Ideologies*, 24(3), 221–240. DOI: 10.1080/13569317.2019.1633100

Kirton, M. (2010). *Political culture of democracy in Trinidad and Tobago*. Retrieved from Vanderbilt University: https://www.vanderbilt.edu/lapop/trinidad-tobago/2010 -political-culture.pdf

Kjaer, P. (2006). Systems in Context: On the Outcome of the Habermas/ Luhmann Debate, *Ancilla Juris*: 66-77.

Kjaer, P. (2016). From the Crisis of Corporatism to the Crisis of Governance. In P. Kjaer and N. Olson (Ed) *Critical Theories of Crisis in Europe*. Rowman and Littlefield.

Kjaer, P. (Ed.). (2020). The Law of Political Economy: Transformation in the Function of Law. Cambridge University Press.

Kjaer, P. (2013). Transnational Normative Orders: The Constitutionalization of Intra- and Trans-formative Law. *Indiana Journal of Global Legal Studies*, 20(2), 777–803. DOI: 10.2979/indjglolegstu.20.2.777

Kobrin, S. (1998). Back to the future: Neomedievalism and the postmodern digital world economy. *Journal of International Affairs*, 51(2), 361–386.

Kohn, H. (1955). *Nationalism: Its Meaning and History*. Van Nostrand.

Kontopolous, K. (1993). *The Logics of Social Structure*. Cambridge University Press. DOI: 10.1017/CBO9780511570971

Krasner, S. (2001, July). *Abiding sovereignty*. Retrieved from https://maihold.org/ mediapool/113/1132142/data/Krasner.pdf

Krasner, S. (2001, November). *Think again: sovereignty*. Retrieved from Foreign Policy: https://foreignpolicy.com/2009/11/20/think-again-sovereignty/

Krasner, S. D. (1999). *Sovereignty: Organized Hypocrisy*. Princeton University Press. DOI: 10.1515/9781400823260

Krueger, A. O. (2002). *A new approach to sovereign debt restructuring*. International Monetary Fund. DOI: 10.5089/9781589061217.054

Kufuor, K. O. (2005). The Collapse of the Organization of African Unity: Lessons from Economics and Law. *Journal of African Law*, 49(2), 132–144. DOI: 10.1017/S0021855305000112

Kuhn, T. (1963). *The function of dogma in scientific research*. Basic Books.

Kunert, D. (1978). The Role of the Super Powers in Africa. *The South African Journal of African Affairs*, 129–133.

Laarmann, M. (2023). Hybrid Aesthetics and Social Reality: Reading Caribbean Literature in the postcolonial Present. In *De Gruyter eBooks* (pp. 119 136). https://doi.org/DOI: 10.1515/9783110798494-008

Lake, D. A. (1996). Anarchy, Hierarchy, and the Variety of International Relations. *International Organization*, 50(1), 1–33. DOI: 10.1017/S002081830000165X

Lamdan, S. (2019). *Librarianship at the crossroads of ICE surveillance*. In the Library with the Lead Pipe.

Lange, T. (2021). Eine neue» Disease Surveillance «?. FEST, 57.

Lange, T. (2022). Eine neue „Disease Surveillance"? Big Data und die Gefahrenüber- wachung in Global Health. In: Held, Benjamin/ van Oorschot, Frederike Ed.): Digitalisierung: Neue Technik – neue Ethik? Interdisziplinäre Auseinandersetzung mit den Folgen der digitalen Transformation. HeiBooks, Universitätsbibliothek Heidelberg, pp. 57 – 71.

Lange, M., Jeong, T., & Amasyali, E. (2021). The Colonial Origins of Ethinc Warfare: Re-examining the Impact of Communalizing Colonial Policies in the British and French Empires. *International Journal of Comparative Sociology*, 62(2), 141–165. DOI: 10.1177/00207152211023793 PMID: 35228760

Lange, T. (2020). Beyond the'asean-way'? Third-sector driven governance along sars and haze pollution. *Global Health Governance*.

Lange, T., Villarreal, P. A., & Bärnighausen, T. (2023a). Counter-contestation in global health governance: The WHO and its member states in emergency settings. *Health Policy (Amsterdam)*, 131, 104756.

Lange, T., Villarreal, P. A., & Bärnighausen, T. (2023b). The contested authority of international institutions in global health. *Health Policy (Amsterdam)*, 131, 104793.

Lawrence, M. A. (2004). Hot Wars in Cold War Africa. *Reviews in American History*, 32(1), 114–121. DOI: 10.1353/rah.2004.0007

Ledgister, F. (2006). *Democracy in the Caribbean: postcolonial experience*. Retrieved from Academia.edu: https://www.academia.edu/428522/Democracy_in_the_Caribbean_Post Colonial_Experience

Lenoble, J., & Maesschalck, M. (2003). *Toward a Theory of Governance: The Action of Norms*. Hague: Kluwer.

Levi-Faur, , D. (2005). The global diffusion of regulatory capitalism. *The Annals of the American Academy of Political and Social Science, 598*(1), 12-32.

Lewis, D. (1994). Nongovernmental organizations and Caribbean development. *The Annals of the American Academy of Political and Social Science*, 533(1), 125–138. DOI: 10.1177/0002716294533001009

Lewis, G. (2004). *Main currents in Caribbean thought* (2nd ed.). University of Nebraska Press.

Liebowitz, S., & Margolis, S. E. (1995). Path Dependence, Lock-in, and History. *Journal of Law Economics and Organization*, 205–226.

Little, R. (2007). *The Balance of Power in International Relations: Metaphors, Myths and Models*. Cambridge University Press. DOI: 10.1017/CBO9780511816635

Llano, C., Pérez, J., El Khatabi, F., & Steinberg, F. (2021). Weaponized trade policy: The impact of US tariffs on the European automobile sector. *Economic Systems Research*, 33(3), 287–315. DOI: 10.1080/09535314.2020.1804330

Luhmann, N. (1982). The Differentiation of Society (Trans. S. Holes and C. Larmore). Columbia University Press. DOI: 10.7312/luhm90862

Lüthi, L. M. (2008). *The Sino-Soviet Split: Cold War in the Communist World*. Princeton University Press.

MacCormick, N. (1998). Norms, Institutions and Institutional Facts. *Law and Philosophy*, 17, 301–345.

MacCormick, N. (2007). *Institutions of Law: Law, State and Practical Reason.* Oxford University. DOI: 10.1093/acprof:oso/9780198267911.001.0001

MacCormick, N., & Weinberger, O. (1986). *An Institutional Theory of la.* Springer. DOI: 10.1007/978-94-015-7727-4

Maguire, E., Johnson, D., Kuhns, J., & Apostolos, R. (2017). The effects of community policing on fear of crime and perceived safety: Findings from a pilot project in Trinidad and Tobago. *Policing and Society*, 1–20. DOI: 10.1080/10439463.2017.1294177

Maier, C. (2023). *The Project State and Its Rivals: A New History of the Twentieth and Twenty First Centuries.* Harvard University Press.

Makarenko, A., & Chernikova, L. (2020). "New Generation" EU Free Trade Agreements: A Combination of Traditional and Innovative Mechanisms. In: Kovalchuk J. *Post-Industrial Society: The Choice Between Innovation and Tradition*, 109-122.

Maluwa, T. (2012). The Transition from the Organisation of African Unity to the African Union. In Yusuf, A. A., & Ouguergouz, F. (Eds.), *The African Union: Legal and Institutional Framework. A Manual on the Pan-African Organization* (pp. 25–52). Martinus Nijhoff Publishers. DOI: 10.1163/9789004227729_004

Mampilly, Z. (2003). Pacellized Sovereignty: The State, Non-state Actors, and the Politics of Conflict in Africa. *Ufahamu*, 15-62.

Mannheim, K. (1936). *Ideology and Utopia.* Trans. Edward Shils. Harcourt, Brace.

Mansbach, , RFerguson, , Y. (2007). Postinternationalism and International Relations Theory, *Millenium. Journal of International Students*, 35, 529–549.

Margarucci, I., & Roberti, A. (2023). *Anarquismo en América Latina: Historias y conexiones (1890 -1940 ).* Americanía. Revista de Estudios Latinoamericanos.

Martins, H. (1974). Time and theory in Sociology. In Rex, J. (Ed.), *Approaches to Sociology. An Introduction to Major Trends in British Sociology* (pp. 246–294). Routledge & Kegan.

Marx, K., & Engels, F. (1977). *Collected Works* (Vol. 9). Lawrence and Wishart.

Massey, D. (1995). *Spatial Divisions of Labour* (2nd ed.). Routledge. DOI: 10.1007/978-1-349-24059-3

Maull, H. (2011). *World politics in turbulence.* Retrieved from library.fes.de: https://library.fes.de/pdf-files/ipg/ipg-2011-1/2011-1__03_a_maull.pdf

Mazrui, A., & Michael, T. (1984). *Nationalism and the New States of Africa.* Heinemann.

McColloch, W. (1945). A Heterarchy of Values. *The Bulletin of Mathematical Biophysics*, 7, 89–93. PMID: 21006853

McCormick, J. (2023). The role of environmental NGOs in international regimes. In *Routledge eBooks* (pp. 52–71). https://doi.org/DOI: 10.4324/9781003421368-4

McCormick, J. P. (1993). Addressing the Political Exception: Machiavelli's "Accidents" and the Mixed Regime. *The American Political Science Review*, 87(4), 888–900. DOI: 10.2307/2938821

McCoy, J., & Knight, A. (2017). Homegrown violent extremism in Trinidad and Tobago. *Studies in Conflict and Terrorism*, 40(4), 267–299. Advance online publication. DOI: 10.1080/1057610X.2016.1206734

McCulloch, W. S. (1945). A heterarchy of values determined by the topology of nervous nets. *The Bulletin of Mathematical Biophysics*, 7, 89-93.

McDonald, K. (2002). From Solidarity to Fluidarity: Social Movements Beyond 'Collective Identity' —The Case of Globalization Conflicts. *Social Movement Studies*, 1(2), 109–128. DOI: 10.1080/14742830220000106637

McDougall, H. (2023). Colonial internationalism and the governmentality of empire, 1893 1982. *International Affairs*, 99(2), 843–844. DOI: 10.1093/ia/iiad004

McEvoy, J. K. (2022). Power Shift: The global Political economy of energy Transitions. *International Journal, 77*(1), 153 155. https://doi.org/DOI: 10.1177/00207020221097998

McLuhan, M. (1964). *Understanding Media: The Extensions of Man*. McGraw Hill.

McNair, B. (2017). *An introduction to political communication* (6th ed.). Routledge. DOI: 10.4324/9781315750293

McNamara, F. T. (1989). *France in Black Africa*. National Defense University. DOI: 10.21236/ADA229583

Mednick, S. (2023, August 19). *11 Nations of West Africa Commit to a Military Deployment to Restore the Ousted President of Niger*. Retrieved from The Associated Press: https://apnews.com/article/niger-coup-extremists-c4c4024bdd7c d8b7354a448411388137

Melber, H., Bjarnesen, J., Lanzano, C., & Mususa, P. (2023). Citizenship Matters: Explorations into the Citizen-State Relationship in Africa. *Forum for Development Studies*, 50(1), 35–58. DOI: 10.1080/08039410.2022.2145992

Meuleman, L. (2021). Public Administration and Governance for the SDGs: Navigating between Change and Stability. *Sustainability (Basel)*, 13(11), 5914. DOI: 10.3390/su13115914

Meunier, S. (2014). Divide and conquer? China and the cacophony of foreign investment rules in the EU. *Journal of European Public Policy*, 21(7), 996–1016. DOI: 10.1080/13501763.2014.912145

Meunier, S., & Nicolaidis, K. (2019). The geopoliticization of European trade and investment policy. *J. Common Mkt.Stud.*, 57, 103.

Meyer, J., Boli, J., Thomas, G. M., & Ramirez, F. O. (1997a). World Society and the Nation-State. *American Journal of Sociology*, 103(1), 144–181. DOI: 10.1086/231174

Meyer, J., Frank, D. J., Hironaka, A., Schofer, E., & Tuma, N. B. (1997b). The Structure of a World Environmental Regime, 1870-1990. *International Organization*, 57(4), 623–681. DOI: 10.1162/002081897550474

Michael, Z. (2018). *A Theory of Global Governance. Authority, Legitimacy, and Contestation*. Oxford University Press.

Michalopoulos, S., & Papaioannou, E. (2016). The Long-Run Effects of the Scramble for Africa. *The American Economic Review*, 106(7), 1802–1848. DOI: 10.1257/aer.20131311

Middelbeek, L., Kolle, K., & Verrest, H. (2016). Built to last? Local climate change adaptation and governance in the Caribbean – The case of an informal urban settlement in Trinidad and Tobago. *Urban Climate*, 8, 138–154. DOI: 10.1016/j.uclim.2013.12.003

Migdal, J. (1988). *Strong States and Weak States: State-Society Relations and State Capabilities in the Third World*. Princeton University Press.

Migliorati, M., & Vignoli, V. (2022). When politicization meets ideology: the European Parliament and free trade agreements. *Italian Political Science Review/ Rivista Italiana Di Scienza Politica, 52*(3), 346-361.

Miguel, Y. M., & Arias, S. (2020). Between colonialism and coloniality. In *Routledge eBooks* (pp. 1–39). https://doi.org/DOI: 10.4324/9781315107189-1

Milhaupt, C., & Pargendler, M. (2017). Governance challenges of listed state owned enterprises around the world: national experiences and a framework for reform. *Law Working Paper N° 352/2017*. Curtis J. Milhaupt & Mariana Pargendler 2017.

Ministry of Attorney General and Legal Affairs. (1976). *The Constitution of the Republic of Trinidad and Tobago.* Retrieved from Ministry of attorney general and legal affairs: http://rgd.legalaffairs.gov.tt/laws2/Constitution.pdf

Ministry of Finance. (2011, October). *Medium term policy framework 2011-2014 - Ministry of finance.* Retrieved from finance.gov.tt: https://www.finance.gov.tt/wp -content/uploads/2013/11/Medium-Term-Policy-Framework-2011-14.pdf

Ministry of Social Development and Family Services. (2017). *Nongovernmental organization unit.* Retrieved from https://www.social.gov.tt/divisions/nongovernmental -organization-n-g-o-unit/

Minsky, M., & Papert, S. (1972). *Artificial Intelligence Progress Report* (AI Memo 252). Cambridge, MA: MIT Artificial Intelligence Laboratory.

Minsky, H. (1986). *Stabilizing an Unstable Economy.* Yale University Press.

Minto-Coy, I., Cowell, N., & McLeod, M. (2016). Breaking the barriers: Entrepreneurship, enterprise, competitivenes and growth in the Caribbean. *Social and Economic Studies*, 1–13. DOI: 10.1080/08985626.2015.1088727

Miran-Guyon, M. (2006). The Political Economy of Civil Islam in Côte d'Ivoire. In Bestandsaufnahume, E. (Ed.), *Plitical Islam in West Africa* (pp. 82–113). Lit Verlag.

Mistry, P. S. (2000). Africa's Record of Regional Cooperation and Integration. *African Affairs*, 99(397), 553–573. DOI: 10.1093/afraf/99.397.553

Miura, S. (2014, December 1). Heterarchy. *Social Science, Power Structures & Organizations.* Encyclopedia Britannica. https://www.britannica.com/topic/heterarchy

Mnyongani, F. D. (2008). Between a Rock and a Hard Place: The Right to Self-determination Versus Uti Possidetis in Africa. *The Comparative and International Law Journal of Southern Africa*, 463–479.

Mommsen, W. J. (1988). Bismark, the Concert of Europe, and the Future of West Africa, 1883-1885. In Forster, S., Mommsen, W., & Robinson, R. (Eds.), *Bismarck, Europe and Africa: The Berlin Africa Conference, 1884–1885, and the Onset of Partition* (pp. 151–170). Oxford University Press.

Moon, S., Sridhar, D., Pate, M. A., Jha, A. K., Clinton, C., Delaunay, S., Edwin, V., Fallah, M., Fidler, D. P., Garrett, L., Goosby, E., Gostin, L. O., Heymann, D. L., Lee, K., Leung, G. M., Morrison, J. S., Saavedra, J., Tanner, M., Leigh, J. A., & Piot, P. (2015). Will Ebola change the game? Ten essential reforms before the next pandemic. The report of the Harvard-LSHTM Independent Panel on the Global Response to Ebola. *Lancet*, 386(10009), 2204–2221. DOI: 10.1016/S0140-6736(15)00946-0 PMID: 26615326

Moravcsik, A. (2001, April). *Liberal international relations theory: a social scientific assessment.* Retrieved from Weatherhead Center for International Affairs, Harvard University: https://wcfia.harvard.edu/files/wcfia/files/607_moravcsik.pdf

Moreno, A., Bourillon, L., Flores, E., & Fulton, S. (2017). Fostering fisheries management efficiency through collaboration networks: The case of the Kanan Kay Alliance in the Mexican Caribbean. *Bulletin of Marine Science*, 93(1), 233–247. DOI: 10.5343/bms.2015.1085

Morgenthau, H. J. (1948). *Politics Among Nations.* McGraw-Hill.

Morrison, T. H., Bodin, O., Cumming, G. S., Lubell, M., Seppelt, R., Seppelt, T., & Weible, C. M. (2023). Building blocks of polycentric governance. *Policy Studies Journal: the Journal of the Policy Studies Organization*, 51(3), 475–499. DOI: 10.1111/psj.12492

Moscovici, S. (2000). *Social Representation: Explorations in Social Psychology* (Duveen, G., Trans.). Polity Press.

Mostov, J. (2008). *Soft Borders: Rethinking Sovereignty and Democracy.* Palgrave Macmillan. DOI: 10.1057/9780230612440

Mouzelis, N. (1995). *Sociological Theory: What Went Wrong?* Routledge.

Moyo, D. (2009). *Dead Aid: Why Aid Is Not Working and How There Is a Better Way for Africa.* Farrar, Straus and Giroux.

Mueller, B. (2020). Why Public Policies Fail: Policymaking Under Complexity. *Economía*, 21(2), 311–323. DOI: 10.1016/j.econ.2019.11.002

Müller-Crepon, C., Hunziker, P., & Cederman, L.-E. (2021). Roads to Rule, Roads to Rebel: Relational State Capacity and Conflict in Africa. *The Journal of Conflict Resolution*, 65(2-3), 563–590. DOI: 10.1177/0022002720963674 PMID: 33487734

Narlikar, A. (2022). Trade governance: the politics of prosperity, development and weaponization. In: Rüland J. & Carrapatoso A. *Handbook on Global Governance and Regionalism* (pp. 334-349). Edward Elgar Publishing.

Nathan, R. (2001). African Redemption: Black Nationalism, and End of Empire in Africa. *Exchange*, 30(2), 125–144. DOI: 10.1163/157254301X00084

Ndlovu, S., Houston, G., & Magubane, B. (2019). The South African Liberation Struggle. In Temu, A. J. (Ed.), *J. d. Tembe, Southern African Liberation Struggles Contemporaneous Documents:1960–1994* (pp. 101–112). Mkuki na Nyota Publishers Ltd.

Nkrumah, K. (1963). *Africa Must Unite*. Panaf Books.

Norell, M. (2003). A new medievalism? The case of Sri Lanka. *Civil Wars*, 6(2), 121–137. DOI: 10.1080/13698240308402536

Nus, E. (2016). *Strategies, Critique and Autonomous Spaces/15M from an Autonomous Perspective*. <https.//www.degrowth/de/em/dim/degrowth-in-movemrnts/15M>

Nye, J. S.Jr. (2004). *Soft Power: The Means to Success in World Politics*. Public Affairs.

O'Brien, R., Goetz, A. M., Scholte, J. A., & Williams, M. (2000). *Contesting Global Governance: Multilateral Economic Institutions and Global Social Movements*. Cambridge University Press. DOI: 10.1017/CBO9780511491603

O'Connor, T. (1994). Emergent Properties, *American Philosophical Quarterly* 31:18ff

Oakeshott, M. (1976, August). On Misunderstanding Human Conduct: A Reply to My Critics. *Political Theory*, 4(2), 353–367. DOI: 10.1177/009059177600400308

Obi, C. I. (2009). Economic Community of West African States on the Ground: Comparing Peacekeeping in Liberia, Sierra Leone, Guinea Bissau, and Côte d'Ivoire. *African Security*, 2(2-3), 119–135. DOI: 10.1080/19362200903361945

OECD. (2022). Framework for screening foreign direct investment into the EU: Assessing effectiveness and efficiency. OECD report. Available at: https://www.oecd.org/daf/inv/investment-policy/oecd-eu-fdi-screening-assessment.pdf

Okumu, W. (2009). The African Union: Pitfalls and Prospects for Uniting Africa. *Journal of International Affairs*, 93–111.

Olympio, S. (1961, October). African Problems and the Cold War. *Foreign Affairs*, 40(1), 50–57. DOI: 10.2307/20029532

One Caribbean Health. (2016, July 28). *Trinidad and Tobago: civil society rises to the NCD challenge*. Retrieved from onecaribbeahealth.org: http://onecaribbeanhealth.org/trinidad-and-tobago-civil-society-rises-to-the-ncd-challenge/

Onuf, N., & Klink, F. F. (1989). Anarchy, Authority, Rule. *International Studies Quarterly*, 33(2), 149–173. DOI: 10.2307/2600535

Open Government Partnership. (2014). *OGP annual report 2014*. Retrieved from https://www.opengovpartnership.org/stories/ogp-annual-report-2014

Organization of African Unity. (1965, May 22-25). *Resolutions Adopted by the First Conference of Independent African Heads of State and Governments Held in Addis Ababa, Ethiopia, from 22 to May 25 1963*. Retrieved from African Union Common Repository: https://au.int/sites/default/files/decisions/32247-1963_cias_plen_2 -3_cias_res_1-2_e.pdf

Orts, E. (1995). A Reflexive Model of Environmental Regulation. *Business Ethics Quarterly*, 5(4), 799–794. DOI: 10.2307/3857414

Orwell, G. (1938). *Homage to Catalonia*. Secker and Warburg.

Osborne, D., & Gaebler, T. (1992). *Reinventing Government: How the Entrepreneurial Spirit is Transforming the Public Sector, from Schoolhouse to Statehouse, City Hall to the Pentagon*. Addison-Wesley.

Ostrom, E. (1990). *Governing the Commons; The Evolution of Institutions of Collective Action*. Cambridge University Press. DOI: 10.1017/CBO9780511807763

Ostrom, E. (2005). *Understanding Institutional Diversity*. Princeton University Press.

Ostrom, E. (2010a). A Long Polycentric Journey. *Annual Review of Political Science*, 13(1), 1–23. DOI: 10.1146/annurev.polisci.090808.123259

Ostrom, E. (2010b). Polycentric Systems for Coping with Collective Action. *Global Environmental Change*, 20(4), 550–557. DOI: 10.1016/j.gloenvcha.2010.07.004

Ostrom, V., Tiebout, C. M., & Warren, R. (1961, September). The Organization of Government in Metropolitan Areas: A Theoretical Inquiry. *The American Political Science Review*, 55(3), 831–842. DOI: 10.2307/1952530

Oved, I. (1978). *El anarquismo y el movimiento obrero en Argentina*. Siglo XXI.

Oye, K. (1985). Explaining Cooperation under Anarchy: Hypotheses and Strategies. *World Politics*, 38(1), 1–24. DOI: 10.2307/2010349

Ozga, J. (2019). The politics of accountability. *Journal of Educational Change*, 21(1), 19–35. DOI: 10.1007/s10833-019-09354-2

Pahl-Wostl, C. (2015). *Water Governance in the Face of Global Change: From Understanding to Transformation*. Springer International Publishing. DOI: 10.1007/978-3-319-21855-7

Papadopoulos, Y. (2010). Accountability and Multi-Level Governance: More Accountability, Less Democracy? *West European Politics*, 33(5), 1030–1049. DOI: 10.1080/01402382.2010.486126

Parashar, S., & Schulz, M. (2021). Colonial legacies, postcolonial 'selfhood' and the (un)doing of Africa. *Third World Quarterly*, 42(5), 867–881. DOI: 10.1080/01436597.2021.1903313

Parliament, Trinidad and Tobago. (2017, July 12). *Evolution of a nation: Trinidad and Tobago at fifty*. Retrieved from ttparliament.org: http://www.ttparliament.org/documents/2183.pdf

Pawelz, J. (2016). *Violent gangs as social actors in a world of socio-economic inequality. The case of Trinidad and Tobago*. Retrieved from German Institute of Global and Area Studies: https://www.giga-hamburg.de/en/event/violent-gangs-as-social-actors-in-a-world-of-socio-economic-inequality

Payne, A., & Bishop, M. (2010, January 29). *Caribbean regional governance and the sovereignty/statehood problem*. Retrieved from Center for International Governance Innovation: https://www.cigionline.org/publications/caribbean-regional-governance-and-sovereigntystatehood-problem

Peachey, A. (2009, May 2). *Conspicuously Politically Incorrect: The Soft Bigotry of Low Expectations*. Retrieved April 5, 2024, from https://www.nzcpr.com/conspicuously-politically-incorrect-the-soft-bigotry-of-low-expectations/

Perez, O., & Stegmann, O. (2018). Transnational Network Constitutionalism. *Journal of Law and Society*, 45(S1), 13–62. DOI: 10.1111/jols.12107

Perrone, D. (2009, July). *Latin American & Caribbean NGOs: facing challenges for greater participation at the United Nations Economic and Social Council*. Retrieved from http://csonet.org/content/documents/LAC.pdf

Philip, G. (Ed.). (2023). *Cerny. Heterarchy in World Politics*. Rouledge.

Piacentine, C. (2022). Book Review: The Power of Platforms: Shaping Media and Society, by Rasmus Kleis Nielsen and Sarah Anne Ganter. *Journalism & Mass Communication Quarterly*, 100(1), 216–218. DOI: 10.1177/10776990221129838

Pickett, S.T.A., Simone, A.T., Anderson, P. *et al.* The relational shift in urban ecology: From place and structures to multiple modes of coproduction for positive urban futures. *Ambio***53**, 845 870 (2024). https://doi.org/DOI: 10.1007/s13280-024-02001-y

Pierre, J., & Galaz, V. (2017). Superconnected, compex and ultrafast: governance of hyperfunctionality in financial markets. *Complexity, Governance & Networks*, 12-28. doi:DOI: 10.20377/cgn-55

Pineda, A. (2013, May 1). *NGOs and development in Latin American and the Caribbean: A case study of Haiti*. Retrieved from University of New Orleans: http://scholarworks.uno.edu/cgi/viewcontent.cgi?article=1047&context=honors_theses

Pinker, S. (2011). *The Better Angels of Our Nature: The Decline of Violence in History and Its Causes*. Allen Lane The Penguin Press.

Plender, J. (2008). "The Return of the State: How Government Is Back at the Heart of Economic Life," *Financial Times* (August 22)

Postone, M. (1997). *Time, Labor and Social Domination: A Reinterpretation of Marx's Critical Theory*. Cambridge University Press.

Powers, M. (2014, November 23). *Hazel Brown to step down as NGO head*. Retrieved from Trinidad and Tobago Guardian: https://www.guardian.co.tt/news/2014-11-23/hazel-brown-step-down-ngo%E2%80%88head

Premdas, R. (2011). Identity, ethnicity and the Caribbean homeland in an era of globalization. *Social Identities*, 17(6), 811–832. DOI: 10.1080/13504630.2011.606676

Prichard, A. (2010). *Rethinking anarchy and the state in IR theory: the contributions of classical anarchism*. Retrieved from University of Bristol: https://www.bristol.ac.uk/media library/sites/spais/migrated/documents/prichard0310.pdf

Prichard, A. (2010). *Rethinking anarchy and the state in IR theory: the contributions of classical anarchism*. Retrieved from University of Bristol: https://www.bristol.ac.uk/media-library/sites/spais/migrated/documents/prichard0310.pdf

Putnam, R. D. (1988, Summer). Diplomacy and Domestic Policy: The Logic of Two-Level Games. *International Organization*, 42(3), 427–460. DOI: 10.1017/S0020818300027697

Rahman, S., & Tasnim, F. (2023). The role of NGOs in ensuring local governance in Bangladesh: From the perception of other actors of governance. *Asia-Pacific Journal of Regional Science*, 7(3), 1007–1034. DOI: 10.1007/s41685-023-00283-w

Ramadan, A., & Fregonese, S. (2017). Hybrid sovereignty and the state of exception in the Palestinian refugee camps in Lebanon. *Annals of the American Association of Geographers*, 107(4), 2469–4460. DOI: 10.1080/24694452.2016.1270189

Ramdass, A. (2019, March 1). *Amnesty for Venezuelans in Trinidad*. Retrieved from Daily Express: https://www.trinidadexpress.com/news/local/amnesty-for -venezuelans-in-t-t/article_8127756c-3bc7-11e9-b487-e3592eda812c.html

Ramjit, D. (2023). From Post-internationalism to Heterarchy: Turbulence and Distance Proximities in a World of Globalization and Fragmentation. In *"Heterarchy in World Politics"* edited by Philip G. Cerny (2023). Routledge: Taylor & Francis Group.

Ramos, M. (1989). Some ethical implications of qualitative research. *Research in Nursing & Health*, 12(1), 57–63. DOI: 10.1002/nur.4770120109 PMID: 2922491

Rampersad, S., & Julien, J. (2017, June 25). *Speaker under fire from UNC*. Retrieved from guardian.co.tt: https://www.guardian.co.tt/news/2017-06-24/speaker -under-fire-unc

Raphael, C. (2015, January 18). *Accept the disabled*. Retrieved from Trinidad and Tobago Guardian: https://www.guardian.co.tt/news/2015-01-18/accept-disabled

Raphael, J. (2017, August 1). *NGOs must focus on relationships, accountability to survive*. Retrieved from guardian.co.tt: https://www.guardian.co.tt/news/2017-08 -01/ngos-must-focus-relationships-accountability-survive

Rapkin, D. P., Thompson, W. R., & Christopherson, J. A. (1979). Bipolarity and Bipolarization in the Cold War Era: Conceptualization, Measurement, and Validation. *The Journal of Conflict Resolution*, 23(2), 261–295. DOI: 10.1177/002200277902300203

Rappler. (2021). #TunayNaPagbabago: Kuwentong Ex-DDS. Retrieved from: https:// www.rappler.com/nation/elections/video-stories-former-duterte-supporters/

Rappler. Retrieved from: https://www.rappler.com/technology/features/analysis-fake - news-internet-propaganda-2022-philippine-elections/

Rawlins, G. (2017, June 15). *Civil society's overlooked role in natural resource governance*. Retrieved from tteiti.org/tt: http://www.tteiti.org.tt/civil-societys-overlooked -role-in-natural-resource-governance/

Regan, A., & Brazys, S. (2021). Celtic phoenix or leprechaun economics? The politics of an FDI-led growth model in Europe. In Johnston, A., & Regan, A. (Eds.), *Is the European Union Capable of Integrating Diverse Models of Capitalism?* (pp. 79–94). Routledge. DOI: 10.4324/9781003158455-6

Reinisch, A. (2013). The scope of investor-state dispute settlement in international investment agreements. *Asia Pacific Law Review*, 21(1), 3–26. DOI: 10.1080/10192557.2013.11788264

Reis, B. C. (2013). Portugal and the UN: A Rogue State Resisting the Norm of Decolonization (1956–1974). *Portuguese Studies*, 251-276.

Research, B. M. I. (2017). *Local elections deliver little change in political climate.* Latin American Monitor.

Reynolds, J. T. (2015). *Sovereignty and Struggle: Africa and Africans in the Era of the Cold War, 1945-1994*. Oxford University Press.

Riga, D. (2022). Socialization through Interregional Relations: EU's Normative Power in its Dialogue with China. In: *The Twelfth International Convention of Asia Scholars (ICAS 12)*. Amsterdam University Press. 583-593

Risse, T., Börzel, T. A., & Draude, A. (Eds.). (2018). *The Oxford handbook of governance and limited statehood*. Oxford University Press.

Rodrık, D., Subramanian, A., & Trebbi, F. (2004). Institutions Rule: the primacy of institutions over geography and integration in economic development. *Journal of Economic Growth, 9*(2), 131-165. Rhys, J. (1966). *Wide Sargasso Sea*. New York: Norton.DOI: 10.1023/B:JOEG.0000031425.72248.85

Roederer-Rynning, C. (2017). Parliamentary assertion and deep integration: The European parliament in the CETA and TTIP negotiations. *Cambridge Review of International Affairs*, 30(5-6), 507–526. DOI: 10.1080/09557571.2018.1461808

Roger, C., Snidal, D., & Vabulas, F. (2023). The importance of rational institutionalism in the analysis of informal international institutions. *International Politics*. Advance online publication. DOI: 10.1057/s41311-023-00483-3

Rogers, D. (2009). *Postinternationalism and small arms control: theory, politics, security*. Ashgate.

Rosenau, J. (2010). Fragmegration. In J. Rosenau. *Along the Domestic-Foreign Frontier: Exploring Governance in a Turbulent World* (Chapter 6, pp.89-117). Cambridge University Press.

Rosenau, J. N. (2000). The governance of fragmegration: Neither a world republic nor a global interstate system. *Studia Diplomatica*, 15-39.

Rosenau, J. N. (2003). Dynamics beyond globalization. New Jersey: Princeton University Press. 2016.1160599

Rosenau, J. N. (2007). Governing the ungovernable: the challenge of a global disaggregation of authority. *Regulation & Governance, 1*, pp. 88–97. DOI:. 00001. DOI: 10.1111/j.1748-5991.2007

Rosenau, J. N. (1990). *Turbulence in world politics: a theory of change and continuity.* Princeton University Press. DOI: 10.1515/9780691188522

Rosenau, J. N. (1995). Governance in the 21ˢᵗ Century. *Global Governance,* 1(1), 13–43. DOI: 10.1163/19426720-001-01-90000004

Rosenau, J. N. (1997). *Along the Domestic–Foreign Frontier. Exploring Governance in the Turbulent World.* Cambridge University Press. DOI: 10.1017/CBO9780511549472

Rosenau, J. N. (2003). *Distant Proximities: Dynamics Beyond Globalization.* Princeton University Press. DOI: 10.1515/9780691231112

Rosenau, J. N. (2003). *Dynamics beyond globalization.* Princeton University Press.

Roy, R., Denzau, A. T., & Willett, T. D. (Eds.). (2007). *Neoliberalism: National and Regional*

Ryder, H., Baisch, A., & Eguegu, O. (2020, September 19). *Decolonizing the United Nations Means Abolishing the Permanent Five: The Inequalities of the Past Can't Set the Rules of the Present.* Retrieved from Foreign Policy: https://foreignpolicy.com/2020/09/17/decolonizing-united-nations-means-abolish-permanent-five-security-council/

Sabatier, P. (2019). Theories of the policy process. In *Routledge eBooks.* https://doi.org/DOI: 10.4324/9780367274689

Sabel, C. (1996). Constitutional Orders: Trust Building and Response to Change," In Hollingsworth, R. & Boyer, R. (Eds.) eds. *Contemporary Capitalism; The Embeddedness of Institutions* (pp.54-188). Cambridge University Press

Sabel, C. (2004. Beyond Principal-Agent Governance: Experimentalist Organizations, Learning and Accountability. In E. Engelen, E. & M. Sie Dhahien Ho, (Eds.). *Die Staat van de Demokratie. Demokratie voorbij die Staat.* (pp.173-195). WRR. Verkenning 3. University of Amsterdam Press.

Sabel, C. (1994). Learning by Monitoring: The Institutions of Economic Development. In Smelser, N., & Swedberg, R. (Eds.), (pp. 137–168). Princeton University Press.

Sabel, C., & Dorf, M. (1998). A Constitution of Democratic Experimentalism. *Columbia Law Review,* 98(2), 267–473. DOI: 10.2307/1123411

Said, E. (1978). *Orientalism.* Ramdom House.

Saint Ville, A., Hickey, G., & Phillip, L. (2017). How do stakeholder interactions influence national food security policy in the Caribbean? The case of Saint Lucia. *Food Policy*, 68, 53–64. DOI: 10.1016/j.foodpol.2017.01.002

Saka-Olokungboye, N., Ilugbami, J. O., & Olateru-Olagbegi, O. (2023). Traditional Institutions and Good Governance in Nigeria. *British Journal of Multidisciplinary and Advanced Studies*, 4(4), 27–39. DOI: 10.37745/bjmas.2022.0252

Sassen, S. (Ed.). (2007). *Deciphering the Global: Its Scales, Spaces and Subjects.* Routledge.

Scalapino, R. A. (1964, July). Sino-Soviet Competition in Africa. *Foreign Affairs*, 42(4), 640–654. DOI: 10.2307/20029719

Schedler, A. (2007). Mapping Contingency. In Shapiro, I., & Sonu, B. (Eds.), *Political Contingency: Studying the Unexpected, the Accidental, and the Unforeseen* (pp. 54–78). New York University Press.

Schiel, R., Faulkner, C., & Powell, J. (2017). Mutiny in Côte d'Ivoire. *Africa Spectrum*, 52(2), 103–115. DOI: 10.1177/000203971705200205

Schmidt, E. (2013). *Foreign intervention in Africa: From the Cold War to the War on Terror*. Cambridge University. DOI: 10.1017/CBO9781139021371

Scholz, R. (2010). *Internationaler Gesundheitsschutz und Welthandel*. DUNCKER UND HUMBLOT.

Schomerus, M., Englebert, P., & Vries, L. d. (2019). Africa's Secessionism: A Breakdance of Aspiration, Grievance, Performance and Disenchantment. In *L. d. Vires, P. E. Englebert, & M. Schomerus, Secessionism in African Politics* (pp. 1–20). Palgrave Macmillan. DOI: 10.1007/978-3-319-90206-7_1

Sen, A. (1982). Development as Capability Expansion. *Journal of Development Planning*, 19(1), 41–58.

Senel, N. (2014). A postcolonial reading of Wide Sargasso Sea by Jean Rhys. *Journal of Language & Literacy Education*, 38–45. DOI: 10.12973/jlle.11.246

Senior, O. (1994). *Gardening in the tropics*. McClelland & Stewart.

Seremani, T., & Clegg, S. (2016). Postcolonialism, organization and management theory: The rold of epistemological third spaces. *Journal of Management Inquiry*, 25(2), 171–183. DOI: 10.1177/1056492615589973

Sewell, W. H. (1990, October). *"Three Temporalities: Toward a Sociology of the Event"*. Retrieved from University of Michigan: https://deepblue.lib.umich.edu/bitstream/handle/2027.42/51215/448.pdf

Shaw, M. N. (1997). The Heritage of States: The Principle of Uti Possidetis Juris Today. *The British Year Book of International Law*, 75-154.

Sheehan, J. J. (2008). *Where Have All the Soldiers Gone? The Transformation of Modern Europe*. Houghton Mifflin.

Shepperson, G. (2008). The Fifth Pan-African Conference, 1945 and the All African Peoples Congress, 1958. *Contributions in Black Studies*, 35-66.

Sherwood, M. (2012). Pan-African Conferences, 1900-1953: What Did 'Pan-Africanism' Mean? *The Journal of Pan African Studies*, 106-126.

Sherwood, M. (2021). The All African People's Congress (AAPC) was called by Kwame Nkrumah-- and George Padmore. *Contemporary Journal of African Studies*, 63-68.

Shilliam, R. (2011). *International Relations and Non-Western Thought: Imperialism, Colonialism, and Investigations of Global Modernity*. Routledge.

Shimamoto, M. (2021). Unintended Consequences of Government Policy. *Japanese Research in Business History*, 38(0), 1–5. DOI: 10.5029/jrbh.38.1

Siles-Brügge, G., & Strange, M. (2020). National autonomy or transnational solidarity? Using multiple geographic frames to politicize EU trade policy. *Politics and Governance*, 8(1), 277–289.

Silverman, C., Lytvynenko, J., & Kung, W. (2020, January 7). Disinformation for hire: How a new breed of PR firms is selling lies online. BuzzFeed News. https://www.buzzfeednews.com/article/craigsilverman/disinformation-for-hire-black-pr-firms

Sinclair, G. F. (2019). A Battlefield Transformed the United Nations and the Struggle over Postcolonial Statehood. In *J. v. Bernstorff, & P. Dann, The Battle for International Law: South-North Perspectives on Decolonization Era* (pp. 257–277). Oxford University Press. DOI: 10.1093/oso/9780198849636.003.0012

Sklair, L. (2000). *The Transnational Capitalist Class*. Blackwell.

Slaughter, A.-M. (2004). *A New World Order*. Princeton University Press.

Smismans, S. 2004). Reflexive Law in Support of Directly Deliberative Polyarchy/ Reflexive Deliberative Polyarchy as a Normative Frame for OMC." In O. DeSchutter, O. and S. Deakin, (Eds.) *Social Rights and Market Forces:* The Future of Social Europe. Brussels; Bruylant

Smith, A. (1979). *Nationalism in the Twentieth Century*. Martin Robertson / University Press.

Smith, K. (2017). Innovating for the global commons: Multilateral collaboration in a polycentric world. *Oxford Review of Economic Policy*, 33(1), 49–65. DOI: 10.1093/oxrep/grw039

Soederberg, S., Menz, G., & Cerny, P. G. (Eds.). (2005). *Internalizing Globalization: The Rise of Neoliberalism and the Erosion of National Varieties of Capitalism*. Palgrave Macmillan. DOI: 10.1057/9780230524439

SOFRECO. (2009). *Mapping of non state actors in Trinidad and Tobago*. Retrieved from Mapping of non state actors in Trinidad and Tobago: https://www.eeas.europa .eu/archives/delegations/trinidad/documents/1__final_report20131007_01_en.pdf

Spruyt, H. (1994). *The Sovereign State and Its Competitors: An Analysis of Systems Change*. Princeton University Press. DOI: 10.1515/9780691213057

Stalin, J. (2013). *Marxism and the national question*. Prism Key.

Stark, D. (2001). Heterarchy: Exploiting Ambiguity and Organizing Diversity. *Brazilian Journal of Political Economy*, 22-41.

Stark, D., & Sabel, C. (2006). *Heterarchies: Distributed Intelligence and the Organization of Diversity*. Santa Fe Institute.www.santafe.edu/research/heterarchies.php

Stark, D. (2010). Ambiguous Assets for Uncertain Environments: Heterarchy in Postsocialist Firms. *Journal of Economic Sociology*, 1(2), 7–34. DOI: 10.17323/1726-3247-2000-2-7-34

Steinmetz, G. (1998). Critical Realism and Historical Sociology. A Review Article. *Comparative Studies in Society and History*, 40(1), 170–186. DOI: 10.1017/ S0010417598980069

Stephenson, K. (2016). Heterarchy. In *Handbook on theories of governance* (pp. 139–148). Edward Elgar Publishing.

Stone, J. (1942). Peace Planning and Atlantic Charter. *The Australian Quarterly*, 14(2), 5–22. DOI: 10.2307/20631017

Storey, D. (2017). States, Territory and Sovereignty. *Geography (Sheffield, England)*, 102(3), 116–121. DOI: 10.1080/00167487.2017.12094021

Stouck, J. (2005, December). *Gardening in the diaspora: place and identity in Olive Senior's poetry*. Retrieved from https://malcolmliteratureresource.wordpress.com/2012/10/22/gardening-in-the-tropics-journal-essay/

Strachan, H., & Scheipers, S. (Eds.). (2011). *The Changing Character of War*. Oxford University Press. DOI: 10.1093/acprof:osobl/9780199596737.001.0001

Strange, S. (1996). *The retreat of the state: the diffusion of power in the world economy*. DOI: 10.1017/CBO9780511559143

Strokosch, K., & Osborne, S. P. (2020). Co-experience, Co-production and Co-governance: An Ecosystem Approach to the Analysis of Value Creation. *Policy and Politics*, 48(3), 425–442. DOI: 10.1332/030557320X15857337955214

Strongman, L. (2014, October 3). *Postcolonialism and international development studies: a dialectic exchange*. DOI: 10.1080/01436597.2014.946248

Superville, J. (2017, August 12). *Alexandrov: Our forensic pathology systems outdated*. Retrieved from newsday.co.tt: https://www.newsday.co.tt/news/0,247612.html

Sylvester, M. A. (2020). Narratives of resistance in Trinidad's Calypso and Soca music. *Cultural and Pedagogical Inquiry*, 11(3), 105–116. DOI: 10.18733/cpi29507

Tack, C. (2016, June 16). *Hulsie calls for more state support for NGOs*. Retrieved from newsday.co.tt: https://www.newsday.co.tt/news/0,229278.html

Tafotie, J., & Idahosa, S. (2016). Conflicts in Africa and Major Powers: Proxy Wars, Zone of Influence, or Provocating Instability. *Вестник РУДН, серия «Международные отношения», сентябрь*, 451-460.

Tarrow, S. (2010). Dynamics of diffusion: mechanisms, institutions, and scale shift. In Givan, R., Roberts, K., & Soule, S. (Eds.), *The diffusion of social movements: actors, mechanisms, and political effects* (pp. 204–220). Cambridge University Press. DOI: 10.1017/CBO9780511761638.012

Tedeschi, M., Vorobeva, E., & Jauhiainen, J. S. (2020). Transnationalism: Current debates and new perspectives. *GeoJournal*, 87(2), 603–619. DOI: 10.1007/s10708-020-10271-8

Télo, M. (2012). *State, Globalization and Multilateralism: The challenges of institutionalizing regionalism*. Springer Netherlands. DOI: 10.1007/978-94-007-2843-1

Ter Horst, P. (2009).Multiscalar Institutional Complementarity and the Scaling of Clusters," *Belgian Journal of Geography* https://doi.org/ pp. 43-64.DOI: 10.40/belgec7075

Teubner, G. (2002). Hybrid Laws: Constitutionalizing Private Governance Networks. In R. Kagen, R., Krygier, M., & Winston, K. (Eds.). *Legality and Community: On the Intellectual Legacy of Philip Selznick*. Berkeley: Berkeley Public Policy Press

Teubner, G. (2004). Societal Constitutionalism: Alternatives to State-Centered Constitutional Theory, Iin Transnational Governance and Constitutionalism, In C. Joerges, I-J. Sand, & Teubner (Eds.). Oxford: Hart.

Teubner, G. (2011). "Constitutionalizing Polycontexturality." *Social and Legal Studies* 20 (2) 209-252. With Christodoulides, E. et al. (Eds.).

Teubner, G. (2024). *Environmental Law and Ecological Responsibility: The Concept and Practice of Ecological Self-Organization*. With L. Farmer and D. Murphy, (Eds.). Wiley

Teubner, G. (2024). Self-Justifying Law of Constitutionalism. In M. Goldoni & M. Wilkinson, *The Material Constitution in Rudolf Wiethölter's Critical Systems Theory* (Chapter 10, pp. 150-168), Cambridge University Press.

Teubner, G., & Collins, H. (2011). *Networks as Connected Contracts*, Ed./Intro. H Collins. Trans. Michelle Everson. Oxford: Hart.

Teubner, G. (1992). Regulatory Law: Chronicle of a Death Foretold. *Social & Legal Studies*, 1(4), 451–475. DOI: 10.1177/096466399200100401

Teubner, G. (1996). De Collisione Discursuum: Communicative Rationalities: Law, Morality and Politics. *Cardozo Law Review*, 17, 901–918.

Teubner, G. (1998). Legal Irritants: Good Faith in British Law or How Unifying Law Ends Up in New Divergences. *The Modern Law Review*, 61(1), 11–236. DOI: 10.1111/1468-2230.00125

Teubner, G. (2003/2004). *Coincedentia Oppositorium: Networks and the Laws Beyond Contract and Organization. Storrs Lectures.* Yale Law School.

Teubner, G. (2007). In the Blindspot: Hybridization of Contracting. *Theoretical Inquiries in Law*, 8, 51–72.1.

Teubner, G. (2012). *Constitutional Fragments: Social Constitutionalism and Globalization* (Norbury, G., Trans.). Oxford University Press. DOI: 10.1093/acprof:oso/9780199644674.001.0001

Teubner, G. (2015). Transnational Constitutionalism in the Variety of Capitalism. *Italian Law Journal*, 1(2), 219–248.

Teubner, G., & Fischer -Lescano, , A. (2004). Regime Collisions: The Vain Search for Legal Unity in the Fragmentation of Global Law. *University of Michigan Journal of International Law*, 25(4), 999–1046.

The African Union Commission and New Zealand Ministry of Foreign Affairs and Trade/Manatū Aorere. (2014). *African Union Handbook 2021*. The African Union Commission and New Zealand Ministry of Foreign Affairs and Trade/Manatū Aorere.

The New York Times. (1964, July 21). *Nyerere, at Cairo, Assails Nkrumah; Tangangikan Says Ghanaian Only Preaches Unity*. Retrieved from The New York Times: https://www.nytimes.com/1964/07/21/archives/nyerere-atcairo-assails-nkrumah -tangangikan-says-ghanaian-only.html

The New York Times. (2020, June 2). *A Continent Remade: Reflections on 1960, the Year of Africa*. Retrieved from The New York Times: https://www.nytimes.com/ interactive/2020/02/06/world/africa/africa-independence-year.html#:~:text=The%20 year%20was%201960.,for%20this%20project%20was%20born

The Organization of African Unity. (1963, May 25). *OAU Charter*. Retrieved from African Union: https://au.int/sites/default/files/treaties/7759-file-oau_charter_1963 .pdf

The Silver Lining Foundation. (2013). *US Embassy awards $9400USD to The Silver Lining Foundation*. Retrieved from https://www.silverliningtt.com/us-embassy-grant/

Theise, N. (2023). *Notes on Complexity: A Scientific Theory of Connection, Consciousness and Being*. Spiegel and Grau.

Thornhill, C. (2011). *A Sociology of Constitutions" Constitutions and State Legitimacy in Historical-Sociological Perspective*. Cambridge University Press. DOI: 10.1017/CBO9780511895067

Tilly, C. (Ed.). (1975). *The Formation of National States in Western Europe*. Princeton University Press.

Tine, H., & Zangl, B. (2015). *WHO Orchestrates?* Coping with Competitors in Global Health.

Topal, R. (2022). The rise of digital repression: How technology is reshaping power, politics, and resistance. *The Information Society, 38*(1), 77 78. https://doi.org/DOI: 10.1080/01972243.2022.201422

Torfing, J., Peters, G. B., Pierre, J., & Sørensen, E. (2012). *Interactive Governance: Advancing the Paradigm.* Oxford University Press. DOI: 10.1093/acprof:oso/9780199596751.001.0001

Transparency International. (2016). *Corruption perceptions index 2016.* Retrieved from https://www.transparency.org/news/feature/corruption_perceptions_index _2016

*Treaty.* (1975, May 28). Retrieved from The 1975 Treaty of The Economic Community Of West African States: https://www.ecowas.int/publication/treaty/#:~:text =The%20Economic%20Community%20of%20West,in%201975%20in%20Lagos %2C%20Nigeria

Triandafyllidou, A. (2024). Migration and globalization: dynamics and contradictions. In *Edward Elgar Publishing eBooks* (pp. 1–23). https://doi.org/DOI: 10.4337/9781800887657.00007

Trinidad and Tobago News. (2003, January 8). *Trinidad and Tobago emancipation day.* Retrieved from trinidadanadtobagonews.com: http://www.trinidadand tobagonews.com/forum/webbbs_config.pl?md=read;id=1171

Trinidad and Tobago Newsday. (2016, September 30). *Civil society wants transparent governance.* Retrieved from newsday.co.tt: https://www.newsday.co.tt/news/ 0,233921.html

Trommer, S., & Teivainen, T. (2017). Representation beyond the state: Towards transnational democratic nonstate politics. *Globalizations*, 14(1), 17–31. DOI: 10.1080/14747731.2016.1160599

Trondal, J., & Bauer, M. (2017). Conceptualizing the European multilevel administrative order. Capturing variation in the European administrative system. *European Political Science Review*, 9(1), 73–94. DOI: 10.1017/S1755773915000223

Turnhout, E., Metze, T., Wyborn, C., Klenk, N., & Louder, E. (2020). The politics of co production: Participation, power, and transformation. *Current Opinion in Environmental Sustainability*, 42, 15–21. DOI: 10.1016/j.cosust.2019.11.009

Ullah, A. K. M. A. (2024). Struggles for identity formation: Second-generation South Asian diaspora overseas. *South Asian Diaspora*, 1, 16. DOI: 10.1080/19438192.2024.2328465

United Nations Commission of Experts on Reforms of the International Monetary and Financial System. (2009). *Recommendations* (19 March 2009), https://www.un .org/ga/president/63/letters/recommendationExperts200309.pdf

United Nations Digital Library. (2003, March 26). *Report of the Secretary-General on Côte d'Ivoire*. Retrieved from United Nations Digital Library: https://digitallibrary .un.org/record/491307?ln=en&v=pdf#files

United Nations Digital Library. (2017, January 19). *Resolution 2337 (2017) / adopted by the Security Council at its 7866th meeting on January 19 2017*. Retrieved from United Nations Digital Library: https://digitallibrary.un.org/record/856865 ?ln=en&v=pdf

United Nations Treaty Collection. (1963, May 25). *No. 6947. Charter of the Organization of African Unity. Done at Addis Ababa onMay251963*. Retrieved from United Nations Treaty Collection: https://treaties.un.org/doc/Publication/UNTS/ Volume%20479/volume-479-I-6947-English.pdf

United Nations. (1998, November 3). *Agreement between the Government of Guinea-Bissau and the Self-proclaimed Military junta*. Retrieved from United Nations: https://peacemaker.un.org/guatemala-abujaagreement98

United Nations. (2012, December 20). *Security Council Resolution 2085 (2012)*. Retrieved from United Nations: https://www.refworld.org/legal/resolution/unsc/ 2012/en/89613

University of California Press. (1959). Resolutions of the All Africans People's Conference. *Current History*, 41-46.

Untalan, C. (2018). The Curious Case of the Duterte Presidency: Turning the Demos Against Democracy? *Development*. Advance online publication. DOI: 10.1057/ s41301-018-0149-6

van der Pijl, K. (1998). *Transnational Classes and International Relations*. Routledge.

Varela, C. (2017). Africa Finds Voice in the Halls of Manchester. *History in the Making*, 55-87.

Veldman, J. (2017). Self-Regulation in International Corporate Codes. In DuPlessis, J. & Low. (Eds.). *Corporate Governance Codes in the Twentieth Century* (pp.77-95). Springer.

Verheul, J. (2021). The Atlantic Charter: Genesis of the Transatlantic World Order. *Atlantisch Perspectief*, 42-46.

Vlasiuk Nibe, A., Meunier, S., & Roederer-Rynning, C. (2024). Pre-emptive depoliticisation: The European Commission and the EU foreign investment screening regulation. *Journal of European Public Policy*, 31(1), 182–211. DOI: 10.1080/13501763.2023.2258153

Voorn, B., van Thiel, S., & van Genugten, M. (2018). Debate: Corporatization as more than a recent crisis-driven development. *Public Money & Management*, 38(7), 481–482. DOI: 10.1080/09540962.2018.1527533

Voss, J -P. & Kemp, R. (Eds.). (2006). *Reflexive Governance for Sustainable Development*. Cheltenham: Edward Elgar. DOI: 10.1007/978-3-319-51868-8_4

Walcott, D. (1981). *The Fortunate Traveller*. Farrar, Strauss & Giroux.

Walcott, D. (2007). *Selected Poems*. Farrar, Straus and Giroux.

Walker, R. B. J. (1992). *Inside/Outside: International Relations as Political Theory*. Cambridge University Press. DOI: 10.1017/CBO9780511559150

Wallerstein, I. (1974). The Role of the Organization of African Unity in Contemporary African Politics. In Y. El-Ayouty, & H. C. Brooks, Africa and International Organization (pp. 18–28). Martinus Nijhofj. DOI: 10.1007/978-94-010-2050-3_3

Walraven, K. v. (1999, January). Containing Conflict in the Economic Community of West African States. The Hague: Clingendael .

Waltz, K. (1979). *Theory of International Politics*. Addison-Wesley.

Wang, F. (2010). The Evolution of Hierarchy toward Heterarchy. *Frontiers of Business Research in China*, 515-540. doi:DOI DOI: 10.1007/s11782-010-0109-9

Warner, C. M. (2001). The Rise of the State System in Africa. *Review of International Studies*, 27(5), 65–89. DOI: 10.1017/S0260210501008038

Weatherby, J., Arceneaux, C., Leithner, A., Reed, I., Timms, B., & Zhang, S. (2017). *The other world: issues and politics in the developing world* (10th ed.). Routledge. DOI: 10.4324/9781315543383

Webster, C. (2017). Political turbulence and business as usual: Tourism's future. *Journal of Tourism Futures*, 4-7(1), 4–7. Advance online publication. DOI: 10.1108/JTF-11-2016-0045

Weible, M., & Sabatier, P. (2017). *Theories of the policy process* (4th ed.). Westview.

Weinberger, O. (1991). *Institution and Legal Politics. Fundamental Problems of Legal Philosophy and Social Philosophy*. Reidel.

Weinberger, O. (1994). Habermas on Democracy and Justice: Limits of a Sound Conception. *Ratio Juris*, 7(2), 239–253. DOI: 10.1111/j.1467-9337.1994.tb00178.x

Welch, J. C.Jr. (1986). Ethnic Factors in African Armies. *Ethnic and Racial Studies*, 9(3), 321–333. DOI: 10.1080/01419870.1986.9993536

Wendt, A. (1991). *Anarcy is what states make of it: the social construction of power politics*. Cambridge University.

Wendt, A. (1992). Anarchy is what states make of it: The social construction of power politics. *International Organization*, 46(02), 391–425. DOI: 10.1017/S0020818300027764

Wertheim, S. (2024). Internationalism/Isolationism: Concepts of American Global Power. In *Springer eBooks* (pp. 49–88). https://doi.org/DOI: 10.1007/978-3-031-49677-6_3

Wiethölter, R. (1972). *Rechtswissenschaft in Kritik und als Kritik,*.tudienerlin: https://doi.org/DOI: 10.1515/9783

Wiethölter, R. (2005). Justifications of a Law of Society. Paradoxes and Inconsistencies in the Law, 65, 71.

Wiethülter, R. (2013). Politische Rechtstheorie Revisited Rudolf wiethölter zum 100.Semester, In C. Joerges, C. & Zumbansen, P. (Eds.). Zentrum für Europäische Rechts (ZERP) Universität Bremen

Wight, C. (2006). *Agents, structures and nternational relations: politics as ontology*. Cambridge University. DOI: 10.1017/CBO9780511491764

Wiking, S. (1993). *Military Coups in Sub-Saharan Africa: How to Justify Illegal Assumptions of Power*. Scandinavian Institute of African Studies.

Williams, M. J. (2020). Beyond state capacity: Bureaucratic performance, policy implementation and reform. *Journal of Institutional Economics*, 17(2), 339–357. DOI: 10.1017/S1744137420000478

Williams, P., & Chrisman, L. (1988). Can the subaltern speak? In Spivak, G. (Ed.), *Colonial discourse and postcolonial theory* (pp. 66–111). Columbia University.

Willke, H. (2007). *Smart Governance: Governing the Global Knowledge Society*. Campus Verlag.

Wills, M. (2024). *A Messy Divorce: The Sino-Soviet Split*. Retrieved from J Stor Daily: https://daily.jstor.org/a-messy-divorce-the-sino-soviet-split/

Winger, K. (2024). Power from Below in Premodern Societies: The Dynamics of Political Complexity in the Archaeological RecordT. L. Thurston and Manuel Fernández-Götz (eds.): Power from Below in Premodern Societies: The Dynamics of Political Complexity in the Archaeological Record. CambridgeUniversity Press, Cambridge, 2021. 320 pp. ISBN: 9781316515396. *Norwegian Archaeological Review*, 1 2. https://doi.org/DOI: 10.1080/00293652.2024.2324800

Wolfers, A. (1962). *Discord and Collaboration. Essays on International Politics.* The John Hopkins University Press. DOI: 10.56021/9780801806902

Wolin, S. (2008). *Democracy Incorporated: Managed Democracy and the Specter of Inverted Totalitarianism.* Princeton University Press Princeton and Oxford.

Woolcock, S. (2011). *European Union economic diplomacy: The role of the EU in external economic relations.* Ashgate.

Worrel, A. (2016, December 31). *Economic challenges in 2017.* Retrieved from guardian.co.tt: https://www.guardian.co.tt/business/2016-12-30/economic-challenges-2017

Worth, O. (2017). *Hegemony, international political economy and post-communist Russia.* Routledge. DOI: 10.4324/9781315253459

Yolles, M. (2003). The Political Cybernetics of Organizations. *Kybernetes,* 32(9/10), 1253–1282. DOI: 10.1108/03684920310493242

Young, A. R. (2019). Two wrongs make a right? The politicization of trade policy and European trade strategy. *Journal of European Public Policy,* 26(12), 1883–1899. DOI: 10.1080/13501763.2019.1678055

Youssef, A. B. (2024). The role of NGOs in climate policies: The case of Tunisia. *Journal of Economic Behavior & Organization, 220,* 388 401. https://doi.org/DOI: 10.1016/j.jebo.2024.02.016

Zielonka, J. (2006). *Europe as Empire. The Nature of the Enlarged European Union.* Oxford University Press. DOI: 10.1093/0199292213.001.0001

Zielonka, J. (2014). *Is the EU doomed?* Polity Press.

Zolo, D. (1992). *Democracy and Complexity: A Realistic Approach.* Penn State University Press.

Zumbansen, P. (2016). Where the Wild Things Are: Journey into Transnational Legal Orders, University of California, Irvine *(UC, Irvine) Journal of International, Transnational and Comparative Law, Vol. 1 Symposium: Transnational Legal Ordering and Private Law,"* Article 8. [1]

Zürn, M. (2010). Global governance as multi-level governance. In *Handbook on multi-level governance.* Edward Elgar Publishing.

Zürn, M., Binder, M., & Ecker-Ehrhardt, M. (2012). International authority and its politicization. *International Theory,* 4(1), 69–106. DOI: 10.1017/S1752971912000012

Zwitter, A. J., & Hazenberg, J. (2020). Decentralized Network Governance: Blockchain technology and the future of regulation. *Frontiers in Blockchain*, 3, 12. Advance online publication. DOI: 10.3389/fbloc.2020.00012

# About the Contributors

**Dana-Marie Ramjit** is a Politics and Public Policy professor at St. Mary's University and the University of New Brunswick, Canada. She is a leading voice in examining the evolving dynamics of global politics and policymaking. Her research and publications focus on governance structures, multi-nodal systems, and collaborative policymaking, providing valuable insights into the shifting landscapes of global governance.

***

**Philip G. Cerny** is Professor Emeritus of Politics and Global Affairs at the University of Manchester and Rutgers University-Newark. He was educated at Kenyon College, Sciences Po (Paris) and the University of Manchester, where he received his Ph.D. in 1976. He has also taught at the Universities of York and Leeds, and has been a visiting scholar or professor at Harvard University, Sciences Po (Paris), Dartmouth College, New York University and the Brookings Institution. He is the author of The Politics of Grandeur: Ideological Aspects of de Gaulle's Foreign Policy (Cambridge University Press 1980; French translation 1984), The Changing Architecture of Politics: Structure, Agency and the Future of the State (Sage 1990) and Rethinking World Politics: A Theory of Transnational Neopluralism (Oxford Univeristy Press 2010), and he has been editor or co-editor of several books on French politics, international political economy, global finance and international political theory, most recently Rethinking World Politics: A Theory of Transnational Neopluralism (2010) and Heterarchy in World Politics (Routledge 2023). His most recent book chapter is "The Limits of Global Global Governance" in Raffaele Marchetti, ed., Partnerships in the European Union and Global Policymaking (2014), and his most recent articles are "The New Anarchy: Globalisation and Fragmentation in World Politics" (with Alex Prichard), in the Journal of International Political Theory (2017), "In the Shadow of Ordolliberalism: The Paradox of Neoliberalism in the 21st Century", in the European Review of International Studies (2016), "Rethinking Global Environmental Policy: From Global Governance to Transnational Neopluralism" (with Gabriela Kütting), in Public Administration (2015) and "Reframing the International", in ERIS (2014). He received the Distinguished Scholar Award of the I.P.E. Section of the International Studies Association in 2011 and until recently chaired Research Committee No. 36 (Political Power) of the International Political Science Association.

**Adrian David Cheok** is Full Professor at i-University Tokyo, Director of the Imagineering Institute, Malaysia, Visiting Professor at Raffles University, Malaysia, Visiting Professor at University of Novi Sad-Serbia, on Technical faculty "Mihailo Pupin", Serbia, and CEO of Nikola Tesla Technologies Corporation.

**Nene-Lomotey Kuditchar** is a senior member at the Department of Political Science University of Ghana. He is also a co-opted instructor at the Legon Centre for International Affairs and Diplomacy, the Institute for Statistical Social and Economic Research and Centre for Migration Studies (all at the University of Ghana) as well as the Ghana Armed Forces Command and Staff College. He is also a former research associate at the Ghana Centre for Democratic Development on an ETH Zurich project focused on Ethnic Power Relations and Conflict in Fragile States, visiting scholar at the Geneva Graduate Institute, Fellow at the Merian Institute for Advanced Studies in Africa, University of Ghana and visiting Professor at the Fletcher School of Law and Diplomacy, Tufts University and currently an associate fellow at the Africa Centre for Transregional Research, Albert-Ludwig-Universität Freiburg and Academy of International Affairs, NRW.

**Aileen Joy Pactao** is a full-time faculty member in the Social Science Department, College of Arts and Humanities at Palawan State University, Palawan, Philippines. She is particularly interested in conducting research works about foreign policy, political economy, security issues, local politics, and international relations.

**Dealan Riga** is a Ph.D. candidate and part-time Teaching Assistant at the Center for International Relations Studies (CEFIR) in the Department of Political Science at the University of Liège (ULiège) in Belgium. My research focuses on EU economic diplomacy, particularly examining its trade policy towards China. The core of my Ph.D. thesis evaluates how EU geopoliticization either hampers or strengthens negotiations for a Comprehensive Agreement on Investment. I am actively involved in the International Political Economy section of the Belgian Association of Political Sciences (BAPS) and hold a role in executive board of RC 03 "European Unification" within the International Political Science Association (IPSA).

# Index

Milton Keynes UK
Ingram Content Group UK Ltd.
UKHW051843221024
449899UK00008B/69